# The Maghrib in Question

T0341970

# The Maghrib
*in*
# Question

ESSAYS IN HISTORY & HISTORIOGRAPHY

*Edited by Michel Le Gall and Kenneth Perkins*

THE UNIVERSITY OF TEXAS PRESS
AUSTIN

Copyright © 1997 by the University of Texas Press
All rights reserved
Printed in the United States of America
First edition, 1997

Requests for permission to reproduce material from this work should be sent to
Permissions, University of Texas Press, P.O. Box 7819, Austin, TX 78713-7819.

∞ The paper used in this publication meets the minimum requirements of American
National Standard for Information Sciences—Permanence of Paper for Printed Library
Materials, ANSI Z39.48-1984.

Library of Congress Cataloging-in-Publication Data

The Maghrib in question : essays in history and historiography / edited by Michel
Le Gall and Kenneth Perkins. — 1st ed.
       p.      cm.
Includes bibliographical references.
ISBN 978-0-292-72391-7
    1. Africa, North—Historiography.    I. Le Gall, Michel.    II. Perkins, Kenneth J.
DT193.95.M34    1997
961'.072—dc20                                                    96-44825

# Contents

# Preface and Acknowledgments

Our apprenticeships in Maghribi history began roughly a quarter of a century ago. At the time, if it were not exactly true that one could count on the fingers of a single hand the scholars in the United States and Europe (excluding France) who were primarily engaged in the writing of North African history, it was true that the fingers of the second hand provided quite sufficient reinforcements for the enumeration. In the Maghrib itself, a somewhat larger cadre of historians had emerged in the years since European political control had ended, but with only a handful of exceptions, the work of these pioneers was difficult to obtain and was not widely known outside the Maghrib, even among their historian colleagues.

A number of significant developments occurred in the field of North African history in the 1970s and 1980s: the annual publication of more monographs than one could read; the appearance of specialized journals; and the organization of scholarly associations. The expansion of Maghrib-related panels at professional conferences underscored how dramatically the situation was changing, not only in these quantifiable terms, but also—and more importantly—with respect to the nature of the discourse within this enlarged community of historians of the Maghrib.

After participating in an especially thought-provoking seminar entitled "The Historiography of the Maghrib" held in 1989 at the Unité de Recherche en Anthropologie Sociale et Culturelle (URASC) at Oran University under the joint sponsorship of the Centre d'Etudes Maghrébines à Tunis (CEMAT) and the American Institute of Maghrib Studies (AIMS), we concluded that the time was ripe for a serious assessment of the state of our field—a project which, somewhat to our surprise, had not been previously attempted in any systematic fashion. The result is the collection of essays contained in this volume. In it, we have endeavored to develop an overview of historiographical production in the years since the Maghrib states won their independence, to assess the quality of that work, and to identify its most salient trends.

To render our inquiry as inclusive as possible, we solicited contributions from historians of the Maghrib from Tunisia, Algeria, Morocco, and the United States. Their chronological expertise ranges from the ancient, pre-Islamic Maghrib through the medieval, early modern, and Ottoman periods, to the contemporary era. The views on the nature and condition of their discipline that they express in these essays constitute a unique collective statement that reflects the prevailing intellectual discourse in each country and indicates how each scholar's own research and thinking have contributed to it. In their previous writings, some of these historians have developed overviews of a particular period or place; others have tended to focus on case studies; and still others have concentrated on more theoretical and methodological themes.

Thus, the scope of this work is broad, both in terms of chronology and technique. While it is not comprehensive in the usual sense of that term, the book does survey many of the principal historical questions, types of sources, and methodological problems that have shaped the parameters of the historiography of the Maghrib. As a result, these essays should prove a useful guide to both the beginner and the seasoned student of Maghribi history.

The book speaks to a broader audience as well, for the historiography of the Maghrib invariably touches upon connections between North Africa and Europe (especially the Mediterranean lands), West and Central Africa, and the Arab Middle East. In the process of exploring these links, our contributors relate the historiography of North Africa to such wider political and intellectual issues as European colonialism, the internal contests in the Maghribi states over national historical identities, the agendas of professional historians, and, perhaps most fundamentally, the possibilities and limitations imposed by the raw materials of history from archives to archeological digs. It is our hope that the attentive reader will acquire insights into the complexity of Maghribi history and will come to recognize the region as more than merely a poor western cousin of the Islamic Middle East or a stepchild of the European Mediterranean or sub-Saharan Africa worlds.

One general theme that emerges in this volume is the common challenge facing historians of the Maghrib as well as other regions of the once-colonized world: the search for an authentic and balanced view of the past. But the test of authenticity and balance is not a simple one. It transcends the summons issued to an earlier generation to "decolonize" history. That enterprise, launched in the 1960s, has not proven entirely satisfactory, since decolonizing history all too often meant simply embracing the so-called indigenous forces while rejecting those labeled as foreign, colonial, or extraneous. The varieties of the history and historiography of the Maghrib reveal the limits of this earlier dialectic, largely because the region has been both victim and beneficiary of the interaction of numerous political and cultural legacies from the Berbers to the Byzantines, from the Muslims to the officials of metropolitan France.

Of course, this reality has not deterred some historians and politicians from pursuing efforts to refashion the past in light of what they understand as powerful national imperatives. Consequently, historians have, willy-nilly, become engaged—indeed, sometimes locked—in a difficult struggle to counter political expediency with historical truth, a process that echoes what Lucien Febvre described in a different context as "combats pour l'histoire." The events that have shaken Algeria in the 1990s give eloquent testimony to the ongoing relevance of the debate over history and historiography in the Maghrib and much of the rest of the developing world. The end results of this process may vary, but professional historians must never lose sight of the impact of such controversies.

While this volume does not directly concern itself with the political ramifications of historical debates, it does proffer an invitation to appreciate the intricacy and sophistication of the historiography of the Maghrib. For those who study what is now termed "Western history," this book opens a window onto the field of Maghribi history and its maturation over the past forty years. In the process, it demonstrates convincingly that a subject once labeled "area studies" has evolved into a multifaceted discipline that can take stock of its accomplishments, assess historical agendas, and offer suggestions to that universal enterprise known simply as History.

In arranging this volume, we have opted not to adhere to a rigidly chronological format. We have done so because many of the essays offer, on both historical and historiographical issues, comparative perspectives that overstep chronological determinants. Instead, we have brought together essays focusing on different periods in order to throw into relief important continuities, patterns of interaction, and linkages between eras that might otherwise escape notice. The volume is divided into three parts. Part One groups several general pieces on the nature and scope of the historiography of the Maghrib; Part Two delves into a series of specific issues related to the modern history of the Maghrib; and Part Three explores the range of possibilities offered by the sources for Maghribi history.

Several technical notes are in order here. Transliteration in any book on the Maghrib is a thorny problem. We have tried to simplify matters by following these rules: works in Arabic and the names of their authors have been transliterated according to the system used by the *International Journal of Middle East Studies,* but with one modification—the omission of diacritical marks. In transliterating the names of Maghribi scholars who have written in French or English, we have adhered to the spellings that they themselves have adopted. Occasionally, however, the same author's name appears on his or her publications in variant forms. In such instances, we have adopted the most frequently cited version and utilized it throughout this volume. With respect to well-known political figures, we have again opted for the most commonly used spelling rather than the more esoteric standardized Arabic transliteration which would, for example, render Bourguiba as Abu Raqiba.

Other Arabic words in this book are italicized (and accompanied by a brief definition intended to assist nonspecialist readers) at their first usage in each essay. A few Arabic common nouns that are in the *Merriam-Webster's Collegiate Dictionary* (10th ed.), for example, amir, suq, ulama, and sheikh, are treated as English words when given in the plural, and these are not italicized. A list of the abbreviations used in this work is found at the end of the essays.

The essays by Professors Bergaoui, Carlier, Chapoutot-Remadi, El Moudden, Mahjoubi, and Touati were originally written in French. As we translated them into English, we were aided by the invaluable advice of Louis Le Gall, who placed his many years of experience as a translator at our disposal. We gratefully acknowledge his assistance.

We have benefitted from the services of many others in preparing this volume. First and foremost, we thank our contributors for the quality of their work and the depth of their patience. We are deeply appreciative of the faculty and staffs of URASC, CEMAT, and AIMS for organizing the conference in Algeria that sparked the idea for this volume. The warm reception extended by our Algerian hosts in both Oran and Tlemcen to their Maghribi colleagues and those of us from the United States ensured that a stimulating and exciting intellectual experience was also a delightful social occasion. Thanks are also due to Dr. Ali Hossaini of the University of Texas Press for shepherding this volume through the acceptance process; to Jane H. Chamberlain for a superb job of editing that brought uniformity and consistency to the work; and, finally, to Professor L. Carl Brown who has been our mentor in things Maghribi and who has done much to forge links among the members of the guild of Maghribi historians scattered throughout North Africa, Europe, and North America.

*Michel Le Gall*, St. Olaf College
*Kenneth Perkins*, University of South Carolina

# Introduction

*Wilfrid J. Rollman*
Harvard University

ᶜ*A sabiyya,* the group solidarity described by Ibn Khaldun and so familiar to students of the Maghrib, has been a somewhat fragile and precarious concept among historians of the region. Until quite recently, the
limited knowledge of English in North Africa, even in intellectual circles,
restricted the impact of British and North American scholarship. Conversely, excellent articles by North African historians sometimes appeared
in periodicals with little or no circulation outside the Maghrib and their
monographs were often published by presses with equally circumscribed
distribution networks. Moreover, European and North American publications have frequently proven prohibitively expensive for Maghrib university
libraries, let alone individual scholars. All of these factors have impeded free
access to, and exchange of, information vital to sustaining a scholarly bond.
The widespread view of the Maghrib as peripheral to other major cultural
areas—the Arabo-Islamic Middle Eastern heartlands, sub-Saharan Africa,
or southern Europe and the Mediterranean world—has further exacerbated
matters by its implicit threat to marginalize the study of the region.

Owing to the fragmented intellectual environment these dilemmas created, historians of the Maghrib have often wrestled with questions concerning sources, methodologies, and the objectives of their work in something
of a vacuum. The assessments of the current state of Maghrib historiography that are presented, from a variety of perspectives, in the essays of this
book make it very apparent, however, that all historians of North Africa,
regardless of their chronological or geographical specialization, do face remarkably similar challenges and would benefit enormously from more con-
certed interaction.

## DOCUMENTATION

Whatever their period of specialization, for example, historians face thorny
problems regarding the documentation they study. At best, the survival of
written records from every historical period has been haphazard. Even for

the study of the modern era, where the quantity of material already accessible, or steadily becoming available, is very large in comparison with what
historians of earlier periods have at their disposal, great gaps are obvious.
But beyond the issue of locating and classifying new textual materials to fill
lacunae in their fields, most historians of North Africa are aware of still-
unexploited sources. Large quantities of inscriptions have eluded systematic
study by ancient historians. Some, including much of the material from ancient Libya, remain undeciphered. North African medievalists reap great
rewards from the discovery of previously unknown manuscripts, such as the
biographies of Andalusian and North African saints compiled by Abu Tahir
Saddafi and discovered a few years ago in Berlin, but scholars can hardly
rely upon such windfalls for their evidential materials. Increasing numbers
of researchers in both the medieval and ancient fields have striven to offset
deficiencies of these kinds by generating new information through archeological studies. Work now underway at such sites as Tahert in Algeria and
Sijilmasa in Morocco, in the Kasserine region of Tunisia, and at UNESCO-
sponsored projects in Libya confirms that this rich source will continue to
yield valuable information.

Specialists in the early modern and modern periods must also cope with
chronological gaps in, and the sometimes marginal quality of, currently
available documentation. They, however, can harbor greater optimism about
overcoming at least some of these shortcomings as new sources do come to
light and as they gain access to existing collections once closed to research
for one reason or another. The libraries and state archives of Europe—
especially in Italy, the Netherlands, and Spain—house copious documentation that remains to be analyzed. Relatively few scholars have consulted
Turkey's extensive Ottoman government archives pertaining to the Maghrib, but the work they have done has clearly revealed the wealth and variety of information there. The state archives of Tunisia and Morocco are
facilitating access to their considerable holdings, especially for the eighteenth and nineteenth centuries. Despite the havoc that Algeria's independence struggle visited on historical records, important materials bearing on
that country's precolonial period have survived—some in Algeria itself,
others in France—and merit more serious attention than they have thus far
received.

Private collections of documents have proven increasingly important,
particularly in the study of local and regional history. Not only do they
bring to light frequently overlooked information, but they also provide a
fresh viewpoint often at variance with that expressed in the state-generated
documentation on which many historians of the modern period have customarily depended. Throughout the Maghrib, archival records, memoirs,

and other documentation germane to the nationalist campaigns against European rule are more readily attainable than in the past. The cataloguing of such materials held in the Archives de la Wilaya d'Oran; the extensive microfilming of documents from the interwar years by the Centre National Universitaire de Documentation Scientifique et Technique in Tunis; and the multifaceted work of the Commission des Sources de l'Histoire Tunisienne en France all illustrate this positive trend.

In recent years, other disciplines have substantially contributed to modifying historians' traditional approaches to identifying, locating, and examining sources. Paleobotany, zooarcheology, numismatics, and geomorphology are among the many fields to have exerted valuable influence on the study of ancient and medieval history. The methodologies and conceptual frameworks of anthropology have offered historians of all periods insights that have enriched their studies. Affected by colleagues in anthropology and by the *Annales* historians of France, more and more historians of the Maghrib are evincing an interest in questions that no longer privilege politics and ruling groups. As a result, legal documents, oral accounts, literary works, hagiographies, and other written materials have acquired new significance. Recent developments in literary criticism have also had an impact on the historical community, prompting some of its members to reevaluate the very notion of texts as a source of truth and to reexamine familiar sources in ways that make them, in practice, new sources. In sum, whatever the inadequacies of documentation—and these exist in generous measure—the range and quantity of source materials available to today's historian of North Africa could not even have been hoped for twenty-five years ago.

## STRUCTURES

A wide variety of organizations and institutions promoting research and higher education, many of which include among their activities historical research and publishing or instruction on regional history, have been created since the Maghrib states attained their independence. A remarkable numerical and qualitative growth of universities, research institutes, libraries, laboratories, and researchers has occurred in every country. That such expansion has been accomplished in the face of a truly formidable array of obstacles, some of which remain to be fully overcome, makes the process all the more striking and impressive. As university systems expanded rapidly after independence, state scholarships played a critical major role in training a cadre of teachers and scholars to staff the faculties at the new institutions. Now, after more than three decades, Maghribi students are as likely to pursue advanced degrees in historical studies at home as abroad, and studies written for such degrees (Diplôme d'études supérieures; Doctorat du troisième cycle) are beginning to fill library shelves. Many of these recent graduates have chosen aspects of their own countries' history as topics for their projects.

An informal analysis of the content of dissertations produced in recent years reveals that they have, through their emphasis on the use of internal documentation, significantly advanced our understanding of North African history while producing a new generation of historians eager to carry on the work they began as students. The same analysis suggests that although the number of individuals holding advanced academic degrees has increased noticeably in all fields of historical specialization, most of them have focused their work on the nineteenth and twentieth centuries. Important gaps remain to be filled. Archeologists trained to work in the Islamic period are in extremely short supply, for example, as are Ottomanists. Colonial regimes long neglected these fields, while early nationalist governments were often either ill disposed toward them or uninterested. Only time and the infusion of substantial financial resources will overcome the serious deficiencies that continue to characterize these areas of study.

The states have also championed the development of historical studies through their administrative and programmatic participation in the study, preservation, and management of monuments and other aspects of the cultural patrimony within their national borders. Whatever the dangers of "patrimonialisation" or "folklorisation" of the past inherent in such an approach, state support for archeological projects, the restoration of monuments, the preservation of documents, the development of museums, and the sponsorship of academic meetings have undoubtedly promoted historical study. This is not to say that the private sector has not contributed, but its comparatively modest resources have limited the extent of its participation.

Specialized research institutes are yet another illustration of structural support for the study of North African history. Many of these are North African, but several important European and American ones have also emerged. The American Institute of Maghrib Studies (AIMS), with its North African affiliate, the Centre d'Etudes Maghrébines à Tunis (CEMAT), and the Tangier American Legation Museum (TALM) exemplify the latter category. Other centers and institutes outside the Maghrib that have made major contributions to the advancement of North African historical studies include the Centre de Recherches et d'Etudes sur les Sociétés Méditerranéennes (CRESM) in Aix-en-Provence and the Centre National de la Recherche Scientifique (CNRS) in Paris. Each Maghribi country has established a national documentation center to encourage and facilitate historical work through the preservation and classification of documentation. Institutes of archeology similar to the Institut National des Sciences et de l'Archéologie et du Patrimoine in Rabat now function in each country and have made considerable progress in training personnel for fieldwork, the analysis of artifacts, and the preservation of sites and findings for future study and exhibition. Organizations with more general missions include the Centre d'Etudes de Recherches Economiques et Sociales (CERES) in Tunis; the Centre d'Etudes et de Recherches Ottomanes, Morisques, de Documentation et d'Information (CEROMDI) in Zaghouan; L'Institut Agronomique et Vétérinaire Hassan II in Rabat; and the Unité de Recherche en Anthropologie Sociale et Culturelle (URASC) in Oran.

Publications printed in the region are another aspect of structural support. Well-established journals such as the *Cahiers de Tunisie, Revue de l'Institut des Belles Lettres Arabes* (IBLA), and *Hespéris Tamuda* have served as excellent outlets for the history and historians of North Africa over many years. More recently, other periodicals published by university faculties and institutes have assumed importance as forums for the discussion of historical issues throughout the region. The *Majallat Kulliyyat al-Adab,* produced by the Faculté des Lettres at Université Mohammed V in Rabat, is only one noteworthy example of this trend. Among the European periodicals that have consistently presented high quality material on the Maghrib are *Annales, économies, sociétés, civilisations* (AESC); *Revue de l'Occident musulman et de la Méditerranée* (ROMM); and the *Annuaire de l'Afrique du Nord.*

Government presses play a major role in the publication of historical and other academic works in North Africa. The Algerian Société Nationale d'Edition et de Diffusion and the Société Tunisienne de Diffusion are perhaps the two best known government publishers, but there are others, particularly if presses subsidized in whole or part by state funds are included. Especially in Morocco, private publishing houses have become important outlets for scholarly work, including history. Toubqal, Afrique Orient, al-Najjah al-Jadida, and al-Afaq al-Jadida have all given a prominent place to Maghribi history in their lists.

Both state-run and private firms have published works of importance to historians that had long been out of print. The Ministry of Awqaf (pious endowments) in Morocco, for example, is publishing an edition of the *Mi'yar al-Mu'rib* of Ahmad ibn Yahya al-Wansharisi. In a new series called "Collection Archives," Afrique Orient of Casablanca is republishing such "classics" as Robert Montagne's *Les Berbères et le makhzen, La Berbérie musulmane et l'Orient au moyen-âge* by Georges Marçais, and *Les Historiens des chorfas* by Evariste Lévi-Provençal. Between 1974 and 1983, the Imprimerie Royale in Rabat reprinted those portions of the ten-volume biographical dictionary *al-ʿIlm bi-man hal Marrakush wa-ʾAghmat* of al-ʿAbbas bin Ibrahim al-Marrakishi that had appeared between 1936 and 1938, as well as publishing the parts still in manuscript. For each North African country, there are numerous other examples. Since access to the earlier editions is often difficult, owing to the ravages of time and a world book market that has rendered these valuable items scarce or unavailable, such publication projects, provided they are undertaken with care, are invaluable to historians, regardless of their theoretical or methodological approaches.

The publication of manuscripts has enjoyed similar attention, as have the efforts by a small number of dedicated scholars in each country to produce inventories of manuscript collections held in public and private libraries. In the latter category, the works of ʿAbd al-Hafiz Mansur (*Catalogue général des manuscrits,* 1974– ) in Tunisia, Muhammed Manuni (*al-Masadir al-ʿarabiyya li-ta'rikh al-Maghrib,* 1983– ) in Morocco, and Abdeljelil Temimi (*Inventaire sommaire des registres arabes et turcs d'Alger,* 1979) for Algeria have proven extremely useful. A number of guides to sources have appeared or are in preparation in a variety of formats, but especially as periodical articles.

Despite the work of the postindependence decades, there remains a need for the most basic information about many sources. The search for new sources must certainly continue, but equal attention must be given to making what has already been discovered in North Africa, Europe, and the United States more readily available and "usable" to students of history. In the past, certain kinds of sources have been privileged, with chronicles and "classical" texts in each field receiving priority attention in publication projects and the preparation of critical editions.

Newly discovered sources coupled with methodological innovations have enabled historians to understand well-known sources in quite different and highly productive ways. They have also encouraged scholars to appreciate categories of sources—customary law, oral accounts, juridical texts, literary works, and statistical materials—which, until recently, were not given serious attention. While presenting historians of all periods with a new opportunity, this development also complicates the choices that must be made in the process of distributing meager financial resources and marshaling the skills and time needed to preserve materials and make them accessible to scholars. By organizing microfilm projects intended to preserve archival materials from all of these genres, national documentation centers have made a start at grappling with this problem.

In summation, although considerable progress has been made in the development of cadres, facilities, and sources throughout the region, as well as outside it, much remains to be accomplished. For every collection microfilmed, every book published or republished, every manuscript edited or archeological expedition launched, many more might be proposed and justified. Scholars, government officials, and interested parties in the private sector face contracting budgets and increasing demands. Everywhere, they are finding it more difficult to make decisions about what is to be studied, reconstructed, restored, and preserved and what is to be left aside and frequently, in cases such as oral history and some archeological sites, allowed to perish. The task is rendered more painful by the general absence of consensus among professionals about precisely what is historically significant, worthy of attention, and essential to preserve for the cultural and political well-being of generations to come.

Nor is this a question posed in isolation from politics and the broader cultural and intellectual contexts peculiar to each country involved. The need to contribute to (or at least not to detract from) the process of national reconstruction and the ongoing effort to "decolonize" North African history strongly influences decisions on the choice of themes and methodologies for historical study. Thus, decisions about the type and extent of support given to any of the fundamental components essential to the advancement of historical research and production are seldom made without reference to these broader criteria, as well as to more strictly intellectual and financial ones. Professional historians often view the results of this politicization of their efforts with little enthusiasm. This situation is not, of course, unique to historians in North Africa; but in the Maghrib, as in other parts of the recently decolonized world, the pressure to consider national politics and issues of cultural identity in the conduct of research and writing is often quite explicit.

INTERPRETIVE ISSUES

Despite the obvious relationship between documentation and support structures on the one hand and matters of interpretation and methodology on the other, a much clearer consensus exists among historians of North Africa on the former than on the latter. In method and focus, the historiography of the Maghrib is so diverse that some of its practitioners have worried that the dispersal of efforts and resources inevitably entailed in such a multiplicity of inquiries will lead to fragmentation rather than the construction of national histories or other useful works of general significance. Neither the approach of the traditional Orientalists—with its focus on the normative, the literary, and the ruling elites—nor more recent methodologies that concentrate on social history, local history, the community, the family, and the individual have yet done much to allay these concerns.

In fact, the challenge to the production of critical, documented national history has, if anything, intensified in recent years. The very coherence of such key concepts as "society" and "culture," or of such notions as "continuity" and "consciousness," has come under fire, no longer from a colonial policy that sought to divide, marginalize, subjugate, and rule, but rather from a set of theoretical propositions—again originating in Europe—that seems to oppose any form of hegemony. One might go so far as to speak of histories, rather than *the* history, of the Maghrib or its national units. At the same time, however, North African governments and their intellectual elites have become more secure in their identity as Tunisians, Moroccans, and Algerians. With this has come a greater willingness to acknowledge and appreciate the diversity of their past, which they recognize as a source of richness and cultural potential rather than as a threat.

In dealing with the colonial regimes, a unified political stand was essential for Maghribi historians, as was a consensus on the singularity of the nation and the commonality of its historical origins, culture, and experience. With the prize of independence won and endowed with some substance on the cultural and political levels, however, it has become possible for many North African historians to see their pasts as more shared and less homogeneous than participants in the independence struggle and the early years of national consolidation would have had it. Many different constituencies can, and do, legitimately claim the North African past. If history is not to be an enterprise primarily engaged in the production of a particular ideological perspective—or of several with competing hegemonic pretensions—these claims and differences must be recognized, accepted, and studied with the same attention to methodological rigor and documentation accorded to other, hitherto more privileged, aspects of the past. Doing so faithfully will create a more nuanced and substantive account of the past than now exists—one that more faithfully depicts the historical experiences that continue to have a formative influence on the entire region.

## THE UNIT OF ANALYSIS

Although most historians of the Maghrib, North African and otherwise, tend to formulate their inquiries and focus their documentary research in terms of presently existing nation-states, many find such an analytical framework unsatisfactory. The nation-state remains the unit of choice for historians from the generation of nationalist struggle and for those who, because of their skepticism about the stability and durability of the nation-state and the national community, insist that history should, above all else, serve to defend and reinforce those concepts.

The continued reliance on a scheme of artificial compartmentalization imposed by a colonial regime has distressed some historians and provoked a search for alternative spatial definitions of the units they study. Some scholars have engaged in comparative analyses of existing national units as a method of downplaying artificially imposed discontinuities that does not, at the same time, necessitate the formulation of an altogether different set of parameters. Others, basing themselves on substantial geographical, cultural, and historical evidence, have suggested that the Maghrib could best be studied in the context of Africa, as an extension of the Middle East, or as a part of the Mediterranean world. Yet a third group has emphasized that the notion of the Maghrib is itself a historical-cultural construct whose spatial content has changed over time and must, therefore, be considered historically. The history of this concept and its use over centuries by various political regimes and cultural entities has yet to be undertaken, despite long-standing calls for such work.

The unit of analysis problem has taken on new urgency in recent years owing, in part, to the revival of activity designed to create a "Grand Maghrib" and the emergence of this goal as an important element in state policy. The formulation of sweeping theories has lost popularity among historians, and the greater emphasis on projects with more modest goals and more narrowly defined units of analysis has also stimulated thinking on this issue. A trend toward local history and historical-anthropological projects that make, at most, only cursory reference to larger social, political, and cultural entities and processes, has posed new problems of defining the appropriate object of historical research and analysis. For reasons outlined above, many North African historians worry that an "excessive" focus on local history might bolster regional identities at the expense of maturing— but still fragile—national ones. Even historians for whom this is not a serious concern are skeptical or ambivalent about such an approach, seeing in it the danger of uncoupling local questions from the "national" or other larger frameworks and processes in a way that makes meaningful generalizations impossible and renders local history less comprehensible by isolating it from the broader context which undoubtedly had some formative influence on it.

Proponents of local history regard it as ideally suited to the task of reconstructing North African history on the basis of concrete, documented examples. They argue that their approach, if carefully employed, has the capacity to produce a history closely attuned to the values, constraints, and opportunities experienced by North Africans at a given time. On the other hand, local history is, no less than other models, conceptualized and executed by human beings living in specific cultural, political, and social settings and sharing a particular set of values. Consequently, it constitutes neither a polar opposite nor a reliable antidote to ideological or teleological versions of history—the chronicles, biographical dictionaries, and other writings produced by Muslim scholars who conceived, and still conceive, of history as a means of religious edification, demonstrating how God works in the world, or as a vehicle for bringing deeds considered exemplary to the attention of the faithful. Nor is it a strategy that has yet proven its adequacy for reconstructing history on a larger scale. Despite some hopeful analogies to pointillism, no one is yet certain that the proliferating number of microstudies will add up to anything more significant and reliable than the historiography that grappled with questions raised by grand theories. Whether or not local history is obliged thus to justify itself is another question, although most scholars believe that it should if it is to secure a place as a legitimate unit of historical analysis. Similarly, practitioners of local history must also maintain a continuous dialogue with larger theoretical discourses to prevent their work from "degenerating" into ethnography or folklore. With these caveats taken into account, the North African historical community appears to support the trend toward a sharper focus on local history, acknowledging it as a methodological approach potentially more productive than, and less susceptible to the shortcomings of, the paradigms of Weberian sociology, structuralism, the political economy tradition of Marx, or the methods employed by "traditional" Arabo-Muslim historians.

Akin to the question of appropriate units of analysis is the matter of the chronological division of North African history. Once again, there is general dissatisfaction with the widely used periodization—Roman, Arab, Ottoman, French (or Spanish or Italian), Independent—based primarily on dynastic or racial criteria. Such categories as ancient, medieval, and modern are even less useful because of their extreme imprecision and the heavy cultural baggage accompanying them. Unfortunately, these conventional terms are so deeply embedded in the historical discourse that their usage persists, even in the face of the near-universal acknowledgment of the overlap and continuity between, for example, the Roman and early Islamic periods, or colonial and postcolonial history. Any examination of periodization serves to highlight the virtual absence of historical work on some periods, most notably the first centuries of the Islamic period, the Ottoman era, and the eighteenth century. Historians must devote more attention to the continuities and connections between periods and places in the history of the Maghrib if an accurate comprehension of the interpenetration of cultures over time and the evolution of the Maghrib's most salient political, social and cultural features is to be achieved.

## HISTORY AND THE COLONIAL LEGACY

Although the effort to "decolonize" North African history and historiography and the critique of Orientalism have scored significant successes in replacing Eurocentric interpretations and preoccupations with North African priorities and perspectives, concerns about this legacy persist. French and Italian historians and archeologists continue to play influential roles in the study of pre-Islamic North African history, for example, while scholars of all periods still make extensive use of many Orientalist studies which have, in some sense, attained the status of classics and are judged authoritative on a wide range of topics in which further original research might revise their findings. The interpretations of colonial historians are still well-represented in such works as the third (1987) edition of Jamil Abun-Nasr's *History of the Maghrib in the Islamic Period*. The texts and methodologies of previous generations have given way only slowly to newly developed sources for, and approaches to, the study of history, although substantial progress has occurred since the 1960s.

Ironically, several decades after independence, the conviction that this earlier corpus of work should be replaced entirely is no longer so readily answered in the affirmative. Instead, there is a growing awareness that, despite its grounding in methodological and ideological frameworks now considered flawed and perhaps even reprehensible, this body of literature remains a storehouse of material for historians utilizing newer methods and speaking in different ideological contexts. The use and reevaluation of this material is an important part of the contemporary historian's task.

Many historians now practicing their craft in North Africa received their training in France under the guidance of mentors imbued with ideological and methodological traditions with which their former students are now clashing. The small but growing group of North African scholars trained in the United States are also, to some extent, heirs to this colonial tradition, given their wide exposure to the production of French scholars writing within it. In many ways, the rhetorical commitment to the decolonization of history and a rigorous critique of "Orientalist" prejudices and methods have crystallized well in advance of the actual work of reinterpretation. Much remains to be done to regulate this stubborn intellectual heritage.

The resilience of the colonial legacy poses especially acute problems for

North African scholars by virtue of its intersection with such other issues as the choice of language for historical discourse, national politics, and the continuing influence of academic trends and models generated in Europe. Michel Foucault, the *Annales* School, Anglo-Saxon social science, and a variety of Marxist and neo-Marxist approaches to the study of society and history have all left their marks on the recent historiography of the Maghrib, once again raising questions about external influences in defining North Africa's present and past. The determination of scholars to engage in dialogue with significant intellectual traditions that may contribute to a more sophisticated and coherent understanding of their own fields of research and study makes the maintenance of autonomy vis-à-vis the intellectual and historiographical traditions of Europe—whether viewed as colonial, neocolonial, or something other—extremely difficult.

The works of Jacques Berque illustrate this point. His writings on North African history continue to stimulate interest, guide research, and provoke lively debates. A French native of Algeria who spent his entire career studying the Maghrib, Berque has been viewed as authoritative by several generations of scholars in North Africa and elsewhere. His last works earned high praise for their innovative use of manuscript sources and their contribution to local history. Yet, for North African scholars, many of whom were his students, admiration for Berque's achievements is tempered by a disillusionment with his attempts to sustain comparisons between early modern Europe and North Africa during the same period. At times, they find his use of language and imagery to be paternalistic, even as they applaud his rejection of "Orientalist assumptions" and "revolutionary history," or his contributions to the development of local identity and self-critique.

## THE LEGACY OF NATIONAL STRUGGLE

The obverse of historians' need to guard against misleading interpretations fostered by the colonial legacy is their obligation to take a discerning view of the historiography produced within the context of, and often for the explicit purpose of legitimating, the national struggle. As might be anticipated, critical evaluations of the nationalist legacy can impose burdensome political and professional liabilities on North African historians, many of whom feel the need to position themselves in such a way as to avoid giving any appearance of detracting from the achievement of nationhood and communal solidarity. Consequently, little attention was given to Berber studies or to Islamic reform and militancy in the years following independence. Developments in Algeria in the 1990s have rendered an interest in such topics even less viable than previously. This neglect, as well as the general lack of interest in ancient history since independence or in Ottoman history throughout the modern era, stems in part from the difficulty of fitting these groups and periods into the historical framework fashioned to support the nationalist struggle, and in part from the belief that the disproportionate emphasis accorded to them in the colonial period justified their relegation to a status of secondary importance by postcolonial scholars.

Assessing the contribution of religious reformers to the nationalist struggle has presented an especially acute dilemma of both a political and a methodological nature. Scholars of the Salafiyya tradition, whose historical writing marked a new departure for North Africans, played a pivotal role in the nationalist movement. Combining methodologies borrowed from European practice with others drawn from their own Arabo-Islamic tradition, they wrote about North Africans for North Africans with the explicit purpose of providing them with a mirror on their past—a mirror that showed them heroes of their own, gave them proof of their existence as a people, and offered a new scale of values by which to comprehend and evaluate their condition under colonial rule in the twentieth century. These scholars intended for their history to serve as a pedagogical tool in the reawakening of Algerians, Tunisians, and Moroccans to their potential strength as a community and their worth as persons. In short, they sought to affirm the "historicity" of the conquered people and their brilliant past while providing the tools with which to confront colonial historiography and prove that they were not French.

For all these contributions, Tawfiq al-Madani, Mubarak al-Mili, and other practitioners of a "reformed" Arabo-Islamic historical tradition deserve recognition. But their methods and production (not to mention their politics) in the postindependence setting all but compel a new generation of scholars, intent on a more "scientific" and critical study of North African history and anxious to avoid the production of history as propaganda for a particular form of nation-state or political system, to formulate criticisms.

Acutely aware that this debate, like the one concerning the colonial legacy, is about much more than methodological issues, North African historians are cautious in broaching these subjects. They know full well that in each country of the Maghrib, the retrieval and definition of the past is an integral part of the ongoing process of constructing (or reconstructing) the society, culture, and political system. Their academic study is enmeshed in the larger search for symbols of authenticity and political legitimacy and the manipulation of these symbols for their own purposes by political parties, ethnic groups, religious movements, and governments. Whatever their individual preferences or the strength of their wish to remain detached from these debates, historians who are not themselves North Africans must take these issues into account in their work. This will inevitably, albeit indirectly, feed back into the debates by contributing to the continuing historical discourse that provides their context.

## HISTORY AS A DISCIPLINE

Delimiting the boundaries of history has become something of a growth industry in Europe and the United States. Nor has history in, and of, North Africa escaped this debate. Historians of the region generally advocate an interdisciplinary approach to the study of historical problems, arguing that ancillary sciences (most obviously, but not exclusively, archeology and anthropology) can make enormous contributions to creating new opportunities for historians and to providing them with valuable data and methodological assistance. Many of these same scholars have expressed their malaise with historiography that focused primarily on political events or the activities of ruling elites, or that which was teleological or evolutionary. Having fallen short of their promise, the grand paradigms of Marxist and Weberian inspiration, which pulled history in the direction of political economy and other social sciences, have, for the moment receded into the background, although they continue to inspire and guide many historians. The challenge to the identity of history posed by anthropology and sociology has been offset by the sustained critique of structuralism and the call, even among some anthropologists closely identified with the structuralist approach, for greater attention to the diachronic aspect of social experience. Hence, the question arises for all historians of what, exactly, they are engaged in and how, if at all, it is distinct from other ways of analyzing and describing human societies.

Historians of North Africa have certainly not reached a consensus on what history is or should be, but they agree that history, in the sense of a study of change over time and the use of chronological structure, has been an essential ingredient in the process of reconstructing the past—perhaps not so much at the level of individual memory, but certainly at that of the collective memory of groups and institutions. History, then, should interact with other disciplines and they with it. Historians should avoid articulating a particular ideological perspective, be critically aware of the context in which they are producing their work, emphasize a rational approach to research and analysis, and eschew involvement in the unrealistic quest for comprehensive explanatory theories.

All of this relates back to the issue of local history. Although some historians of the Maghrib believe that the need to know more about many broad—but still inadequately studied and poorly understood—issues concerning government, the state, the economy, and the like makes an emphasis on local history premature at this juncture, a larger number seem sympathetic to the move to narrow the focus of historical research to something less than such unwieldy categories as nation, state, and society. At the same time, however, they recognize the need to keep the analysis of local history linked to broader historical and theoretical contexts. Maghribi historians of this school clearly regard the goal of specificity and the careful documentation of cases from local sources to be not merely the acquisition of knowledge about particular places, groups, and processes, but the application of that new knowledge in a way that illuminates larger entities, provides comparative examples, and tests theoretical assumptions and previous historical analysis.

Nevertheless, even the advocates of local history have not agreed on a rigorous definition of the concept. For some, it means a concern for small groups—the oasis, village, city quarter, or family. For others, it has a wider definition that includes the study of regions, cities, minority groups, mentalités, and a variety of cultural phenomena, all of whose spatial domains are smaller than such categories as state, society, and nation. The accessibility of new archival sources in North Africa has stimulated interest in and provided support for increasing numbers of projects devoted to variously defined studies of local history, as have theoretical developments pertaining to social and cultural history in the United States, Great Britain, and France. The works of such scholars as E. P. Thompson, Peter Brown, Natalie Zemon Davis, Clifford Geertz, and Michel Foucault are reaching an ever-widening audience among younger North African scholars now entering the academy and embarking on research careers.

The essays that follow provide a very encouraging look into the future of North African historical studies. The discipline promises to be productive and engaging, both in terms of the significant advances likely to occur in what is known about the Maghrib's history in all periods and in terms of the heightened level of comprehension of this history and its place in the larger world of Africa, the Middle East, and Mediterranean Europe.

# The Maghrib in Question

PART I

# *Reconnoitering the Terrain*

The heavy legacy of colonialism in the Maghrib and, indeed, in the entire Arabic-speaking world, has made itself felt in many realms. Those most commonly studied by historians are the political, the social, and the economic. Still, one of the more profound and lasting, although often neglected, legacies of colonialism is the intellectual one. This intellectual legacy is particularly important, for it was through the prism of French power that much of the Maghrib was first exposed to the intellectual traditions, both contemporary and past, of the West. There are several reasons—none justified—why the intellectual impact of colonialism has been left in some measure understudied. First, the preoccupation with Orientalism has, ironically, focused on western scholarship about Islam, with little regard for the effect of this scholarship on Middle Eastern and Maghribi intellectual developments. Second, the keepers of the intellectual property of any nation are frequently a small elite, and the current trend in history is to study the broader segments of society at the grass-roots level. Finally, the intellectual effects of colonialism are often diffuse and defy efforts to relate developments in a scheme consistent with the standard notion of cause and effect.

The effects of French and, to a much lesser degree, Spanish and Italian intellectual colonialism on the historiography of the Maghrib are particularly pronounced. The reasons for this originate with the task that the French administrations in Algeria, Tunisia, and Morocco set for themselves. One of their priorities was to instill French language and culture in their colonial subjects, especially the urban dwellers. In Algeria, this process was remarkably successful because the structures of settler colonialism advanced the frontiers of French colonialism and culture in unprecedented ways before the appearance of the modern media. "The torch of French civilization," as Victor Hugo termed it, found its way into all facets of everyday life, including education and research. The study of history was no exception. After all, history, as Paul Valéry noted, has the dangerous potential of leading—or misleading—nations and entire peoples. In the century and a half of French involvement in the Maghrib, both direct and indirect, the study and writing of history was, and continues to be, an integral part of the Maghribi and French experience. But the Maghrib was no tabula rasa upon which to imprint French views of history or in which to apply newly developed historical methodologies. In the Maghrib, there were well-established historiographic traditions that had emerged as early as the first century after the Arab conquests of North Africa and Spain. These historical genres included chronicles of battles and dynasties, biographical dictionaries of famous men (and occasionally women), and geography manuals which described roads and regions.

Likewise, history in Europe had developed long-standing practices and traditions. These began to change profoundly in the eighteenth century. And in nineteenth-century France, history, archeology, and geography underwent a renewal and reevaluation which combined often contradictory intents—scientific methods with the extolling of national virtues. Indeed, Michelet, Taine, and others saw in the study of history in the broadest sense a call to build a national identity and patrimony. Geography underwent similar developments in the late nineteenth century and, early in this century, was connected even more closely with history following the publication in 1922 of Lucien Febvre's *La Terre et l'évolution humaine*. In the course of the colonial and postcolonial experience, French and Maghribi traditions have sometimes clashed and sometimes complemented one another. The result has been both a writing and a rewriting within several generations of the history of the Maghrib.

The first section of this collection, entitled "Reconnoitering the Terrain," sets out to study some of the lasting effects of French intellectual colonialism in regard to the practice of history by North Africans, Europeans, and, recently, Americans. L. Carl Brown begins the analysis with the very definition of the Maghrib as a unit of study developed during the period of French rule and considers both the benefits and shortcomings of the notions of the Maghrib as a unit of inquiry. Ammar Mahjoubi then offers an appreciation of the highly political nature of archeology in the period of direct French rule: the unearthing of the ancient past as a rationalization of French rule. The establishment of numerous universities in the nineteenth and twentieth centuries, first in France and later in the Maghrib, along with the awarding of doctorates by Maghribi and French institutions, has fostered a new era in the study of the medieval Islamic period, one to which French historians such as William Marçais and Henri Terrasse first gave shape starting in earnest after World War I. Mounira Chapoutot-Remadi reviews recent publications dealing with the medieval Islamic period and relates them to the efforts of Maghribi historians to reevaluate and repossess their past independently of the work of "les grands maîtres" to whom we are still profoundly indebted. Finally, Wilfrid Rollman considers how the study of modern North Africa has in some measure escaped the influence of French intellectual traditions thanks to a conscious effort on the part of native Maghribi historians to "decolonize" history and, in addition, to the entry of non-Francophones into the field.

# Maghrib Historiography:
# The Unit of Analysis Problem

### L. Carl Brown
Princeton University

*The ideal, of course, would be to start with a history of
historiography; to trace the genesis of the concept of the Maghrib
and discover how it ultimately took on an objective definition.*
— ABDALLAH LAROUI [1]

Among the aims of all North African historians should be to advance
this ideal proposed almost two decades ago by our Moroccan colleague Abdallah Laroui. Differently stated, why do we speak of "the Maghrib" as if it were an accepted term not requiring further definition? Why
not the Arab world? Or the southwestern portion of the Mediterranean
world? Or Muslim Africa? Or Dar al-Islam? Or, since it is argued by many
that we are increasingly living in a compact "global village," why not go for
a broader definition such as "Third World"?

Each of the above alternatives to "the Maghrib" brings with it a specific
political agenda; so, too, does the term "Maghrib." Exposing the political
implications of the different regional definitions, including, of course, definitions used by historians themselves, is one of the basic tasks of the historian. Certainly, the Maghrib in modern times has witnessed an abundance
of politicized history. Note the way a French scholar at the time of the 1930
centennial of the French conquest of Algeria depicted his country as completing the work of the Romans:

> As for the Romans, during a period of domination that lasted for six
> centuries, they knew how to exploit North Africa admirably and how
> to Romanize it, at least superficially. But their ability to populate the
> region was so limited that the transformations they effected lacked
> deep roots. . . . Rome achieved splendid material successes whose pre-
> cious vestiges we must preserve, in that they constitute a glorious artis-
> tic heritage and confer on us, in a sense, "letters of patent". But history

has proven that the moral work of Rome was deficient and its impact on the natives ephemeral. Even its material accomplishments were spatially limited. Ours, by contrast, are immense, stretching widely and penetrating deeply. After only a century, unimpeachable evidence of the moral, educational, social, and resolutely humanitarian impact of our work is everywhere abundant.[2]

Such uses of history to justify conquest create, of course, responses from those conquered. As French colonial ideologues assumed the Roman mantle, Tunisian nationalists came to celebrate their Punic past. Or, as early as the 1930s, young Moroccan nationalists adopted, at least in their propaganda wars with colonialism, the usage *malik* (king) and went on to propose that the young Prince Hasan might be dubbed "Prince of the Atlas" (with this Moroccan equivalent of "Prince of Wales" calling attention to the deep historical roots of Morocco's Alawite dynasty, older indeed, by one way of reckoning, than that of Great Britain). And in Algeria the classic retort of Ben Badis undermined the policy of those Algerians who would consider assimilationism as either a stage or an ultimate goal:

> We, too, have searched in history and in the present and have found that the Algerian Muslim nation has been formed and it exists. . . . This nation has its history illustrated by lofty deeds. It has its religious and linguistic unity, its culture, its traditions. We thus say that this Algerian Muslim nation is not France, cannot be France and does not wish to be France.[3]

The effort to "decolonize" history was clearly one of the goals Abdallah Laroui set for himself in proposing a new interpretative synthesis of North African history. Yet, he chose to avoid writing "une histoire de l'historiographie," calling such an effort "premature." In my view, Laroui was suggesting that only a team of scholars working toward common aims could achieve progress in this regard. Only specialists for the different time periods are in a position to answer the basic question: What was the territorial and group identity held by the people whom we now identify as Maghribis in, say, Roman times, the Byzantine period, the early centuries of Islam, the age of the Ottoman Empire, and so on? Surely such an effort will begin to uncover significant differences in group identifications and loyalties over the centuries. No one historian can be expected to trace this cultural and geographical pedigree.

At the same time, historians today must not fall into the trap of concentrating so much on historiography as to overlook history. Doing so puts us at risk of concentrating so heavily on the "hidden agendas" of past historians that we overlook the basic, mundane work that all historians must accomplish. The American historian Samuel Eliot Morison, writing many years ago in a context far removed from the Maghrib (and thus without any "hidden agenda" as regards the Maghrib) offered a challenge still worth considering:

> So much has been written in recent years about these limitations on "Scientific" objectivity as to obscure the plain, outstanding principle that the historian's basic task is one of presenting a corpus of ascertained fact. This is the hardest thing to get across to students today, especially to those who have been to the so-called progressive schools. Somewhere along the assembly-line of their education, these students have had inserted in them a bolt called "points of view," secured with a nut called "trends," and they imagine that the historian's problem is simply to compare points of view and describe trends. It is not. The fundamental question is, "What actually happened, and why?"[4]

Morison's definition of the historian's task as that of reconstructing, to the extent evidence makes this possible, "what actually happened" is in the best tradition of the German historian Leopold von Ranke (1795–1886), usually deemed the father of modern scientific history. The methodology proposed by the school of history that we associate with Ranke does, however, raise as many problems as it answers. Even a later historian who would see himself as a disciple of Ranke has pointed out the limitations of scientific history:

> . . . we return to our revered master Ranke. The historian should attempt to tell us, without fabrication or prevarication, how it actually happened. But he must never forget that *it* is made up of passions and dreams, of myths and legends, which alone give human events their significance. In the beginning was not the word, not the deed, but the pain, the love and the dread.[5]

All of this amounts to a series of working rules that might seem contradictory or even paradoxical but actually serve as keys to the complex guidelines that the sophisticated historian must seek not just to apply but to internalize to such an extent that they become second nature. Neither history nor historiography, by itself, presents a sufficient perspective on the past. Working in tandem, each enhances the sweep of the other; history without historiography would be like a mason laying brick upon brick without bothering to draw up a plan of what is to be constructed.

The historian can never be completely objective. We are all too much the prisoners of our own personalities, our own times, and our own environments. Nevertheless, the historian who consciously strives for objectivity will surely come closer to objectivity than one who willfully chooses to advance individual prejudices and political programs.

Historians are not, however, so many white-coated scientists observing inert matter in their laboratories. They belong to the species that they undertake to observe, analyze, and interpret. Accordingly, historians must strive not only for optimal scientific objectivity but also for empathy.[6]

Finally, historians need to advance various generalizations as explanatory frameworks: for example, in the context being considered here, the Maghrib, the Mediterranean world, Dar al-Islam, Africa, or the Arab world. These generalizations should, to the extent possible, be based on the actual reality and placement in time of the people being studied, as well as the perceptions of reality by those same people at the time under examination. Even while doing this basic historical spadework, historians must be on guard against the common human tendency to retroject today's prevailing assumptions into earlier times.

Having attempted to define the historiographer's role, let us now turn to the issue set for this discussion: Is "Maghrib" the most effective unit of analysis? In posing this question, I hope to set in motion a new consideration of an old issue, a view that seeks to be aware of the potential political implications of the way the question is answered but that attempts to transcend politics in reaching for at least an approximation of scientific objectivity. Approaches once viewed with suspicion or even opposed outright because of their implicit political agenda can, with the passing of time and new developments, become depoliticized.

This will be at best only a partial "histoire de l'historiographie." What follows is as much prospective as it is retrospective; it is concerned with future historiography as much as historiography to date.

Is the Maghrib the most effective unit of analysis? My own tentative answer is a guarded "yes" with nuances and reservations to be pointed out in the discussion that follows.

There is, first, the geographical argument. That regions or countries vary in the degree to which they possess geographically significant or "natural" borders is an old idea among historians. Who can deny, for example, that Japan and Great Britain owe much of their distinctiveness to their being island kingdoms in close contact with, but still separated from, Eurasia? The Maghrib, in a sense, can be seen as an island surrounded by seas of sand as well as of salt water, for the Atlantic and the Mediterranean link up with the world's largest desert, the Sahara, to give the Maghrib reasonably distinct borders. The phrase adopted by early Muslim geographers—*jazirat al-Maghrib*—indicates their perception of this reality.

Only in the east is the Maghrib's natural border somewhat indeterminate, leaving present-day scholars to wrestle with the question of whether Libya belongs to the Maghrib or the Mashriq. The answer historical geographers would be inclined to give is that Tripolitania best fits with the Maghrib and Cyrenaica with Egypt and the Mashriq. And, in fact, until modern times the broad historical developments in what is now Libya have been bifurcated along these geographical lines, with western Libya more oriented toward the Maghrib and eastern Libya more linked to Egypt and the Mashriq.

Moreover, within these boundaries set by seas of sand and salt water, the Atlas Mountain chain gives the Maghrib a configuration that sharply distinguishes it from its neighbors. One geographer has even suggested that "Atlas Land" might well be the name of choice for the entire region, so important is this imposing mountain chain in determining Maghrib history. The Atlas Mountains give the region its backbone, extending from the Moroccan-Mauritanian borders in a northeasterly direction to the Rif chain in northern Morocco, moving as two distinct chains eastward across Algeria, and receding into foothills in Tunisia. The obtuse angle thus traced is as distinctive a geographical characteristic of the Maghrib as is the image of the Fertile Crescent in the Mashriq.

The distinctive juxtaposition of cities, and their agricultural hinterlands, with mountains and deserts has given the Maghrib a special cachet. The mountains and deserts combine to offer refuge areas for peoples who would escape the homogenizing and centralizing impulses coming from the cities and the plains. The slow and still incomplete Arabization of the Maghrib—as contrasted with, say, Egypt—is thus explained, as is the fact that Berber speakers even to this day trace their roots to mountains and deserts. The Berbers of North Africa can usefully be compared with the Druze, the Maronites, and the Kurds of the Middle East.[7]

Here we touch upon one of those enduring historical themes characterizing the Maghrib. Note, for example, the following appraisal of Roman North Africa:

> If Roman civilization appeared to have conquered cities and the lowlands of the Maghrib, it did not reach the pockets of mountainous settlement. The garrisons that encircled the mountain chains and the roads that cut through them were not means of acculturation but re-

pression. In the Aurès, Kabylia, the Biban, Dahra, Ouarsenis, Tessela and the Rif, the Berbers kept their customs. They never gave up their dialects, their tools nor even their funeral practices.[8]

Then, skipping across the centuries from Roman to Ottoman North Africa, one finds the following appraisal:

> In the central Maghrib the Turks occupied only a few towns where they left garrisons responsible for guarding the surrounding region. These towns, chosen for their strategic value, either commanded the sea routes, as Dellys, Cherchell, or Mostaganem, or the essential routes of the interior such as Blida, Médéa, or Tlemcen. Thus the Turks practiced . . . a policy of limited (or partial) occupation.[9]

These two examples separated by over a millennium of history provide the setting for Germaine Tillion's argument during the period of the Algerian war of independence that, whereas French administration in most of Algeria was inflated, the Kabylia suffered from being woefully underadministered.

Mountains and deserts also serve as human reservoirs for hinterland challenges to the urban-based centers, and here the historian can trace a chain from the Donatists to the FLN in Kabylia or from the Almohades to ʿAbd al-Krim. The Dutch Orientalist Reinhart Dozy understood this imprint of geography with history, of terrain with theology, when he remarked of the Kharijite revolt in the Maghrib that the Muslim equivalent of Calvinism had found its Scotland.

That geography can explain much of its distinctiveness is an old theme in the historiography of the Maghrib. The basic ideas and themes were captured first and most strikingly by the Maghrib's own Ibn Khaldun. It is often overlooked that Ibn Khaldun was as much a brilliant historian of the Maghrib as he was a philosopher of history. Certainly, his would-be universal rules of historical change fit most neatly with the medieval Maghrib that he knew so well.[10]

Yet, this emphasis on geographical determinants of Maghrib history evokes ghosts of partisan controversies that inflamed the period of colonial rule and decolonization. An example of this kind of writing was Le Passé de l'Afrique du Nord, by the French geographer Emile Félix Gautier, which gained considerable notoriety in its presentation of a North Africa lacking true cultural centers, resisting civilizing influence from Rome to France, made up of indigestible blocs of "old cities, Arab nomadic tribes, sedentary Kabyles, and Berber transhumants," doomed to repeated cycles of "aborted evolution." Gautier used geography as a crude tool to condemn the Maghrib to domination and to justify, seemingly, any and all tactics employed to maintain French rule:

> This land is the eternal partner; it has never succeeded in freeing itself from some master or other. But of all our predecessors here, not a single one has managed to ensure its stability or achieve its ultimate objective. The conquerors have never been able to merge into a single people with the conquered; not once in 3,000 years. It is not simply a question of noting that this is ominous; but let us hope for the best, since there is no other way of proceeding.[11]

Moreover, Gautier was simply more outspoken than most of his compatriots involved in the colonial enterprise. In other forms, some subtle, others crude, various colonial administrators, scholars, and ideologues adopted their own deterministic notions of geography to justify both the French presence and the harsh tactics of rule often used. Thus, the "politique de grands caids," the idea that the rural Maghrib was the "true" Maghrib, idealized as possessing its own form of chivalry (the baroud d'honneur) but still presented as uncivilized (savages, even if at times noble savages) and understanding only force.[12] From the same bag of geographical and ecological maxims that passed for colonial experience also came the notion of "Berber policy" dividing "good Berbers" from "bad Arabs."[13] This kind of thinking also underlay the colonialist support for the brotherhoods, seen as defenders of Maghrib particularism.

The historiography of tomorrow, it might be argued, can dispense with the likes of Gautier and all other examples of geographical determinism. Certainly, no case can be made for the crude geographical reductionism that amounted to what Ageron and, later, Edmund Burke III dubbed the colonialist "vulgate."[14] On the other hand, colonialism is over. Instead of fighting the old battles of yesteryear, why not attempt to filter out what may be useful from the colonialist scholarship? Indeed, in a way that might surprise a Gautier, a late-twentieth-century scholar could put forward the not-inconsiderable geographical constraints on state-building and modernization in the Maghrib as a means of providing a more sympathetic and understanding appraisal of Maghribi states since independence.

Back, then, to the issue of the Maghrib as the most appropriate unit of analysis. A few alternative frames of reference can, for present purposes, be readily dismissed as too large or too diverse (if not, indeed, both). This is surely the case as regards "Third World," or Dar al-Islam, or Africa. Although

Braudel and several other scholars have contributed useful new insights to our historical knowledge by seeing the lands washed by the Mediterranean as a single region, this category does cluster an unnecessarily cumbersome combination of languages, religions, and ecologies, added to which are quite different histories and quite different collective "historical memories."

The alternative deserving more consideration is "Arab world." What, in sum, would be the advantages and disadvantages of a historiography that treated the entire Arab world as a single entity, instead of the conventional Maghrib-Mashriq bifurcation? After all, the Arab world is increasingly a political reality. Historians should rightly be on guard against "reading back" existing circumstances into past time but, on the other hand, historians fail if they fastidiously abstain from working to clarify the past roots of present circumstances. Moreover, there are today approximately 200 million people divided into twenty-two different states, the overwhelming majority of whom speak Arabic, are Muslim, and share a common culture marked by such basic, mundane matters as cuisine, housing style, child rearing, relations between the sexes, and patterns of politesse.

Certainly, at one time the choice between Maghrib-Mashriq and a single Arab entity involved a political agenda. To concentrate on Maghrib separateness and distinctiveness was to play into the hands of the French colonial establishment that consistently sought to stifle all ties between the two parts of the Arab world.[15] Yet, just as we would propose to "depoliticize" old colonialist arguments based on geography so, too, should we dismiss as no longer relevant the old colonialist attempts to keep the Maghrib sealed off from Mashriqi influences.

Indeed, more history writing that takes the entire Arab world as its frame of reference would be welcome, especially if done in an ideology-free spirit. That is, to make the case for (or against) Arab unity will serve no legitimate historical purpose, but to trace the evolution of such political ideas within the context of a clearly defined Arab cultural world must be very much a part of the historian's task.

Even so, the historian must be on guard against any implicitly or explicitly "teleological" history. It has been well said that to choose is also to reject, and substituting a common Arab frame of reference for that of the Maghrib is necessarily to pay more attention to the former and less to the latter. That is a choice that can certainly be defended, but it may not be the most effective way to advance our historical knowledge. This line of thought can be followed to another step. Even the emphasis on the Maghrib can be challenged. Is it not possible to argue that recent political and social developments argue for increased historical attention to the fostering and institutionalization of specific states and civil societies in the Maghrib—Algeria, Morocco, and Tunisia, plus Libya and, to a much lesser extent thus far, Mauritania?

Several comparisons come to mind. Some important groups of English-speaking nations—for example, Canada and the United States or Australia and New Zealand—share a common culture as strongly as do the various Arab countries. Yet, it seems much more logical for the historian to stay essentially within the framework of the individual nation-state, not of the larger English-speaking world. A second example: Kemal Ataturk, in working to create the Republic of Turkey, induced his compatriots to turn their back on Pan-Turanism. In that country, the ensuing years have deepened the sense of "Turkishness" without, however, eliminating the sense of fellow feeling for Turks living in the Balkans, the central Asian states of the former Soviet Union, or elsewhere. Except for the very exciting developments underway in western Europe (a major exception, admittedly), the broad historical tendency worldwide would seem to favor increased nation-state building over merger into larger superstates. This would appear to be especially marked in the Arab world, including the Maghrib.[16]

Another important consideration argues against using the entire Arab world as the unit of analysis. It obscures the formative influence of the Ottoman Empire in shaping political institutions and attitudes of much, but not all, of the Arab world. The difference in historical legacy between a Morocco (never part of the Ottoman Empire) and the rest of the Maghrib (sharing the Ottoman legacy for roughly four centuries) cries out for historical examination. In the same way, it is essential not to lose sight of the quite different experiences of Ottoman rule in the largely autonomous provinces of North Africa (in this case from Egypt to Algeria) as contrasted with conditions in Anatolia and the Fertile Crescent.

Equally, as part of the historian's task of "depoliticizing" and thus correcting previously politicized historical interpretations, it is important to note the sharply different view of those Ottoman years held by Arabs now living in the Mashriq as opposed to citizens of the Maghrib. To the former—except for a few professional scholars who know better—the Ottoman period represents four centuries of backwardness, oppression, and alien rule. The Maghribi perception is more benign. In each case it is a matter of "reading back" into earlier times latter-day political attitudes and perceptions. The eastern Arabs went through the traumatic Young Turk period of rule and formulated an Arab nationalist ideology that took its distance from political "Turkism" emanating from Istanbul. To the Maghrib, the Ottoman Empire was seen as the despoiled Muslim state valiantly fighting the battle of Muslims against western colonialism.[17]

Moreover, as specialists on the premodern period of Maghrib history will affirm, Maghrib history is really distinct from that of the Mashriq. Witness the Aghlabid dynasty, the Spanish Umayyads, the Zirid breakaway from Fatimid rule after the Fatimids had moved eastward to found Cairo, the end of a native Christian presence in North Africa during the time of Almohade rule as contrasted with the continued presence of Christian minorities in the Mashriq. Many other examples of Maghribi distinctiveness could be cited.

What, then, is the best answer to the unit of analysis question? Perhaps Alexander Pope's conservative couplet is not bad advice for the historian:

> *Be not the first by whom the new are tried,*
> *Nor yet the last to lay the old aside.*

The Maghrib as a unit of analysis has proven useful. It clearly helps historians carry out their principal task of presenting a coherent ordering of complex historical data. That spokesmen for French colonial rule once sought to isolate the Maghrib from its Arab and Muslim neighbors and worked to provide a historical interpretation fostering such isolation can now be deemed no more than an interesting historical datum. It is no longer relevant to the question of determining the utility of organizing historical facts in a Maghribi context.

At the same time, historians should look to other possible frames of reference that may, in certain cases, provide coherence and ordering. These other orders will certainly include both the smaller units of individual Maghrib states and such larger frameworks as the entire Arab world.[18]

So, just as later historians can use Gautier in ways that he would not have imagined nor desired, they can also turn even that quintessential imperialist, Rudyard Kipling, to serve their purposes by asserting that for the true historian there can be no fixed borders. For the historian

There is neither East nor West, Border, nor Breed, nor Birth . . .

## Notes

1. *L'histoire du Maghreb: un essai de synthèse* (Paris: François Maspero, 1979), p. 14.

2. Gustave Mercier, *Le Centenaire de l'Algérie: Exposé d'ensemble* (Algiers: P. G. Soubiron, 1931), p. 23.

3. *al-Shihab,* June 1936.

4. Samuel Eliot Morison, "Faith of a Historian," *American Historical Review* LVI (January 1951), p. 263.

5. Albert Guérard, "Millennia," in Alexander V. Riasonovsky and Barnes Riznik, eds., *Generalizations in Historical Writing* (Philadelphia: University of Pennsylvania Press, 1963), p. 197.

6. "It represents therefore a contribution that historical science itself has added to our interpretation of life—one which leads us to place a different construction on the whole human drama, since it uncovers the tragic element in human conflict. In historical perspective we learn to be a little more sorry for both parties than they know how to be for one another." Herbert Butterfield, "The Tragic Element in Modern Conflict" in his *History and Human Relations* (London: Collins, 1951), p. 17.

7. As noted long ago by the French geographer Jean Despois, who wrote: "North Africa is distinct from the arid lands to which it is linked. It is very different from Libya, whose flat terrain extends to the sea and where, except in Cyrenaica, the desert or the steppe extends all the way to the coast. Nor does North Africa have anything in common with Egypt, a ribbon of oasis unrolled within a framework of arid plateaux. North Africa has sometimes been compared with Asia Minor or the Iberian Peninsula, but an analogy with the country of Syria would be both more exact and far more suggestive." Jean Despois, *L'Afrique du Nord* (2d ed.; Paris: PUF, 1958), pp. xi–xii.

8. Charles-André Julien, *Histoire de l'Afrique du Nord. Tunisie-Algérie-Maroc. (Des origines à la conquête arabe),* vol. I [revised by Christian Courtois] (Paris: PUF, 1956), p. 194.

9. Fernand Braudel, "Les Espagnols en Algérie" in *Histoire et historiens,* Collection du Centenaire de l'Algérie, vol. IV (Paris: F. Alcan, 1931), pp. 244–245.

10. Historians have a duty to combat the tendency of later generations to strip political philosophers from their specific historical contexts. Just as Machiavelli makes sense only as an inhabitant of Renaissance Italy, so Ibn Khaldun must be firmly set within the fourteenth-century Maghrib. A more recent example: The political philosophy of Franz Fanon can only be completely understood within the framework of the harsh Algerian armed struggle for independence from 1954 to 1962. Especially useful commentary on the relevance of Ibn Khaldun's great work for the study of Maghrib history (and Mus-

lim history in general) is to be found in several articles by Ernest Gellner, including "Flux and Reflux in the Faith of Men" and "Cohesion and Identity: The Maghreb from Ibn Khaldun to Emile Durkheim" in his *Muslim Society* (Cambridge: Cambridge University Press, 1981), pp. 1–85 and 86–98.

11. Emile F. Gautier, *Le Passé de l'Afrique du Nord: Les siècles obscurs* (Paris: Payot, 1952). The citations are from pp. 438, 440, and 28.

12. It would be useful to compare the colonial administrator's preference for the tribesman over the urbanite in modern European colonialism. Although there is nothing quite like the full-throttle romanticism of the British (from Rudyard Kipling to T. E. Lawrence) in French rule, something of the same mystique prevailed. Or, to put the matter in the Maghribi context, the spirit of the Bureaux Arabes remained alive to the end. Now that European colonialism is over, the subject can be studied with both greater empathy and greater objectivity. Nor was this colonialist romanticism consistently a bad thing. Given the harsh fact of alien domination, paternalistic colonialism could serve to mitigate the iron fist in a way that what might be labeled bureaucratic colonialism could not. On the other hand, paternalistic colonialism did serve to stifle the development of modernizing, urban-based nationalist forces. Thus, the issue of which form of colonialism best served the postcolonial needs of the society affected is not easily resolved.

13. See, on France's Berber policy, Charles-Robert Ageron, "La France a-t-elle eu une politique Kabyle?," *Revue Historique* CCXXIII (1960), as well as his "La Politique Berbère du protectorat marocain de 1913 à 1934" in his *Politiques coloniales au Maghreb* (Paris: PUF, 1972), pp. 109–148.

14. See the several articles by Burke developing this theme, including "The Image of the Moroccan State in French Ethnological Literature. A New Look at the Origin of Lyautey's Berber Policy" in Ernest Gellner and Charles Micaud, eds., *Arabs and Berbers: From Tribe to Nation in North Africa* (London: Duckworth, 1972), pp. 175–199.

15. The significant role of one individual, Shakib Arslan, in fostering the Maghrib's sense of Arabism is well brought out in William L. Cleveland, *Islam Against the West: Shakib Arslan and the Campaign for Islamic Nationalism* (Austin: University of Texas Press, 1985). See especially chapter 4, "Mentor to a Generation: North Africa."

16. See L. Carl Brown, "The Middle East: Patterns of Change, 1947–1987," *Middle East Journal* XLI, no. 1 (Winter 1987), pp. 26–39.

17. I well remember during my first field research in Tunisia (1960–1961) the late Uthman Kaak's telling me that for weeks after the French occupation of Tunisia in 1881, Tunisians would go to the seashore hoping to see the arrival of Ottoman ships.

18. A few suggestions for comparative Maghrib-Mashriq historiography:

(1) The fascinating concatenation of similarities linking Tunisian and Egyptian history during the nineteenth century, as first noted by the Egyptian historian Shafiq Ghorbal in his introduction to the Arabic edition of *Initiation à la Tunisie*. See also the elaboration of that theme in L. Carl Brown, "Toward a Comparative History of Modernization in the Arab World: Tunisia and Egypt," in *Identité culturelle et conscience nationale en Tunisie: Actes de Colloque de Tunis—1974* (Cahiers du CERES, Série Sociologique II, June 1975).

(2) The comparative possibilities of "reform from the top" modernization in Egypt, Tunisia, and the central Ottoman Empire. Suggestions of how this might be done are contained in the conclusion to L. Carl Brown, *The Tunisia of Ahmad Bey* (Princeton: Princeton University Press, 1974).

(3) The difference between settler colonies as in the Maghrib and nonsettler colonization in the Mashriq. See, for example, L. Carl Brown, "The Many Faces of Colonial Rule in French North Africa," *ROMM,* nos. 13–14, (1st semester 1973), pp. 171–191. See also Edmund Burke III, "Morocco and the Middle East: Reflections on Some Basic Differences," *Archives européennes de sociologie* X (1980), pp. 70–94.

# Reflections on the Historiography
## of the Ancient Maghrib

*Ammar Mahjoubi*
Université de Tunis

For many years, the historiography of the ancient Maghrib commanded only a limited following. In the past three decades, however, interpretations of the Roman period developed by both historians and archeologists from the French colonial era to the present have elicited considerable interest that has resulted in the appearance of numerous scholarly studies and some polemical works as well. Among the publications stimulating this attention to the Maghrib's ancient history were the works of two Moroccan scholars—Abdallah Laroui's sweeping *Histoire du Maghreb* (1970) and Marcel Benabou's 1976 thesis, *La résistance africaine à la romanisation*. More recently, Paul Albert Février devotes the first two chapters of his *Approches du Maghreb romain* (1989) to a discussion of the historiography of the Roman period.

Two explanations for this sudden interest in the ancient Maghrib stand out. First, the process of decolonization, with its attendant political events, inevitably invited a reassessment of the view of the Maghribi past, both as it had been fashioned by historians and archeologists working with the Department of Antiquities in "French North Africa" or with academic centers in Paris or Rome and as it had emerged from the accounts and observations of seventeenth-, eighteenth-, and nineteenth-century European travelers. Second, the dramatically revised picture of North African Antiquity that began to develop fueled not only new research, but also advances in prospecting and excavating techniques, materials analysis, and methodology.

Following the independence of their countries, the very few North Africans who undertook archeological research could not avoid being struck by the remarkable parallels between the characterizations made by partisans of French colonization and those which appeared in the historiography of Roman Africa.[1] Unfavorable comments on Arabs and Kabyles and the importance ascribed to the benefits of French civilization (or that of Italy in Tripolitania) faithfully echoed judgments on the barbarity of Libyans and Numidians and the emphasis on the civilizing influences of Rome which brought urban life and economic development to the area.[2]

The writings of the nineteenth century—and sometimes those of the twentieth—often opened with a discussion of the salience of North Africa's geography, emphasizing its importance in shaping the virtually static traits of the local culture. Then followed relentlessly repeated axioms about the immutability of customs from the dawn of history to modern times: tribes whose way of life was endlessly perpetuated without alteration;[3] populations incapable of organizing, governing, or unifying themselves;[4] a permanent state of rebellion among bands led by utterly fractious men bent upon raiding and plundering;[5] a country introduced into History only thanks to Carthage and Rome, and whose own past is no more than an interminable succession of Semitic invaders from the East or Greco-Roman or Judeo-Christian invaders from the West.[6] As a final verdict, Gilbert Charles-Picard concluded in 1954 that "the disconcerting sterility of their [the Libyans] nature renders them incapable, unless compelled by some external authority, to move beyond the most primitive manifestations of human activity, as is clearly revealed in the realm of the religious just as it is in that of politics or economics."[7]

It seemed never to occur to these historians that Gaul and the Iberian peninsula, which had experienced the penetration of an "imported" civilization in much the same way as had the Maghrib, manifested features congruent with those ascribed to North Africa, including tribal divisions and armed resistance to the Roman conquest by tribes led by equally fractious men. Nor did it matter that certain European religious traditions, habits, and customs that are as persistent as those in the Maghrib may be looked upon—with an identical dose of imagination—as derived from the earliest Antiquity.

The Berbers' exposure to alien cultures allegedly brought out the remarkable "aptitude for civilization" of these otherwise "backward" and "restless" people, leading Jérome Carcopino to assert that "there exists, deep in the Berber mentality, and in spite of the mobility so often condemned by Latin writers, the ability to understand the benefits of a superior civilization, the flexibility to absorb them and, above all, the obstinate dedication to preserve them, even after the departure of the benefactors. . . ."[8] Carcopino goes on to amass arguments justifying his contention: ceramics from Kabylia display such "rectilinear decorations that one would deem them descendants of Hellenic ceramics;" the longevity of Punic influences in language, the arts, and religion is exceptional; many "Muslim" customs in fields as diverse as city planning, clothing, and social practices (such as *diffa*, the hospitality accorded to guests) correspond to Hellenistic and Roman customs. Finally, the author praises "the stubborn commitment that sufficed to enable the Numidians to claim from Latin culture and the Church such illustrious names as Minucius Felix, Tertullian, Saint Cyprian, Saint Optat of Milev, and Saint Augustine. It was the same stubborn commitment that romanized Moors gave with all their heart to the empire and to Christianity." [9]

This presumed attachment of the Africans of Antiquity, both Numidians and romanized Moors, to Latin culture and Christianity boded well for the modern resumption of the Church's interrupted work. Archeologists and clerics joined forces to restore the Christian past in North Africa following the 1867 appointment to the See of Algiers of Charles Cardinal Lavigerie, who proclaimed "May God grant that this victory of France be also the final victory of Christian civilization in these barbarous lands." [10] In 1875, Lavigerie sent missionaries to Carthage to watch over the tomb of Saint Louis. Among them was Père Alfred Louis Delattre who, along with many men of the cloth, suddenly discovered a talent for archeology. Brimming with enthusiasm, he plowed the soil of Carthage in search of basilicas and Christian inscriptions, founded a museum, and ordered the construction of the primatial church of Saint Louis. But the Church experienced a severe disappointment as it came to realize that Islam had erased the very memory of Christian Africa.

An overview of archeological exploration and research from the early modern European travelers (whose interest in the relics of the past echoed the curiosity of their Arab predecessors) [11] to the middle of this century is a prerequisite for assessing the present state of ancient historiography in the Maghrib. This essay focuses primarily on Tunisia but, owing to its affinity with Algeria, both physically and in terms of the issues raised, also takes that country's past into account.

From the end of the nineteenth century to the middle of the twentieth, it is possible to discern the birth and development—initially under the influence of policies of colonial conquest and later those of direct rule over "French North Africa"—of two perspectives. One concentrated on the native, "Barbary," and colonization, while the other, in parallel fashion, emphasized Africa, its people, and the influence of Rome. Paul Albert Février, in reviewing the reports and observations of such early visitors as Thomas d'Arcos in the seventeenth century and Ximenes, Peyssonnel, and, especially, Shaw in the eighteenth, has provided a broad analysis of the context of this era and the activities of its principal "actors," to whom we owe the discovery of many of the epigraphic and archeological riches of the Maghrib, but also much of their destruction and looting. [12]

With the conquest of Algeria in 1830, archeological exploration took another form. It fell to a commission of the expeditionary force to discover ancient ruins and gather inscriptions, antiquities, and objets d'art. This amateurish military undertaking was supplemented by the work of such able and experienced individuals as the paleographer and archivist Louis Adrien Berbrugger, the illustrator Delamare, the architect Ravoisie, and Léon Renier, the assistant librarian at the Sorbonne, who greatly influenced research by stressing the importance of epigraphic texts as distinct from their archeological context. Later, learned societies and the clergy assumed many of these same tasks, but the military always remained active in them.

In Tunisia, following the initial work of the Danish Consul C. T. Falbe, his British consular colleague Sir Thomas Reade, and the latter's compatriot Nathan Davis, the visit of Victor Guérin in the middle of the nineteenth century expanded the knowledge of both Tunisia and its antiquities, thereby providing valuable insights for those who would later occupy the country. Later came the missions of Charles Ernest Beulé to Carthage, and of A. Daux and Evariste Charles Pricot de Sainte-Marie. Finally, Père Delattre displayed his religious zeal in Carthage just prior to, and after, Tunisia's occupation by French troops.[13] The efforts of officers in the army of occupation, such as Captain Vincent and Lieutenant Espérandieu, greatly increased the extent and number of explorations and the gathering of inscriptions.[14] But the most important figure was Charles Tissot. This diplomat, historian, and geographer, after initial inquiries in Tunisia and Constantine province, returned to Morocco in the early 1870s and studied the Bagrada in 1879. His monumental *Géographie comparée de la province romaine d'Afrique* was published in 1888, after his death, by Salomon Reinach. As Février points out, at the same time that all these works made the country better known, they paved the way for its occupation. "Politics and archeology," he noted, "shared the same purpose."[15]

As early as 1881, topographical detachments of the French Army began the identification and mapping of archeological remains, thereby establishing the bases of two atlases. *L'Atlas archéologique de l'Algérie* by Stéphane Gsell and *L'Atlas archéologique de la Tunisie*. The former remains a valuable source of information and is of much greater use than the latter. A beylical decree of 1882 established the national museum at the Bardo Palace and the Tunisian Department of Antiquities, under the control of the Académie des Inscriptions et Belles Lettres and the French Ministry of Education through a "North African Commission" created within the Committee for Historical Research. As the archeological missions multiplied (Reinach and Babelon in Carthage and in Gigthi gathering inscribed stones from Phoenician sanctuaries; Cagnat roaming the country in search of inscriptions; Saladin setting down the architectural plans of monuments, especially pagan temples and Christian basilicas), René Ducoudray, nicknamed "La Blanchère," was appointed director of the Department of Antiquities in 1885. His chief contribution was to assemble in the Bardo Museum the Manouba Palace collection of former Prime Minister Mustapha Khaznadar Bey, along with other pieces, many of them from Gigthi. In this respect, Tunisian archeology differed significantly from Algerian. Despite the remarkable work of Stéphane Gsell, who was appointed inspector of antiquities in 1900, the architects of the Algerian Department of Historical Monuments kept a tight rein on the management of the monuments as well as of the digs.

The decade between 1880 and 1890 marked a turning point in the accumulation and the organization of the archeological heritage in both Tunisia and Algeria. Important excavations were started in Algeria, particularly at Thamugadi and Lambaesis, where well-preserved forums and public buildings were brought to light. The contemporary preoccupation with Christian basilicas is best explained by ideological motivations. In Tunisia, this interest centered on the beautiful mosaics of the Sorothus House in Sousse and those of the Labirii house in Oudhna and corresponded with the contemporary enthusiasm for "fine artistic works." Paul Gauckler's tireless activity and the rigorous quality of his research made him a remarkable director of the Department of Antiquities. In addition to Christian basilicas and mosaics, however, he also devoted considerable attention to Punic sites. Two of his books remained for a long time the basic references for Punic chronology. In southern Tunisia, which remained under military control until the eve of independence, the army undertook archeological investigations. As might be expected, the primary archeological concern of army personnel was for the small fortifications of the ancient defensive line along the Saharan frontier.

Extensive research continued until the First World War, benefiting from the contributions of young members of the French School of Rome, who initiated a tradition carried on by agreements between the school and the Archeological Institute in Tunis after independence. Among the best known of these scholars were Auguste Audollent, Maurice Besnier, Jérome Carcopino, Léon Pol Homo, Alfred Merlin, and Jacques Toutain. In Algeria, the continuation of excavations at Thamugadi and their commencement at Cuicul allowed Stéphane Gsell and the architect Charles Albert Joly to publish three volumes on Thibilis, Thurbisicu, and Madauros. Alfred Merlin, the next director of the Department of Antiquities in Tunisia, began the series entitled "Notes et Documents" with the publication of the inscriptions of Uchi Maius. There followed publications on the temple of Apollo in Bulla Regia, the forums of Thuburbo Maius and Althiburos, and the "mosaic homes" at the latter site. This attests to an unflagging interest in epigraphy, in "Roman" public monuments, and in elegant mosaic work. In Dougga (Latin: Thugga) Dr. Carton, a dedicated amateur, started the excavation of the theater. He was also active at Bulla Regia, where he discovered houses with underground quarters, and in Carthage, where he brought to light a Punic chapel.

In fact, archeologists' greatest interest resided in the necropolises and the religion of "Dido's Carthage." At about the same time, Merlin published a work on the sanctuaries of Ba'al and Tanit near Siagu. In the course of excavations near Thignica, Carcopino found the inscription of Ain Djemala concerning the management of imperial estates and the condition of the colonizers. He thus presented an opportunity—to specialists and nonspecialists alike—to stress the theme of the great prosperity of "the granary of Rome" and to observe the region's subsequent decline. Other excavations were initiated in Gigthi, Simitthu, Thina, Sousse, and on the Bou Kornein mountain near Tunis.

When Louis Poinssot succeeded Merlin in 1921 at the Department of Antiquities, he made Dougga his favorite site, clearing the better part of the location and restoring its important monuments. Yet, despite the fact that interest remained concentrated on the Roman period at the expense of medieval and later periods buried in soil layers that disappeared with ongoing excavations, it was Poinssot who oversaw the restoration of the famous Numidian mausoleum and the great mosque of Kairouan, as well as the publication of Qur'an bindings discovered in that mosque, some of which dated to the Aghlabid era. Poinssot's investigative spirit and scientific integrity compelled him to an interest in the periods before and after the Roman one. Even so, the pre-Islamic era retained pride of place, as demonstrated by a beylical decree issued at Poinssot's initiative in 1921. Wishing to strengthen the archeological laws, he arranged to have the Tunisian state become the owner of all antiquities henceforth discovered. But antiquities, in this case, referred only to sites and items predating the Arab conquest.

When Gilbert Charles-Picard succeeded Poinssot in 1941, he attempted to show greater interest in the Punic and medieval periods. Inspector of Antiquities Pierre Cintas worked at Utica, on Cape Bon, and in Carthage, where he conducted a search of the tophet and attempted to establish a chronology. Imperfect though his work may have been, he pioneered the study of Punic ceramics, on which he wrote numerous essays. On the other hand, Slimane Mostafa Zbiss, as inspector of Muslim antiquities, worked in Mahdia, organizing and protecting the historical monuments that had been preserved. The architect Alexandre Lézine published a study on the *ribat* (fortified monastery) of Sousse. Charles-Picard and his wife themselves augmented the staff of the Department of Antiquities with their digs at Mactaria, Acholla, and Carthage, where they discovered the public baths of Antoninus Pius. Charles-Picard assigned to the Bardo Museum two former members of the Ecole Française de Rome, Pierre Quoniam and Edmond

Frezouls, who continued the development and organization programs started by Poinssot. He also placed departmental representatives in Sousse (Louis Foucher), Acholla, the Sfax area (Mohamed Fendri), and in Dougga, where he named Claude Poinssot to follow in his father's footsteps.

Beginning in the middle of the nineteenth century, the expansion of learned societies in Algeria multiplied the number of publications appearing. In the *Recueil de Constantine,* a review of the Société Archéologique de Constantine, most of the articles were accounts by soldiers of their explorations, digs, and the inscriptions they had gathered. But some civilians— mostly amateurs who worked in the civil service—also contributed studies on Latin and ancient topics, along with some on the Arabic language, literature, and epigraphy. This made it possible to record some of the countless vestiges that were excavated but then destroyed or lost without a trace. Such instances occurred frequently in the course of public works projects and the construction of settlement villages. The same learned society is credited with creating a museum in Constantine and even of undertaking some clearing work, notably in Cuicul.

The Société Historique d'Alger was not founded until 1856, a few years after that of Constantine. But the title of its journal—*La Revue africaine*— clearly indicates that its scope was encyclopedic. Sharing with its sister institution in Constantine the desire to pursue both Latin and Arabic studies, it named as its vice-president William MacGuckin, Baron de Slane, the translator and editor of al-Bakri and a translator of Ibn Khaldun. At first, Roman archeology was its main concern. The society participated in the preservation of collections housed in museums established in Algiers, Cherchell, and Tipasa, and prevented them from being shipped to Paris. Subsequently, the focus of its journal's articles shifted increasingly towards Muslim religious monuments, jurisprudence, and law, and medieval and modern history.

In Bône (now Annaba), the *Bulletin de l'académie d'Hippone* appeared in 1865. Primarily devoted to Roman archeology, it later published many reports sent from Tunisia by officers of the expeditionary force. A learned society, whose first bulletin appeared in 1878, was subsequently founded in Oran, as was a museum.

Aside from these journals, other important works included the *Recueil d'inscriptions libyco-berbères* published in 1870 by Captain Victor-Constant Reboud and the *Collection complète des inscriptions numidiques* by General Louis Léon Faidherbe, which came out in the same year but is of lesser value. In Paris, studies appeared in *Revue archéologique, Comptes-rendus de l'Académie des inscriptions et belles-lettres, Nouvelles archives des missions,* and *Mémoires de la Société des antiquaires.* Nor did the Berlin Academy overlook the rich epigraphic crop harvested by Germans. Gustav Wilmanns, who was responsible for preparing Volume VIII of the *Corpus Inscriptionum Latinarum* which was devoted to Africa, personally went to check the epigraphic texts in the field, only to learn of the loss of many of them and the deplorable condition of the unprotected ruins.[16] The great German historian of Rome, Theodor Mommsen, completed Wilmanns's work, which appeared in 1881.

For obvious reasons, the French scientific establishment was embarrassed by the defeat of 1870 and resolved to make North African archeology its exclusive preserve. Convinced of the importance of keeping epigraphy within the sole purview of France, even after World War I, René Cagnat published *Inscriptions latines d'Afrique*. Such an attitude persisted among many French archeologists long after the countries gained their independence. The Church also shared in this jingoism. Although Giovanni Bernardo De Rossi could include in the *Bolletino di archeologia cristiana* in the 1870s news from Algeria, sent mainly by the Bishop of Constantine, Cardinal Lavigerie would not tolerate foreigners conducting digs in the area. In Tunisia, for instance, he attempted, through Père Delattre, to have the Italian Capuchins evicted.

One must take note, however, of a very sharp slowdown in the rate of scientific publications between World War I and the post–World War II years. The *Notes et documents de la Direction des antiquités de Tunis* concluded its publications in 1929 with *L'Autel de la gens Augusta*. The only other publication after World War I was the proceedings of a symposium on Thuburbo Maius which appeared in 1922. The same year saw the publication of the first volume of Stéphane Gsell's *Inscriptions latines de l'Algérie*—a collection much closer to the quality of the *Corpus Inscriptionum Latinarum* of the Berlin Academy than its counterpart book of Tunisian inscriptions by Cagnat. During this period, the archeological services of Algeria contented themselves with episodic accounts and reports on the currently active digs. All that remains of these are a few supervisors' reports and very cursory information. The same unfortunate conditions prevailed in Tunisia where, following the suspension of the Notes et Documents series, there appeared between 1921 and 1934 only the slender articles of the *Bulletin de la société archéologique de Sousse,* along with a few articles in *Revue tunisienne,* which displayed only a passing interest in archeology and ancient history in its publications series of 1894–1923 and 1930–1943.[17]

This brief retrospective has clearly shown that archeology very often pursued the same goals as colonial policy, laying the groundwork for the occupation of the country by revealing crucial geographical, ethnographical, and social aspects of its past. This approach gave birth, whether consciously and intentionally or not, to an ideological interpretation that dominated studies of the native population and analyses of historical development until the acquisition of independence.

Such was the case with the 1955 Franco-Tunisian agreements that ushered in the short-lived interlude of internal autonomy. In those agreements, the French imposed a specific division of responsibilities between the Tunisian Department of Antiquities and the French Archeological Mission in Tunisia. To the Tunisians fell that part of their history after the Arab conquest, while the French mission kept for itself the field of ancient history. Behind the prejudices, the pretentions, and the interests of French archeological circles in Tunis and within the North African Commission, as well as in the Committee for Historical Research, was there not the obdurate survival of the idea that French colonial policy was the legitimate heir to the Roman colonization it intended to revive? Was there not also the bizarre habit of slicing the history of the Maghrib into discontinuous segments, to the point not only of depriving North Africans of their ancient history, but also of the right to manage and study that history in any capacity except as mere foreigners?

Other, purportedly "scientific" interpretations have also prevailed, even though their true origin lies in the views and experiences of the first archeologists. Février has shown that, very often, comments on the vulnerability of Roman settlements and the importance of their fortifications are nothing but reflections of the views and concerns of the French army and the archeologists who followed in its footsteps. For them "the antagonism between Romans and natives, between people of the plains and people of the mountains, between the Kabyle (or the Berber) and the Arab, between the army and the rest of the populace, often remained present in the collective subconscious of researchers."[18] One scarcely need add that such interpretations are rooted in information derived from literary traditions, especially Latin histories and geographies on the one hand and archeological studies and the abundant epigraphic evidence on the other. But in the days of scientism, these interpretations bore no rebuttal.

However, the advances previously made in textual analysis and critique, as well as in the publishing of historical texts, had not yet enabled scholars of the period to avoid the pitfalls of a text. They often contented themselves with repeating, word for word, the comments of Tacitus or Ammianus Marcellinus, taking at face value a hodgepodge of facts, images, or ideas the author wished to convey about a specific situation or within a specific context.[19] Similarly, the official language and standard dedications found in epigraphic texts were rarely seen primarily as indications of power or expressions of an ideology. Their idyllic picture of prosperous towns and a harmoniously dynamic society fit perfectly with the magnificent public monuments and beautiful mosaics uncovered by the digs. This was because the digs concentrated on the main monuments in the forum and other public monuments with, at best, an occasional foray into a few other temples, Christian basilicas, or homes in which care was taken to show only the superb floors made of pictorial polychromatic mosaics.

A dearth of official epigraphic texts, whether absent or lost, was taken as a sign of decadence unless it could be proven that the region had been affected only slightly, or not at all, by the Roman presence. It is only quite recently that attention has been paid to the vagaries of the discovery and preservation of texts, the relative extent of digs from one area to another or one town to another, the scarcity or abundance of stone, or the diversity in the execution and use of epigraphy from one period to another.

For a long time, the tendency of European scholars imbued with classical educations and views to search almost exclusively for the beautiful, the spectacular, and the well known exerted considerable influence on historical interpretation. This bias reduced the history of archeological sites to the Roman period. That the depth of digs rarely went below the level of the second century A.D. is a case in point. Thus, archeological data on the Punic-Numidian period were virtually absent except for a few mausoleums, such as the one in Dougga; a few monumental tombs, such as the Medracen; and the Punic necropolises and Numidian graves located on the outskirts of towns and, therefore, not covered by layers dating from the Roman period.

Consequently, Stéphane Gsell, in his remarkable and monumental history which regrettably stopped at the very beginning of the Roman conquest, could rely only on texts and a few digs in the Punic necropolises or sanctuaries. The opportunity to compare the data from the literary tradition with archeological finds from the Punic-Numidian period would probably have been of great benefit in the writing of the eight volume *Histoire ancienne de l'Afrique du Nord* published between 1913 and 1928, if only that historical period had enjoyed some of the attention monopolized by the Roman era.

Yet another factor is even more serious and has most unfortunate consequences for the writing of the Maghrib's history. Not only did colonial scholars continue to insist that the vast majority of the Libyan population, including the Numidians, consisted of nomadic tribes which, as Tacitus had asserted, did not live in cities[20] (so that the towns of the ancient Maghrib were, with the exception of Punic coastal settlements, Roman from their inception), but they also vigorously claimed that the towns, after an admirable blossoming, fell victims to a long period of decadence at the end of Antiquity, only to disappear entirely following the Arab conquest. So authoritative were these assertions that care was taken to "clear" properly the vestiges of Roman times and eliminate all the "warts" (such as walls built with recycled materials or crude mortar)—in a word, the very strata which told the history of a city from the end of Antiquity to at least the Arabo-Muslim High Middle Ages.

Take Dougga, for instance. Every trace of the Arab period has been irretrievably lost save for a few glazed lamps, a few enameled fragments of glass, and the vestiges of the Arab baths below the forum.[21] Yet Arab geographers whose works were being translated by the likes of Baron de Slane could easily have been cited to prove the ongoing urbanism and prosperity of transit towns such as Hadrumetum (Sousse) or Vaga (Béja). Equally worthy of mention would have been numerous hydraulic works, such as the open-air basins and the systems for collecting water from springs found in the Sahel and the Lower Steppes, all of which date back to the medieval period. Unfortunately, those were classified by the *Atlas archéologique de la Tunisie* as "Roman ruins." In any event, the "destruction" of Roman towns, held to be quite evident and explained by the incursions, looting, and *ghazawat* (plural of *ghazwa*, "raid") of the Berber tribes or the Arab "hordes," was apparently confirmed by the process of "gourbification" and by the "warts" so hastily removed to cleanse the "Roman" monuments. But there is no need to belabor this point, which has been dealt with at length in articles on permanence and change in urban life at the end of Antiquity and the beginning of the Arab Muslim period.[22]

The introduction to this article mentioned the substantial progress over the past thirty years in the study of the ancient Maghrib and of the knowledge gathered thanks to dramatic advances in archeology. But while it is too soon to assess the various aspects and trends of the most recent historiography, it is possible, nonetheless, to point to those that seem the most important.

It must first be said that, unlike the situation before the Second World War, scholars have since had at their disposal bibliographical catalogues covering all the studies dealing with ancient Africa. As things now stand, thanks to the nearly exhaustive bibliography amassed in 1951 by Charles Courtois in the second edition of Charles-André Julien's *Histoire de l'Afrique du Nord des origines à la conquête arabe,* there is practically no need to resort to other bibliographical sources for works written prior to the middle of this century. This undertaking was followed in 1953 by the bulletin of the Department of Antiquities of Algeria, *Libyca,* whose bibliographical section was regularly written by Marcel Glay until 1961. Then, starting in 1965, the Mediterranean Archeology Section of the French CNRS in Aix-en-Provence began publishing *Archéologie de l'Afrique antique,* one of whose recent issues provides a list of works published in 1984 and 1985. The *Bibliographie analytique de l'Afrique antique* prepared by Jehan Desanges and Serge Lancel has long been a particularly useful tool despite several years' delay between the publication and recording of new works (recent issues list studies that appeared some five years earlier). These bibliographical reviews do not, of course, replace the general bibliographies of the *Revue historique* or, especially, those of *Année philologique*. There are also extremely important specialized bibliographical reviews such as the *Rivista di studi fenici* for Carthage and the Punic world and the *Bulletin de l'AIEMA* for studies on mosaic decor.

Even more numerous are editions of literary sources, epigraphic collections, and archeological and iconographic repertories such as editions of the works of African authors and texts relative to Africa, all of which have greatly facilitated research. Most worthy of note are Desanges's edition of Book V of Pliny;[23] the numerous collections of inscriptions, from the first installment of Volume II of the *Inscriptions latines de l'Algérie,* published in 1957 by Hans Georg Pflaum, to the catalogue of the Latin inscriptions of the Bardo Museum by Zeineb Ben Abdallah, published in 1986; and the successive installments of the *Corpus des mosaïques de Tunisie* edited primarily by Margaret Alexander and Aicha Ben Abed.

On the other hand, since the publication in 1953 of *Libyca, archéologie épigraphique* and its counterpart dealing with prehistory and ethnology, several other African archeological reviews have been published more or less regularly. In Tunisia, the first issue of *Karthago* appeared in 1950. After the creation of the National Institute of Archeology and Arts in Tunis, this journal was published under the auspices of the French Archeological Mission, first in Tunis, then in Paris. The Tunis Institute published its own review, *Africa,* while the French CNRS began publishing *Antiquités africaines* in 1967.

Also beginning in the 1960s, numerous theses and books treated various periods of Maghribi antiquity. At the same time, the foci of scholars diversified. The pre-Roman period enjoyed a heightened interest, initially from North Africans whose motivation was ideological as well as scientific. To the search for cultural roots, the assertion of national identity, and the reaction against the neglect—not to say the contempt—displayed by some towards that period during the colonial era, was added the desire to strengthen knowledge previously limited to funeral monuments and a few sanctuaries. Explorations were conducted in the Sahel and on Cape Bon, where Punic monuments and sites were discovered on the coast. The digs in the Punic town of Kerkouane, whose remains had not been covered by the building of a city after the Roman occupation, were conducted with special diligence.

The Tunisian government received financial help from UNESCO to undertake an international program of digs at Carthage. At the same time, Punic studies enjoyed an increasing degree of attention from scholars, especially in

Italy. Numerous papers raised anew questions regarding the foundation of Carthage, Punic religion and institutions, and Phoenician and Punic expansion. Our understanding has especially been broadened by archeological contributions in Kerkouane and Carthage that have enhanced our knowledge of urban topography and aided the study of living conditions and architecture, including wall and floor decorations. The household utensils thus collected are a rich source of information on the way of life and culture in this society. In Carthage, Serge Lancel, working on the hills of Byrsa, and Friedrich Rakob, closer to the sea near the old beylical palace, have succeeded in studying the various stages in the evolution of these districts within the overall evolution of the city itself. They have looked at the different phases of construction and the successive reapportionment of land, including some sort of resettlement area in Byrsa shortly before 146 B.C. Along the coast were large tracts of land and luxurious villas that were later replaced by narrower houses clinging together along the coastal rampart. Unfortunately, the urban landscape, with its rich, poor, and even destitute districts, each with its own architecture, decor, and everyday objects betokening social relationships, has not received, in the monograph on Kerkouane, all the attention it deserves.

Ceramics, once neglected except for those beautiful specimens gathered whole in necropolises, also became an important subject of socioeconomic studies, as well as a chronological and stratigraphic standard. Besides the Punic-Libyan ceramics, for which an attempt at classification was made in the 1950s, the black varnish ceramics, whether imported from Greater Greece or imitated locally, have been the object of much attention, especially in the work of Jean-Paul Morel.

Among the new historical overviews of the Punic period, those of Sabatino Moscati and Maurice Sznycer deserve particular mention, even if the latter, prepared by a Semitic specialist in Phoenician and Punic studies and appearing in Claude Nicolet's *Nouvelle clio,* does not make sufficient allowance for archeological data.

In Numidian country, the probes that have been extended down to previously unexplored levels at Simitthu and Belalis Maior have made it possible to go back to the origins of urban development, especially around the third century B.C. The study of Caesarea, capital of Juba II and of Ptolemy, was significant for the interest it displayed in the countryside, in that rural archeology had remained, ever since the colonial period, a stepchild of research. Furthermore, the study of the architectural decor of the Numidian princes' altars and monumental tombs, still often looked upon as "Hellenistic dressing on a native model," has revealed the remarkable degree of integration of upper Numidian society with ancient Greek culture.[24]

Many earlier interpretations of the Roman period have also been revised. Without going into detail on a wide variety of topics, suffice it to note the progress made in the knowledge of ceramic features, especially regarding African pottery and its economic role.[25] The extensive research on urban architecture and late Antiquity, stretching chronologically from the fourth century A.D. to the Arab High Middle Ages, has made it possible to follow the evolution and transformations of cities.

To conclude this particular theme, the thesis of Marcel Benabou on "African Resistance to Romanization," which precipitated a rich and sometimes passionate debate, should be mentioned. It should also be noted that this study has not been criticized for "standing history on its head," as some North Africans have at times been tempted to do in reaction to the interpretations and prejudices of the colonial period. But if one cannot deny the agricultural accomplishments of the Romans any more than one can deny the reality and evolution of African culture, neither can one deny the influence of the dominant Mediterranean civilizations—Greek during the Numidian-Punic period, then Greco-Roman. Indeed, such influence was sometimes pronounced, especially for the ruling classes at both the provincial and urban levels.

In fine intellectual tradition, contemporary researchers have continued to build on the foundations laid in the best work of the nineteenth-century pioneers of the study of the Maghrib's ancient history. At the same time, scholars of the postindependence years have shed the most debilitating of their predecessors' assumptions and prejudices, enabling them to transcend the colonialist mentalities that limited the capacity of earlier generations of historians and archeologists to present a full and accurate picture of the region in Antiquity. Among other benefits, this new outlook has generated a greater emphasis on the medieval Arab and Punic eras, both of which had suffered neglect in the interest of underscoring the supposed links between ancient Rome and imperial France and Italy. Today's scholars have broadened their outlook not only chronologically, but also with respect to identifying components of the past that may hold important keys to a richer understanding of its complexity. New methodologies, many of them grounded in the most up-to-date technology, and the development of entire new fields such as rural archeology have expedited their work, frequently enabling them to portray rich colors where once there were only monochromes. An immensely useful next stage for today's admirably equipped scholars would be a more detailed analysis of the questions broached in this overview and elsewhere in a thorough state-of-the-field examination of ancient Africa's historiography.

## Notes

1. See Ammar Mahjoubi, "Pour une histoire ancienne décolonisée de l'Afrique du Nord," in *La Construction du Maghreb* (Tunis: CERES, 1983), pp. 56–61.

2. As late as 1959, Pietro Romanelli, in his *Storia delle province romane dell'Africa,* reverted to themes presented in the writings of such ancient historians as Sallust and Tacitus and of such geographers as Strabo when he portrayed the armed resistance of the North Africans as a clash between barbarism and civilization, between instinct and rationality—in a word, between absolute evil and supreme good.

3. From the *mapalia* (the hut of the nomadic Africans described by Sallust) to today's *gourbi* (a crude stone dwelling found in southern Tunisia), or from the bread oven found in a Punic tomb to the *tabouna* of the contemporary Tunisian countryside—not to mention the cult of the jinn or that of the martyrs—this is seen not in terms of traditions becoming extinct nor of constants in comparable circumstances (as happens in Europe), but rather in terms of the local population lingering in a primitive stage of development.

4. Paul-Albert Février notes that Gabriel Camps still spoke, in 1961, of "the historical inability of North Africa to achieve unity." *Approches du Maghreb romain* (Aix-en-Provence: Edisud, 1989), p. 24.

5. These themes, which have been bandied about since the nineteenth century, eventually seduced even the former president of Tunisia, Habib Bourguiba. He prided himself in having founded the first truly Tunisian state and in unifying a land that had, since the dawn of history, been stifled by tribalism and anarchy. At the same time, he compared himself to Jugurtha, but a Jugurtha who succeeded. See, for example, Bourguiba's remarks during a 1968 state visit to Rome as cited in Sophie Bessis and Souhayr Belhassen, *Bourguiba,* vol. 2: *Un si long règne* (Paris: Jeunes Afriques Livres, 1988–1989), p. 82.

6. "Islam founded Kairouan (670), destroyed Carthage (698), and rejected Africa for twelve centuries in the Oriental and Semitic cycle of history," concluded Charles Saumagne in his introduction to "La Tunisie antique" in *Atlas historique, géographique, économique et touristique de la Tunisie* (Paris: Horizons de France, 1936), p. 27. Février, *Approches,* p. 24, cites the views of two well-known French scholars in this regard. Léon Galibert remarked that "'Abd el-Kader was Jugurtha, Tacfarinas, and Firmus. Men are always the same; only the names change." Emile Félix Gautier, explaining that Barbary "has always been a province of an empire," observed that "although this race may have some fundamental vitality . . . it has no positive individuality." According to Abdallah Laroui, "The dilemma imposed on us is this: Either you deal with the history of the foreign invaders or you confine yourself to pre-

history and protohistory." *Histoire du Maghreb* (Paris: Maspero, 1970), p. 30, n. 22.

7. Gilbert Charles-Picard, *Les Religions de l'Afrique antique* (Paris: Plon, 1954), p. 25. More nuanced judgments appear in the conclusion of his book *Civilisation de l'Afrique romaine* (Paris: Plon, 1959), pp. 354–358. Similar assertions may be found in the citations referred to by Joseph Mesnage in *Romanisation de l'Afrique* (Paris: Gabriel Beauchesne, 1913), pp. 175 and 214.

8. Jérome Carcopino, *L'Aptitude des Berbères à la civilisation, d'après l'histoire ancienne de l'Afrique du Nord. Actes du VIIIè Congrès Volta* (Rome: Ecole Française, 1939), p. 629.

9. Ibid., p. 637.

10. Cited in Février, *Approches,* p. 57.

11. The accounts of these Arab travelers and geographers go back to the ninth century. Among the most important are Yaqubi, Ibn Hawqal, al-Bakri, al-Idrisi, Ibn 'Idhari, and al-Tijani.

12. To acquire the bilingual (Punic-Libyan) inscription from the Dougga mausoleum and ship it to England, the British consul Thomas Reade did not hesitate to demolish the monument. See Claude Poinssot, *Les Ruines de Dougga* (Tunis: Institut Archéologique, 1958), p. 61. Paul Albert Février maintains that when the Académie des Inscriptions et Belles-Lettres instructed Evariste de Sainte Marie to undertake excavations in search of inscriptions for French museums, he "harvested more than 2,300 epigraphic texts and seven chests of antiquities and sculpted blocks" which were dispatched to Algiers. Another thirty-nine chests filled with steles were sent to France. (Sadly, the ship that was carrying them exploded at Toulon and five to six hundred items were lost.) Such government-sanctioned plunder was typical of the acquisition policies of Europe's museums and private collections. Février, *Approches,* p. 39.

13. "When the French forces occupied Tunisia, many columns used archeological studies as a guide, whereas the 1857 map served them poorly" wrote Salomon Reinach. Cited in Février, *Approches,* p. 49.

14. See, for example, the description of the activity of Captain Vincent, as well as others in the Béja region, in Ammar Mahjoubi, *Recherches d'histoire et d'archéologie à Henchir el-Faouar. La Cité des Belalitani Maiores* (Tunis: Université de Tunis, 1978), p. 30. For overviews of the origins of archeological work in Tunisia, see Serge Lancel, *Carthage: A History,* trans. Antonia Nevill (Oxford: Blackwell, 1995), pp. 438–446, and Gilbert Charles-Picard, "La recherche archéologique en Tunisie des origines à l'indépendance," *Cahiers des études anciennes* XVI (1984), pp. 11–20.

15. Février, *Approches,* p. 53. The work of Charles Tissot, which was the standard for a long time, is a synthesis of work prior to 1881.

Its maps pinpoint the results of explorations undertaken by missionaries and army officers interested in topography and archeology.

16. Février, *Approches*, p. 47.

17. Aside from the work of Février, other sources for the period prior to 1950 include the bibliographical essay "Histoire et historiens de l'Algérie" published by *Revue historique* in 1931 in its Collection du Centenaire (with particularly noteworthy contributions by Eugène Albertini and Jacques Zeiller on ancient Algeria and Christian Africa); an article by A. Truillot on the bibliography of the Tebessa region in *Recueil de la société de préhistoire et d'archéologie de Tébessa*, 1936–1937, pp. 321–353; and another by E. Janier on Tlemcen and its region in *Revue africaine*, 1940, pp. 314–334. By contrast, no bibliography specifically on ancient Tunisia was available at that time, but only a volume devoted to Morocco and Tunisia in the *Encyclopédie de l'empire français*, under the direction of Eugène Guernier, that included a bibliography. Fortunately, the rich and detailed bibliography of the second edition of Charles-André Julien, *Histoire de l'Afrique du Nord des origines à la conquête arabe*, reviewed and updated in 1951 by Charles Courtois, fills this gap.

18. Février, *Approches*, p. 88.

19. See Pietro Romanelli, *Storia delle province romane dell'Africa* (Rome: L'Erma di Bretschneider, 1959), pp. 227 ff. (for the account of Tacitus) and pp. 565 ff. (for that of Ammianus Marcellinus).

20. For Tacitus' discussion, see his *Annals*, Book II, Chapter 52.

21. "After the destruction of the forum, the site was occupied by very poorly built houses of recycled materials and graves were dug there. The clearing of the forum led to the disappearance of these structures, some of which predated the Byzantine occupation and which, in and of themselves, were of little interest. . . . Later, small baths were built to the west of the southern bastion of the fort, although to the detriment of the street that ran along its south wall. These baths, constructed of rather mediocre materials, can be dated to the Aghlabid era (ninth century) by virtue of the designs carved in the stucco that covers the walls. They consist of a vestibule and a caldarium built over a basement heated by a fireplace." Poinssot, *Les Ruines de Dougga*, pp. 40–41.

22. Ammar Mahjoubi, "Permanence et transformation de l'urbanisme africain à la fin de l'Antiquité: l'exemple de Belalis Maior," in *Mitteilungen des deutschen archaeologischen Instituts*, no. 25, pp. 77–83; and "De la fin de l'Antiquité au haut Moyen Age, héritages et changements dans l'urbanisme africain," in *110è Congrès national des sociétés savantes. IIIè Colloque sur l'histoire et l'archéologie de l'Afrique du Nord* (Montpellier, 1985), pp. 391–406.

23. Pliny the Elder, *Histoire naturelle* (in the text translated and edited by J. Desanges) (Paris: Les Belles Lettres, 1980), V, 1–46.

24. See Filippo Coarelli and Yvon Thèbert, *Architecture funéraire et pouvoir: réflexions sur l'hellénisme numide* (Mélanges de l'Ecole française de Rome, 100, 1988), pp. 761–818.

25. See especially the definitive study by Andrea Carandini, "Pottery and the African Economy," in Peter Garnsey, Keith Hopkins, and C. R. Whittaker, eds., *Trade in the Ancient Economy* (London: Chatto and Windus, 1983), pp. 145–162.

# Thirty Years of Research on the History of the Medieval Maghrib (Seventh to Sixteenth Centuries)

*Mounira Chapoutot-Remadi*
Université de Tunis

B ecause of the extensive but widely dispersed research on North Africa in the Middle Ages, carried out not only in the three countries of the Maghrib, but also in France, England, Germany, Italy, Spain, the United States, and elsewhere, this sketch cannot by any means be exhaustive. Further adding to the difficulty of compiling a survey such as this is the poor circulation of information, especially within the three Maghrib countries. For the purposes of this paper, "the Maghrib" means Morocco, Algeria, and Tunisia. The information available on Libya is too fragmentary to take into account in an analysis of this kind.

Researchers in several countries share common preoccupations: virtually everywhere, they have felt the need to sketch an overview, whether complete (that is, Maghrib-wide) or partial (Tunisian, Algerian, or Moroccan). Needless to say, I have relied on these important works, many of which are mentioned below.

### REFERENCE WORKS

The national libraries of all three Maghrib countries have published bibliographies.

The *Bibliographie Nationale Tunisienne* was established in 1970. Two retrospective series (1958–1968 and 1969–1973) were issued in 1974–1975, and regular periodical publications have appeared since in Arabic and French. The National Library has also published some fifty specialized bibliographies in conjunction with cultural or political events. Among their subjects have been Ibn Hani al-Andalusi (the first such publication, in 1973); Imam Mazri (1975); Ibn Khaldun (1980); Ibn Sina (1980); and Ibn Jazzar (1983). The Algerian National Library, created after independence in 1962, also maintains bilingual listings.

Other useful works include the bilingual *Catalogue de la bibliothèque: Occident musulman* (3 vols.; Casablanca: King Abdul Aziz ibn Saud Foundation for Islamic Studies and the Humanities, 1987); Marcelle Beaudiquez, ed., *Inventaire général des bibliographies nationales rétrospectives* (Munich: K. G. Saur, 1986); and Jean Déjeux, *Dictionnaire des auteurs maghrébins de langue française* (Paris: Karthala, 1984).

Overviews and broad historiographical surveys published in North Africa include ʿAbd al-Salam ibn Suda, *Dalil muʾarrikh al-Maghrib al-Aqsa* (Tetouan: Institut Moulay Hassan, 1950. 2d ed.; 2 vols.; Casablanca: Dar al-Kitab, 1960–1965); Muhammed Manuni, *Al-Masadir al-ʿarabiyya li-taʾrikh al-Maghrib* (Rabat: Manshurat Kulliyyat al-Adab wa-l-ʿUlum al-Insaniyya, 1983); Université de Tunis, *Esquisse d'un bilan de la production scientifique, 1958–1983* (Tunis: Ministère de l'Enseignement Supérieur et de la Recherche Scientifique, 1983); Jean Fontaine, *Fihris taʾrikh al-muʾallifat al-tunisiyya* [with Arabic text by Hammadi Sammud] (Tunis: Bait al-Hikma, 1986); and Mohamed Yalaoui, "Les Recherches sur la Tunisie médiévale au cours des trentes dernières années (1956–1986)," in *IBLA,* no. 159 (1986), pp. 61–72, an overview done on the fiftieth anniversary of the journal.

Among the surveys compiled or published abroad are those of the Association Française des Arabisants, *Dix ans de recherche universitaire française sur le monde arabe et islamique* (Paris: Editions Recherche sur les Civilisations, 1982); *Mille et une livres sur le monde arabe* (Paris: Maison des Sciences de l'Homme, 1984); and Mohamed Ben Madani, "Thèses soutenues sur le Maghreb dans les universités françaises en 1987," in *The Maghreb Review* XIII, nos. 1–2 (1988), pp. 136–140. Claude Cahen, *Introduction à l'histoire du monde musulman médiéval, VIIè–XVè siècles. Méthodologie et éléments de bibliographie* (Paris: Maisonneuve, 1982) is, as the author indicates in the introduction, the third of its kind, the first being Jean Sauvaget, *Introduction à l'histoire de l'Orient musulman: Eléments de bibliographie* (Paris: Adrien-Maisonneuve, 1943), which Cahen updated in 1961 and which was revised again in 1982. Also by Cahen is "L'Historiographie arabe des origines au VIIè siècle H" in *Arabica* XXXIII, fasc. 2 (1986), pp. 133–197. Other articles and books of note are Jean-François Clément, "L'Historiographie récente du Maroc. Réunion d'Aix-en-Provence, 2–4 juillet 1987," in *Bulletin de l'Association française d'études sur le monde arabe et musulman,* no. 2 (December 1987), pp. 117–132; Bernard Rosenberger, "Vingt ans de recherches sur l'histoire médiévale marocaine," in *Arabisant,* no. 26 (1987), pp. 9–43; and Pessah Shinar, *Maghrébin contemporain: Essai de bibliographie sélective et annotée sur l'Islam. Maroc, Algérie, Tunisie, Libye (1830–1978)* (Paris: CNRS, 1983).

## SPECIALIZED INSTITUTIONS AND THEIR PUBLICATIONS

In Morocco, the Institut Universitaire de la Recherche Scientifique (IURS, previously known by the acronym CURS) publishes the Arabic language journal *Majallat al-Bahth al-'Ilmi*. The Faculté des Lettres at the Université Mohammed V in Rabat puts out two journals: *Hespéris-Tamuda*, which dates from 1960 when it consolidated *Hespéris*, published by the Institut des Hautes Etudes Marocaines since 1921, and *Tamuda*, which had appeared from 1953 to 1960 in Tetouan; and the *Majallat Kulliyyat al-Adab wa-l-'Ulum al-Insaniyya bi Ribat*. Since 1984, the Université de Fès has also had its own publication, the *Majallat Kulliyyat al-Adab wa-l-'Ulum al-Insaniyya bi-Fas*. The faculties at Casablanca, Marrakesh, Kenitra, Oujda, and Agadir will likely have publications of their own in the future.

Other Moroccan periodicals include the *Majallat Dar al-Niyaba* (Tangiers); and *al-Kitab al-Maghribi*. The *Bulletin de la société d'histoire du Maroc* has appeared in Arabic since 1986, with the title *Majallat Jam'iyyat Ta'rikh al-Maghrib*.

The Service des Antiquités, which became the Service de l'Archéologie et du Patrimoine and then the Institut National des Sciences de l'Archéologie et du Patrimoine, publishes the *Bulletin de l'archéologie marocaine*.

Algeria, like Morocco, has a number of universities and institutions of higher learning. The four biggest are Algiers, Oran, Constantine, and Annaba. From 1934 to 1964, the Faculté des Lettres et Sciences Humaines in Algiers published *Annales de l'Institut des études orientales d'Alger*, which was replaced by the *Revue d'histoire et de civilisation du Maghreb* from 1966 to 1970. *La Revue africaine*, published by the Algerian Historical Society from 1856 until 1962, was the oldest Algerian journal. Between 1953 and 1971, the Centre de Recherche Anthropologie, Préhistoire, et Ethnographie published *Libyca: Revue d'anthropologie, histoire, ethnographie*. Recently, the Université d'Oran has been particularly active in its support of anthropological publications and has attracted a group of researchers interested in modern and contemporary history.

In recent years, Tunisia has experienced a process of decentralization. The Faculté des Lettres et Sciences Humaines in Tunis, the successor in the 1960s of the Institut des Hautes Etudes de Tunis, is responsible for *Cahiers de Tunisie*, which replaced the *Revue tunisienne* in 1953. This journal was originally open to all disciplines but since 1982 its content has been confined to the humanities. In fact, most of the articles in *Cahiers de Tunisie* are historical. Ten-year tables appeared in vol. XVI, no. 68 (1968), covering 1953 to 1963; in vol. XXI, nos. 83–84 (1973), covering 1963 to 1972;

and in vol. XXXI, nos. 125–126 (1983), covering 1973 to 1982. See also the 1985 Mémoire en documentation (DBA) of S. Hafsa, "*Les Cahiers de Tunisie,* Index, 1er trimestre 1953–2è trimestre 1984." The tables and index permit an analysis of the nature of the journal's content. The tables' classification of material by discipline, author, and rubric (articles, reviews, and chronicles) provides quick access to this information. Most of the articles are in Arabic or French, but the journal also accepts articles in English, Italian, and Spanish. The historical contributions generally deal with Tunisia, the Maghrib, the Mediterranean world, and the Arabo-Muslim world.

In Table 1, the figures that follow the slash indicate the number of Tunisian contributions. The decade ending in 1982 saw an upsurge of articles in Arabic: twelve on the history of the Middle Ages; one on modern history; and two on contemporary history. The Faculté des Lettres—called the Faculté des Sciences Humaines et Sociales since 1986—has an Arabic language review, *al-Hawliyyat,* which appears yearly and contains articles primarily on language and literature but also includes pieces on history.

Three other facultés des lettres are located in Tunis—at Manouba, in Kairouan, and in Sfax—but only the first currently has a department of history. There is also an Ecole Normale Supérieure at Sousse; however, none of these relatively new institutions yet has its own publications.

The *Revue de l'Institut des belles lettres arabes (IBLA),* published in Tunis since 1937, celebrated its fiftieth anniversary by publishing several surveys of publications on Tunisian history. The *Revue d'histoire maghrébine,* founded by Abdeljelil Temimi in 1973, has recently published its seventy-fifth number. It also publishes articles in several languages and, while it has tended to emphasize modern and contemporary history, it also accepts studies on other periods. The *Revue tunisienne des sciences sociales,* published by the

TABLE I

Contents of *Cahiers de Tunisie*

| YEARS | MIDDLE AGES | ANCIENT | MODERN | CONTEMPORARY |
|---|---|---|---|---|
| 1953–62 | 33/8[a] | 40/3 | 20/0 | 27/2 |
| 1963–72 | 26/10 | 52/7 | 20/3 | 27/6 |
| 1973–82 | 44/26 | 30/19 | 19/8 | 46/22 |

[a]The first number represents the total number of articles; the number following the solidus indicates the number by Tunisian authors.

Centre d'Etudes et de Recherches Economiques et Sociales (CERES), welcomes historical contributions, and the Center maintains a department of research historians. From 1972 to 1976, when CERES invited teachers to serve as research associates, its department of history published a large number of articles in the *Revue tunisienne des sciences sociales*. That department established the Congrès d'Histoire et de Civilisation du Maghreb in December 1974 and published that organization's *Actes*. Other reviews that occasionally publish articles on history include *al-Hayat at-thaqafiyya, al-Hidaya,* and *al-Fikr.*

Still other institutions that are interested in history and publish some works in the field are the Publications de l'Université de Tunis, a service attached to the Faculté des Sciences Humaines et Sociales and which publishes the theses of faculty members; the Bait al-Hikma (or al-Mu'assasa al-Wataniyya li-l-Tarjama wa-l-Tahqiq wa-l-Dirasah), which has a double mission of translating basic texts from other languages and editing Arabic manuscripts; the Société Tunisienne de Diffusion, which publishes some works of history and some editions of texts; and the Institut National d'Archéologie et d'Art (INAA), which has many researchers and an important Islamic department devoted to the study of the archeological patrimony of the Islamic era.

Tunis also boasts two professional associations for historians: the Association d'Histoire et d'Archéologie and the Société Tunisienne des Historiens Universitaires (STHU). The latter, founded more than twenty years ago, has taken over the management of the Congrès d'Histoire et de Civilisation du Maghreb and organizes historical seminars and congresses. It has regularized the meetings of the Congrès, bringing Maghrib specialists together every three years. To promote as broad a participation as possible, themes that cut across all historical periods have been selected as topics. The first congress, in December 1974, lacked a precise theme but permitted the opening of contacts between specialists; the second (1980) had as its theme "Dépendances, résistances et mouvements de libération au Maghreb." The third, held in Oran in 1983, was focused on "Sociétés rurales." The fourth congress (1986) looked at "Villes et sociétés urbaines"; and the fifth, held in Tunis in November 1989, considered the issue of "Echanges et contacts entre les pays méditerranéens et le Maghreb." The *Actes* of some of the congresses have been published. The first, in two volumes, was done by CERES in 1979 and includes six essays in French and eight in Arabic on medieval history. The second and fourth constitute special issues of *Cahiers de Tunisie*—nos. 117–118 (1981) and nos. 137–138 (1986), respectively. The former has seven contributions on the history of the Middle Ages, three of which are in Arabic; the number of articles on the Middle Ages and the language distribution among them are very similar for the *Actes* of the fourth congress.

Tunis is the location of two other institutions that are very useful for all researchers. One is the Centre de Documentation Tunisie Maghreb (CDTM), which organizes conferences of specialists from the Arabo-Muslim world and makes available to researchers a library that attempts to collect all publications pertaining to the Maghrib. The second, relatively new, center is the Centre d'Etudes Maghrébines à Tunis (CEMAT), which provides facilities and services similar to those of the previous center but complements it with its excellent stock of American publications.

In France, the most productive research institutes are the universities, the Centre National de la Recherche Scientifique, the Ecole Pratique des Hautes Etudes, the Centre de Recherche et d'Etudes sur les Sociétés Méditerranéennes, the Institut de Recherches et d'Etudes sur le Monde Arabe et Musulman (IREMAM), the Association Française des Arabisants (AFDA), the Union Européenne des Arabisants et Islamisants (UEAI), and the Société Asiatique. Much of this research takes the form of theses, and a central catalogue of theses lessens the problems arising from the tremendous geographical dispersion of the material and the people.

Several French periodicals provide outlets for such research. The *Revue de l'Occident musulman et de la Méditerranée* (*ROMM*) in Aix-en-Provence, the *Cahiers de la Méditerranée* of Nice, *Arabica*, *Studia Islamica*, and the *Revue des études islamiques*, with its supplement of abstracts called *Islamica*, are open to work on the Arab and Muslim world regardless of specialization. In addition, *Revue historique*, *Annales, économies, sociétés, civilisations*, and *Revue d'histoire économique et sociale* sometimes publish articles on Maghrib history.

In Spain, the Instituto Hispano-árabe de Cultura, the Consejo Superior de Investigaciones Científicas (CSIC), and the universities all do work on Muslim Spain and the Maghrib, especially Morocco. The review *al-Qantara*, which has replaced *al-Andalus*, the *Cuadernos de historia del Islam*, the *Revista del Instituto de estudios islámicos*, and *al-Awraq* all publish articles on the Maghrib.

In Great Britain, the School of Oriental and African Studies is interested in research on the Maghrib and publishes a journal, the *Bulletin of the School of Oriental and African Studies*. Other important periodicals from Great Britain are the *Journal of African History* and the *Maghreb Review*.

In the United States, the difficulties of geographical dispersion are overcome to a large extent by the existence of a professional organization, the American Institute of Maghrib Studies (AIMS).

## HISTORICAL RESEARCH IN THE THREE
## MAGHRIB COUNTRIES AND ABROAD

Before discussing the postindependence evolution of the historiography of the Maghrib in the Middle Ages, a reminder of the legacy of colonial history, which differed markedly from contemporary trends, is in order. There is no point in reproaching the medievalists of the colonial period for their failure to learn Arabic, which deprived them of access to important sources. A work such as Emile Félix Gautier, *Le Passé de l'Afrique du Nord: Les Siècles obscurs* (Paris: Payot, 1927) certainly generated lively debate. In retrospect, some studies from the colonial era retain their value. The Tunisian scholar Mohamed Yalaoui has paid fitting homage to the memory of "Marçais, Fagnan, Bercher, Lézine, and many others who, by editing important texts, undertaking essential corrections, and generally breaking the ground, blazed the way for the following generations while indicating fruitful directions for research."[1]

### Sources for the History of the Middle Ages

To study the period from the seventh to the sixteenth centuries, researchers must have access to the manuscript sources. Editions that make such sources readily available to the greatest number of scholars are, therefore, of the utmost importance. On the occasion of a 1988 colloquium held in Rabat, "Les Manuscrits Arabes de l'Occident Musulman," the King Abdul Aziz Foundation published a list of catalogues of Arabic manuscripts throughout the world. Perhaps the most valuable work of this kind, however, is Kurkis Awwad, *Faharis al-makhtutat al-ʿarabiyya fi-l-ʿalam* (2 vols.; Kuwait: Institute of Arab Manuscripts, 1984).

Also of importance are the previously mentioned guide of ʿAbd al-Salam ibn Suda; Muhammad Bu Khabzah, *Fihris makhtutat khizanat titwan* (Tetouan: Wizarat al-Dawlat al-Mukallafa bi-l-Shu'un al-Thaqafiyya, 1981); Muhammed Manuni, *Dalil makhtutat dar al-kutub al-nasiriyya bi-tamkrut* (Mohammedia: Matbaʿat Fidala, 1985); Mukhtar al-Saddiq Bel-ʿArbi, *Fihris makhtutat khizanat Ibn Yusuf bi-marrakush* (Marrakesh: Université d'al-Qadi ʿIyadh, n.d. [mimeographed]); Muhammad Hajji, *Fihris al-khizanat al-ʿilmiyya al-sabihiyya bi-sala* (Kuwait: Institute of Arab Manuscripts, 1985); *Makhtutat kulliyyat al-adab wa-l-ʿulum al-insaniyya* (Rabat: Université Muhammad V, 1980 [mimeographed]); and two catalogues edited by ʿAbd al-Hafiz Mansur, *Fihris makhtutat al-maktabat al-ahmadiyya bi Tunis* (Beirut: Dar al-Fatah li-l Tabʿa wa-l-Nashr, 1969) and *Fihris al-ʿam li-l makhtutat rashid Hasan Husni ʿAbd al-Wahhab* (Tunis: Institut National d'Archéologie et d'Art, 1975).

Within North Africa itself, there are no archives for the Maghribi Middle Ages. But Charles Emmanuel Dufourcq has made extensive use of the Archives of the Crown of Aragon in his books *L'Espagne catalane et le Maghrib aux XIIIème et XIVème siècles* (Paris: PUF, 1966); *La Vie quotidienne dans les ports méditerrannéens au moyen âge* (Paris: Hachette, 1975); and *La Vie quotidienne dans l'Europe médiévale sous domination arabe* (Paris: Hachette, 1978). These archives contain a wealth of untapped and useful information on commercial relations between Spain and the Maghrib.

Noteworthy collections of archival materials include Maximiliano Agustín Alarcón y Santón, *Los Documentos árabes diplomáticos del Archivos de la corona de Aragón* (Madrid: E. Maestre, 1940); Angeles Masia de Ros, *La Corona de Aragón y los estados del Norte de Africa* (Barcelona: Instituto Español de Estudios Mediterráneos, 1951); Louis de Mas-Latrie, *Traités de paix et de commerce et documents divers concernant les relations des chrétiens avec les arabes de l'Afrique septentrionale au moyen âge* (Paris: Plon, 1865); Michele Amari, *I diplomi arabi* (Florence: Le Monnier, 1863); and two collections edited by Evariste Lévi-Provençal, *Documents inédits d'histoire almohade* (Paris: Geuthner, 1928) and *Trente-sept lettres almohades* (Rabat: Matbaʿat al-Iqtisadiyya, 1941).

Many other archives, the most promising of which are in the important Italian trading centers of Venice, Florence, Genoa, and Pisa, have hardly been exploited at all, but as scholars investigate their resources, our knowledge and understanding of the medieval Maghribi economy will undoubtedly improve greatly. Some studies have already appeared—for example, those on Venice by Bernard Doumerc, who in 1982 defended a thesis at the Université de Toulouse-Le Mirail entitled "Venise et la Barbarie de 1230 à 1510." He is now preparing a thèse d'état on a related topic. Doumerc participated in the 1980 and 1986 sessions of the Congrès d'Histoire et de Civilisation du Maghreb, resulting in the publication of "Venise et la dynastie hafside à la fin du XVème siècle," in *Cahiers de Tunisie* XXIX, nos. 117–118 (1981), pp. 573–580; and "La Ville et la mer: Tunis au XVème siècle," in *Cahiers de Tunisie* XXXIV, nos. 137–138 (1986), pp. 111–130. An exploration of the Genoese archives resulted in Georges Jehel, "Catalogue analytique et chronologique des actes du notaire Petrus Batifolius," in *Cahiers de Tunisie* XXV, nos. 99–100 (1977), pp. 69–137. Philippe Gourdin has worked in the same collection, while material from the Pisan archives is central to Mékia Bensaci, "Familles et individualités pisanes en relations avec le Maghrib," in *Cahiers de Tunisie* XXVIII, nos. 113–114 (1980), pp. 57–75.

It may still be possible to discover some *waqf* (a pious endowment, usually called *habus* in North Africa) documents that date to the Middle Ages, at least to the Hafsid era. Family archives will certainly continue to shed precious light on this institution. Abdelhamid Henia, who works on such records with a group of researchers in Tunis, has discovered some, and another young Tunisian researcher has published part of a private archive in Muhammad Hassan, "Wathiqa fi-l-ta'rikh al-rifi: tahbis hanshir Ibn Mansur bi-l-Mahdiyya ʿala ribat al-Munastir 825/1422," in *Revue d'histoire maghrébine* XV, nos. 49–50 (1988), pp. 221–248. Perhaps one day notarial archives will be found that will bear comparison with Ibn al-ʿAttar's book edited by Pedro Chalmeta and F. Corriente, *Kitab al-Watha'iq wa-l-sijillat* (Madrid: Academia Matritense del Notariado and Instituto Hispano-árabe de Cultura, 1983).

The Geniza Documents are also a good source for the history of the Maghrib. Such works of S. D. Goitein as "La Tunisie au XIème siècle à la lumière des documents de la Geniza du Caire," in *Etudes d'orientalisme dédiées à la mémoire de Lévi-Provençal* (2 vols.; Paris: G.-P. Maisonneuve et Larose, 1962), II, pp. 559–579 and "Medieval Tunisia, the Hub of the Mediterranean," in *Studies in Islamic History and Institutions* (Leiden: E. J. Brill, 1966), pp. 308–328, more than amply demonstrate the value of the Geniza records.

*Published and Translated Sources*

Despite its importance and the veritable infatuation of which it was the object some years ago, the work of Ibn Khaldun, while accessible, still requires a solid, scholarly critical edition. The Arabic text most widely used now was published in 1956 in Beirut by Dar al-Kitab al-Lubnani. The work consists of seven volumes: one for the *Muqaddimah* and six for the history itself.

There are, of course, translations of Ibn Khaldun. William MacGuckin, Baron de Slane, *Histoire des berbères et des dynasties musulmanes de l'Afrique septentrionale* (4 vols.; Algiers: n.p., 1852–1856) was the first into French. A more recent translation is by Vincent Monteil, *Discours sur l'histoire universelle* (3 vols.; Beirut: Commission Libanaise pour la Traduction des Chefs-d'oeuvre, 1967–1968; new ed.; Paris: Sindbad, 1978). Perhaps the best translation is Frantz Rosenthal, *Ibn Khaldun: The Muqaddimah; an Introduction to History* (3 vols.; Princeton: Princeton University Press, 1967). There is also a translation of Ibn Khaldun's "autobiography" by Abdesselam Cheddadi, *Le Voyage d'occident et d'orient* (Paris: Sindbad, 1985). Several North African colloquia have focused on Ibn Khaldun; one particularly noteworthy study to have emerged from them is Ali Oumlil, *L'Histoire et son discours, essai sur la méthodologie d'Ibn Khaldun* (Rabat: Faculté des Lettres et des Sciences Humaines, 1983).

The medieval Arab geographers who described the Maghrib are almost all known to us through the work of Michael Jan de Goeje, *Bibliotheca Geographorum Arabicorum* (Leiden: Brill, 1870–1894). The writings of some of them—particularly al-Idrisi and al-Bakri—have been reprinted. Italian researchers have published al-Idrisi, *Nuzhat al-mushtaq fi khitraq al-afaq*, A. Bombaci, Umberto Rizzitano, R. Rubinacci, and Laura Veccia Vegliari, eds. (Naples: Instituto Universitario Orientale di Napoli, 1970– ). Another translation of those parts of al-Idrisi dealing with the Maghrib in the sixth century A.H. (twelfth century C.E.) is Mohamed Hajj Sadiq, *al-Maghrib al-ʿarabi min "Kitab nuzhat al-mushtaq" li-l-Idrisi* (Paris: Publisud, 1983). Those portions of al-Bakri concerning the Maghrib were translated by de Slane, *Description de l'Afrique septentrionale* (Paris: n.p., 1859). This was reprinted, along with the Arabic text, in 1965 in Paris by the Librairie d'Amérique et d'Orient. The work of Ignatii Iulianovich Krachkovsky, *Arabskaya geografitcheskaya literatura* (Moscow: Academy of Sciences of the USSR, 1957), which was translated into Arabic by Salah al-Din ʿUthman Hashim as *Taʾrikh al-adab al-jughrafi al-ʿarabi* (Cairo: Lajna al-Taʾalif wa-l-Tarjumat wa-l-Nashr, 1963) and then reprinted in Beirut by Dar al-Gharb al-Islami, remains very valuable; so does André Miquel, *Géographie humaine du monde musulman jusqu'au milieu du XIème siècle* (Paris: Ecole des Hautes Etudes des Sciences Sociales, 1963–1988), the deepest and most magisterial analysis of Arabic geographical literature.

Critical editions of several important texts appeared in the 1980s. Muhammad Ibn Marzuq, *al-Musnad al-sahih al-hasan fi muʿathir mawlana Abi-l-Hasan*, Maria J. Viguera, ed. (Algiers: Sharika Wataniyya li-l-Nashr wa-l-Tawziʿ, 1981) and by the same editor in a Spanish edition, *El Musnad: Hechos memorables de Abu al-Hasan, sultan de los Benimerines* (Madrid: Instituto Hispano-árabe de Cultura, 1977. Parts of this important work had earlier been translated by Evariste Lévi-Provençal and Pedro Chalmeta). Ibn ʿIdhari al-Marrakushi, *al-Bayan al-mughrib fi akhbar muluk al-andalus wa-l-maghrib*, Muhammad Ibrahim al-Kettani et al., eds. (Casablanca and Beirut: Dar al-Gharb al-Islami and Dar al-Thaqafa, 1985); Ibn al-Zayyat, *al-Tashawuf ila rijal al-tassawuf*, Ahmad Tawfiq, ed. (Rabat: Université Muhammad V, 1984); and the anonymous *Kitab al-istibshar fi ʿajaʾib al-amsar*, ʿAbd al-Hamid Saad Zaghlul, ed. (Casablanca: Dar al-Nashr al-Maghribi, 1985).

A group of *fuqaha'* (plural of *faqih*, an interpreter of Islamic law) under the direction of Muhammad Hajji has published a collection of *nawazil* (plural of *nazila*, a legal action) that is very helpful in understanding the social history of the Maghrib. This is the work of Ahmad ibn Yahya al-Wansharisi, *al-Miʿyar al-muʿrib wa-l-jami ʿal-mughrib ʿan fatawa ʿulamaʾ ifriqiyya wa-l-andalus wa-l-maghrib* (13 vols.; Beirut: Dar al-Gharb al-Islami, 1983). This edition replaces a lithographed, less legible version of the text.

The long list of other important published texts includes Ibrahim al-Raqiq al-Qayrawani, *Ta'rikh ifriqiyya wa-l-maghrib,* Mongi Kaabi, ed. (Tunis: n.p., 1968); and the Shiʿi theologian al-Qadi al-Nuʿman ibn Muhammad, *Iftitah al-daʿwa,* Wadad al-Qadi, ed. (Beirut: Dar al-Thaqafa, 1970). At about the same time, this text was also edited by Farhat Dachraoui (Tunis: STD, 1975). Other important Shiʿi works are al-Qadi al-Nuʿman ibn Muhammad's *al-Majalis wa-l-musayarat,* edited by Habib al-Faqih, Ibrahim Subbuh, and Mohamed Yalaoui (Tunis: Université de Tunis, 1978) and the text of Idris al-Daʿi ʿImad al-Din, *Ta'rikh al-khulafa' al-fatimiyyin bi-l-maghrib,* Mohamed Yalaoui, ed. (Beirut: Dar al-Gharb al-Islami, 1985). Also deserving of mention is Abu'l ʿAbbas Ahmad Ibn Qunfudh, *al-Farissiyya fi mabadi' al-dawlat al-hafsiyya,* Mohamed Naifar and ʿAbd al-Majid Turki, eds. (Tunis: Dar al-Tunisiyya li-l-Nashr, 1968).

A few collections of *tabaqat* (biographical compilations) have been published, for example, Mohamed Talbi, *Les Biographies aghlabides du Qadi Iyad* (Tunis: Université de Tunis, 1968); al-Maliki, *Kitab riyad al-nufus,* Bashir Baccouche, ed. (3 vols.; Beirut: Dar al-Gharb al-Islami, 1981–1984); al-Darjini, *Tabaqat al-mashayikh bi-l-maghrib,* Ibrahim Tallay, ed. (Beirut: Dar al-Fikr al-ʿArabi, 1980?- ); Abu Zakariyya, *Siyar al-ayyima,* Ismail Larbi, ed. (Beirut: Dar al-Gharb al-Islami, 1982), with another edition by ʿAbd al-Rahman Ayyoub (Tunis: Dar al-Tunisiyya li-l-Nashr, 1985); and ʿAbd al-Rahman al-Dabbagh and Ibn Naji al-Tanukhi (who completed al-Dabbagh's unfinished work), *Maʿalim al-imam fi maʿrifati ahl al-qayrawan,* Ibrahim Sabbuh, ed. (Cairo: Maktaba al-Khanaj, 1968). Said Dahmani has also edited this work, but his edition remains unpublished. For still more sources, see Bernard Rosenberger, "Vingt ans de recherche sur l'histoire médiévale marocaine," in *Arabisant,* no. 26 (1987), pp. 33–34.

A somewhat unusual illustration will serve to round out this survey—the case of Leo Africanus (Hassan al-Wazzan al-Fasi al-Gharnati). The work of this early sixteenth-century traveler has been edited and translated into several European languages since its initial appearance in the Tuscan dialect in Venice in 1558. Originally from Grenada and then a resident of Fez, this citizen of the Arab world was enslaved and then presented to Pope Leo X, who adopted him, in theory converted him, and bestowed his name on him. Apart from an article or two that appeared in the interwar years in Morocco, Leo Africanus generated little interest until the 1980s. Then, more or less simultaneously at both ends of the Arab world, in Morocco and Saudi Arabia, researchers began working with the French text of *Description de l'Afrique,* Alexis Epaulard et al., eds. (2 vols.; Paris: Adrien-Maisonneuve, 1956), which had gone out of print soon after its publication. The Moroccan historians of the Saadian era Muhammad Hajji and Mohammed Lakhdar prepared an Arabic version of the text, *Wasf Ifriqiyya li-l-Hasan ibn Muhammad al-Wazzani al-Fasi* (Beirut: Dar al-Gharbi al-Islami, 1983). Thus was the Arabic-speaking world exposed for the first time to this intriguing travelogue. In Saudi Arabia, another researcher, ʿAbd al-Rahman Hamida, was charged with preparing a translation to mark the First Arab Congress of Geography in Riyadh in 1979. In general, the work of the Moroccan authors is superior. Shortly after this "recovery" of Hassan al-Wazzan al-Fasi al-Gharnati, a novel about him was published by the Lebanese author Amin Maalouf, *Léon l'Africain* (Paris: Lattès, 1986) and a Tunisian film director contemplated making a movie about this extraordinary man's extraordinary adventures. An English translation of the novel was published by W. W. Norton and Company in 1989.

## THE HISTORY OF THE MIDDLE AGES

For the sake of an orderly presentation, these works will be classified as general histories, dynastic histories, and thematic studies.

In the first category, the long-acknowledged standard by Charles-André Julien, revised by Christian Courtois and Roger Le Tourneau, *Histoire de l'Afrique du Nord* (Paris: Payot, 1966) has been superseded, as has Georges Marçais, *La Berbérie musulmane et l'Orient au moyen âge* (Paris: Aubier, Editions Montaigne, 1946). Throughout the Maghrib, the appearance of national histories has indicated the intention of North African scholars to write their own. Among these is Hichem Djait, et al., *Histoire de la Tunisie* (Tunis: Société Tunisienne de Diffusion, 1960). Abdallah Laroui, *L'Histoire du Maghrib: un essai de synthèse* (Paris: Maspero, 1970), goes beyond the goal of rewriting history to engage broad conceptual issues. Perhaps for this reason, the book has found a receptive audience among the generation of Maghribi intellectuals imbued with attitudes of revisionism and protest, acquired especially in the French universities of the 1960s.

A colloquium with the theme "How to Write the History of the Maghrib" was held in Hammamet in May 1972; in the following year, the Association d'Histoire et d'Archéologie organized a second such gathering. A report by the late Béchir Tlili, "La Recherche historique en Tunisie," in *Cahiers de Tunisie* XX, nos. 77–78 (1972), pp. 125–133, summarizes some of the debate on this topic. Laroui tended to downplay the ancient history of the Maghrib, denying it any influence. Other Arab intellectuals adopted this view in the 1970s, arguing that the history of their countries began only with the Arab conquest. It is worth noting that in ancient times historical developments in the Maghrib were concentrated in its eastern portion—

what would later be Ifriqiyya—while in the Middle Ages more was happening in the west—the region that is so important to Laroui.

Other general histories include J. F. P. Hopkins, *Medieval Muslim Government in Barbary until the Sixth Century of the Hijra* (London: Luzac, 1958), which has been translated into Arabic by Amin Tawfiq al-Tibi as *Nuzum islamiyyat fi-l-Maghrib fi-l-qurun al-wusta* (Tunis and Tripoli: Maison Arabe du Livre, 1980); and Jamil M. Abun-Nasr, *A History of the Maghrib in the Islamic Period* (Cambridge: Cambridge University Press, 1987), which gives its strongest emphasis to the colonial era. A new general history taking account of the progress in scholarship over recent years would be most welcome. Finally, the articles in the *Encyclopaedia of Islam* on the countries and dynasties of the Maghrib are, for the most part, well executed.

Among the dynastic histories of what is now Tunisia are: Robert Brunschvig, *La Berbérie orientale sous les Hafsides, des origines à la fin du XVème siècle* (2 vols.; Paris: Adrien-Maisonneuve, 1940–1947); Lucien Golvin, *Le Maghreb central à l'époque des Zirides, recherche d'archéologie et d'histoire* (Paris: Arts et Métiers Graphiques, 1957); and Hadi Roger Idris, *La Berbérie orientale sous les Zirides, Xème–XIIème siècles* (2 vols.; Paris: Librairie d'Amérique et d'Orient, 1962). M. Vonderheyden, *La Berbérie orientale sous la dynastie des Banou'l Arlab, 800–909* (Paris: Geuthner, 1927) has been partially supplanted by the work of Mohamed Talbi, *L'Emirat Aghlabide, 184–196/800–909, histoire politique* (Paris: Librairie d'Amérique et d'Orient, 1966). Talbi's study has been translated into Arabic as *al-Dawla al-aghlabiyya* (Beirut: Dar al-Gharb al-Islami, 1985). A final study is Farhat Dachraoui, *Le Califat fatimide au Maghrib* (Tunis: Société Tunisienne de Diffusion, 1981). For this book, also, an Arabic translation is anticipated. In all these works, which nicely survey the dynastic history of medieval Ifriqiyya, the contemporary Tunisian authors have rejected the term "Berbérie" as inappropriate because of its many implications which have no relevance to present-day Tunisia.

The dynastic history of Algeria is less fully covered. One can begin with Abbé Bargès, *Complément de l'histoire des Beni-Zayyan, rois de Tlemcen, ouvrage du Cheikh Mohamed 'Abd al-Djalil al-Tenessy* (Paris: Leroux, 1887), which has been revised by the works of Atallah Dhina, beginning with his thèse de troisième cycle, defended at Paris in 1971, "Essai sur les structures politiques, sociales et économiques de l'état tlemcenien à l'èpoque d'Abu Hammu Musa I et Abu Tashfin I." Dhina has also written a number of good articles, including: "Actes de 'chancellerie' tlemcenienne," in *Revue d'histoire et de civilisation du Maghrib*, XII (1974), pp. 5–33; "Visage de l'ancienne société musulmane," in *Révolution africaine*, no. 559 (8–14, November 1974), pp. 49–51; and "Le Royaume 'Abd al-Wadide: quelques aspects de sa vie économique," in *Majallat al-Ta'rikh* [Algiers] VI (1978), pp. 11–21, that round out our information on Tlemcen. His richest work can be found in his thèse d'état, defended in 1980 and published in an abridged version as *Le Royaume Abdelouadide à l'époque d'Abou Hammou Moussa Ier et d'Abou Tachfin Ier* (Algiers: Office des Presses Universitaires, 1985).

It remains to speak of the great Moroccan dynasties: the Almoravids, Almohades, and Merinids. A significant imbalance exists in the historiography of Morocco between the period from the eighth to the eleventh century and that from the thirteenth to the fifteenth, with far more studies on the latter era. On the Almoravids, there is Jacinto Bosch Vilá, *Los Almorávides, historia de Marruecos* (Tetouan: Editoria Marroqui, 1956), which has been updated by such works as Husayn Munis, "Les Almoravides, esquisse historique," in *Revista del Instituto de estudios islámicos,* XIV (1967–1968), pp. 49–102; and P. F. de Moraes Farias, "The Almoravids: Some Questions Concerning the Character of the Movement During Its Closest Contact with the West Sudan," in *Bulletin de l'Institut français de l'Afrique noire* XXIX (1967), pp. 794–878. On the Almohades, the first item to mention is Roger Le Tourneau, *The Almohad Movement in North Africa in the Twelfth and Thirteenth Centuries* (Princeton: Princeton University Press, 1969). Also important is the work of Rachid Bourouiba, "La Doctrine Almohade," in *ROMM* XIII–XIV (1973), pp. 141–158; *Ibn Tumart* (Algiers: Société Nationale d'Edition et de Diffusion, 1974); and *'Abd al-Mu'min, flambeau des Almohades* (Algiers: Société Nationale d'Edition et de Diffusion, 1974).

The Merinids and Wattasids have also been studied extensively. A good starting point is Maya Shatzmiller, *L'Historiographie mérinide, Ibn Khaldun et ses contemporains* (Leiden: E. J. Brill, 1982). Other articles by Shatzmiller are "Les Premiers mérinides et le milieu religieux de Fès: l'introduction des médersas," in *Studia Islamica* XLIII (1976), pp. 109–118; and "Islam de campagne et Islam de ville: le facteur religieux à l'avènement des Mérinides," in *Studia Islamica* LI (1979), pp. 123–136. Also of value are the books of Mohamed Benchekroun: *Le Milieu marocain et ses aspects culturels* (Rabat: n.p., 1970); and *La Vie intellectuelle marocaine sous les Mérinides et les Wattasides, XIIIème, XIVème, XVème, XVIème siècles* (Rabat: n.p., 1974), which gathers very important documentation on the question addressed. Another useful study is Maria J. Viguera, "Le Maghrib Mérinide: un processus de transfèrement," in *Actes de la huitième congrès de l'Union européenne arabisants et islamisants* (1976), pp. 309–322; and the Moroccan scholar Muhammed Manuni has published a collection of articles entitled *Waraqat 'an al-hadara al-maghribiyya fi 'asr Banu Marin* (Rabat: Manshurat Kulliyyat al-Adab wa-l-'ulum al-insaniyya, 1979). Finally, the very innovative book of Mohamed Kably, *Société, pouvoir et religion au Maroc à la fin du moyen âge, XIVème–*

*XVème siècles* (Paris: Maisonneuve et Larose, 1986), that won the Prix d'Histoire du Maroc in 1987, deserves special mention.

This strong interest on the part of Moroccan historians in the Merinid era is partly ideological; for, in many respects, that period corresponds with the apogee of Moroccan history. Some foreigners have also been drawn to this era, notably Rudolf Thoden, *Abu-l Hasan Ali, Merinidenpolitik zwischen Nordafrika und Spanien in der Jahren 710–732/1310–1331* (Freiburg: Schwarz, 1973). Similarly, the work of Charles E. Dufourcq has long focused on relations between the Maghrib and Spain. Two final publications of note are Ahmed Khaneboubi, *Les Premiers sultans mérinides, 1269–1331, histoire politique et sociale* (Paris: Harmattan, 1987); and A. Diallo, "Les Relations commerciales et diplomatiques entre le Maghreb et l'Occident chrétien à la fin du moyen âge" (Université de Paris I, 1987).

A number of works emphasize thematic research in urban or social history, numismatics, or archeology, and should be discussed separately from the "classical" studies—although some of those do examine many of these same questions. In urban history, for example, pioneers such as Marçais and Terrasse led the way. An example of an older work still deserving of attention is Lucien Golvin, *Recherches archéologiques à la Qal'a des Banu Hammad* (Paris: G.-P. Maisonneuve et Larose, 1965). More recently, Golvin has co-authored with Jacques Revault, *Palais et demeures de Fès: époque mérinide et saadienne, XIVè–XVIIè siècles* (Paris: CNRS, 1985). Alexandre Lézine has written *Deux villes d'Ifriqiyya, Sousse et Tunis: Etudes d'architecture, d'urbanisme, de démographie* (Paris: Geuthner, 1971), as well as a number of other books and articles on similar topics. Abdelaziz Daoulatli, *Tunis sous les Hafsides: Evolution urbaine et activité architecturale* (Tunis: Institut National de l'Archéologie et d'Art, 1976), with an Arabic translation in 1985, exhibits the same spirit of linking urban history and architecture.

Some years ago, Dominique Chevallier organized two seminars on urban questions. A study by Roberto Berardi, "Espace et ville en pays d'Islam," in *L'Espace social de la ville arabe,* Dominique Chevallier, ed. (Paris: G.-P. Maisonneuve et Larose, 1979), pp. 99–123, draws on the personal architectural experience of the author who, since the 1960s, has worked closely with the Association de Sauvegarde de la Médina de Tunis. For the second colloquium, Berardi used the example of Tunis for another interesting essay on urban planning, "Signification du plan ancien de la ville arabe," in *La Ville arabe dans l'Islam,* Abdelwahab Boudhiba et al., eds. (Tunis and Paris: CERES and CNRS, 1982), pp. 165–192. One fact that emerged clearly from these conferences was that the Middle Eastern Arab city has garnered far more attention than its Maghribi counterpart.

Paul-Louis Cambuzat defended his thesis on medieval North African cities in 1971. An abridged version was published posthumously as *L'Evolution des cités du Tell en Ifriqiyya du VIIème au XIème siècle* (Algiers: Office des Publications Universitaires, 1986). In it, Cambuzat provides something of a catalogue of the cities of this region, listed alphabetically, with each entry containing data arranged under a variety of headings. Consequently, the book constitutes a useful reference manual for many urban centers. Christian Ewert and Jens P. Wisshak, *Forschungen zur almohadischen Moschee* (3 vols.; Madrid: Deutsches Archäologisches Institut, 1981–1987) is another very important work on Islamic architectural history.

Several works are available on Tunisian monuments—mosques, *madaris* (plural of *madrasa*, traditional school), *zawayya* (plural of *zawiyya*, a building used for religious rituals, usually by sufis or mystics) and *rubut* (plural of *ribat*, a fortified monastery)—of the Islamic era, most notably Slimane Mostafa Zbiss, *al-Funun al-islamiyya fi-l-bilad al-tunisiyya/L'Art musulman en Tunisie* (Tunis: Institut National d'Archéologie et d'Art, 1978); and Michel Terasse, "Recherches archéologiques d'époque islamique en Afrique du Nord," in *Comptes-rendus de l'Académie des Inscriptions et Belles Lettres*, 1976, pp. 590–611. By the same token, Rachid Bourouiba has published many studies, among which a fine example is *L'Art musulman en Algérie* (Algiers: Société Nationale d'Edition et de Diffusion, 1972).

A short study of my own on the cities, "Fronte Sahariano e Fronte Mediterraneo," in *Hinterland* [Milan] XV–XVI (July–December 1980), pp. 10–20, contains some reflections on the evolution, during the Middle Ages, of Islamic cities from their original inward-turning orientation to a focus on the sea. This work originated with a colloquium on "Les Villes musulmanes et la mer" organized by the Société des Cultures Méditerranéennes on Djerba in 1980. The Arab League's Educational, Cultural, and Social Organization is now in the process of overseeing a collected work on Arab cities.

In the fields of numismatics and economic history, essential works include: Claudette Vanacker, "Géographie économique de l'Afrique du Nord selon les auteurs arabes du IXème au milieu du XIIème siècles," in *Annales, économies, sociétés, civilisations* XXVIII (1973), pp. 639–680; and two articles by Jean Devisse, "Routes de commerce et échanges en Afrique Occidentale en relation avec la Méditerranée, XIème–XVIème siècles," in *Revue d'histoire économique et sociale* L (1972), pp. 42–73 and 357–397; and "Comment restitut-t-on l'histoire des relations transsahariennes?," in *Sociétés africaines, monde arabe, et culture islamique* (Paris: CERMAA, 1979 [mimeographed]), pp. 9–56.

The problem of supplies of precious metals is studied by Claude Cahen, "L'Or du Soudan avec les Almoravides, mythe ou réalité?" in *Le Sol, la pa-*

*role, l'écrit; 2000 ans de l'histoire africaine; mélanges en hommage à Raymond Mauny* (Paris: Société Française de l'Histoire d'Outre-Mer, 1979), pp. 539–546. Also of great utility is Bernard Rosenberger, "Les Vieilles exploitations minières et les anciens centres métallurgiques du Maroc," in *Revue de géographie du Maroc* XVII (1970), pp. 71–108 and XVIII (1970), pp. 59–102, as well as "Tamdult cité minière et caravanière présaharienne, IXème–XIVème siècles," in *Hespéris-Tamuda* XI (1970), pp. 103–139.

On the economy, an important starting point is Habib Janhani, *Dirasah maghribiyya fi-l-ta'rikh al-iqtisadi wa-l-ijtimaʿi li-l-Maghrib al-islami* (Beirut: Dar al-Taliʿa li-l-Tibaʿa wa-l-Nashr, 1980) which gives a good summation of the state of knowledge on the four cities of Kairouan, Tahert, Sijilmasa, and Aoudaghoust. On Kairouan, there is no notable new work, but on Tahert there is Brahim Zerouki, *L'Imamat de Tahart, premier état musulman du Maghrib: Histoire politico-socio-religieuse* (Paris: L'Harmattan, 1987). For Sijilmasa, to the article by J. Lessard, "Sijilmasa: la ville et ses relations commerciales au XIème siècle d'après al-Bakri," in *Hespéris-Tamuda* (1969), pp. 5–36, should be added the more recent one of Jean Devisse, "Sijilmasa: les sources écrites, l'archéologie, le contrôle des espaces," in *Les Actes du quatrième colloque euro-africain sur l'histoire du Sahara et des relations transsahariennes entre le Maghreb et l'Ouest africain du Moyen-Age à la fin de l'époque coloniale* [held at Erfoud, Morocco, in October, 1985] (Paris: Institut International d'Anthropologie, 1986), pp. 18–25. The study of Denise Jacques-Meunie, *Le Maroc saharien des origines à 1670* (2 vols.; Paris: Klincksieck, 1982) is of lesser value.

In numismatics, little work has been done since the publication of the catalogue of Henri-Michel Lavoix, *Catalogue des monnaies musulmanes de la Bibliothèque nationale,* Vol. II: *Espagne et Afrique* (Paris: Imprimerie Nationale, 1891), but those items that have appeared have been important. They include Daniel Eustache, *Corpus des dirhams idrisides et contemporains* (Rabat: Banque du Maroc, 1972); and a second catalogue, Mohamed Abu-l-Faraj al-ʿUsh, *Monnaies Aghlabides, étudiées en relation avec l'histoire des Aghlabides,* (Damascus: Institut Français de Damas, 1982).

Two other important studies remain unpublished: Khaled Ben Romdhane, "Les Monnaies almohades, aspects idéologiques et économiques" (Université de Paris VII, 1978); and Hamid al-ʿAjabi, "Corpus des monnaies hafsides du musée du Bardo."

In the realm of social and religious history, there are the collected articles of Robert Brunschvig, *Etudes d'Islamologie* (2 vols.; Paris: G.-P. Maisonneuve et Larose, 1976) and ʿAbd al-Majid Turki, ed., *Etudes sur l'Islam classique et l'Afrique du Nord* (London: Variorum Reprints, 1986). Mohamed Talbi, *Les Etudes d'histoire ifriqiyenne et de civilisation musulmane médiévale* (Tunis: Université de Tunis, 1982) gathers together several important studies on social and religious history. Talbi belongs to a group of researchers who regularly participate in the discussion of Islamo-Christian encounters and to whom we are indebted for a book coedited with Olivier Clément, *Un respect têtu: Islam et christianisme* (Paris: Nouvelle Cité, 1989). Talbi has directed theses on Islamo-Christian polemics in the Middle Ages, some of which have been published. Notable among these is ʿAbd al-Majid al-Sharfi, *al-Fikr al-islami fi-l-radd ʿala-l-nasara ila nihayat al-qarn al-rabi ʿal-ʿashur* (Tunis: Maison Tunisienne de l'Edition, 1986). He also directed the 1986 thesis of Farhat Jaʿbiri, "Tahlil ma yataʿalliq bi-'usul al-din min al-turath al-ʿibadi bi-l-Maghrib fi-l-qurun al-taliyya X–XII/XVI–XVIII" which, regrettably, has not yet been published, although Jaʿbiri has published *Nizam al-ʿazzaba ʿinda al-ʿibadiyya al-wahbiyya fi Jarba / L'Organisation des Azzaba chez les ibadites wahbites de Jerba* (Tunis: INAA, 1975).

General studies of the Jewish and Christian minorities include André Chouraqui, *Histoire des juifs en Afrique du Nord* (Paris: Hachette, 1985); and David Corcos, *Studies in the History of the Jews of Morocco* (Jerusalem: R. Mass, 1976); and an article by Charles E. Dufourcq, "Chrétiens et musulmans durant les derniers siècles du moyen âge," in *Annales de estudios medievales* X (1980), pp. 207–225. Mention should also be made of the book of Philippe Senac, *L'Image de l'autre: l'Occident médiéval face à l'Islam* (Paris: Flammarion, 1983), which builds on the research of Alain Ducellier. The subject would be definitively covered if a study of the image of the other in Islamic societies, perhaps based on the seminar led by André Raymond, were to be made.

Also of note is the collection by Mohamed Kably, *Murajaʿat hawla al-mujtamaʿ wa-l-thaqafa bi-l-Maghrib al-wasit* (Casablanca: Dar Tubqal li-l-Nashr, 1987), which includes a methodological discussion that suggests revisions of thinking on such important and diverse matters as the nature of power, Merinid madrasas, and attempts to unify the Maghrib. Also of great importance are Vincent Lagardère, "Le Gouvernorat des villes et la suprématie des Banu Turgut au Maroc et en al-Andalus," in *ROMM* XXV (1978), pp. 49–65; "La Tariqa et la révolte des Muridun en 539/1144 en Andalus," in *ROMM* XXXV (1983), pp. 157–170; and "La Haute judicature à l'époque almoravide en al-Andalus," in *al-Qantara* [Madrid] VII (1986), pp. 135–228, in which he makes use of the *Miʿyar* of al-Wansharisi.

## UNPUBLISHED RESEARCH

The remainder of this paper will survey unpublished dissertations and theses written in France and the Maghrib. While there may be official records of the dissertations and theses defended in the various facultés des lettres of Maghribi universities, they are difficult to obtain. Despite real progress in some areas, information is still poorly distributed and is subject more to the accident of personal relations than to any interfaculty or interuniversity conventions and agreements.

Even so, general trends appear. Both in North Africa and abroad, the modern and contemporary periods are more intensively studied than the Middle Ages, with more and better-supported research teams working in those areas closest to the concerns of the present. For example, between 1978 and 1987, five thèses de troisième cycle (called in Tunisia the "diplôme de recherche approfondie") have been defended in medieval history, as opposed to seven in ancient history and twenty-two in modern and contemporary history. The situation is modified somewhat when Tunisian mémoires (called "certificat d'aptitude à la recherche") defended between 1970 and 1987 are taken into account: thirty-two on medieval history, fourteen on ancient history, and eighty-one on modern and contemporary history. In 1988, twenty-two mémoires were presented, of which six were in medieval history, one in ancient history, and the rest in modern and contemporary history.

Much the same situation holds true for Morocco. At Rabat, of thirty theses defended between 1977 and 1987, only two deal with the Middle Ages. Since 1979, when university reforms took effect, only one of six doctorats d'état, and fifteen of seventy-two doctorats de troisième cycle, have had a medieval focus. In France, according to the Association Française des Arabisants, *Dix ans de recherche française sur le monde arabe et islamique* (Paris: Recherche Civilisations, 1982), there were thirty-two such theses.

With regard to France, Paul Balta has called attention to the problems caused by the steady decline in the number of academic specialists on the Arab world.[2] The number of advanced students remains high, but the majority are from North Africa and the Middle East. Recent reforms in the thèse d'état generated a sudden avalanche of defenses, but it has not yet been possible to measure the impact of this on Maghribi research. The survey of unpublished French research which follows is certainly not exhaustive but does faithfully reflect the general orientation of current research.

Some of these dissertations have concentrated on editing or translating texts. Among the better examples are the theses of Said Dahmani on Ibn Naji al-Tanukhi's *Ma'alim al-iman fi ma'rifati ahl al-qayrawan,* translated as "La Conquête de l'Ifriqiyya et ses artisans" (Université de Paris I, 1973); Roger Deladrière, "La Profession de foi d'Ibn 'Arabi" (Université de Paris IV, 1974; subsequently published, Paris: Editions Orientales, 1978), an edition, translation, and commentary on Ibn 'Arabi's important work; and Alfred-

Louis du Mouchel de Prémare's "Contribution à la connaissance du Maroc au XIVème siècle: les notes de voyage d'Ibn al-Hadj al-Numayri" (Université de Lyon II, 1981), which is a critical edition of the text with a partial translation and a commentary. Two other theses based on travel narratives are S. Maghribi, "Les Voyageurs de l'Occident musulman du XIIème siècle à la fin du XIVème siècle," which analyzes the data on people, cities, flora, and fauna from travelers' accounts in the spirit of the work done by André Miquel on geographical literature; and M. Escoute, "Les Voyageurs chrétiens au Maroc au XVème et XVIème siècles" (Université de Toulouse, 1984).

In the field of Islamic studies, special mention must be made of Saʿad Ghrab, "Ibn ʿArafa et le Malékisme en Ifriqiyya au VIIIème/XIVème siècles" (Université de Paris III, 1985), which is not only a biography of Ibn ʿArafa, but also a sketch of religious and intellectual life in Ifriqiyya. The thesis of Mohamed al-Habib al-Hila, "L'ascèse et son influence sur la société ifriqiyenne jusqu'à l'époque aghlabide" (Université de Paris IV, 1976) heightens our understanding of religious life in the early days of Islam. Two other theses on the ʿIbadis will significantly add to an area of scholarship long studied only by the Polish historian Tadeusz Lewicki—whose very important work should be gathered into a volume or two in order to make it more accessible to researchers. These are Gérard Dangel, "L'Imamat ibadite de Tahert (761–909): Contribution à l'histoire de l'Afrique du Nord devant le haut moyen âge" (Université de Strasbourg I, 1977) and Brahim Fekhar, "Les communautés ibadites en Afrique du Nord depuis les Fatimides" (Université de Paris III, 1971).

Among the better theses in economic history are B. Y. Rhozali, "Recherche sur le mode de production au temps des Almohades," defended in 1987; and A. el-Alaoui, "Le Maghrib et le commerce transsaharien: milieu XIème–milieu XIVème siècles," defended in 1983.

In archeology and the history of monuments, several studies focus on specific cities. They include M. Fatha, "Contribution à l'étude de la ville marocaine des Merinides aux Wattasides" (1982); and the very interesting work of Faouzi Mahfoudh, "La Ville de Sfax, recherche d'archéologie monumentale et évolution urbaine" (Université de Paris IV, 1988), which contains an overview of the city's history in the Middle Ages and a systematic study of its monuments, accompanied by plans, illustrations, and documents, many drawn from the private archives of great Sfaxi families. Another thesis in the same mold which deserves mention, although it goes beyond the chronological limits of the Middle Ages, is Ahmad Saʿdawi, "Testour du XVIIème au XIXème siècle: Histoire monumentale d'une ville morisque de Tunisie" (Université de Paris, 1987).

In archeology and art history, S. Dargouth on the oratories of the Tunis medina; and A. Bouyahyaoui, "Evolution de la grande mosquée médiévale dans la région de Tlemcen" (1985) clarify the evolution of religious art in the Maghrib. Two theses by Tunisians, Mustafa el-Habib, "Stèles funéraires kairouanaises d'époque Fatimide et Ziride" (Université de Paris IV, 1972) and K. Mawdoud, "L'Art funéraire de Tunis sous les Banu Khurasan (454/1062–554/1159)" examine funeral art.

The only available indices of unpublished research compiled in North Africa itself are lists of theses and dissertations published by L'Association des Auteurs Marocains pour la Publication in Rabat in 1987 and covering the period from 1953 to 1984; a mimeographed copy of unpublished research done at the Université de Constantine; and a *Répertoire chronologique des thèses et mémoires soutenus* (Tunis: Université de Tunis, 1987).

With respect to research in the Maghrib, a few preliminary observations are in order. The relatively recent establishment of the universities limits the number of dissertations and theses that have been completed. Most of this work has been done in departments of Arabic and history in the facultés des lettres; but, especially in topics related to Islamic studies, the faculties and special schools of theology have also been active. Finally, it is worth noting that the inclination to write in Arabic is on the increase.

To my knowledge, there are only two Moroccan theses: Muhammad ʿAbid Jabiri, "al-ʿAsabiyya wa-l-dawla: maʿalim nazariyya khalduniyya fi-l-taʾrikh al-islami" (Université Muhammad V, 1971; subsequently published, Casablanca: Dar al-Thaqafa, 1971); and M. Miftbah, "al-Tayyar al-sufi wa-l-mujtamaʿ fi-l-andalus wa-l-Maghrib athnaʾ al-qarn 8H/14JC." There have also been some mémoires done in the departments of Arabic and history, most of which are textual editions.

The University of Constantine's records indicate thirty-two theses in history, six of which were on the Middle Ages. None of these, however, were defended at Constantine proper. One was done in France, the others in universities in the Middle East. Among these are three theses in Islamic studies: Muhammad Khalid Istanbuli, "Edition et commentaire de la deuxième partie du *Kitab mashariʾ al-ashawaq ila masariʾ al-ʿusaq wa muthir al-gharam ila dar al-salam*," done at Mecca in 1985; a *fiqh* (Islamic jurisprudence) study by M. Busaq al-Madani, "al-Taʿwid ʿan al-sarf fi-l-fiqh al-islami" (1982); and J. al-Kolli, "La Polémique islamo-chrétienne en Espagne, 1492–1640, à travers les réfutations de l'Islam de Juan Andréa et Lopé Obrégon" (Université de Montpellier, 1983). Three others address topics of classical history: Bahaz I. Bakir, "al-Dawla al-rustumiyya (160–296/777–909): Dirasah fi-l-awdaʿ al-istiqsadiyya wa-l-hayat al-fikriyya" (1983); Filali ʿAbd al-ʿAziz

Nawwar, "al-'Alaqat al-siyasiyya bayna al-dawla al-'umawiyya fi-l-andalus wa dawla al-Maghrib" (1977); and Khalidi 'Abd al-Hamid, "al-Haraka al-fikriyya fi-l-maghrib al-awsat 408–547/1018–1152" (1983).

One particularly interesting thesis, Nur al-Huda' Buhalfa, "al-Islam wa-l-ta'rib fi shamal ifriqiyya fi-l-qurun al-thalatha li-l-hijra" (1986), focuses on the problem of the Arabization of North Africa. It looks into important questions first posed by William Marçais in two seminars, in 1938 and 1958, on "Comment l'Afrique de Nord a été arabisée." Michael Brett has examined the issue from the perspective of Islamization in "The Spread of Islam in Egypt and North Africa," in Michael Brett, ed., *Northern Africa: Islam and Modernization* (London: Cass, 1973); and, more recently, it has attracted the attention of Richard Bulliet, *Conversion to Islam in the Medieval Period: An Essay in Quantitative History* (Cambridge, Mass.: Harvard University Press, 1979).

More research needs to be done on the impact of the Arab tribes on the peopling and history of the Maghrib. Thus far, it has predominantly been the Berbers who have been studied, as in Richard Bulliet, "Botr et Baranès, hypothèse sur l'histoire des Berbères," in *Annales, économies, sociétés, civilisations* XXXVI (1981), pp. 106–116; Gabriel Camps, *Berbères aux marges de l'histoire* (Toulouse: Editions des Hespérides, 1980), and Maya Shatzmiller, "Le Mythe d'origine berbère, aspects historiographiques et sociaux," in *ROMM* XXXV (1983), pp. 145–156; and in a few articles by Tadeusz Lewicki and Mohamed Talbi.

In the Faculté des Lettres at Tunis, only five thèses de troisième cycle have been defended in the department of history, two of which are not related to the Maghrib. Among the remaining three is Muhammad Hassan, "*Kitab al-Siyar* (al-qism al-thani): fuqaha' al-'ibadiyya bi-l-Maghrib; tahqiq wa dirasah" (Université de Tunis, 1979), a critical edition of Sammahi's collection of biographies of 'Ibadi sheikhs. Hassan has also published several articles on the Ibadis, including "Ibadiyyat Jirba wa 'alaqatuhum bi-l-fatimiyyin wa-l-ziriyyin," in *al-Hayat al-thaqafiyya*, no. 24 (1982), pp. 70–77; and "Les Sectes ibadites," in *Jerba, une île méditerranéenne dans l'histoire* (Tunis: Institut National d'Archéologie et d'Art, 1982). He is particularly interested in the rural world and has published "Malamih min al-rif al-maghribi min khilal *Kitab al-Nawazil*," in *Cahiers de Tunisie*, nos. 131–132 (1985), pp. 5–34; and "Wathiqa fi-l-ta'rikh al-rifi: tahbis hanshir Ibn Mansur bi-l-Mahdiyya 'ala ribat al-Munastir, 825 H /1422 M," in *Revue d'histoire maghrébine*, nos. 49–50 (1988), pp. 221–248, an edition and study of habus documents at the end of the Middle Ages.

Mohamed al-Baji ibn Mami has written a superb thesis on "Madaris medinah Tunis min al-'ahd al-hafsi ila-l-'ahd al-husaini" (Université de Tunis, 1981), which gives a history of the madrasas of Tunis along with a detailed architectural study of each of them. Ibn Mami, currently a researcher at the Institut National de l'Archéologie et d'Art, has written a history of the mausoleum of Sidi Mahrez which the Ministry of Culture has published as a brochure. He has also published some inscriptions from Hafsid Era funeral steles.

Mourad Rammah also defended a thesis on archeology and history, "Susa min al-fatah al-islami ila maji' al-muwahidin: dirasah ta'rikhiyya wa hadariyya wa athriyya" (Université de Tunis, 1982). The author is now responsible for the archeological work and the museum at Kairouan.

An as-yet uncompleted thesis by Ibrahim Jadla on urban society in the Hafsid era will enrich our understanding of the social history of that era. Another thesis in progress, by Hussain Ben Abdallah, deals with Andalusian immigration in the Hafsid era and promises to be most interesting. Despite a traditional interest in immigration from Muslim Spain, only a few articles, such as Mohamed Talbi, "Les Contacts culturels entre l'Ifriqiyya hafside (1230–1569) et le sultanat nasride d'Espagne (1232–1492)," in *Actas del II Coloquio Hispano-Tunecino* (Madrid: Instituto Hispano-árabe de Cultura, 1973), pp. 63– 90; and Muhammad Belkhodja, "al-Hayat al-thaqafiyya bi Ifriqiyya sadr al-dawlat al-hafsiyya," in *al-Nashra al-'ilmiyya*, IV (1976–1977), pp. 9– 80 give insight to the importance of this immigration and its impact on the ethnic composition of the population, on agriculture, and on literary production.

Admittedly, this essay has largely overlooked Muslim Spain, only because of the impossibility of covering every facet of the topic. The important work of Pedro Chalmeta, especially his thesis on the *"sahib al-suq"* (market overseer), subsequently published as *El Señor del zoco en España* (Madrid: Instituto Hispano-árabe de Cultura, 1973); the intriguing studies of Lucie Bolens on the cultural practices of Andalusian farmers, for example, "La Révolution agricole andalouse du XIème siècle," in *Studia Islamica* XLVII (1978), pp. 121–141, or "L'Agriculture hispano-arabe au moyen âge," in *Wirtschaftsgeschichte des vorderen Orients in islamischer Zeit* I (1977), pp. 55–275; and the book by Dominique Urvoy, *Le Monde des ulemas d'andalous du Vème/XIème au VIIème/XIIIème siècles: Etude sociologique* (Geneva: Droz, 1978) all richly deserve notice.

A brilliant thesis combining social history and religious studies is Amor Ben Hamadi, "al-Fuqaha' fi 'asr al-murabitin" (Université de Tunis, 1987). Its author has published "Abu-l-Hassan 'Ali, le qadi almoravide mentionné dans une inscription de la grande mosquée de Tlemcen," in *IBLA*, no. 155 (1985), pp. 133–140; and "Encore sur la rencontre Ghazali et Ibn Tumart," in *IBLA*, no. 156 (1985), pp. 297–311.

Among the mémoires worthy of note is that of Ahmad Sa'dawi, "al-Afat wa-l-kawarith al-tabiʿiyya bi-l-Maghrib al-wasit" (Université de Tunis, 1982), which verifies Talbi's assertions on demographic disruptions laid out in "Effondrement démographique du Maghrib du XIème au XVème siècle," in *Cahiers de Tunisie* XXV, nos. 97–98 (1977), pp. 51–60. Many of the mémoires are sharply focused urban or regional studies—for example Hadi Sayadi, "al-Mahdiyya des origines à la conquête normande;" H. Zarrad, "La Ville de Sfax au moyen âge;" and Hamdi Maouia, "Le Djérid à l'époque hafside." Others, such as Mohamed Anqazu, "Mujtamaʿ al-mudun al-ifriqiyya min khilal *Kitab riyad al-nufus* li-Abi Bakr al-Maliki" (Université de Tunis, 1987), analyze classical literature, including also the *Tabaqat* of Abu l-ʿArab.

The impact of the "Hilalian Invasion" on North Africa has been the focus of no fewer than three mémoires: Radi Daghfous, "Recherches sur l'origine des tribus arabes (Hilal et Sulaym) et les conditions de leur émigration au Maghreb" (1970); Saif al-Din Daghfous, "al-Sirat al-hilaliyya baina 'l-mashriq wa-l-Maghrib" (1987); and Mohamed Saʿid, "al-Qabaʾil al-hilaliyya wa-l-sulaimiyya wa ʿalaqatiha bi-l-mujtamaʿ al-hafsi" (Université de Tunis, 1987). These studies carry on the celebrated international scholarly debate aroused by this question since the days of Gautier, Poncet, Idris, and Jacques Berque.

Most of the research in the departments of Arabic bears on textual editions, but several theses in literary history are of considerable importance. Chedly Bouyahya blazed a path with "La Vie littéraire en Ifriqiyya sous les Zirides, pp. 362–555 H/972–1160 JC" (Université de Paris I, 1969; subsequently published with the same title, Tunis: Société Tunisienne de Diffusion, 1972); followed by Ahmed Touili, "al-Hayat al-adabiyya bi Tunis fi-l-ʿahd al-hafsi" (Université de Tunis, 1985). Poets have been the objects of such studies as Mohamed Yalaoui, *Un Poète chiite d'occident au IVème/Xème siècle: Ibn Hani al-Andalusi* (Tunis: Publications de l'Université, 1976); and ʿAbd al-Rahman Yaghi, *Diwan Ibn Rashiq al-Qayrawani* (Beirut: Dar al-Thaqafa, 1961) on Ibn Rashiq; while a second work by the same author, *Hayat al-Qayrawan wa mawqif Ibn Rashiq minha* (Beirut: Maktabat al-Maghribiyya, 1962) examines life in Kairouan in Ibn Rashiq's time. The completion of a thesis in preparation on literary life in Ifriqiyya in the Aghlabid epoch will give us an almost continuous knowledge of medieval literary production in Ifriqiyya. A last thesis to be noted is Ahmad Chtioui, "al-Mazahir al-hadariyya min khilal rahalat al-mugharibah wa-l-andalusiyyin wa thaqafati-him" (Université de Tunis, 1989), which analyzes the content of travel literature in much the same way as Miquel has done.

## THE NEW HISTORY

The work reviewed up to this point has been, on the whole, quite traditional, but several major projects in Tunisia, where much innovative work is underway, serve to introduce a discussion of "the new history." The first is an important project on the history of the national movement, facilitated by a convention with the French government that has made possible the repatriation of crucial archives. This project has generated significant accomplishments, including several annual seminars on the history of this era.

The second project, centering on habus records, will ultimately allow research on Tunisian social and economic history to proceed more quickly and efficiently. The classification and analysis of documents may enable us to learn more about the Middle Ages, and especially the Hafsid era. The third project is an attempt by historians and geographers to establish a map of agricultural production in medieval Ifriqiyya. Toward that end, a very useful mémoire that indexes inhabited places mentioned by the medieval Arab geographers is Fawzia Shaqrun, "al-Fihris al-zamani li-l-amakin bi-l-Maghrib hasab jughrafi al-'asr al-wasit" (Université de Tunis, 1978).

The Commissariat Général à l'Aménagement du Territoire has commissioned a team of researchers to establish an archeological map of the country, and some preliminary maps have already been completed. When completed, this project will update our information about both Muslim and Ancient sites, as well as provide a census of urban buildings from the Muslim era.

A team under the direction of this author is collaborating in an international project on Arabic onomasty which will utilize computers to study the data in Arabic biographical dictionaries. The work on Ibn Sakir al-Kutubi's *Fawat al-wafayat* is underway, with over four hundred biographies finished. Four scholars are at work on the *Durar al-kamina* and have gone through more than five hundred biographies. The work of researchers looking at Jubrini's *'Unwan al-diraya* and the *Tabaqat* of Abu-l-'Arab is at an earlier stage.

## CONCLUSION

This survey has attempted to convey a reasonably complete and accurate idea of the research that will permit scholars in the future to better understand those centuries of the Middle Ages that were once so abusively described as "obscure"—such was the minimal state of knowledge at the beginning of the current century. The time for syntheses based on solid research has already arrived. It is now possible to envisage an accurately interpreted general history of the Maghrib in the Middle Ages. Given the breadth of work involved in such an undertaking, the ideal would be to do it collectively, with each researcher working within the chronological limits most familiar to him or her.

Another vision for the future is a spirit of greater cooperation between North African researchers and Maghribi specialists elsewhere to avoid the redundancy of scholars working on the same subject. It should be quite clear that in many instances texts have been translated or edited at the same time in France, the Maghrib, and perhaps even the Mashriq, while even within a single faculty there is often an overlap or repetition of topics covered by mémoires.

It would also be helpful to promote work on the period of the early conquest of North Africa, which remains very poorly known. A few articles by Hichem Djait constitute the bulk of our information on this era: "L'Afrique arabe au VIIIème siècle," in *Annales, économies, sociétés, civilisations* XXVIII, (May–June 1973), pp. 600–611; "Note sur le statut de la province d'al-Andalus de la conquête à l'instauration de l'émirat omayyede," in *Cahiers de Tunisie* XVI, nos. 61–64 (1968), pp. 7–11; and "La Wilaya d'Ifriqiyya au IIème/VIIème siècle: étude institutionnelle," in *Studia Islamica* XXVIII (1968), pp. 79–107.

The time of the traditional historians, no matter how respectable they were, has passed. It is now essential to acknowledge the preoccupations of western historians and address questions concerning women (one such mémoire, based on the *Nawazil* of al-Wansharisi is now underway); daily life (Mohamed Talbi is preparing a book on daily life in the Hafsid era); on death (a mémoire in preparation considers this question through an analysis of published funeral inscriptions); and the family. Several Tunisian researchers interested in Arab medicine organized a colloquium on Ibn Jazzar, while mathematicians, historians, philosophers, and lexicographers all participated in a seminar on Arab mathematics held in Tunis in 1989.

Inevitably, this paper has omitted, whether deliberately or by accident, some important works. Following the example of classical Arab authors, let this be attributed to "khawfan min al-tatwil" (the fear of overextending oneself). After all, "al-kamal li-l-Sayyid al-Khalq" (perfection belongs only to God).

## Notes

1. Mohamed Yalaoui, "Les Recherches sur la Tunisie médiévale au cours des trente dernières années (1956–1986)," in *IBLA,* no. 159 (1987), p. 61.

2. "Etudes arabes et islamiques connaissent une grave crise en France," in *Le Monde* (December 17, 1987), p. 23.

# Some Reflections on Recent Trends
# in the Study of Modern North African History

*Wilfrid J. Rollman*
Harvard University

O ver the past quarter century, scholars have made numerous assessments of the state of historical studies on North Africa. Some have attempted to provide general overviews giving analytical attention to works considered of salient importance. Among the best of these are Edmund Burke III, "Towards a History of the Maghrib," *Middle Eastern Studies* XI, no. 3 (October 1975), pp. 306–323; and the special fiftieth anniversary issue of the *Revue de l'Institut des belles lettres arabes* 159 (1987), which contains articles on historiography in Tunisia by Habib Ben Younes, Mohamed Yalaoui, Taoufik Bachrouch, Mohamed Hédi Chérif, and Zeineb Cherni-Ben Said. Other similar surveys include Jacob M. Landau, "Russian Works on the Maghrib," *Middle East Studies* XXIII, no. 1 (January 1987), pp. 116–119; André Martel, "Etat des recherches historiques françaises sur le Maghreb contemporain," in *Atti del Terzo congresso di studi arabi e islamici* (Naples, 1967), pp. 493–509; Jean-Louis Miège, "Historiography of the Maghrib," in *Reappraisals in Overseas History,* Pieter C. Emmer and Henk L. Wesseling, eds. (The Hague: Martinus Nijhoff, 1979), pp. 69–83; and Béchir Tlili, "La Recherche historique en Tunisie: Bilan et perspective," *Cahiers de Tunisie* XX (1972), pp. 77–78; 125–133.

Other reviewers have taken a more thematic approach. Ernest Gellner, "The Struggle for Morocco's Past," in *Man, State and Society in the Contemporary Maghreb,* I. William Zartman, ed. (New York: Praeger, 1973), pp. 37–49; David C. Gordon, *Self-determination and History in the Third World* (Princeton: Princeton University Press, 1971); Mohamed Sahli, *Décoloniser l'histoire: Introduction à l'histoire du Maghreb* (Paris: François Maspero, 1965); and John Wansbrough, "Decolonization of North African History," *Journal of African History* IX (1968), pp. 643–650, focus on the process of "decolonizing" history. In "Problématique du féodalisme hors l'Europe: Le Maghreb pré-colonial," a chapter of *Sur le féodalisme* (Paris: Editions Sociales, 1971), pp. 145–270, René Gallissot and others discuss works devoted to the definition and analysis of social formations and modes of production, as does

Jean-Claude Vatin, "Introduction générale: Appréhensions et compréhensions du Maghreb pré-coloniale (et colonial)," *Revue de l'Occident musulman et de la Méditerrannée* XXXIII (1982), pp. 7–32.

Taken together, these earlier contributions constitute the unstated background and introduction to the remarks that follow and have provided invaluable guidance in forming these concepts. This essay opens with a brief overview and discussion of some aspects of the scholarship on modern North African history as it has evolved over approximately the past twenty years. Many of these observations will refer particularly to Morocco in the precolonial period (1750–1912)—the "longue dix-neuvième," as it has been called. However, a recognition of the limitations of strictly "national" history makes it imperative to keep the broader framework of the Maghrib (à quatre) in view.

Of course, given the space available, nothing even approaching a comprehensive and balanced overview of the great volume and diversity of work on modern North African history that has been published in recent years could be attempted. Hence, this essay will touch on only a limited number of developments in the areas of archival sources, research tools, theoretical approaches, and foci of scholarly research which seem especially significant.

The past few decades have witnessed a most impressive—not to say overwhelming—outpouring of publications of an almost luxuriant variety in scholarly quality, subjects of investigation, themes, and theoretical or methodological approaches. There is much in all of this that is encouraging, brilliant, informative, and stimulating. Abundant evidence indicates that historians on both sides of the Mediterranean and Atlantic have been influenced by a multiplicity of conceptual frameworks. Social history; Anglo-Saxon social science; structuralism; the writings of Karl Marx, Max Weber, and their disciples; the broad and challenging projects advanced by what has come to be known as the *Annales* school of history; the Orientalism debate; the discourse analysis of the French historian-philosopher Michel Foucault; and others all have their practitioners in the field of North African historical studies. A preliminary survey of this work also confirms that no particular theoretical approach or research goal has come to definitively dominate the study and interpretation of the history of the Maghrib since 1500. Many heirs to the Arabo-Islamic tradition of historiography of the precolonial ulama and many practitioners of political and dynastic history continue their work virtually unaffected by the intense intellectual debates and the variety of theoretical influences engaging other scholars of history. Increasingly, too, historians have found none of the approaches mentioned above adequate to their needs. Consequently, their works often reflect a combination of approaches which, in effect, results in a kind of histoire composite[1] that is, nonetheless, original, interesting, and valuable for its refusal to impose any single paradigm.

While the diversity of frameworks and efforts has obviously not thwarted the production of high-quality work, it has tended to encourage a degree of conceptual fragmentation and the dissipation of effort and resources. Certainly it has made the goal of producing "*a* history of the Maghrib"[2] seem much further from reach today than might have been imagined in the 1970s, when two histories of the Maghrib first appeared, one by Abdallah Laroui, *L'Histoire du Maghreb: Un essai de synthèse* (Paris: François Maspero, 1970), subsequently translated into English as *The History of the Maghrib: An Interpretive Essay* (Princeton: Princeton University Press, 1977); and the other by Jamil M. Abun-Nasr, *A History of the Maghrib* (Cambridge: Cambridge University Press, 1st ed. 1971; 3d ed. 1987, with the revised title *A History of the Maghrib in the Islamic Period*). This is true despite the near quantum leap forward that has since been made in our knowledge about the region's precolonial modern period, and despite the fact that the quantity and variety of sources available to researchers today was something only hoped for at that time. The profound differences in style, content, and conceptualization between these two important and influential works seem in many ways to symbolize the struggle for the definition, valuation, and transmission of North Africa's precolonial past that is presently engaged along a broad front at once intellectual, social, political, and cultural.[3]

All parties in this struggle have made some contribution (in the form of edited texts, published documents, analyses or descriptions of new archival sources, the investigation of new topics, the testing of new theoretical approaches, or the use of new methodologies) toward reconstructing the factual outline of the precolonial past that is indispensable for any serious effort toward a coherent reading. At one very basic level, all of these writers and researchers are participants in the urgent and crucial project of retrieving what precious evidence remains of this period.

At another level, much of the work of the past twenty years has also demonstrated an accelerated convergence between history and the other social sciences, particularly anthropology, sociology, and political science. Increasingly, we have seen what Clifford Geertz called a blurring or a mixing of genres, almost a "jumbling" of discourse that makes the definition of what is and is not history increasingly difficult for the modern scholar striving for scientific rigor and precision—a striving which may be ill-fated, perhaps even ill-founded, and which, ironically, reflects back on the "interdisciplinary" practice of the *maddah* (eulogists) or *jawwal* (itinerant storytellers), who should be counted as predecessors and colleagues of those engaged in the task of reconstructing, preserving, transmitting, and interpreting history, the social fact.[4]

To be sure, the influence of the other social sciences on the history of this region is a fact of long standing. Many of the works which have played a formative role in its study have been produced by scholars from other disciplines, or those whose work has combined its history with some other discipline. Jacques Berque, *L'Intérieur du Maghreb, XV–XIX siècles* (Paris: Editions Gallimard, 1978); and *Ulemas, fondateurs, insurgés du Maghreb, XVII siècle* (Paris: Sindbad, 1982), to cite only two of his later works, comes readily to mind, as do Jean-Claude Vatin, *L'Algérie politique, histoire, et société* (Paris: Fondation Nationale des Sciences Politiques and Armand Colin, 1974); Paul Pascon, *Le Haouz de Marrakech* (2 vols.; Rabat: CURS, 1977); Lucette Valensi, *Fellahs tunisiens: L'Economie rurale et la vie des campagnes aux 18è et 19è siècles* (Paris: Mouton, 1977); and much of the writing of Abdallah Laroui.

Anthropologists and sociologists from Europe and North America have long maintained a keen interest in North African society. Having begun work in the region in the 1940s, primarily within the theoretical confines of their principal disciplines, they have increasingly moved to add a historical dimension to their analyses, especially in the face of persuasive critiques based on structuralist analysis and segmentary theory. Some examples of the latter trend are Abdallah Hammoudi, "Segmentarité, stratification sociale, pouvoir politique et sainteté," *Hespéris-Tamuda* XV (1974), pp. 147–179; Ellen Titus Hoover, "Among Competing Worlds: The Rehamna of Morocco on the Eve of French Conquest" (unpublished Ph.D. diss., University of Michigan, 1978); and John Chiapuris, *The Ait Ayash of the High Moulouya Plain: Rural Social Organization in Morocco* (Ann Arbor: University of Michigan Museum of Anthropology, 1969).

Whether embarked on studies of economic history, investigations of dependency and the processes of economic development, or the nature of the state and its relationships to society, to name but a few important themes central to their work, social scientists have all generally come to accept the importance—if not always the necessity—of including the historical dimension in their analyses.[5] For, as E. J. Hobsbawm has argued concerning social history, the social or societal

> aspects of man's being cannot be separated from the other aspects of his being, except at the cost of tautology or extreme trivialization. They cannot, for more than a moment, be separated from the ways in which men get their living and their material environment. They

cannot, even for a moment, be separated from their ideas, since their relations with one another are expressed and formulated in language which implies concepts as soon as they open their mouths.[6]

Still greater communication between history and the other social sciences should be fostered by the multidisciplinary and interdisciplinary efforts required to pursue research and analysis within some of the more complex paradigms, such as those formulated in discourse analysis models or by the historians and social scientists of the *Annales* school. Such prominent historians as Fernand Braudel and E. J. Hobsbawm see such communication and cooperation as essential to the very survival of history as a practice.[7] Notes the former,

> Whether it [history] wants to or not, it must assimilate all the discoveries made by the different social sciences, of more or less recent birth, in the inexhaustible field of man's existence. A difficult task, but an urgent one, for only if history decisively commits itself to this path can it be of any substantial use in understanding the world of today.[8]

An increasing number of historians of North Africa would seem to agree, despite the magnitude of the task Braudel sets for them and the limited and dispersed resources at their disposal for its accomplishment.[9]

As has been indicated, students of North African history have been steadily expanding the range of their inquiry in many directions over the past twenty years. Their research has been greatly facilitated by the substantially increased availability of internal and external archives and other manuscript sources.

In Tunisia, the work of Abdeljelil Temimi, founder and editor of the *Revue d'histoire maghrébine* (1974– ) and director of the Centre d'Etudes et de Recherches Ottomanes, Morisques de Documentation et d'Information in Zaghouan, has made numerous valuable contributions to the collection, publication, and analysis of documentation of all genres relating to early modern and modern history.[10] Further description and analysis of the archival materials available in Tunisia can be found in the works of some of the best known historians of the precolonial period, such as Lucette Valensi, *Fellahs tunisiens: L'Economie rurale et la vie des campagnes aux 18è et 19è siècles* (Paris: Mouton, 1977); Mohamed Hédi Chérif, *Pouvoir et société dans la Tunisie de Husayn Bin 'Ali (1705–1740)* (2 vols.; Tunis: Publications de l'Université de Tunis, 1984 and 1986), especially II, pp. 219–230; Khelifa Chater, *Dépendance et mutation pré-coloniales: La Régence de Tunis de 1815–1857* (Tunis:

Publications de l'Université de Tunis, 1984); Rashad al-Imam, *Siyasat Hamuda Basha fi Tunis* (Tunis: Manshurat al-Jami'at al-Tunisiyya, 1980); and Abdelhamid Henia, *Le Grid: Ses rapports avec le Beylik de Tunis (1676–1840)* (Tunis: Publications de l'Université de Tunis, 1980). Of similar interest is F. Robert Hunter, "Capital Accumulation and Provincial Power in Pre-Protectorate Tunisia (1850–1881): Notes from the Tunis Archives," *Middle East Studies* XXIII, no. 1 (January 1987), pp. 108–115.

Among the most helpful guides to Tunisian manuscript collections are the catalogues of 'Abd al-Hafiz Mansur, *Catalogue général des manuscrits*, vol. I: *Fonds Hassan Husni Abdelwahab;* vol. II: *Fonds Ahmadiyya* (Tunis: Institut National d'Archéologie et Arts, 1975 and 1986, respectively). As an overall introduction to Tunisian historians and their work, Ahmed Abdesselam's *Les Historiens tunisiens des XVIIè, XVIIIè et XIXè siècles* (Tunis: Librairie C. Klincksieck, 1973) is still the most useful and informative volume available.

Archival materials for the study of precolonial Algeria are scattered in many repositories outside the country. Notable collections are to be found in France and in Turkey, as well as, to some extent, in Tunisia. Efforts are underway in Algeria to repatriate some of these materials and to gather and organize what has been preserved in the country. A good introduction to the manuscript sources on Algeria can be found in the works of Aboul-Kassem Saadallah, especially *Ta'rikh al-jaza'ir al-thaqafi* (2 vols.; Algiers: SNED, 1981), his two-volume cultural history of Algeria from the sixteenth to the twentieth centuries.

Moroccan archival and manuscript collections have proven extremely rich sources, particularly for historians of the nineteenth century. New materials are being added to what is available for study every year, making it difficult to give an account that is current. Articles by Daniel Schroeter, "The Royal Palace Archives of Rabat and the Makhzen in the 19th Century," *The Maghreb Review* VII, nos. 1–2 (January–April 1982), pp. 41–45; and Thomas K. Park, "A Report on the State of Moroccan Archives," *History in Africa* X (1983), pp. 395–409 are, however, indicative of the wealth and nature of the materials that are known to exist.

The large manuscript collections housed in the Royal Palace Library, the National Library, and the Qarawiyyin Library in Fez have all become more accessible to scholars during the past decade. Multivolume catalogues for the Royal Palace Library—*Faharis al-Khizanat al-Hasaniyya bi-l-Qasr al-Maliki* (Rabat) (6 vols.; various compilers to 1987)—and for the Qarawiyyin collections—Muhammad al-'Abad al-Fasi, *Fihris Makhtutat Khizanat al-Qarawiyyin* (3 vols.; Casablanca: Matba'at al-Najjah al-Jadida, 1979–1983) are in progress. As shown by the work of Muhammad Hajji, *Fihris al-Khizanat al-'ilmiyya al-Sabihiyya bi Sla* (Kuwait: Manshurat Ma'had al-Makhtutat al-'Arabiyya,

1985), smaller libraries, both private and public, are also beginning to provide catalogues or guides to their manuscript and book collections. The indefatigable Muhammed Manuni, whose knowledge of the manuscript and archival resources of his country is itself a national treasure, has been in the forefront of efforts to preserve, classify, and describe these materials. A prolific writer and lecturer on this subject, Manuni has produced several book-length manuscript catalogues and numerous shorter descriptions, including *Al-Masadir al-ʿArabiyya li Taʾrikh al-Maghrib,* vol. I (Rabat: Manshurat Kulliyyat al-Adab wa-l-ʿulum al-insaniyya, 1983; *Faharis Makhtutat al-Khizanat al-Hasaniyya,* vol. I (Rabat: Al-Matbaʿat al-Malikiyya, 1983), all of which are valuable tools for the historian. For a bibliography of some of Manuni's other works see Abdallah Laroui et al., *Fi al-Nahda wa-l-Tarakum: Dirasah fi Taʾrikh al-Maghrib wa-l-Nahda al-ʿArabiyya Muhadatan li-l-ʾUstadh Muhammad al-Manuni* (Casablanca: Dar Tubqal li-l-Nashr, 1986).

Lastly, the existence of several hitherto underexploited or unexploited European sources must be mentioned. The publication of a series of articles and books by the Spanish scholar Ramón Lourido-Díaz on the period during which Sidi Muhammad bin ʿAbd Allah al-ʿAlawi reigned as sultan of Morocco (1757–1790) have brought to light the importance of the Spanish archival sources (in this instance, the archives of the foreign ministry) for the economic and political history of Morocco. One of the most important of these is *Marruecos en la segunda mitad del siglo XVIII* (Madrid: Instituto Hispano-árabe de Cultura, 1978). There is reason to believe that they will be equally helpful for the other countries of the Maghrib as well. If the work of Lourido-Díaz is indicative of their value, they will, for example, provide a good deal of new data on the region's maritime commercial relations (such as the export of cereals) with Iberia in the eighteenth and nineteenth centuries. As Mariano Arribas-Palau suggests in "La Documentación del Archivo histórico national relativo al Norte de Africa," *Revista del Instituto egipcio de estudios islámicos* (Madrid) XX (1978–1980), pp. 69–95, they can also offer a valuable supplement and point of comparison for the English and French documents which have served as the principal sources of information on these matters until now.

Other guides to and selections of European sources for the eighteenth and nineteenth centuries which seem particularly useful include the work on eighteenth-century French documents by Chantal de La Veronne, *Documents inédits sur l'histoire du Maroc. Sources françaises, tome I, 1726–1728* (Paris: Geuthner, 1975); and the continuing UNESCO series of guides to sources on North African history in Europe: UNESCO and the Conseil International des Archives, *Guide des sources de l'histoire d'Afrique du Nord, d'Asie et d'Océanie*, vol. I, pt. 1 [Belgium] (Brussels, 1976); vol. II, pt. 2 [Bibliothèque Nationale, Paris] (Paris: K. G. Saur, 1981); vol. III, pts. 1 and 2 [Denmark, Finland, Norway, and Sweden] (Paris: K. G. Saur, 1980); vol. VI [Germany] (Munich: K. G. Saur, 1984); vol. VIII [Austria] (Munich: K. G. Saur, 1986). Further guides to materials on North Africa are anticipated. Arnaud de Menditte, *Répertoire des archives du Maroc (Série 3H: 1877–1960)* (Paris: Service Historique, Etat Major de l'Armée de Terre, 1982), which lists items housed in the Ministry of Defense collection at the Chateau de Vincennes, is a much needed starting point for research in that collection.

In addition to the works of Ahmed Abdesselam, Muhammed Manuni, and others already mentioned, several bibliographies of secondary sources and manuscript sources should be mentioned as examples of the improved research tools that have become available to historians since 1970. Mohammed Lakhdar's study of the literary sources for the history of the Alawite Dynasty (to 1894), *La Vie Littéraire au Maroc sous la Dynastie 'Alawide (1075–1311/1664–1894)* (Rabat: Editions Techniques Nord-Africaines, 1971) and Muhammad Hajji's similar work on the Sa'di Dynasty, *Al-Haraka al-Fikriyya bi-l-Maghrib fi 'Ahd al-Sa'diyyin* (2 vols.; al-Muhammadiya: Matba'at Fadala, 1976 and 1978) have made important additions to the classic works of Evariste Lévi-Provençal, *Les Historiens des Chorfa* (Paris: Larose, 1922) and 'Abd al-Salam ibn 'Abd al-Qadir ibn Suda, *Dalil Mu'arrikh al-Maghrib al-Aqsa* (2 vols.; 2d ed.; Casablanca: Dar al-Kitab, 1960 and 1965).

Lionel Galand has provided researchers with a critical introduction to the resurgent field of Berber studies, *Langue et littérature berbères: Vingt-cinq ans d'études* (Paris: Editions du Centre National de la Recherche Scientifique, 1979), while Robert Attal has written a similarly essential guide to the literature on the Jews of North Africa, *Les Juifs d'Afrique du Nord: Bibliographie* (Jerusalem: Ben Zvi Institute, 1973). Pessah Shinar's annotated bibliographical essay on Islam in North Africa, *Essai de bibliographie sélective et annotée sur l'Islam maghrébin contemporain: Maroc, Algérie, Tunisie, Libye (1830–1978)* (Paris: CNRS, 1983) gives substantial attention to works on the nineteenth century. For works written by anthropologists and sociologists, but of interest and value in the task of the historian, André Adam's bibliography, *Bibliographie critique de sociologie, d'ethnologie et de géographie humaine* (Algiers: Centre de Recherches Anthropologiques, Préhistoriques, et Ethnographiques, 1972) is especially important, the more so as it contains copious references to material produced earlier in this century which is sometimes difficult to locate.

Though not, strictly speaking, research tools in the same sense as the works just noted, the reedited and republished biographical dictionary of al-'Abbas bin Ibrahim al-Marrakishi, *Al-I'lam bi man Hala Marrakish wa*

*Aghmat* (10 vols.; Rabat: Matbaʿat al-Malikiyya, 1974–1983) and Muhammad Dawud, *Ta'rikh Titwan* (6 vols.; Tetouan: Matbaʿat al-Mahdiyya, 1959–1970; then Rabat: Matbaʿat al-Malikiyya [vols. 7 and 8], 1975–1979), the previously unpublished volumes of which were brought out posthumously, are two major sources of information on the precolonial period in Morocco. The *Ta'rikh Titwan* also includes reproductions of a large number of documents. It is to be hoped that these kinds of endeavors will continue and that some of the other critical sources for this period, such as Muhammad bin Jaʿafar al-Kattani's *Salwat al-anfas* and ʿAbd al-Rahman ibn Zaydan's *Ithaf aʿlam al-nass,* both now extremely difficult to find, might receive similar attention.

Finally, it should be noted that the periodical literature and scholarly journals of interest to the historian have increased in quality and quantity to a remarkable degree over the past twenty years. University faculties and institutes in all of the North African countries, as well as other institutions and organizations, are publishing journals on a wide range of issues, sources, and analytical and methodological debates relating to precolonial history, thus making accessible discussion forums and sources of information never before so abundantly available to scholars of this period.

New interpretive methodologies, originating in the critique of western European Orientalism, the movement among North African scholars and others in the 1950s and 1960s to "decolonize" North African history and, most recently, the writings on discourse analysis by anthropologists from the United States and Great Britain—and Michel Foucault in France—have also opened up new sources for scholars.[11] In two recent books organized around a selection of manuscripts and their analysis, *L'Intérieur du Maghreb, XV–XIX siècles* and *Ulemas, fondateurs, insurgés du Maghreb, XVII siècle,* Jacques Berque has done ground-breaking work in the "rereading" of such commonly known sources as chronicles, genealogies, and hagiographies.

Abdelahad Sebti has produced a study of equal importance on Sharifian genealogies (*ansab*), "Au Maroc: Sharifisme citadin, charisme et historiographie," *Annales, économies, sociétés, civilisations* (March–April 1986), pp. 433–457, and Magali Morsy has been able to suggest a reinterpretation of the so-called "interregnum" (1727–1757) following the death of the Alawite sultan Mawlay Ismaʿil through the application of some of the principles of this approach to internal and external sources for the period in "Réflexions sur le discours historique à travers l'examen d'un document sur le Maroc au milieu du XVIIIè siècle," *Revue de l'Occident musulman et de la Méditerrannée* XX (1975), pp. 67–103. Lucette Valensi, in the introduction to her new edition of the travel account of Jean André Peyssonnel, *Voyage dans les ré-*

*gences de Tunis et d'Alger* (Paris: La Découverte, 1987), has made a timely and instructive contribution concerning some of the dangers inherent in rereading texts, specifically travel accounts, to fit contemporary ideological positions. Like Sebti and Berque, Valensi calls for special attention to the need to preserve the historical specificity of the contexts in which such works were written.

Two studies by Edmund Burke III on the connections between French scholarship on the Maghrib and French colonial policy there—"The Image of the Moroccan State in French Ethnological Literature: A New Look at the Origin of Lyautey's Berber Policy," in Ernest Gellner and Charles Micaud, eds., *Arabs and Berbers* (London: Duckworth, 1973), pp. 175–199, and "The First Crisis of Orientalism, 1890–1914," in Jean-Claude Vatin, ed., *Connaissances du Maghreb* (Paris: Editions CNRS, 1984), pp. 213–226—have pointed out the role, in the case of Morocco, of implicit and explicit cultural perspectives, their influence on the scholarly analysis of the Maghrib, and their links with broader political and cultural projects. Similar or related work on this problem for North Africa generally has been the subject of *Connaissances du Maghreb,* the excellent anthology in which one of the Burke articles appears.

The number of studies on the "image" of the Maghrib in European literary and historical works has increased in recent years. Several examples, of varying quality and utility but with useful bibliographies and discussions indicative of this trend, are Ann Thomson, *Barbary and Enlightenment* (Leiden: E. J. Brill, 1987), which examines eighteenth-century European stereotypes of the Maghrib that served as part of the intellectual milieu in which the French decision to invade Algeria was taken and rationalized; Alf Andrew Heggoy's edited collection, *Through Foreign Eyes* (Washington: University Press of America, 1982), a group of essays dealing especially with American perspectives on North Africa; and Guy Turbet-Delof's well-known critical bibliography on the image of the Maghrib in French literature to 1715, *Bibliographie critique du Maghreb dans la littérature française, 1532–1715* (Geneva: Droz, 1973).

Interest in external relations persists in the form of diplomatic history, although this field now has only a small number of practitioners. Monumental works like Pierre Guillen's study of German-Moroccan relations, *L'Allemagne et le Maroc de 1870 à 1905* (Paris: Presses Universitaires de France, 1967); Frederick V. Parson's *The Origins of the Morocco Question, 1880–1900* (London: Duckworth, 1976); and Jean-Louis Miège's *Le Maroc et l'Europe* (4 vols.; Paris: PUF, 1961–1963) have not had—perhaps could not have— imitators. A great deal of interest remains in some of the specific issues raised in these works, and particularly in the forms of European political and economic intervention, but these issues are now treated with a different emphasis, if not always with substantially different results, by historians with access to local archives. Their research has produced such contributions as Mohammed Kenbib, "Structures traditionnelles et protections étrangères au Maroc au XIXème siècle," Hespéris-Tamuda (1984), pp. 79–101 and Mustafa Bu Shaʿaraʾ, Istitan wa-l-Himayat bi-l-Maghrib, 1863–1894 (2 vols.; Rabat: al-Matbaʿat al-Malikiyya, 1984, 1987). Scholars also remain engaged in research on external relations with countries like the United States and Spain, which have not previously received much attention in the histories noted above, or elsewhere. Two of the more significant publications in this regard are Manuel Fernandez Rodríquez, España y Marruecos en los primeros años de la restauración (1875–1894) (Madrid: Consejo Superior de Investigaciones Científicas, Centro de Estudios Históricos, 1985) and Aurora Valadez and Laila Hajoui, comps., A Selected Bibliography of Moroccan American Relations (Rabat: EDINO, 1987).

In general, the works in this category which have made extensive use of consular and economic, as well as diplomatic, documents (those of Miège and Guillen, for example) contain much information that historians cannot and should not ignore, even though the sources on which they are based are external and hence, now, often "problematic." Despite their perspective on North African history and society, which may raise serious issues with contemporary readers, these sources can serve as valuable points of comparison with internal sources in matters of internal economic, social, and political processes.

Though the historiography of the Maghrib produced over the past two decades reflects many perspectives and a wide variety of interests and goals, the object of its inquiry remains, decidedly, the Maghrib itself. There are many reasons for this. In part, it is the natural development of the drive for self-determination, self-definition, and reorganization begun by nationalist activists and intellectuals earlier in this century. Not that they shared from the start a consensus on how to go about this task; rather, the contrary was true. They did, however, all share an appreciation of the need to reconstruct from local materials a past of their own and to find a suitable framework or frameworks for the creation of the new nations they envisioned. And, to varying degrees in different countries, investigations into the past have elucidated patterns of government-society relations that provide a window on contemporary politics.

Also, in part, the persistent focus on the Maghrib has been the product of the efforts of influential scholars such as Abdallah Laroui, whose work has posited the primacy of internal dynamics and structures in the explanation of critical questions about, for example, the internal origins of colonial domination, economic dependence, and the fragility of political legitimacy. In three books, *L'Histoire du Maghreb* (1970), *Les Origines sociales et culturelles du nationalisme marocaine (1830–1912)* (Paris: Maspero, 1977), and *La Crise des intellectuelles arabes: Traditionalisme ou historicisme?* (Paris: Maspero, 1974) which was translated into English as *The Crisis of the Arab Intellectual* (Berkeley: University of California Press, 1976), Laroui has leveled a strong and sustained— sometimes brilliant and often polemical—critique of Arabo-Muslim society in Morocco and elsewhere and has posed a challenge to historians and intellectuals everywhere in the region to rethink basic issues concerning culture, society, government, and economy that has been difficult to ignore. His seminal and critical work has served to reinforce the trend toward a sharper focus on internal history already underway in Morocco and elsewhere.

Many others have encouraged and participated in this move to focus more attention on internal history. An example of such work in Tunisia is Taoufik Bachrouch, "L'Historiographie tunisienne de 1968 à 1985: L'Epoque moderne," *Revue de l'institut des belles lettres arabes* L, no. 159 (1987), pp. 75–90; in Algeria, Jean-Claude Vatin, *L'Algérie politique: histoire et société* and Aboul-Kassem Saadallah, *Ta'rikh al-Jaza'ir al-Thaqafi;* and in Morocco, Germain Ayache, *Etudes d'histoire marocaine* (Rabat: SMER, 1983) and Muhammed Manuni, *Mazahir yaqzat al-Maghrib al-hadith* (2d ed.; 2 vols.; Casablanca: Shirkat al-Nashr wa-l-Tawzi'a al-Mudaris, 1985).

Historical research across the Maghrib has also developed in response to the findings, methods, and theoretical assumptions of western researchers working in the region and reflects the influences of different educational experiences. The *Annales* "school," with its emphasis on large-scale changes in fundamental structures such as class, households, and kinship, has become increasingly influential. Moreover, its interest in demography, the study of local communities, regions, "out groups" of all kinds (slaves, sharecroppers, and women), crime, climate, food, and mentalités converges throughout the Maghrib with already strong interests in the local and internal, the cultural, the religious, and the socioeconomic. In some places, archival materials, public and private, may be available in sufficient measure to further pursue some of these lines of inquiry and thereby strengthen this approach to the study of history.[12]

The ongoing debate about rural Morocco, based on the extensive work already done, especially concerning tribes, by English and American anthropologists and sociologists, has also generated considerable response in the region, which is effectively summarized in Lilia Ben Salem, "Interêt des analyses en termes de segmentarité pour l'étude des sociétés du Maghreb," *Revue de l'Occident musulman et de la Méditerrannée* XXXIII (1982), pp. 113–135. As suggested by Abdallah Hammoudi, "Segmentarité, stratification sociale, pouvoir politique et sainteté," *Hespéris-Tamuda* XV (1974), pp. 147–179, this discussion has served to stimulate further "readings" of local sources, ecological and legal evidence, and oral accounts aimed at sustaining or refuting the validity of tribe and kinship categories as operational concepts in rural North Africa in precolonial times as well as later.

In addition, the debate has been enlarged to consider alternatives to the notion of "tribe" and kinship lineage systems as actual structures, a position championed by David Hart, *The Ait Waryaghar of the Moroccan Rif: An Ethnography and History* (Tucson: University of Arizona Press, 1976). The conceptualization of kinship as an ideological category or as an ad hoc explanation of association and demands for protection and support has emerged as a strong alternative over the years since Jacques Berque posed the essential and still vexing question, "Qu'est-ce qu'une 'tribu' nord africaine?" in *Eventail de l'histoire vivante: Hommage à Lucien Febvre*, vol. I (Paris: Librairie Armand Colin, 1956), pp. 261–271.[13] Subsequently, more ecologically determined explanations, such as Henry Munson, Jr., "The Mountain People of Northwestern Morocco: Tribesmen or Peasants?," *Middle Eastern Studies* XVII, no. 2 (April 1981), pp. 249–255, have been put forward, particularly with respect to the Rif.

The great interest in the development of states and in issues of economic development after independence prompted European and American political scientists and political economists to devote considerable attention to North Africa. Many of these scholars' research projects had a marked contemporary focus and concern for policy; hence, much of what they have generated has little to say concerning the past. The most interesting and useful bits of this work, from the historian's point of view, are precisely those in which some account has been taken of the historical dimension. Prominent examples of this approach are Lisa Anderson, *The State and Social Transformation in Tunisia and Libya* (Princeton: Princeton University Press, 1986); Elbaki Hermassi, *Leadership and National Development in North Africa* (Berkeley: University of California Press, 1972); Clement H. Moore, *Politics in North Africa* (Boston: Little Brown and Co., 1970); and John Waterbury, *The Commander of the Faithful* (New York: Columbia University Press, 1970).

Even these works, however, tend to concentrate on the colonial and the postindependence periods. They are concerned primarily with political elites and the "center." Nonetheless, the interest of political scientists in government, the bureaucracy, the army, and state-sponsored efforts to strengthen government, extend its scope, and seize control of the economy, has raised a number of important issues and generated propositions concerning the state which have served as helpful starting points for historians interested in similar themes in earlier periods. Examples of this genre include the work on nineteenth-century reform in Tunisia by L. Carl Brown, *The Tunisia of Ahmad Bey, 1837–1855* (Princeton: Princeton University Press, 1974); and Wilfrid Rollman's study "The 'New Order' in a Pre-Colonial Muslim Society: Military Reform in Morocco, 1844–1904" (2 vols.; unpublished Ph.D. diss., University of Michigan, 1983).

Finally, a number of scholars working within a Marxist perspective have focused attention on internal history and the nature of local social structures, economies, and governments, as well as the relations between state and society, as they have striven to place precolonial and precapitalist North Africa into some sort of Marxist framework. Their interest in charting the emergence of capitalist forms of production and exchange and their inquiries into the possibility that feudalism, in the Medieval European sense of that institution, might have existed in North Africa have helped elucidate patterns of economic exchange such as long-distance trade, forms of labor, and the production of commodities for export. Studies by Rahamin Benhaim, "L'Etat, la paysannerie et la colonisation au Maroc XIX–XX siècles," *Mediterranean Peoples* VII (April–June 1979), pp. 141–155, and David Seddon, *Moroccan Peasants: A Century of Change in the Eastern Rif* (Folkstone, England: William Dawson and Sons, 1981), among others, have also posed useful questions and provided information about land ownership and land use in the region.

Although the *Annales* approach may prove to be an exception, virtually all of these paradigms have tended to impose categories and assumptions that, in the end, simply do not fit the Maghrib, or do not do so entirely. This has limited their utility. On the other hand, all of them continue to encourage useful debate, new research, and increased cross-fertilization between historians and other social scientists. Singly or in combination with other theoretical perspectives they have helped to push historical research to new frontiers. The concern of anthropologists about tribal society and of political economists about peasants has generated a host of studies on the rural sector throughout the region. Research on peasants and other local groups within the context of state-society relations has yielded very interesting work on political protest, banditry, and political communications between and among various strata of society. Several works on these themes worthy of particular attention are David Hart, *Banditry in Islam* (Wisbech, England: MENAS Press, 1987), pp. 1–45; Edmund Burke III and Ira Lapidus, eds.,

*Islam, Politics, and Social Movements* (Berkeley: University of California Press, 1988); Donald Crummey, ed., *Banditry, Rebellion and Social Protest in Africa* (London: James Currey, 1986); and Bruce Cumings, "Interest and Ideology in the Study of Agrarian Politics," *Politics and Society* X, no. 4 (1981), pp. 469–495.

Increased attention to the groups—rural and urban—that were the components of the larger society has also facilitated, and perhaps stimulated to some degree, the growth of scholarly interest in the study of Berbers and Jews. While such interest has not been wholly academic, by any means, serious studies are now underway. It may take some time before the results of this labor are integrated into the broader tapestry of North African history or the respective national histories of its member states, but the study of these groups can add much that is important to the broader history all serious students of the past are striving to reconstruct.

Some helpful titles focusing on historical themes within the Jewish community are Michel Abitol, ed., *Judaïsme d'Afrique du Nord aux XIXè–XXè siècles* (Jerusalem: Ben Zvi Institute, 1980); *Les Relations intercommunautaires juives en Méditerranée occidental, XIIIè–XXè siècles. Actes du Colloque internationale de l'Institut d'histoire des pays d'outre-mer (Aix-en-Provence) et Centre de recherche sur les juifs d'Afrique du Nord (Jerusalem)* (Paris: Editions CNRS, 1984); and Mohammed Kenbib, "Musulmans et juifs au Maroc, 1850–1945: Essai bibliographique," *Hespéris-Tamuda* XXIII (1985), pp. 5–26. On the Berbers, there are, in addition to Lionel Galand's *Langue et littérature berbères: Vingt-cinq ans d'études,* H. T. Norris, *The Berbers in Arabic Literature* (Harlow, England: Longman, 1982); and Mohammed Abès, "Recherches historiques sur les berbères de la banlieue de Meknès: Les Aït Idrasen," *Etudes et documents berbères* I (1986), pp. 27–40.

Endowed with archival resources that are extensive, albeit not without major gaps, Moroccans and Tunisians, joined by a small number of European and American colleagues, have forged ahead in the study of local and regional history. While a final assessment of this trend would be premature, outstanding contributions by Ahmad Tawfiq on Inoultan and the region south of Marrakesh, *al-Mujtamaʿ al-Maghrib fi-l-qarn al-Tasiʿ ʿashr (Inultan, 1850–1912)* (Casablanca: Matbaʿat al-Najjah al-Jadida, 1983); Naʿima Harraj Tuzani on the *ʿumana'* (financial administrators) during the reign of Mawlay al-Hassan I (1873–1894), *al-ʿUmana' bi-l-Maghrib fi ʿahd al-Sultan Mawlay al-Hasan* (Rabat: Matbaʿat al-Fadala, 1979); and Umar ʿAfa's impressive study of the Moroccan currency and monetary policies during the nineteenth century, *Masa'ila al-nuqud fi ta'rikh al-Maghrib fi-l-qarn tasiʿ ʿashr* (Casablanca: Matbaʿat al-Najjah al-Jadida, 1988) constitute a most fruitful beginning.

Other scholars—Bourqiya Rahma, "La caidalité chez les tribus Zem-mour aux XIXè siècle," *Bulletin économique et sociale du Maroc*, nos. 159–161 (1987), pp. 131–140; E. G. H. Joffé, "Local Society in Morocco on the Eve of the European Occupation: The Southern Jhala in 1911," *Revue d'histoire maghrébine* XXV–XXVI (1982), pp. 51–64; and Abderrahmane El Moud-den, "Etat et société rurale à travers la harka au Maroc du XIXè siècle," *The Maghreb Review* VIII, nos. 5–6 (1983), pp. 141–145, to name a few—have produced numerous studies of the nature of, and changes over time in, rela-tions between the centralizing government and its subjects in the provinces during the nineteenth century.

Still others, whose research concentrates on the socioeconomic and cul-tural transformations that were in progress during this period, have gener-ated studies on commerce, agriculture, and the role of local religious fig-ures. The best of these include Dale F. Eickelman, *Moroccan Islam: Tradition and Society in a Pilgrimage Center* (Austin: University of Texas Press, 1976); Abdallah Hammoudi, "Sainteté, pouvoir, et société: Tangrout au XVIIè et XVIIIè siècles," *Annales, économies, sociétés, civilisations* XXXV (May–August 1980), pp. 615–641; and Hassan El-Boudrari, "Quand les saints font les villes," *Annales, économies, sociétés, civilisations* (May–June 1985), pp. 489–508.

The cumulative effect of all this, it is hoped, will be to bring Moroccans, Tunisians, Algerians, and Libyans from all social sectors, ethnic groups, and religious affiliations into their history. Local history, however defined, should serve as a building block for reconstructing a fuller and more nuanced aware-ness of how communities interacted among themselves, felt the forces of change, and responded to them. Learning more about everyday life, the family, the town quarter, and the life of the soldier should not obscure the fact that all these were components of a larger community, in contact with government with increasing regularity, and involved in politics, commerce, and other forms of exchange. To understand their experiences properly, and to represent them accurately, historians must learn about them and present them in relation to each other.

For the historian, the challenge is also to take advantage of the perspec-tive that local history gives. Archives and other sources of documents and oral accounts from the period now offer us the opportunity not simply to answer questions posed by the theoretical paradigms inherited from the past, but to generate new questions. With a view "from below" as well as one "from above," might we have a chance to reexamine such fundamental notions as "crisis" in the nineteenth century? Might we be able, ideally working together, to reassess notions about "national" economy, political legitimacy, and "colonizability"?

## Notes

1. To borrow the late Paul Pascon's term for the coexistence of the dissymmetrical components that, in combination, constitute Moroccan rural society. Paul Pascon, "Segmentation et stratification dans la société rurale marocaine," in *Actes de Durham: Recherches récentes sur le Maroc moderne* (Rabat: Bulletin Economique et Sociale du Maroc, 1973), pp. 105– 119. See also Abdelkebir Khatibi, "Mémoire d'une quête," *Bulletin économique et sociale du Maroc,* pp. 159–161 (1987), p. 11.

2. The reference to *a* history is from Edmund Burke III, "Towards a History of the Maghrib," *Middle Eastern Studies* XI, no. 3 (October 1975), p. 306.

3. As discussed in Ernest Gellner, "The Struggle for Morocco's Past," in *Man, State and Society in the Contemporary Maghreb,* edited by I. William Zartman (New York: Praeger, 1973), pp. 37–49.

4. Clifford Geertz, *Local Knowledge: Further Essays in Interpretive Anthropology* (New York: Basic Books, 1983), pp. 19–23.

5. Note, for example, the copiously documented essay by Habib al-Malki and Abdelali Doumou, "Réflexions méthodologiques sur le problématique des réformes au Maroc du 19è siècle," in *Actes du Colloque: Réformisme et société marocaine au XIXè siècle* (Rabat: Publications de la Faculté des lettres et des sciences humaines, 1986), pp. 447–473; and Jean-Claude Vatin, "Les examens contradictoires: Esquisse de bilan des recherches sur les formations étatiques et identités nationales au Maghreb (XIXè–debut XXè siècle)," *ROMM* XXXVI, no. 2 (1983), pp. 177–200.

6. E. J. Hobsbawm, "From Social History to the History of Society," *Daedalus* C (Winter 1971), p. 25.

7. Fernand Braudel, *On History* (Chicago: University of Chicago Press, 1980); Hobsbawm, "From Social History," p. 24.

8. Braudel, *On History,* p. 200.

9. Note, for example, the variety of work recently presented in homage to Paul Pascon in the *Bulletin économique et sociale du Maroc,* pp. 159–161 (1987).

10. Xavier Yacono, "L'Histoire moderne et contemporaine du Maghreb dans les archives arabes et turques," *Revue historique* CCL (October–December 1973), pp. 403–416.

11. Edward Said, *Orientalism* (New York: Vintage Books, 1979); Philippe Lucas and Jean-Claude Vatin, *L'Algérie des anthropologues* (Paris: Maspero, 1982); Mohamed Sahli, *Décoloniser l'histoire: Introduction à l'histoire du Maghreb* (Paris: Maspero, 1965); Kevin Dwyer, *Moroccan Dialogues: Anthropology in Question* (Prospect Heights, Ill.: Waveland Press, 1982).

12. For an interesting and informative introduction to the basics of social history and the work of *Annales* historians, see William B. Tay-

lor, "Between Global Process and Local Knowledge: An Inquiry into Early Latin American Social History, 1500–1900," in Oliver Zunz, *Reliving the Past: The Worlds of Social History* (Chapel Hill: University of North Carolina Press, 1985), pp. 115–190, especially p. 119; and Charles Tilly, "Retrieving European Lives," ibid., pp. 11–52.

13. On this general subject, see Dale Eickelman, *The Middle East: An Anthropological Approach* (Englewood Cliffs, N.J.: Prentice Hall, 1981), pp. 85–134.

# PART II

# Modern History and Historiography

The development of any nationalist movement entails a reassessment of the past. This process is a critical one that goes to the heart of creating a nation-state with a national identity and, eventually, citizens who partake of that identity in the belief that it expresses both their individual aspirations and their collective will. The development of the study of history is an integral part of this undertaking.

In the case of the Maghrib, a number of issues related to the creation of a "national" history had to be taken into consideration. First, while the fate of each emerging state had, clearly, to be associated with the general course of Islamic history, there was an equal need for a history that was peculiar and distinct to that country. Second, there was a need to enshrine national heroes who were universally recognized and credited with advancing the national liberation movement. As several of the pieces in this section suggest, it was sometimes easier to reach a consensus on figures of the nineteenth century than on those who were more immediately contemporary. Finally, given the nature of contemporary history, its writing is rarely the monopoly of the nationals of any particular country. Foreigners, both members of the former colonizing power and others, invariably take an interest in the history of any given country. As a consequence, a third problem arises: How does one reconcile, or simply make peace with, the often contradictory demands of the need for a national history and the practice of good, unbiased history?

Since nationalism is a European invention, there is a tendency to analyze and evaluate the development of nationalist movements against the pattern of events in eighteenth- and nineteenth-century Europe. While this may appear justified in some regards, the important role of Islam as a defining cultural and political force in all the nationalist movements of the Maghrib, no matter how secular they may appear, belies any attempt to superimpose the case of Europe on North Africa. The same holds true for the study of the historiography of the Maghrib. For there are several obvious differences between the case of Europe and that of the Maghrib. First, in the nineteenth century, European historians tended to concentrate on, or monopolize, the history of their own countries. Frenchmen wrote about France; Germans wrote about Germany, and so forth. This was equally true of French or German studies of the remoter periods, such as that of Roman rule. Somehow this ancient past was shaped so that it related to the history of the nation-state. By contrast, modern Maghribi historiography was first created by Europeans—particularly French historians—while Maghribi historians continued to pursue the models of classical Islamic history or tried to integrate some European methodologies into their traditional frameworks.

If they did adopt wholesale European historical traditions, it was often in the service of a national history and the nationalist struggle. Consequently, while these works served the intellectual needs of the nationalist movement, they did not always satisfy the standards of good history.

In this section, "Modern History and Historiography," the essays focus on the problem of creating a decolonized history and the long journey that historians of the Maghrib, both native and foreign, have followed to forge this history. Two articles, those of Houari Touati and Omar Carlier, deal with the complexities of writing the history of Algeria. Touati addresses the difficult and uncertain transition from traditional Islamic historiography to a more modern or scientific view of history as it emerged in the Arabic language works of Algerian historians at the turn of this century. Carlier focuses on the tensions that exist between, on the one hand, nationalism and politicians-turned-historians as the makers of historical myth and, on the other, history as the conscience of scientific "reality." The pieces by Kenneth Perkins, Mohamed El Mansour, and Michel Le Gall focus on the specific problems of the postindependence writing of history. All three authors suggest how the postindependence climate has allowed the former victims of colonization to look at their past afresh, sometimes on their own and sometimes assisted by sympathetic outsiders with no linguistic or cultural links to the former colonizer. What emerges is a picture of the diverse nature of the historical analysis. But equally significant is the uneven nature of the development of the historiography. The historiography of Algeria in this century is particularly rich, while that of Libya remains very much in its initial stages, due in part, no doubt, to the traditional Islamic-style monarchy of King Idris, which lasted until 1969. In the case of Morocco, a rather singular situation exists. While there are still many gaps, several Moroccan historians have ventured to produce broad syntheses of the history of the Maghrib, offering at once an agenda for historiography and an appreciation of its current shortcomings. What all these contributions point to is the fact that while the history of the Maghrib has made immense strides in the past three decades, it is still very much a historiographical tradition in the making.

# Algerian Historiography in the Nineteenth and Early Twentieth Centuries: From Chronicle to History

*Houari Touati*

Ecole des Hautes Etudes en Sciences Sociales (Paris)

## THE AGE OF THE CHRONICLERS

Until the end of the nineteenth century, the intellectual bases of North African historical writing were the very ones on which Arab Muslim historians had built their studies during the classical period. For these historians, history was, above all, the representation of Providential time. Beholden as it was to an unapproachable Supreme Being, history could only be deciphered through those signs (*ayat*) through which the Supreme Being chose to manifest His Sublime and Immutable Will. Thus, a lost battle signified divine wrath; a victory divine benevolence. The author of *Diwan al-Muttamil* could see in the French conquest of Algeria and the defeat of the Turks in 1830 only one of those ayat with which the Almighty customarily punished sinners.

In fact, the notion of catastrophe is central to premodern thinking. In the *Anis al-Gharib wa-l-Musafir* of Muslim b. 'Abd al-Qadir, for example, there is "a sign from God most High" (ayat min Allah ta'ala)[1] every time He wants to express His disapproval or dissatisfaction with tyranny, injustice, sinful acts against morality or religion, and sundry other *manakirat* (plural of *munkar*, 'reprehensible act.') It is through this intervention in the temporal sphere that God attributes to events a meaning He alone can decree. The theory of divine punishment finds its transcendental justification in these same "signs." In the discursive Qur'anic form, the concepts of divine punishment and history operate on an identical plane where history, conceived of as the milieu for divine punishment, draws from such punishment its semantic and mythological significance. The stories in Sura XI (Hud) relate in the same archetypal pattern the saga of Noah and his people, of Hud and the 'Ad, of Salih and the people of Thamud, assigning to history the tasks of edification and fashioning "normative models."

The histories of apostles that We relate to you are meant to strengthen your heart. Through them has the truth come to you, and guidance, and reminder to those who believe. (XI: 120)

This concept elicits, in the text of the chronicler, what one might call an edification syndrome. For example, consider the description of the famous "Snow Storm Expedition" launched by Abu Kabus Bey against the Darqawa insurgents and their chief, Ibn Sharif, in 1806. Muslim b. ʿAbd al-Qadir writes:

> The Bey arrived in the village governed by Abu Tarfas (a holy man sympathetic to the Darqawa insurgency) and destroyed it entirely, along with the gardens. On the return road, as he arrived by the banks of the Wad Tafna, he was caught unexpectedly by a horrendous snow storm such as had never happened in man's memory. Nearly all the horses of the makhzan died. Thus was the Bey compelled to return hurriedly to Tlemcen. His armies scattered in the most complete disarray, some men losing their horses, some their saddles, others their firearms, in the heavy snow. Rivers started overflowing, disaster gripped the whole surrounding countryside and trees split asunder. Praise be to the One Almighty who punished the Pharaohs and humiliated the giants, the God whose punishment knows no limit or temporal bounds. For there is no God beside Him and none worshipped other than Him.[2]

We are still within the framework of Sura XI: The giants are certainly those semimythical ʿAd from southern Arabia who were "accursed in the world and . . . will be damned on the Day of Doom" (XI: 60). It is on this preestablished archetypal model, with cosmic catastrophe at its center, that the historian Muslim b. ʿAbd al-Qadir bases his narrative of the "Snow Storm Expedition." The concept evoked by this catastrophe is also archetypal and emblematic. It could very well apply to the disaster that befell the "People of the Elephant" in the time of the Prophet Muhammad. The fact is that, from the perspective of the believer, cosmic catastrophe is the spiritual equivalent of what we call historical determinism.

In the *Dalil al-Hayran wa Anis al-Sahran* of Muhammad b. Yusuf al-Ziyani,[3] there is yet another technique characteristic of premodern historiography—one that some western historians have denigrated, but others have applauded. Emile Félix Gautier, for example, was appalled by the way in which Abu Zarʿ had crafted his *Rawd al-Qirtas* in the fourteenth century.

Gautier found the style of his historical narrative, which brought together, helter-skelter, major facts and minor incidents, and which tolerated contradictory versions of the same event, puzzling.[4] Gustave von Grunebaum, on the other hand, saw in this apparent confusion a mark of honesty and noted that "the overall objectivity of Arab historiography is remarkable."[5] What, then, is one to make of *Dalil al-Hayran?* If one chooses to read it from the perspective of Gautier, one can only be disturbed by the apparent structure of the narrative. At first glance, one might find the end of the chapter entitled "Fourth Dynasty: The Merinides" shocking. Following a catalogue of heroic war deeds comes an account of the introduction of coffee and tobacco in Morocco—a juxtaposition which interrupts the flow of the narrative for no apparent reason.

In another example from al-Ziyani, the reader confronts a cascade of contradictory passages. The chronicler saw no problem in giving five different dates, mentioned in the following order, for the arrival of the Turks in Algiers.

1) The year 1 of the tenth century A.H., according to Abu Ras al-Nasiri and Abu ʿAbdallah Muhammad b. ʿAskar al-Sharif;

2) The year 15 of the tenth century A.H., according to ʿAbd al-Razzaq al-Jazaʾiri;

3) The year 20 of the tenth century A.H., according to al-Yafrani;

4) About the year 20 of the tenth century A.H., according to ʿAbd al-Rahman al-Jamiʿi.

5) The year 10 of the tenth century A.H., according to Muslim b. ʿAbd al-Qadir.

After this list, al-Ziyani gives another one, of the rulers of Algiers, again without commentary on the contradictory dates that he has furnished.

Behind this type of historical narrative are two basic concepts: a desire, imparted to Arabo-Islamic historiography by the writers of the eighth and ninth centuries C.E., to be exhaustive and objective; and the absence of causal sequencing in the reporting of events. For the early historians, the core of Arabo-Islamic historiography was the *Sirat al-Rasul (The Biography of the Prophet)*. The need to relate all the facts and all the trustworthy accounts in the reconstruction of the life of the Prophet gave rise to the now-familiar historiographical archetype: around a given fact all the credible versions were gathered haphazardly. Al-Masʿudi offers an example. In the chapter of *Muruj al-Dhahab* entitled "Account of the Caliphate of Abu Bakr," a section with the title "Oath of Allegiance of ʿAli" reads as follows:

There are discrepancies in the date of the oath of allegiance of ʿAli b. Abi Talib. Some people claim that he paid allegiance to Abu Bakr ten days after Fatima's death (that is, some seventy days after the death of the Prophet). But others maintain that it was three months afterwards, and some even say six months. There are others who offer other dates.[6]

Not wishing to make any comment, al-Masʿudi moves on to something else.

Al-Tabari displays this same attitude, although he adopts the formula *wa huwa al-athbathu ʿindana* ('this seems most reliable to us') each time he wants to take a position. This expression is not, of course, entirely affirmative, nor does it contradict our contention of impartiality, in that the expression refers not to the substance of the *matn* (facts reported), but rather to the *silsilat al-isnad* (chain of authorities) reporting them. In the end, al-Tabari allows his *dhawq*, the sixth sense of an experienced scholar, to prevail, rather than dealing with the historical information in a manner that would enable him to offer a sustained assessment.[7]

According to Gaston Bachelard, the establishment of causal sequencing is an epistemological hurdle on the route to scientific formulation, since "it is through a rationally established sequence that random facts acquire the status of scientific facts."[8] In premodern Arabo-Islamic historiography, the absence of causal sequencing is, in intellectual terms, the very organizing element of the historical text. No fact is a fact in and of itself; a fact exists only to the extent that God grants it substance. Moreover, there can be no independent certification of fact because history, as a sequence of events, is conceived as the recurrence of an archetypal beginning.

These are some of the epistemological constructs which helped shape premodern Arabo-Islamic historiography. For over a thousand years, they were at the root of the transcendental Muslim vision of the past, a vision regulated by a God-given normality and periodically recalled by various "signs." Such a vision was progressively abandoned only after the start of the twentieth century.

## THE MAGHRIB'S TRANSITION TO THE QUEST FOR HISTORICAL CONTINUITY

The publication by Editions Fontana of the first volume of *Kitab taʿrif al-khalaf bi-rijal al-salaf* by Abu al-Qasim al-Hafnawi (Algiers, 1907) was a major intellectual event—the first time that an Algerian historian had had a manuscript printed. This breakthrough, along with the content of the work, made the event doubly important for an Algerian scholarly elite keenly interested in history. In 1906, Ahmad b. Murad Turk, an Algiers bookseller, had begun disseminating the three volumes of the *Ta'rikh al-tamaddun al-islami,* a pioneering book in late nineteenth–century Arabo-Islamic historiography in that it combined Khaldunian concepts and western evolutionism.[9] Mohammed Ben Cheneb, who had very favorably reviewed this work in the *Revue Africaine,* undertook the task of recovering from obscurity the written works of Algeria's past, especially those of historians. He began with the publication in 1907 of Ibn Maryam's *al-Bustan* (dating from the late sixteenth or early seventeenth century); then the *Rihla* of al-Wartilani (eighteenth century) in 1908; and the *'Unwan al-diraya* of al-Ghubrini (late thirteenth or early fourteenth century) in 1910. Even earlier, the *Nihlat al-labib bi akhbar al-rihla ila al-habib* of Ibn 'Ammar (eighteenth century) had appeared. And in 1903, Abu Rabi' Sulayman b. Yakhlaf al-Mazati published in Tunis a lithographed edition of his *Kitab al-Siyar.*

Al-Hafnawi's work is organized following the model of the *tabaqat* (categories) common in classical Arabo-Islamic history. Such works are a compendium, often in tedious detail, of biographies of scholars and famous men of a given period.[10] In this respect, al-Hafnawi's work exhibits neither a new concept nor a new discursive mode. Indeed, its style bears the imprint of the past with its imitation of *saj',* a grandiloquent, rhythmic, and assonated prose. This is the work of a compiler, content with reporting lists of facts without any critical examination. Thus, his method remains that of the historiographers of the distant Muslim past, lining up sets of mythicohistorical facts strung together in incongruous bunches, not necessarily immune to chronological disorder. In that sense, al-Hafnawi is a man of the past.

But there is more to al-Hafnawi. On closer scrutiny, one discovers that his work is a source of innovation—indeed, of modernity. Historicist though he may be, he has two objects in mind: first, to inform the reading public, with its short memory, of its glorious past by relating the deeds of its most illustrious ancestors (*rijal al-salaf*) and consequently to instill in it a sense of historical continuity; second, to assert, in the face of the ideologues of the colonial conquest, the authentic historicity of the conquered land, even though its star may have paled considerably. In his introduction, al-Hafnawi writes:

It would appear that Algeria [*al-qutr al-Jaza'iri*] has, in the past, progressed in the study of the various branches of science from the most varied horizons. It developed great skill in scientific methods and fully assimilated their results. Algeria was a center of learning that held high the banner of science, as did its neighbors in the Maghrib. Algeria's star shone in all nations and its place in history was secured by the dedication of scientists who had built their work upon perfectly buttressed foundations. These scholars were, in their time, guiding lights widely consulted for their superior knowledge. But times have changed. Today they are cast into oblivion. Yet the poet has written: "We shall not leave without a trace / Behold what has been left behind us."[11]

At the root of this historicist commentary lies a consciousness shaken by the western world. For if such a commentary acknowledges the fact that the conquered people have been surrounded (*inhittat*), it challenges the denials of colonial historiography with reminders of the glories of their own past. They are not a people deprived of history, as colonial historiography tried to imply. On the other hand, al-Hafnawi's discontent over his people's indifference to their past turns into a pedagogical discourse within the context of history and genealogy, at the center of which now lies Algeria (*al-qutr al-Jaza'iri*) a modern concept totally absent from the old historiography. Thus, with al-Hafnawi a new conception of history emerges, although it remains constrained by the forms and conceits of classical Arabo-Islamic historiography.

## THE EMERGENCE OF NATIONAL HISTORY

When the first volume of Mubarak al-Mili's *Ta'rikh al-Jaza'ir fi-l-qadim wa-l-hadith* was published in 1929,[12] Algerian historiography was in the process of absorbing certain positivist notions, as well as breaking away from the old forms of historical writing. This was because the opening to modernity in the 1920s had profoundly disturbed the practice of politics in Algeria. The collapse of the old structures of political socialization such as the brotherhood, *zawiyya* (building used for religious rituals, usually by sufis, or mystics), mosque, guild, and the like, made way for the emergence of new groups issuing from the civilian bourgeois society—clubs, associations, labor unions, and political parties. Cultural socialization in the schools popularized new basic constructs that were to shape the secular intellectual elite, while the Nahda (Arab cultural renaissance) movement converted a part of the religious elite to the rationalism espoused by proponents of the Salafiyya (an Islamic movement espousing a return to the values of the ancestors, or *salaf*). In the end, the Algerian political process transformed itself into a nationalist movement informed by the idea of the nation-state such as it had existed in western European thinking since the eighteenth century.

Historians also responded to these breaks with the past. They were compelled to reformulate their role in society, their methods, and their goals. Moreover, they were obliged to equip themselves with new intellectual tools suitable for the history and genealogy of a nation driven by incipient nationalism, a nation in search of secure moorings. This manner of "making history" was absolutely new. For historians searching for tools in the past, the only resource to help formulate a new style of historical writing was Ibn Khaldun. In contrast to these historians was the "Ecole historique d'Alger." Even though the members of this truly compelling group sought to write a history of Algeria that conformed, naturally enough, with the dictates of the occupier, they nevertheless proposed the only epistemological model capable of supporting the emergence of a national history. In appropriating this model, modern historians had to challenge the concept of divine ordinance giving meaning to worldly events and, at the same time, recognize the sheer reality, or "positivism," of events. Suddenly, then, God's presence in history gave way to the idea of the "evolution" of events.

A historian cannot make these breaks with the past without a profound upheaval of intellectual habits. Al-Mili believed that nothing was more painful for an Arab historian than writing history according to the modern method, adding that he himself had toiled over checking facts, gathering material, clarifying historical perspectives, and integrating modern methods. Yet al-Mili responded boldly to this challenge by introducing his work with an outline of his critical method; by adding illustrations; by adopting—albeit awkwardly—the formal apparatus of notes and references; and, finally, by resorting, thanks to the summaries and translations of Tawfiq al-Madani and of Amar Dhina, to the works of French historians (some twenty of which he cites in his bibliography).

But what is national history for al-Mili? According to him, it is

the mirror of the past and the ladder by which one rises to the present. It is the proof of the existence of people, the book in which their power is written, the place for the resurrection of consciousness, the way to their union, the springboard for their progress.

This pragmatic definition is governed entirely by its new pedagogical responsibilities. For when members of a nation study their history, when the young get to know its cycles, they know their own reality, and so insatiably greedy nationalities in their neighborhood do not absorb their nationality. They understand the glory of their past and the nobility of their ancestors and accept neither the depreciations of their depreciators, nor the discrediting of falsifiers, nor the lies of the prejudiced. They awake to the blessings of sovereignty to rise against the oppressors, their rule and their humiliations.[13]

Thus, history becomes not the history of kings, princes, and governments, but of peoples. Consequently, the task of the historian is to put himself "at the service of his country" (*fi sabil al-watan*). It further behooves him to do battle, at once, with the historiography of the oppressors and with the native myths which clutter the history of the country, since most earlier historians simply wrote down everything they heard and compiled everything they found without making the effort to check their stories.

Al-Mili attributes to colonialist historiography three cardinal biases: its dogmatism; its superiority complex and fondness for subjugating others; and its disregard for authentic sources. In the case of Algerian history, one area in which these biases operated especially strongly was ancient history. For that reason, al-Mili decided to begin at the beginning. Following al-Mili's foray into the past, the reader discovers that yesterday's colonialism—aggressive and spoliatory—closely resembles that of more recent times. Thus, for instance,

> when the Romans arrived (in North Africa) they took all the possessions of the kings and princes. The state retained part of the loot and the rest was divided among Roman soldiers and mercenaries. The possessions of the people were taxed. As for those who rose in revolt, their possessions were confiscated by the state which distributed them in the usual manner.[14]

This reassessment of Algeria's national past also appears in Tawfiq al-Madani's *Qartajina fi arba'at 'ushur*. The central theme of this work revolves around the incompatibility of two basic notions: Roman imperialism on the one hand, Berber nationalism on the other. "The Roman state," writes al-Madani,

> was an entirely colonialist state founded upon a large Roman colony within the country. This colony knew the Berber only in terms of his

productivity, his usefulness at the service of colonialism, his payment of taxes, and his compulsory enlistment in the fight against his brothers in blood, if, somewhere, they rose against "Rome."[15]

The inevitable replacement of "Rome" with "France" in the minds of al-Madani's readers gave this picture a strikingly contemporary impact. The main task of history, then, is obvious: to dig farther into the past, the better to question the future. The fact is, everything in Algeria's history symbolizes its national identity. The difficulty, as al-Madani observed in his 1932 *Kitab al-Jaza'ir*, is that

the sons of the Arabs [*al-ʿarabiyya*] know nothing of their past. They do not know their history, they do not know their geography, they know neither the administration nor the laws; they do not know the groups that make up our population, they know neither their cultural circumstances nor their economic assets—as if they lived in a house not their own.[16]

Al-Madani's discourse is, again, heavily pedagogical (that is to say, educational and activist), since the nationalism of which it is a discursive byproduct demands the Salvation of the Nation, which can only "rise again by remaining faithful to its faith, its traditions, its language, its culture." Thus, in his view, Arab Muslim Algeria would only gain its freedom within its nationalism, its Arabism, and its Islamism.

In the wake of World War II, new historians educated by dint of circumstances in colonial schools began to make their mark. They included Abdelaziz Khaldi, Mohamed Chérif Sahli, and Mostefa Lacheraf. Their historical orientation was precisely that advocated by Mubarak al-Mili in his program for the nationalist movement: to take the anticolonialist struggle into the field of history. Abdelaziz Khaldi, in his book *Le Problème algérien devant la conscience démocratique* (1946), took stock of the colonization of Algeria in the same way as Tawfiq al-Madani had done in his *Kitab al-Jaza'ir*. Sahli wrote books about two prominent heroes of anticolonialism, ʿAbd al-Qadir and Jugurtha,[17] and Mostefa Lacheraf published an article about anticolonial resistance in the nineteenth century.[18] Thus, Algerian historiography continued to bring historical dignity to the people, as well as to their great leaders.

In 1954, another ʿalim (Islamic scholar) turned historian, Abderrahmane Djilali, sought to awaken the young Algerian generation by guiding it towards the study of its rich history in order to inspire in it a respect for its "forefathers." Towards that end, he wrote *Ta'rikh al-Jaza'ir al-ʿam,* covering the period from prehistoric times to the twentieth century.[19] Not surprisingly, since the key objective was no longer to refute the Latin heritage of Algeria, but rather to emphasize the glories of the Islamic era, so severely mistreated and denigrated by colonial historiography, the bulk of the book was given over to an analysis of the Islamic period.

The fact of the matter is that Algerian historiography has always operated as the *inverse* of colonial historiography. At the start, it was national and nationalist; however, leavened by the nationalist movement, it developed its own political and cultural program. Evolving from the Islah (Islamic Reform) movement headed by the ulama, it has still not entirely freed itself from that influence. But Algerian historians today are vastly indebted to their historiography for formulating a *transcendental* historical vision of their past and, more specifically, for having invented the means toward the historical continuity that has justified and legitimized Algeria's emancipation.

From the point of view of the historian's discourse, this vision rests upon four epistemological pillars: recovering Ibn Khaldun; treating the historical event as a positivist entity; using the techniques and methods of western historical science; and establishing the national entity as fundamentally significant. This history-genealogy of the nation has, from the very beginning, organized the Algerians' relationship to their past within the *transcendental and historical* vision because it tried to explain nothing and, instead, legitimized everything; because it had nothing to explain but everything to legitimize; and because it was nothing more than a fragment of the nationalist ideology that found its adequate expression in the historical narrative.

## Notes

1. Muslim ibn ʿAbd al-Qadir, *Anis al-Gharib wa-l-Musafir* (Algiers: SNED, 1974).

2. Ibid.

3. For a discussion of this important unpublished manuscript concerning western Algeria in the early nineteenth century, see Mehdi Bouabdelli, "Documents inédits sur la révolte des Derqawa en Oranie," in *Les Arabes par leurs archives,* Jacques Berque and Dominique Chevallier, eds. (Paris: CNRS, 1976), pp. 93–100.

4. Emile Félix Gautier, *Le Passé de l'Afrique du Nord: Les Siècles obscurs* (Paris: Payot, 1952), pp. 51–67.

5. Gustave von Grunebaum, *Medieval Islam* (Chicago: University of Chicago Press, 1946), p. 283.

6. Abu'l-Hasan ʿAli Ibn al-Husayn al-Masʿudi, *Muruj al-dhahab wa maʿadin al-jawhar,* Muhammad Muhyi al-Din, ed. (4 vols.; Cairo: al-Maktabat al-Tijariyyah, 1964–1967), II, 308.

7. For a general discussion of the writings of al-Tabari, see *The History of al-Tabari,* vol. 1: *General Introduction and From the Creation to the Flood,* Franz Rosenthal, ed. (Albany: SUNYP, 1989), pp. 5–147.

8. Gaston Bachelard, *Le Rationalisme appliqué* (Paris: PUF, 1962), p. 123.

9. Jurji Zaydan, *Ta'rikh al-tamaddun al-islami,* (5 vols.; Cairo: Dar al-Hilal, 1902–1906).

10. For a brief discussion of tabaqat literature in classical Islamic historiography, see Franz Rosenthal, *A History of Muslim Historiography* (Leiden: E. J. Brill, 1968), pp. 93–95.

11. Abu al-Qasim al-Hafnawi, *Kitab taʿrif al-khalaf bi-rijal al-salaf* (Algiers: Editions Fontana, 1907).

12. Mubarak al-Mili, *Ta'rikh al-Jaza'ir fi-l-qadim wa-l-hadith* (2 vols.; Constantine: 1929–1932; repr. Algiers: SNED, 1976).

13. Quoted from David Gordon, *Self-Determination and History in the Third World* (Princeton: Princeton University Press, 1971), p. 155.

14. al-Mili, *Ta'rikh al-Jaza'ir.*

15. Tawfiq al-Madani, *Qartajina fi arbaʿat ʿushur* (Tunis: n.p., 1926; repr. Algiers: al-Mu'assasat al-Wataniyyah li-l-Kitab, 1986), p. 105.

16. Tawfiq al-Madani, *Kitab al-Jaza'ir* (Algiers: Al-Matbaʿat ʿarabiyya fi-l-jaza'ir, 1932).

17. Mohamed Sahli, *Le Message de Jugurtha* (Algiers: Imprimerie Générale, 1947); and idem., *Abdelkader, chevalier de la foi* (Algiers: En-Nahda, 1953).

18. Mostefa Lacheraf, "Colonialisme et féodalités indigènes en Algérie," in *Esprit* XXII, no. 213 (April 1954), 523–542.

19. Abderrahmane Djilali, *Ta'rikh al-Jaza'ir alʿam* (repr.(?) 2 vols.; Algiers: Dar al-Thaqafa, 1982).

# Forging the Nation-State: Some Issues in the Historiography of Modern Libya

*Michel Le Gall*
St. Olaf College

## INTRODUCTION

The nation-state is widely accepted by modern historians of western and nonwestern civilizations alike as a common unit of historical inquiry. Various multivolume series exist on the modern histories of most European countries, some notable examples being the exhaustive *Oxford History of Modern England* or Georges Duby's edited survey *Histoire de la France*. Counterparts of these works exist, although in briefer form, for most countries of the Middle East and North Africa; in the case of Libya, the works of Wright and Rossi come to mind.[1]

The evolution of the nation-state in European history extends over a period of three or four centuries. Hence, the very study of national history assumes that the events of these centuries exhibit a coherence and follow a progression which gives birth to something called "modern France" or "modern England."

As a matter of convenience, historians of the Mashriq and Maghrib have adopted the European conceit of national history to provide a focus for their respective fields of study—Algeria, Tunisia, Libya, and so on. As a consequence of adopting this historical license, they speak of sixteenth-century Algeria or eighteenth-century Tunisia, although they readily admit that, for the inhabitants and rulers of these areas, the national concept implicit in these turns of phrase would have been unknown and unintelligible. Until the nineteenth century, the political references and loyalties of Maghribi politics encompassed, in addition to an allegiance to Islam, personal loyalty to the ruler, identification with a professional group or guild such as the Janissaries or ulama, and a commitment to family, clan and town. "L'Algérie" or "la Tunisie" as Ben Bella or Bourguiba came to speak of them in the current century were forged, in good measure, by the policies and political failures of French administration and the reactions of Algerians and Tunisians to these colonial and protectorate practices.

Nevertheless, the case for speaking of sixteenth- or seventeenth-century Algeria, Tunisia, or Morocco is strengthened by the relative independence that the dey, bey or sultan enjoyed from the major Islamic power of the time, the Ottoman Empire. Indeed, Morocco never came under the rule of the House of Osman, and the Turkic-Mongol institutions of the Ottoman patrimonial state never cast a shadow over the western extremity of the Mediterranean.[2] Algeria and Tunisia did, however, succumb to the rule of Istanbul. Janissary troops manned garrisons there; for a time governors were appointed directly by the Porte and the customary recognition of the Ottoman sultan in prayers and coinage prevailed.

By the late seventeenth century, Algeria and Tunisia had established regimes that were largely independent of Ottoman sovereignty in almost every regard, although the Porte continued, in strictly legal terms, to exert minimal rights of sovereignty. In Algeria, these ended with the French invasion of 1830, whereas Tunisia considered itself an integral part of the Ottoman Empire as late as 1871.[3] Like the Khedive of Egypt, the Husaynid beys enjoyed several privileges, including the right to conduct a separate foreign policy, contract loans, and negotiate the terms of trade. Many of these advantages were lost after the creation of a French protectorate in 1881.

The history of Libya, by virtue of this country's inclusion in the Maghrib, has been cast in a similar historical framework: It enjoyed semi-independence from the Ottoman sultan under the Qaramanlis (1711–1835), underwent a brief transitional period—commonly called the "Second Ottoman Occupation" (1835–1911)—and then a stretch of Italian colonialism before achieving full independence in 1951, several years before the French dependencies to its west.

On the face of it, Libya's modern history shares features common to its North African neighbors: an extended period of evading direct Ottoman rule; occupation by a European colonial power (Italy 1911–1943); and a nationalist struggle ultimately rewarded with independence.

My intent here is to furnish a number of reasons why this apparent progression of events is, in fact, somewhat different from what it appears to be; to review—although admittedly not exhaustively—some of the literature on nineteenth- and twentieth-century Libyan history; and, finally, to suggest those areas of Libyan history which need further exploration.

At the outset, there is a need to emphasize the misconceptions engendered by the expression "Libya." *Libya* is a word of Greek origin applied to the former Ottoman provinces of "Trablus Garb" and "Bingazi" by Italy and adopted by the United Nations to refer to the newly created kingdom over which King Idris ruled after 1951. Before 1911, no European, Ottoman, or indigenous authority ever used the term "Libya." We may, then, speak of

Libyan history for reasons of convenience; but as an integrated political, economic, and administrative reality, Libya is barely forty years old. Consequently, historians must tread carefully when speaking about earlier Libyan history, for stark regional, economic, political, and administrative differences must be addressed. Likewise, the variegated policies of the Ottoman, Italian, Idrisi, or Jamahariyyan governments cannot be reduced to a common denominator simply for reasons of convenience or national history. The regional differences throughout Libya are far more marked and political than were those between, say, Burgundy and Provence in nineteenth-century France.

## NINETEENTH-CENTURY LIBYA:
### OTTOMAN AND SANUSI HISTORY

The current scholarship on nineteenth-century Libya faces several dilemmas because of the political and economic disparities between Tripolitania, Cyrenaica, and, to a lesser degree, the Fezzan. One of the central problems has been to determine the respective spheres of authority of the Ottoman regime and the Sanusiyya. The received wisdom—which is largely derived from Evans-Pritchard's *The Sanusi of Cyrenaica*—contends that the Ottoman government was relatively effective in Tripolitania, whereas in Cyrenaica it resigned itself to the apparent supremacy of the Sanusiyya.[4] Such an allegedly agreed-upon division of labor is reiterated or assumed in most works dealing with nineteenth-century Libya.[5]

This is certainly the case with the widely cited works of Ahmad Sidqi al-Dajani, *Libya on the Eve of the Italian Occupation* and *The Sanusi Movement*.[6] The first volume, despite use of the word Libya in its title, deals only with Tripolitania between 1881 and 1911 and combines a survey of commercial, agricultural, and social life with an account of Ottoman administration, governor by governor. The Sanusiyya hardly figure in this work, and there is no discussion of any Ottoman civil or military presence in Cyrenaica. Dajani's second volume on the Sanusiyya provides an in-depth account—some of it based on unpublished Sanusi manuscripts—of the foundation stories, lore, tradition, and ideas associated with and formulated by Muhammad b. 'Ali al-Sanusi (1783–1856) and his son, Muhammad al-Mahdi (1844–1902). Although brimming with interesting anecdotes of early encounters between Muhammad b. 'Ali and religious and secular authorities, and tales of remarkable political clairvoyance, the book fails to provide a solid account of the relations of the *tariqa* (sufi brotherhood) with Ottoman officials and successive sultans. Neither does it deal with matters of administrative import such as tax collection, nor with the Sanusiyya expansion. On these critical issues, Dajani, like most of his Arab or European colleagues, relies on Evans-Pritchard or the dubious work of nineteenth-century explorer turned authority on Islam, Henri Duveyrier.[7]

A more recent study, a dissertation, addresses some of these issues and focuses on the career of Ahmad al-Sharif al-Sanusi in the years preceding his accession to the leadership of the Sanusiyya.[8] Drawing on a number of Sanusi manuscript sources, it tries to explain the contribution of Ahmad al-Sharif to the history of the Libyan hinterland in the last few decades of the nineteenth century. The argument is, in certain respects, flawed because of its reliance on the structure of national history to discern the significance of Ahmad al-Sharif's contribution. It necessarily sees in Ahmad al-Sharif's quietist proselytization work the seeds of opposition to French colonialism in Chad, the more severe opposition to Italian colonialism, and the birth of the Sanusi monarchy.

Such a reading of events anticipates and may exaggerate the contribution of the Sanusiyya to the long war against Italy, especially in the first phase, from 1911 to 1919, which has received careful attention from Rachel Simon.[9] Simon, as well as Lisa Anderson in an article on the short-lived Republic of Tripoli (1919–1920),[10] emphasizes the contribution of the Ottoman command and those notables who still shared a common political loyalty with the post-1908 Ottoman regime, despite sometimes-severe differences over its provincial policies. These studies indirectly raise two significant questions. The first is the relative importance of events in Cyrenaica and, implicitly, of the Sanusiyya. Were they crucial to the general history of Libya before the implementation of a more consistent Italian colonial policy after 1920? The second question revolves around the very nature of the Sanusiyya. Was the tariqa as politically minded or astute as most European observers since the nineteenth century have assumed it to be? If this is a given, the activities of the nineteenth-century Sanusiyya are merely a prelude to events after 1911. If, however, one acknowledges a different balance between the contribution to pre-1911 politics of the Ottoman state and the Tripolitanian notables as against that of the Sanusiyya, one may well ask whether the emergence of Sanusi opposition to Italian colonialism was a natural extension of earlier events or the result of a brutal apprenticeship under Italian policy.

My reading of events would suggest that the answer to both these questions is negative. The nineteenth-century Sanusiyya was not as powerful or influential as has been commonly assumed, and the role of the Ottoman regime and Tripolitanian families has been underestimated. Second, the Sanusiyya did not develop any keen political sense until Ahmad al-Sharif struggled to improve his relations with the post-1908 Ottoman regime, commonly known as the Young Turks. This last point has been made quite clear, albeit indirectly, by Orhan Kologlu in his book *Two Libyan Leaders at the Side of Mustafa Kemal.*[11]

The currently available historiography in Arabic or European languages, on the other hand, has yet to explore the reasons behind the common wisdom that the Sanusiyya was so powerful in the late nineteenth century. Instead, its answers have been formulated by the mold of national history, which would seem to dictate a linear progression of events towards the eventual creation of the nation state. And since, for a time, Idris and his followers created havoc for the fledgling Italian colonial regime, and since Idris became the first (and only) king of the postwar entity called Libya, the historiography has been driven to seek the roots of the later Sanusi victory in the nineteenth century. Other more immediate explanations for the success of the Sanusiyya are also germane, such as the argument that the Sanusiyya was *the* leadership element that remained after the first destructive decade of Italian colonialism between 1919 and 1929, or the assertion that Great Britain turned its back on the urban notables and instead chose to support Idris and the bedouins after World War II because of British strategic interests.

The concept of state building and state formation, which is finding a wider following in the study of late nineteenth-century Ottoman provinces, is a useful vehicle of analysis, as Lisa Anderson has clearly demonstrated for Libya in her book *The State and Social Transformation in Tunisia and Libya, 1830–1980.*[12] In particular, it helps to identify the priorities which informed Ottoman provincial policies. Nevertheless, the use of such a model may also be misleading. The very idea of state building presupposes that the region or "state-to-be" had relatively defined borders and that its local political leadership shared a common political outlook and agenda with the ruling Ottoman regime. But this was not the case in Libya, especially after the Ottomans tried to introduce rigorous tax reform in the 1880s. More troubling in Anderson's analysis, however, is the underlying assumption that French notions of colonialism as applied in Tunisia are in some fashion comparable to Ottoman notions of empire—a difficult leap of faith for those versed in the Ottoman notions of empire, government, and society.

Although in the most general terms, the priorities and objectives of the government were similar in Tripolitania and Cyrenaica, the methods and policies employed in dealing with the urban notables of Tripolitania were very different from those used in the largely rural-village society of Cyrenaica's al-Jabal al-Akhdar. This difference is underlined by the fact that the governors-general of Tripolitania were all civil governors until the onset of the Italian threat, whereas in Cyrenaica they were all military governors who bore the rank of divisional commander (*ferik*).

A partial answer to (and a further complication of) the historiographical and methodological issues outlined above lies in the Libyan National Archives housed in Tripoli. In al-Saray al-Hamra', once the headquarters of the Ottoman bureaucracy, is a vast collection of uncatalogued and unindexed Ottoman archival materials which cover the period from the late eighteenth century to the end of World War I. Included are tax records, court transcripts, municipal records, intraprovincial correspondence, and official correspondence between Tripoli and Istanbul. Although much of the material is in Arabic, all official documents, including communications with the imperial capital, are in Turkish. Yet most of the material has gone untouched for lack of competent cataloguers and a dearth of researchers capable of tackling its voluminous mass. To date, no monograph on Ottoman Libya has systematically mined these rich sources, and Libyan archival materials are used primarily to season works built largely around secondary sources.

Political problems also attend the use of these archives. The Libyan government remains reluctant to open the sources of its national past to the unrestricted scrutiny of Libyan or foreign researchers. There are several reasons for this. First, government officials remain highly sensitive about Libya's role in the trans-Saharan slave trade of the nineteenth century, and the regime of Colonel Qadhdhafi is clearly very conscious of its image as an African nation and power. Second, the regime and some Libyan researchers that serve its purposes are clearly ambivalent about the Sanusi family. On the one hand, the dictates of the national historical construct require that the Sanusis be idealized as the founders of the state and the first line of resistance to foreign aggression. At the same time, the Sanusi family is ultimately held responsible for betraying the national interest by courting the United States and American petroleum concerns.

The problem of access to archives is not singular to Libya. Yet the political tensions inherent in the building of a national history are of relatively recent origin there and are thus more pronounced in Libya's case than in those of its neighbors. Until the political custodians of Libya's past yield the right of way to professional historians, these rich archives will go little used.

## THE YEARS OF ITALIAN COLONIALISM
## AND THE IDRISI MONARCHY

The study of Italian colonial rule in Libya has, to a large degree and for obvious reasons, been dominated by Italian historians. Their primary concern has been the origins of Italian colonialism and its relationship to the fascist fiasco which beset Italy in the 1930s and early 1940s. Specifically, their works have tended to focus on two issues. The first of these is the political debate that racked Italy in the decade between the first Franco-Italian accord on the Mediterranean (1900) and the invasion of Libya in 1911. The second issue that has provoked authors' attention is the war itself: its military aspects, the diplomatic denouement, and its function as a prelude to World War I.[13] In this category, the work of Francesco Malgieri stands out as perhaps the best, although it can be supplemented by several works in English.[14]

Two studies offer a full survey of the Italian period in Libya: Claudio Segrè, *The Fourth Shore* and Angelo Del Boca, *Gli Italiani in Libia.*[15] Segrè provides a full survey of Italian colonial and settler policy and suggests some of the effects of the policies, not only on Italy, but also on Libya. Del Boca, on the other hand, offers a more detailed account of Italy's diplomatic and military struggles to secure, then subdue, Libya.

On the basis of Segrè's work and Anderson's monograph mentioned above, the most fruitful avenue for future research may well be a comparative analysis of French settler colonialism in Algeria with that of Italian settler colonialism in Libya. Still, few historians, Italian or other, have addressed questions that interest those who view Libya as a post-Ottoman, prenationalist Arab state in the making. Scattered articles and monographs provide anecdotal histories of ʿUmar al-Mukhtar,[16] but as yet no book provides a full account of the Italian period as a formative experience in the political development of Libya and its leadership.

In sum, the historiography of the Italian colonial period remains most unsatisfying and lacking in any detailed analysis of indigenous groups. Even in Anderson's thoughtful comparative study of Tunisia and Libya, the politics of the 1920s and 1930s receive only brief coverage. Moreover, the significant differences between Italian policy in Tripolitania and Cyrenaica are too frequently passed over as the Sanusis loom ever larger in the background and the notables of Tripolitania hardly figure at all. The latter emerge again only in the 1950s, when they fill a host of cabinet positions in the newly created government of King Idris. As for today, these family names occasionally appear in western newspaper articles detailing the exiled opposition to Qadhdhafi. But we still know precious little about them as a cohesive political group.

The historiographic lacunae for the 1920s and 1930s can best be addressed by the writing of several biographies, perhaps of Idris and ʿUmar al-Mukhtar, as well as compiling a prosopographical study of the activities of the leading families of Tripoli and Benghazi. The Italian archives would be the easiest source to mine for this purpose; indeed, these contain several files which provide an outline of the prominent political families of Tripolitania and Cyrenaica.[17] At present, the only biographical dictionary for all of

Libyan history is al-Tahir Ahmad al-Zawi's *Notable Men of Libya;*[18] it is, however, far from complete, and its failure to provide any sense of the political and economic standing of various notable families of the late nineteenth and early twentieth century weakens it further. Moreover, it tends to emphasize the lives of war heroes, poets, and sheikhs from Tripolitania while saying little about the prominent families and tribes of Cyrenaica. It can be supplemented by a careful reading of the notes and text of Enrico de Agostini's neglected but outstanding work on the populations of Tripolitania and Cyrenaica published soon after the Italian occupation.[19] Finally, some gaps can be filled by the unpublished doctoral dissertation of Salaheddin Hassan Salem, "The Genesis of Political Leadership in Libya, 1952–1969."[20] A prosopographical study of leading Libyan families in the 1920s and 1930s would serve another purpose as well. It would provide a better sense of the political and ideological setting against which the United Nations fashioned the kingdom of Libya after World War II. The tensions surrounding the choice of King Idris by the British and the relations between his supporters in Cyrenaica and the leading politicians of Tripolitania and their exiled compatriots both need further exploration.

Some of the problems encountered by Idris in forging his new rentier regime cannot have been unlike those attending King Faysal's creation of a government in Syria or Iraq after World War I. As with Faysal, the British chose Idris in part because of their belief that his bedouin followers would be above the political fray and would remain loyal to Great Britain. But like Faysal in Syria and in Iraq, Idris found that the notables of Benghazi and Tripoli were suspicious and were constantly undermining his authority in the regions that they controlled and among the tribes and villagers that formed their retinue. Libya, like Syria and Iraq, was subject to divisive regional and tribal loyalties. Although it was spared many of the religious and ethnic tensions of the other two states, the significance of these problems, while generally overlooked, is just as important as the more obvious economic and educational issues that faced Idris in 1951, or the later challenges associated with the exploitation of oil and the evolution of a monarchy-rentier regime.

In sum, the economic and social problems of Tripolitania, Cyrenaica, and Fezzan during the reign of Idris are known only in the broadest terms. Apart from the information provided by Salem, one is left with the image of Idris as a well-meaning king who was manipulated by U.S. economic and political interests. His demise is explained largely in terms of external political influences, notably the policies and example provided by Nasser, whereas the internal dynamics of Libyan political families and the emergence of a Libyan army go largely unnoticed.

## QADHDHAFI AND THE NATIONAL STATE

Comprehending the complex process through which full-fledged Libyan nationalism and an integrated state would arise in the 1970s requires, then, more work on the rule of Idris. The only studies available are a handful of works written in the 1960s on economic development and constitutionalism. These works, informed by what are now dated and severely criticized notions of economic and political development, provide only a hint of the expectations attending Libya's independence and the later exploitation of its oil.[21]

On the other hand, anthropological field work conducted in the 1950s and 1960s has produced a number of valuable studies on tribal life. A noteworthy piece is that of Emrys L. Peters, a student of Evans-Pritchard's, which was published only recently.[22] These works not only flesh out the structures of bedouin society, particularly in Cyrenaica, on the eve of their demise, but also help us to understand the effect of a centralizing state on tribal habits, living conditions, and occupations.

Qadhdhafi and his regime have, of course, sparked the largest literature on Libya. Part of the early attraction of Qadhdhafi was his youthful appearance, his self-proclaimed accession to the mantle of Nasser, and his commitment to a strong—but idiosyncratic—view of Islam and the state.

After several books on the early years of Qadhdhafi's regime, notably that of South African journalist Ruth First, the literature published in the 1970s and 1980s tended to focus on a common set of issues.[23] The first concern has been the effect of oil wealth, especially after 1973, on state-sponsored development plans and on state-induced popular political participation. The second issue has been the efforts of the new regime to do away with the old structures of Idris's rentier state—the breaking of lingering tribal loyalties and parallel administrative structures, the dismantling of the privileges of the political notables, and the dismissal of Italian and American advisors.[24]

The replacement of the old guard with young (now middle-aged) officials and graduates of Libyan, Arab, and European universities, many with technical backgrounds, helped to forge a new bureaucracy and newly centralized state that has overcome—soccer games notwithstanding—a good measure of the regionalism and parochialism which were the pillars of Idris's political balancing act.

Islam and Qadhdhafi's own ideology, sometimes referred to in Arabic as "Green Thought," have received some scholarly attention, although not as thorough an examination as one might have expected. As far as Islam is concerned, the articles by Ann Elizabeth Mayer on Qadhdhafi's interpretation and application of several aspects of Islamic law stand out as singular contributions for their clarity, the substance of their research, and their ability to rise above the view of Qadhdhafi, perpetuated by both his Arab and western detractors, as simply the "odd bird" of Arab politics.[25] More importantly, these articles avoid the sensationalist tendencies which characterize the popular scholarship on Qadhdhafi and his regime.[26]

Libya's foreign policy has, in the past decade, spurred a greater flow of ink than any other subject associated with Libya. Nevertheless, there is not yet a single work which has captured all the complexities that shape Libya's foreign policy identity vis-à-vis sub-Saharan Africa, the Maghrib, and the Mashriq.[27] The impetus for much of Qadhdhafi's foreign policy comes from a still-underappreciated sentiment that the Libyan regime and, increasingly, the population at large have come to feel: the sense of suffering unheralded martyrdom at the hands of brutal Italian colonialism, serving as a battleground for World War II, and falling victim to unscrupulous British and American political and economic exploitation. Although the sentiment of national victimization is certainly not novel, it has been powerfully implanted in the national psyche by Qadhdhafi's propaganda organs and sometimes appears in subtler forms in history books published in Libya or written by Libyan scholars. An obvious example of such a publication is *The White Book* which appeared in the early 1980s.[28]

## CONCLUSION

The historiography of Libya is still young and relatively underdeveloped compared to the other states of the Maghrib. There are several reasons for this. One has to do with the geographic situation of Libya. Libya is, in many regards, a gateway to North Africa and a route to sub-Saharan Africa. For this reason, many historians of North Africa find it a peripheral state and not as worthy of study as Tunisia, Algeria, and Morocco, all of which have a common and lengthy experience with French colonialism, as against Libya's thirty-year period of Italian rule. Finally, Libya is unique in that in the nineteenth century and early twentieth century it underwent a sustained period of renewed Ottoman rule. The significance of this episode is still being weighed by historians of Libya. Did it radically alter the course of modern Libyan history compared to that of its Maghribi neighbors? Or was it merely an intermezzo of little import? Answers to that question are still pending and will help to forge the agenda of future historians of Libya.

## Notes

1. John Wright's work exemplifies good popular history. See his *Libya* (New York: Praeger, 1969) and *Libya, Chad, and the Central Sahara* (Totowa, N.J.: Barnes & Noble Books, 1989). Ettore Rossi's general work on Libyan history to 1911, *Storia di Tripoli e della Tripolitania dalla conquista araba al 1911*, Maria Nallino, ed. (Rome: Instituto per l'Oriente, 1968), was published posthumously. Its title notwithstanding, the book does include sections on Cyrenaica. For brief general accounts, see also the relevant portions of chapters 6 and 7 in Jamil M. Abun-Nasr, *A History of the Maghrib in the Islamic Period* (Cambridge: Cambridge University Press, 1987). Ali Abdullatif, *The Making of Modern Libya: State Formation, Colonization, and Resistance, 1830–1932* (Albany: State University of New York Press, 1994) must be consulted with extreme caution. In addition to numerous factual errors, the book seriously distorts the past in the service of a nationalist historical agenda which is grounded in the idea that indigenous groups are necessarily the most significant factor in shaping Libya's history. A rather blunt instrument of analysis, this concept neglects the role of the Ottoman government, downplays the contribution of the Tripolitanian notables, and needlessly argues for the existence of a Sanusi state in the nineteenth century.

2. A dated, but still useful, general account of the Ottoman period in North Africa is Aziz Samih Ilter's *Shimali Afrikada Türkler* (Istanbul: Vakit Gazete-matbaa kütuphane, 1934). For the formative sixteenth century of Ottoman rule in North Africa, see Andrew Hess, *The Forgotten Frontier* (Chicago: University of Chicago Press, 1978).

3. For the significance and context of this treaty, see Abdurrahman Çayci, *La question tunisienne et la politique ottomane (1881–1913)* (Erzurum: Edebiyat Fakültesi matbaasi, 1963), pp. 1–16; and Robert Mantran, "Le statut de l'Algérie, de la Tunisie et de la Tripolitaine dans l'empire ottoman," in *Atti del I Congresso internazionale di studi nord-africani* (Cagliari: Facoltà di scienze politiche, 1965), pp. 3–14.

4. E. E. Evans-Pritchard, *The Sanusi of Cyrenaica* (Oxford: Clarendon Press, 1949). For an analysis and critique of some of Evans-Pritchard's research methodology and writing techniques, see Clifford Geertz, *Works and Lives: The Anthropologist as Author* (Stanford: Stanford University Press, 1988), especially chapter 3, "Slide Show: Evans-Pritchard's African Transparencies."

5. For a criticism of this interpretation, see Michel Le Gall, "The Ottoman Government and the Sanusiyya: A Reappraisal," in *International Journal of Middle East Studies* XXI, no. 1 (1989), pp. 91–106.

6. Ahmad Sidqi al-Dajani, *Libya qubayl al-ihtilal al-Itali* (Tripoli: al-Matbaʿa al-fanniyya al-haditha, 1971); and *al-Haraka al-Sanusiyya* (Beirut: Dar al-Lubnan, 1968).

7. Henri Duveyrier and the vast but underestimated influence of his work merit a special study. An explorer and member of the Paris Société de Géographi, Duveyrier was one of several French writers who influenced the outlook of France towards the Muslim sufi orders in North Africa. His most famous piece is *La confrérie musulmane de Sidi Mohammed Ben 'Ali Es-Senousi et son domaine géographique* (Paris: Société de Géographie, 1886). A sympathetic biography of Duveyrier was written some time ago by René Pottier, *Un prince saharien méconnu, Henri Duveyrier* (Paris: Plon, 1938).

8. Abdulmola S. al-Horeir, "Social and Economic Transformations in the Libyan Hinterland during the Second Half of the Nineteenth Century: the Role of Sayyid Ahmad al-Sharif al-Sanusi," (unpublished Ph.D. diss., University of California, Los Angeles, 1981).

9. Rachel Simon, *Libya Between Ottomanism and Nationalism: The Ottoman Involvement in Libya during the War with Italy* (Berlin: Klaus Schwartz, 1987). See also Aghil Mohamed Barbar, "The Tarabulus (Libyan) Resistance to the Italian Invasion" (unpublished Ph.D. diss., University of Wisconsin, 1980).

10. Lisa Anderson, "The Tripoli Republic," in *Social and Economic Development of Libya*, E. G. H. Joffé and K. S. McLachlan, eds. (London: Menas Press, 1982), pp. 43–65.

11. Orhan Kologlu, *Mustafa Kemal'in yaninda iki Libya'li Lider* (Ankara: n.p., 1981).

12. Lisa Anderson, *The State and Social Transformation in Tunisia and Libya, 1830–1980* (Princeton: Princeton University Press, 1986).

13. On this subject, see the bibliographical article of Salvatore Bono, "Dalla Guerra italo-turca alla Guerra italo-libica (1911–1912)" in *Italia-Turchia: Due punti di vista a confronto* (Pavia: Giuffrè Editore, 1992).

14. Francesco Malgieri, *La Guerra libica (1911–1912)* (Rome: Edizioni di Storia e Letteratura, 1970).

15. Claudio Segrè, *Fourth Shore: The Italian Colonization of Libya* (Chicago: University of Chicago Press, 1974); Angelo Del Boca, *Gli Italiani in Libia* (2 vols.; Rome: Editori Laterza, 1988). The first volume covers the years 1860 to 1922; the second from the onset of the fascist period to Qadhdhafi.

16. The best of these are: Rif'at 'Abd al-'Aziz Sayyid Ahmad, *'Umar al-Mukhtar min khilal al-watha'iq al-italiyya* (Cairo: 'Ain Shams University, 1987), an account, as its title suggests, based on a thorough review of Italian sources; and Enzo Santarelli et al., *Omar al-Mukhtar e la riconquista fascista della Libia* (Milan: Marzorati Editore, 1981), a biography which includes an analysis of the trial of 'Umar al-Mukhtar and Italian press coverage thereof.

17. For an overview of Italian archives relative to Libya, see Carlo Giglio, *Inventario delle fonti manoscritte relative alla storia dell'Africa del*

*Nord esisenti in Italia* (Leiden: Brill, 1971). Of special interest to the history of notables in the early period of Italian rule is the series in the Archivio Storico del Ministero dell'Africa Italiana (ASMAI), fasc. 148/1–1 to 148/1–5.

18. Al-Tahir Ahmad al-Zawi, *A'lam Libiyya* (Tripoli: Mu'assassat al-Farjani, 1971).

19. Enrico de Agostini, *Le popolazioni della Tripolitania* (Tripoli: Tipografia Pirotta e Bresciano, 1917); and *Le popolazioni della Cirenaica* (Benghazi: Azienda Tipo-litografica, 1922–23).

20. Salaheddin Hasan Salem, "The Genesis of Political Leadership in Libya, 1952–1969" (unpublished Ph.D. diss., George Washington University, 1973).

21. Examples of this type of literature include Majid Khadduri, *Modern Libya: A Study in Political Development* (Baltimore: Johns Hopkins University Press, 1963); and Ismail Khalidi, *Constitutional Development in Libya* (Beirut: Khayat, 1956).

22. Emrys L. Peters, *The Bedouin of Cyrenaica, Studies in Personal and Corporate Power* (Cambridge: Cambridge University Press, 1990). See also Roy H. Behnke, Jr., *The Herders of Cyrenaica: Ecology and Kinship Among the Bedouins of Eastern Libya* (Urbana: University of Illinois Press, 1980).

23. Ruth First, *Libya: The Elusive Revolution* (New York: Africana Publishing Company, 1975).

24. For a full bibliography of some of the early literature on this topic, see John Videgar, *The Economic, Social and Political Development of Algeria and Libya* (Monticello, Ill.: Vance Bibliographies, 1978). Among this body of literature, we can include the following works which represent some of the better studies: John A. Allan, *Libya: The Experience of Oil* (Boulder, Colo.: Westview Press, 1981); Mukhtar M. Buru, Shukri M. Ghanem, and Keith S. McLachlan, eds., *Planning and Development in Modern Libya* (Boulder, Colo.: Lynne Rienner Publishers, 1985); Lillian Craig Harris, *Libya: Qadhafi's Revolution and the Modern State* (Boulder, Colo.: Westview Press, 1986); G. Albergoni, ed., *La Libye nouvelle: rupture et continuité* (Paris: CNRS, 1975).

25. See, for example, Ann Elizabeth Mayer, "Islamic Resurgence or New Prophethood: The Role of Islam in Qadhdhafi's Ideology," in *Islamic Resurgence in the Arab World,* Ali Hillal Dessouki, ed. (New York: Praeger, 1980), 196–220; and "Islamicizing Laws Affecting the Regulation of Interest Charges and Risk Contracts: Some Problems of Recent Libyan Legislation," in *International Comparative Law Quarterly* XXVIII, no. 4 (1979), pp. 541–59. In the 1970s, when Qadhdhafi proposed a union with Egypt, President Sadat rejected both the idea and Qadhdhafi's brand of revivalist Pan-Arabism, referring to Qadhdhafi and his regime, in a play on the name of the pre-Islamic character Majnun Layla, as Majnun Libya.

26. See for example, Martin Sicker, *The Making of a Pariah State: The Adventurist Policies of Muammar Qaddafi* (New York: Praeger, 1987); and Brian L. Davis, *Qaddafi, Terrorism, and the Origins of the U.S. Attack on Libya* (New York: Praeger, 1990).

27. There are, however, several helpful studies which review the major facts and themes of Libyan foreign policy. See, for example, Mary Jane Deeb, *Libya's Foreign Policy in North Africa* (Boulder, Colo.: Westview Press, 1991); René Otayek, *La politique africaine de la Libye* (Paris: Karthala, 1986); and René Lemarchand, ed., *The Green and the Black: Qadhafi's Policies in Africa* (Bloomington: Indiana University Press, 1988). The recent book edited by Dirk Vandewalle, *Qadhafi's Libya, 1969–1994* (New York: St. Martin's Press, 1995) adds important background to the relationship between foreign and domestic policy in Libya. The many first-rate contributions in this volume provide a framework for future avenues of study and the necessary factual groundwork for understanding the internal dynamics of Libyan politics.

28. See *The White Book: Some Examples of the Damages Caused by the Belligerents of World War II to the People of the Socialist People's Libyan Arab Jamahiriyya* (Tripoli: Libyan Studies Center, 1981).

# Moroccan Historiography
## since Independence

*Mohamed El Mansour*
Université Mohammed V

Within Moroccan historiography, it is possible to distinguish three schools. The first emerged with the Islamization of the country and is generally referred to as the "traditional school." The second dates from the nineteenth century and continues throughout the protectorate period, embracing historical literature that may be designated "colonial." Finally, a third school, which can be termed the "new historical school," developed after independence in 1956. It should be pointed out that, in reality, there has never been a clear-cut chronological distinction among the three schools. Thus, traditional historians continued to produce histories in the traditional pattern throughout the nineteenth and twentieth centuries. On the other hand, it would be unjust to consider everything written by the French before 1956 as colonial. In fact, the seeds of the postindependence "new history" began to germinate well before that date.

## TRADITIONAL HISTORIOGRAPHY

The way Maghribi historians recorded their history did not differ from the general pattern of Islamic historiography elsewhere in the Muslim world. This type of history consisted of chronologies rather than analytical history as it is conceived of today. In other words, the emphasis was on events, with little effort to make assessments or go beyond the chronological succession of events. These *hawliyyat* (chronicles) also concentrated on political and military history, with the ruling dynasty usually at the center of the historian's preoccupations. Historians, or rather *ikhbariyyun* (chroniclers), merely traced the rise of a dynasty to power and described its various military exploits against internal or external enemies until it gave way to another ruling family.

The authors of such chronicles were not professional historians. The "métier d'historien" as such did not exist, since history was never taught as a discipline. Instead, individuals became interested in the history of *akhbar* (events) if they happened to have a strong inclination to *adab* (literature) or to genealogy. In fact, most chronicles were the work of *kuttab* (secretaries) commissioned by sultans to record their glories. As a result, such works were generally biased and strongly apologetic, tending to reflect the views of the ruling elites and rarely questioning their policies or presenting a nonofficial version of events. Historians such as al-Fishtali (d.1621), al-Zayani (d.1833), Akansus (d. 1877) or Ibn al-Hajj (d. 1897) all served as Makhzan secretaries before writing their histories. In some cases, they wrote while still in office. Thus, it was only natural that they concentrated on political history, reserving little room for the economic and social conditions that affected the *ra'iyya* (ordinary people). In their works, references to famines, epidemics, or economic fluctuations are cursory and leave the reader with the impression that a plague epidemic has been mentioned only because some important person died in it. This is why economic and social historians are usually disappointed by such chronicles and must turn to other sources for their information.

## COLONIAL HISTORIOGRAPHY

When the French became involved in Morocco during the latter part of the nineteenth century, history was not their major concern. In fact, compared to ethnographic and linguistic investigations, historical writings were few and far between. During the colonial (or protectorate) period, history was the last discipline on the official list of priorities, but this did not prevent the accumulation of a vast corpus of historical literature.

Historical production before and after 1912 may be termed *colonial* by virtue both of its philosophy and its aims. As interpreted by historians such as Emile Félix Gautier or Henri Terrasse, Moroccan and Maghribi history were subjected to European standards. The North African past was freed from the cyclical conception of history developed by Ibn Khaldun in favor of the concept of linear progress. North African history was no longer perceived as "un cercle vicieux," but was, rather, heading toward "progress," which meant the progress of western civilization. Periodization was likewise subjected to the European yardstick. While for traditional Moroccan historians there were basically only two major eras, the pre-Islamic and the Islamic—one of *jahiliyya* (darkness), the other of salvation—European periodization was based on a different order. Following the glorious days of Rome, a long night of Arab and Islamic domination started in the seventh century and continued until the nineteenth, when the French intervened to free North Africa from its long nightmare and allow it once again to resume the greatness of its Roman past. Both Gautier and Terrasse blamed Islam for not having offered North African peoples the means of achieving moral or political unity.[1] Under Islam, Morocco had never been able to constitute a state worthy of the name. It was no more than "an unstable agglomeration of tribes" subject to a despotic government. These same historians also blamed the "Arab invasion" for introducing instability and undermining the bases of sedentary life.[2]

Such a conception of history clearly reflected a specific ideological orientation. Its purpose was to justify French colonial designs in the region, ultimately aiming at integrating the country into western civilization and giving it the means to achieve the coherence and the unity Islam had been unable to provide. This was made clear by French officials who, by creating "academic" institutions such as the Institut des Hautes Etudes Marocaines, wanted above all to better know *"l'âme marocaine"* (the Moroccan soul) as a first step toward the installation of a western order in place of the sterile Islamic one.

French interest in Moroccan history started in the latter part of the nineteenth century with the editing and translation of some basic chronicles. *Nuzhat al-Hadi* by al-Ifrani (d. 1738) and *al-Turjuman* by Abu al-Qasim al-Zayani were published in Paris during the 1880s.[3] Later, with the establishment of the Mission scientifique du Maroc, important chronicles were translated, in whole or in part, and published in *Archives marocaines. Nashr al-Mathani* by Muhammad ibn al-Tayyib al-Qadiri (d. 1773) and the history of the Alawites in *Kitab al-Istiqsa* by al-Nasiri (d. 1897) both appeared in that journal and provided the raw material for most subsequent historians dealing with the modern period.

However, French historians did not content themselves with the works of Moroccan chroniclers but used other sources as well. Among these were oral traditions collected by ethnographers, archeology, European archives, and travel accounts. In and of itself, this attempt to diversify the historical sources constituted a positive development in Moroccan historiography. Another important contribution of the colonial school was its use of modern methods of historical writing. French historians attempted to make sense of the mass of information contained in the Moroccan traditional histories, although one may ultimately disagree with their interpretations and conclusions. Seen from a purely methodological perspective, the new analytical approach brought about a revolution in the art of historical writing in Morocco.

Another major change accompanying colonial historiography was the extension of the frontiers of history to new horizons. As historians became concerned with the evolution of social and religious institutions, history no longer centered almost exclusively on political events. Ideological and political considerations, for example, sparked the interest shown in the study of tribal and urban institutions. During the early part of the protectorate period, coinciding with the phase of "pacification," much attention was devoted to the study of such tribal forms of organization as the *jama'a* (tribal council) and customary law. Religious brotherhoods and *zawayya* (plural of *zawiyya*, a building used for religious rituals, usually by sufis, or mystics) were also the subjects of much colonial literature. But this interest in the history of institutions resulted not only from ideological motivations; the impact of Emile Durkheim on the French sociological tradition and on ethnography certainly also figured in the process.

However, to label French historical production for the preindependence period as "colonial" does not mean that everything written during that period was "colonial." There is no way, for instance, to overestimate the value of the huge collection of Henry de Castries's *Les Sources inédites de l'histoire du Maroc,* the periodicals *Archives marocaines* and *Hespéris,* or the works of scholars such as Lévi-Provençal or Louis Massignon. Charles-André Julien and Jacques Berque were also able to rise above the official political climate of their time and make valuable contributions to the knowledge of the Moroccan past. Other works, while bearing a clear ideological imprint, nevertheless represent important contributions, particularly in the fields of ancient history and the history of art, neither of which ever figured seriously in the concerns of traditional Moroccan historians.

## POSTINDEPENDENCE HISTORIOGRAPHY

In 1956, there were very few historians who could assume the task of rewriting national history. Unlike Algeria, Morocco did not have a modern university during the colonial period and the number of Moroccans who had had the opportunity to study in French universities was insignificant. When the first modern Moroccan university was created in 1957, many of those who were entrusted with the teaching of history came from other disciplines, such as languages or literature. Apart from a few young French historians, most of the people teaching history at the Rabat university were not professional historians. In fact, the maturation of the first generation of Moroccan historians did not occur until the mid-1970s.

As in most newly independent nations, the political climate in post-1956 Morocco did not favor the writing of academic and objective history. Political elites had their own conception of the past that made them skeptical of any critical interpretation of history that did not take into consideration their immediate political objectives. For the monarchy, the history that was needed was one which could be used to enhance its political legitimacy. As for the nationalist parties, their pressing task was the consolidation of national unity and the achievement of territorial integrity. Indeed, history was very much present in the political discourse of a party such as the Istiqlal, but its aim was to prove that independent Morocco as it stood in 1956 represented only one-fifth of the real historical Morocco. Clearly, this conception of the past did not appeal much to young students of history, especially during the 1960s, when the university became strongly identified with socialist currents of thought. From an official point of view, history and other social sciences were looked upon with suspicion most of the time, since they could be used as a means of undermining the legitimacy of the political order.

In history, as in many other fields, Morocco's transition from the colonial to the postcolonial phase was smooth compared, for instance, with what happened in neighboring Algeria. The fact that the Moroccan university continued to rely on a number of French historians who were under the influence of the *Annales* school proved extremely beneficial. Historians such as Jean-Louis Miège,[4] Jean Brignon, and Bernard Rosenberger filled a gap in Moroccan historiography and contributed to orienting historical research in the direction of economic and social history.

It was only in 1967, more than ten years after independence, that the first attempt was made to write a revised synthesis of Moroccan history. This attempt took the form of a general history by a group of French and Moroccan scholars who felt the need to provide students with a textbook to replace the outdated *Histoire du Maroc* by Henri Terrasse.[5] However, the number of Moroccan contributors working on this new book, which adopted the same title as Terrasse's history, was strikingly small: only two out of six. The influence of the *Annales* school was apparent in the introduction to the new text. Its authors called on Moroccan students "to study the slow evolution of civilizations, economic changes, and interactions in the field of ideas and arts rather than political history or the history of the ruling dynasties."[6] The tone was set for future historical research, but the results took some time to manifest themselves.

In fact, for a number of reasons, the appeal for a global history advocated by the authors of *Histoire du Maroc* had little chance of being heard before the mid-1970s. Although that book, and Abdallah Laroui's synthesis,[7] filled a gap in Moroccan historiography and helped give it focus, each constituted, even for the authors, nothing more than "a premature synthesis" and a blueprint for future investigations, not a set of indisputable conclusions. Moreover, the young generation of history students was skeptical of any premature synthesis as long as the basic foundations of historical research were lacking. Paramount among these was the raw material of every historian, the sources. To dismiss colonial historiography meant that historians had to turn to national sources which were either inaccessible or needed critical editing when in manuscript form. The creation of microhistories, in the form of monographs and particularly regional monographs that would allow the scholar to examine history from below, had to precede the globalization of history. Finally, to look at things from a historical perspective, the time was not yet ripe for the transfer of the *Annales* experience. Before that could take place, accounts had first to be settled with colonial historiography. In other words, a "nationalist phase" was necessary for the decolonization of Moroccan history before it would be possible to think of history as conceived by the *Annales* school.

## NATIONALIST HISTORY

The nationalist trend that dominated historical writing during the 1960s was a challenge to colonial historiography. Its aim was to decolonize Moroccan history by freeing it from colonial stereotypes and interpretations. The underlying objective was to assert the national identity which the colonizer had attempted to undermine by every possible means. The result was a historiography based on the refutation of colonial literature and its tenets.

The work of two scholars may be cited as examples. The first is Muhammed Manuni who, in his book *Madhahir yaqadhat al-Maghrib al-hadith,*[8] attempted to prove that Morocco's situation in the nineteenth century was not as desperate as the colonizer claimed. Far from being on the verge of collapse, the country had actually been on the eve of a renaissance in all fields. Administrative and military reforms were being contemplated by enlightened sultans, the printing press had been introduced, and the intellectual elite were becoming increasingly concerned about reforming the society. The second example is Germain Ayache (d. 1990), who took a leading role in refuting colonial historiography. Strangely enough, this most uncompromising "nationalist" historian was not Moroccan, but French. A former militant of the Moroccan communist party, Ayache became a fervent anticolonialist and, after 1956, chose to remain in Morocco where he supervised the work of a whole generation of history students.

In his various articles, which were published in a book under the title *Etudes d'histoire marocaine,*[9] Ayache took upon himself the task of refuting the principal tenets of colonial historiography. His basic premises can be summed up as follows:

1) The Moroccan people constituted a nation in the fullest sense of the word, and not just a loose confederation of tribes as claimed

by colonial historiographers. Nationalist consciousness in Morocco went back as far as the fifteenth century, with the beginning of nationalist resistance against the threatening Iberians.[10]

2) Tribes, even in the most remote places, never questioned the authority of the sultan as the legitimate ruler and imam. Therefore, there is no room for the Makhzan-Siba or Arab-Berber dichotomies, both of which are purely colonial inventions.[11]

3) Contrary to what was claimed by French historians, the Makhzan was not a parasitic institution solely interested in extorting taxes from the people. In fact, Ayache claimed, the Makhzan was an essential element in the overall political and social equilibrium, fulfilling important functions of arbitration between groups and individuals.[12] Equally wrong was the colonial claim that the Makhzan represented Arab domination over the predominantly Berber population.

4) On the eve of colonialism, the Moroccan state was not crumbling, as alleged by European writers. However, if the Makhzan was facing increasing financial problems and if its authority over the population was becoming weaker, that was essentially the consequence of growing military and economic pressures by the Europeans and their disruptive intervention in domestic affairs.[13]

The objective Ayache set for himself dictated the nature of the sources he relied upon. European sources, both in the form of archives and published literature, were discarded. The usefulness of such sources, Ayache argued, was dubious since their authors merely reflected European interests and preoccupations. Furthermore, European authors were never able to comprehend Moroccan reality, either because they were living on the margin of society in the seaports or because they lacked an adequate knowledge of the country's language and customs. For Ayache, there could be no substitute for national documentation and, in particular, state archives, since they spoke for the country as a whole.[14]

Nationalist history may have been necessary at a particular time in order to refute colonial historiography and clear the way for a more objective national history. However, it soon became clear that such history, by limiting itself to the challenge of colonial arguments, would prove a sterile endeavor. The excesses of Ayache became clear even to his students who could not, for instance, do without European archives. More and more scholars realized that such archives are vital to the study of Morocco's external relations, or even to the study of some aspects of domestic history. Moreover, these

European archives were not all European, since they contained thousands of Arabic documents emanating from Moroccan authorities. De Castries's collection is the best example of this. European ethnographic works and travel accounts are equally important for the study of Moroccan society in the contemporary period. Finally, students of history began to question Ayache's sanctification of the official document. Did this not threaten to distort the assessment of past happenings, since such documents reflected nothing but the official point of view?

Leaving the methodological considerations aside, Ayache faltered in another kind of exaggeration. The idea one gets from his argumentation is that European imperialism was solely to blame for Morocco's past misfortunes. The responsibility for Morocco's decadence and ultimate fall seems to be linked exclusively to outside factors. This might simply distract attention from the contemplation of Moroccans' intrinsic shortcomings in meeting the challenge of the West. Manuni, by contrast, does not fail to point out internal factors that contributed to Morocco's failure to carry out the necessary reforms at the time they were most needed.[15]

## THE EMERGENCE OF SOCIAL HISTORY IN THE 1970S

Without rejecting Ayache's view altogether, the young Moroccan historians realized that perhaps the most effective way to refute the arguments of colonial historians was to study the Moroccan past both from within and from below. This meant that historians had to concentrate on microhistory—studying society at its lowest levels—to discover its internal dynamics and, at the same time, test colonial theses related to Makhzan-tribe relations. In this sense, there was no sudden rupture with the nationalist trend. It should also be mentioned that not all historical production during this phase was oriented towards social history. In fact, a substantial effort was, and still is, devoted to the critical study of Arabic texts. At the university level, this effort represents about one-third of the theses submitted by graduate students. Here, again, the nationalist motivation is not totally absent, since behind the academic concern to provide the necessary raw material for an objective history also lies the eagerness to rehabilitate a national heritage that was not fully appreciated by the colonizer.

Several factors fostered the emergence of social history by the middle of the 1970s. Perhaps the major one had to do with the influence of the *Annales* school. This influence came through two main channels. The first was the works of Jacques Berque who as early as the 1930s began the study of social, juridical, and cultural issues. His monograph on High Atlas society in

1955[16] and his cultural biography of al-Yousi in 1958[17] had a deep impact on the orientation of Moroccan historical research. The second channel for the *Annales* influence was through such French historians as Miège, Rosenberger, and others, either because of their teaching at the Moroccan university or through their publications. Among the latter, *Le Maroc et l'Europe* by Miège was of crucial importance.

In 1975, Abdallah Laroui completed his thesis on the social and cultural origins of Moroccan nationalism.[18] One year later, Ahmad Tawfiq defended the first regional monograph at the Faculté des Lettres of the Université Mohammed V in Rabat.[19] Since then, there has been a proliferation of regional monographs dealing with the social and economic structures of a limited space.

A quick assessment of this social history production reveals the following features:

1) Most social history monographs focused on the nineteenth century and, in particular, its latter part. Strangely enough, Moroccan historians were not lured by the most brilliant periods of their past; rather they chose to examine times of decadence and crisis. How does one account for this? Certainly, the relative abundance of historical sources for the nineteenth century was an incentive, but there was more than that. In fact, the choice was dictated by the nationalist trend which made defeating colonial historiography its main objective. Social historians, as mentioned earlier, were partly motivated by the will to defeat colonial theses by seeking their arguments in the study of society itself. Moreover, these historians could not escape the temptation of trying to recollect the pieces of the shattered image of traditional society in an effort to reconstruct the picture of the "Morocco that was."

2) Most of these social histories were in the form of regional monographs taking as subjects of study either a particular tribe or group of tribes, or a city and its immediate hinterland. Some monographs also focused on a particular sufi order or zawiyya.

3) All of these works relied extensively on national sources, both state and private. In fact, one major contribution of the regional monographs has been to uncover a considerable amount of local documentation belonging to families or to zawayya. However, European sources, both archival and printed, were never dismissed, despite the warnings of Germain Ayache, and in some cases they were primordial in the research process. More and more, historians have realized that European sources are essential

for the rewriting of national history, particularly in fields generally ignored by traditional Moroccan historians, such as economic
history or the ancient history of the pre-Islamic period. A historian like Brahim Boutaleb would even advocate the study and
translation of Lyautey's writings, claiming that Marshal Lyautey is
as much a figure of Moroccan history as he is of French history.
The social history school also attempted to widen the scope of
sources so as to include works that were not written by historians
or were never meant to be part of history. Thus, for example, it
makes frequent use of literary or sufi works, as well as legal re-
sponsa (*fatawa*).

4) Moroccan social historians have shown a great interest in interdisciplinarity, particularly between history and subjects such as
sociology, economics, anthropology, and linguistics. This desire
to benefit from other social sciences is manifest in the various attempts to study social structures, or demographic and monetary
crises, as well as in the analysis of traditional discourse. However,
in Morocco, as elsewhere, the ambition of interdisciplinarity has
not always been matched by satisfactory concrete results. Despite
the good intentions on the part of social scientists to benefit from
each other, the impression one has is that, for most scholars, old
habits are not easily overcome.

## CONCLUSION

The structuralist approach that has dominated Moroccan historical research
for the past two decades seems to have reached a point at which its efficacy
should be questioned. The way this approach has been understood and applied by most young historians has been rather rigid and mechanical. Looking at the numerous monographs on social history produced during the
1970s and 1980s, one has the impression that social structures and institutions are treated in a rather formulaic and descriptive manner which often
disregards the vital problematic and theoretical issues that should be addressed. For most scholars, theoretical concerns seem to be irrelevant, or are
even seen as interfering with historical objectivity. This fossilized structuralism can only impoverish historical research. In fact, the regional monographs
that are accumulating tend to repeat themselves as they follow the same
well-trod paths, answer the same questions and, most of the time, reach the
same conclusions. It is perhaps time to abandon the simplistic view that one

should delay the interpretive effort until one has produced enough "objective" monographs. Refusing to interpret might also mean simply accepting the prevailing interpretations. Just as our positivist knowledge grows as the result of more and more microhistories, our ability to provide sound explanations of our past might also gain from the interpretive effort of each, even when engaged in the writing of microhistory.

Perhaps one way to escape the fossilized structuralism referred to above would be to orient research in the direction of cultural history or the history of mentalités. This would ease the growing dissatisfaction with economic history which, in the view of some historians, can never yield the same results in Morocco as in Europe, since the sources will never provide enough data to allow the writing of satisfactory socioeconomic studies. The first steps in this direction have already been taken, since more and more attention is now given to the study of religious mentalités through the analysis of hagiographic literature.[20] Moroccan history also has much to gain from the comparative approach. Moroccan historians are already taking an increasing interest in the history of the Ottoman Empire, sub-Saharan Africa, and even of far more distant places. Once horizons are extended to include other parts of the world, our assessment of our own history and of the development of our institutions will certainly be done in a much more rewarding fashion.

## Notes

1. Henri Terrasse, *Histoire du Maroc des origines à l'établissement du protectorat français* (2 vols.; Casablanca: Editions Atlantides, 1949–1950) II, p. 423.

2. Ibid., p. 445.

3. Mohammed Esseghir Eloufrani, *Nouzhet Elhadi,* Octave Houdas, ed. (Paris: Ernest Leroux, 1888). Al-Zayani's *al-Turjuman* was also published by Houdas two years earlier under the title *Le Maroc de 1631 à 1812* (Paris: Ernest Leroux, 1886).

4. Jean-Louis Miège, *Le Maroc et l'Europe, 1830–1894* (2 vols.; Paris: PUF, 1961–1963).

5. Jean Brignon, Abdelaziz Amine, Brahim Boutaleb, Guy Martinet, Bernard Rosenberger and Michel Terrasse, *Histoire du Maroc* (Paris and Casablanca: Hatier, 1967).

6. Ibid., p. 2.

7. Abdallah Laroui, *L'Histoire du Maghreb, Essai de synthèse* (Paris: Maspero, 1970). The English translation is *The History of the Maghrib* (Princeton: Princeton University Press, 1977).

8. Muhammed Manuni, *Madhahir yaqadhat al-Maghrib al-hadith* (2 vols.; Rabat: Manshurat Kulliyyat al-Adab wa-l-ʿulum al-insaniyya, 1985). For vol. I, this is a second edition, the original having appeared in the early 1960s.

9. Germain Ayache, *Etudes d'histoire marocaine* (Rabat: Société Marocaine des Editeurs Réunis, 1979).

10. Ibid., p. 180.

11. Ibid., pp. 22–23.

12. Ibid., p. 21. See also Ayache's article "La fonction d'arbitrage du Makhzan," ibid., pp. 159–176.

13. Ibid., pp. 137–138.

14. Ibid., p. 64.

15. Manuni, *Madhahir,* I, pp. 385–387.

16. Jacques Berque, *Structures Sociales du Haut Atlas* (Paris: PUF, 1955).

17. Jacques Berque, *Al-Yousi. Problèmes de la culture marocaine au XVIIè siècle* (Paris and The Hague: Mouton, 1958).

18. Abdallah Laroui, *Les Origines sociales et culturelles du nationalisme marocain, 1830–1912* (Paris: Maspero, 1977).

19. Tawfiq's thesis was published under the title *Al-Mujtamaʿ al-maghribi fi-al-qarn al-tasiʿ ʿashar* (Rabat: Faculté des Lettres, Université Mohammed V, 1983).

20. *Histoire et hagiographie* (Rabat: Association Marocaine pour la Recherche Historique, 1989).

# Recent Historiography of the Colonial Period in North Africa: The "Copernican Revolution" and Beyond

*Kenneth Perkins*
University of South Carolina

## INTRODUCTION

Two significant, and interrelated, changes have characterized the historiography of North Africa's colonial period over the past thirty-five years. With the independence of the Maghrib countries, scholars and others from the colonial powers lost the near monopoly they had long enjoyed on the study of the region. A new cadre of researchers, many of them Anglophone and none encumbered by the intellectual and political baggage borne by their French, Italian, and Spanish predecessors merely by virtue of who they were and the times in which they lived, showed less inclination either to act as apologists for the colonial regimes or to criticize them out of a sense of national guilt.[1] In time, a younger generation of scholars from the former colonial powers swelled the relatively thin ranks of these newcomers. But by far the most significant development during these years—and the second agent of the historiographic transformation—has been the dramatically heightened role North African scholars, with their unique perspective, have played in the analysis of their past. The collective efforts of all of these students of Maghribi history have succeeded in engineering a major historiographical reorientation.

In an early reinterpretation of modern Maghribi history, Mohamed Chérif Sahli, *Décoloniser l'histoire. Introduction à l'histoire du Maghreb* (Paris: Maspero, 1965), spoke of the need for a "Copernican Revolution" in historiography that would displace the colonizers from the center of the colonial universe and insert in their stead the colonized people themselves. To write the history of those who had been assumed not to have a history reversed the existing order of things much as did the attainment of political independence. Like the acquisition of independence, it was a sign of maturity and of equality. In the words of Mehdi Ben Barka,

When a nation begins to speak about itself and about its past, it has reached maturity. In recent centuries, it has been the Europeans who have written and expounded about us. . . . Today, we are beginning to speak about the West and to judge its actions. In this way, equality is reestablished.[2]

For those who wished to carry out this historiographical revolution, there was no shortage of advice on how to proceed. Between 1964 and 1976, at least eight articles on the decolonization of North African history appeared. Of these, however, half were published in periodicals not widely read in North Africa or by North African specialists. They were Douglas Johnson, "Algeria: Some Problems of Modern History," in *Journal of African History* V, no. 1 (1964), pp. 221–242; John Wansbrough, "The Decolonisation of North African History," in *Journal of African History* IX, no. 4 (1968), pp. 643–650; Michael Brett, "The Colonial Period in the Maghrib and its Aftermath: The Present State of Historical Writing," in *Journal of African History* XVII, no. 2 (1976), 291–305; and John Wansbrough, "On Recomposing the Islamic History of North Africa," in *Journal of the Royal Asiatic Society*, no. 2 (1969), pp. 161–170. The fact that African historians were then grappling with precisely these sorts of issues, and the relative paucity of periodicals devoted exclusively to the Maghrib, help account for the articles appearing where they did.

The remaining articles, Béchir Tlili, "La recherche historique en Tunisie: bilan et perspectives," in *Cahiers de Tunisie* XX (1972), pp. 125–133; two by Edmund Burke III, both in *Middle East Studies* [London], "Recent Books on Colonial Algerian History," in VII (1971), pp. 241–250, and "Towards a History of the Maghrib," in XI (1975), pp. 306–323; and Abdelkader Zghal and Hachmi Karoui, "Decolonization and Social Science Research: The Case of Tunisia," in *Middle East Studies Association Bulletin* VII (1973), pp. 11–27 were in more likely sources, although the latter article focused on the social sciences in general, not merely on history.

In the years that followed, the research and writing of historians of North Africa, the increase in journals focusing on the region, and the successful efforts to repatriate archival materials all served to advance Sahli's "Copernican Revolution," but the revolution itself commanded surprisingly little attention, at least in print. In January 1979, *Revue d'histoire maghrébine* devoted a double issue (nos. 13–14) to "Méthodologie et sources d'histoire maghrébine." Just under half the articles in western languages addressed issues of the colonial era; none of those in Arabic did. In the same year, the *Annuaire de l'Afrique du Nord* published a superb study of colonial Algerian historiography by Jean-Claude Vatin, "Science historique et conscience historiographique de l'Algérie coloniale. I. 1840–1962," in *Annuaire de l'Afrique du Nord* XVIII (1979), pp. 1103–1122. The postcolonial period was to be covered in a subsequent article which, to date, has not appeared. Of more recent vintage is Mohamed Hédi Chérif, "L'histoire du XXème siècle tunisien: sources et études," in *IBLA* L (1987), pp. 91–114. In that same year, the *Lettre d'information de l'Association française pour l'étude du monde arabe et musulman* published two essays that included discussions of the colonial era: Annie Goldzeiguer, "Historiographie de l'Algérie, 1830–1970," no. 2, pp. 107–115; and Jean-François Clément, "L'Historiographie récente du Maroc," no. 2, pp. 117–132.

With respect to historiography, historians of sub-Saharan Africa may provide not only intellectual stimulation, but also suggestions about fruitful lines of inquiry. Among those scholars, historiographical debate, including the presentation (and challenging) of new methodologies, is both more institutionalized and more lively, occasionally bordering on the vituperative. Although some of the questions addressed are not directly relevant to the Maghrib, others do provide food for thought, especially for historians anxious to understand the nonurban, nonliterate components of society. For almost twenty years, the journal *History in Africa* has focused on

> source criticism and evaluation and the nature of history and historical thought, surveys of the historiography of themes and events, archival and bibliographic reports, review essays of methodological works, and studies of problems which are comparative in focus or approach.[3]

In June 1987, the *African Studies Review* published a special issue with eight articles devoted to "African History Research Trends and Perspectives on the Future." General studies on African historiography are fairly plentiful, in fact,[4] while the library shelves that might house similar studies for the Maghrib (and the Mashriq, for that matter) are distressingly bare.

## IMPLEMENTING THE "COPERNICAN REVOLUTION"

Historiographical debate aside, the themes that have attracted historical investigation in recent decades reveal the success of efforts to reorient the study of Maghrib history. The survey that follows is representative rather than inclusive and cites, whenever possible, works in English.

Foremost among the themes treated over recent decades has been resistance to colonialism, with particular attention devoted to the genesis and development of the nationalist movements that ultimately secured independence. In much the same way that pre-"Copernican" North African history concentrated on those who held power, the focus of this theme has been on what might be termed "mainstream" movements of resistance and nationalism. In the wake of independence, historians sought to elucidate the background and thinking of the leaders whose movements had triumphed and who now controlled the destiny of the new states. Inasmuch as such studies helped to forge national identities and lent legitimacy to as-yet unproven postcolonial political structures, the new governments frequently encouraged them. The opposite side of the coin was that the victors in the anticolonial struggle, because of the intranationalist rivalries that inevitably ensued, had little interest in the formulation of any interpretation of the recent past that differed with their own "official" version ascribing to them a preeminent, if not exclusive, role in national liberation. Their control over access to information, especially in newly created archives whose initial direction often fell to nationalist party loyalists rather than professional historians or record managers, determined, to a considerable extent, what serious researchers could feasibly investigate.

In Lisa Anderson's essay "Legitimacy, Identity, and the Writing of History in Libya," in Eric Davis and Nicolas Gavrielides, eds., *Statecraft in the Middle East: Oil, Historical Memory, and Popular Culture* (Miami: Florida International University Press, 1991), she discusses this issue in the Libyan context.[5] During the monarchy, historical and anthropological studies—most written by westerners—concentrated overwhelmingly on the role of the Sanusi order, which the king headed, in resisting Italian colonialism. By downplaying or entirely overlooking such other critical components of the opposition to the Italians as the leaders of the Tripoli Republic (1918–1922), these writers helped enshrine a national Sanusi myth. In the decade or so after the 1969 revolution, with a cadre of Libyan historians completing their education and beginning to publish, a more comprehensive picture of the resistance, and of Libyan history in general, emerged.

The government-sponsored Center for the Study of the Jihad of the Libyans Against the Italian Occupation played a major role in facilitating this revisionist approach, at least until the mid-1980s, when a number of its practitioners exasperated Qadhdhafi by failing to gear their writings to the promotion of his ideology and policies. Non-Libyan scholars, among them Lisa Anderson, *The State and Social Transformation in Tunisia and Libya, 1830–1930* (Princeton, N.J.: Princeton University Press, 1986); and "The Tripoli Republic, 1918–1922," in *Social and Economic Development of Libya*, E. G. H. Joffé and K. S. McLachlan, eds. (London: Middle East and North African Studies Press, Ltd., 1982), also contributed to this reinterpretive exercise, although the West's often perverse fascination with the Qadhdhafi regime resulted in a far greater corpus of material on contemporary issues (much of it insubstantial) than on the colonial era.

Two studies of the years of Italian rule by Claudio Segrè, *Fourth Shore: The Italian Colonization of Libya* (Chicago: University of Chicago Press, 1974); and *Italo Balbo: A Fascist Life* (Berkeley: University of California Press, 1987) take an Italian perspective, concentrating on administrative policies, especially those related to rural settlement and development. Given the scarcity of material on Libya, such works serve a useful purpose, offering points of departure for the further consideration of Italian rule from the vantage point of Libyans. Other authors, such as John Wright, *Libya, A Modern History* (Baltimore: Johns Hopkins University Press, 1981); Juliette Bessis, *La Libye contemporain* (Paris: Editions L'Harmattan, 1986); and André Martel, *La Libye, 1835–1990: Essai de géopolitique historique* (Paris: PUF, 1991) give the colonial period limited, but generally adequate, treatment.

Tunisia provides the most notable exception to the tendency to neglect secondary elements of the nationalist cause. Mustapha Kraiem has written extensively about aspects of the nationalist movement outside the framework of the Dustur and the Neo-Dustur in the *Revue d'histoire maghrébine*. His studies include "Aux origines du parti communiste tunisien," in no. 2 (1974), pp. 116–137; "Le Parti réformiste tunisien, 1920–1926," in no. 4 (1975), pp. 150–162; and "Le Parti communiste tunisien dans les années trente," in nos. 21–22 (1981), pp. 7–23. Many of the themes first presented in these articles are reprised in the author's *Pouvoir colonial et mouvement national. La Tunisie dans les années trente* (Tunis: Alif, 1990).

In a related vein, the impact of European liberals on the Tunisian political environment has provided the focus for Claude Liauzu, *Aux origines des tiers-mondismes. Colonisés et anti-colonialistes en France, 1919–1939* (Paris: Editions L'Harmattan, 1982); Ali Mahjoubi, "Le Cartel des gauches en France et le mouvement national tunisien," in *Cahiers de Tunisie* XXIV, nos. 95–96 (1976), pp. 187–215; and Béchir Tlili in a series of articles in *Cahiers de Tunisie*, "Socialistes et Jeunes-Tunisiens," in XXII, nos. 85–86 (1974), pp. 47–134; "La Fédération socialiste et la 'Tunisie-Martyre' (1919–1925)," in XXV, nos. 99–100 (1977), pp. 139–215; and "La Fédération radicale-socialiste de Tunisie à la veille de la deuxième guerre mondiale (1937–1938)," in XVIII, nos. 111–112 (1980), pp. 75–203.

Despite this moderately receptive climate, very little has been written, inside or outside Tunisia, on Salah Ben Yusuf, whose tactical approach to acquiring independence and whose policy recommendations for the new state contrasted sharply with the Bourguibist principles that, in the end, carried the day. Since the rift between Bourguiba and the Yusufists in the 1950s (which continued until Ben Yusuf's assassination in 1961) set the tone for Bourguiba's approach to opposition movements throughout his lengthy presidency, the topic deserves study. Even with Ben Yusuf's rehabilitation by President Ben Ali after the removal of Bourguiba—his remains were returned to Tunisia for reburial in 1991—only a single article, in Arabic, has wrestled with this issue.[6]

Algeria's revolutionary explosion drew a disproportionate measure of attention that, in many respects, detracted from the study of earlier periods of nationalist activity, if not from the nineteenth-century resistance that offered clear-cut parallels with the revolution itself. Among the studies on Algerian primary resistance are Raphael Danziger, *Abd al-Qadir and the Algerians* (New York: Africana Press, 1977); Yahya Bouaziz, *La Révolution de 1871. Le Rôle des familles el-Mokrani et el-Haddad* (Algiers: Société Nationale d'Edition et de Diffusion, 1979); Djilali Sari, *L'Insurrection de 1881* (Algiers: Société Nationale d'Edition et de Diffusion, 1981); Peter von Sivers, "The Realm of Justice: Apocalyptic Revolts in Algeria (1849–1879)," in *Humaniora Islamica* I (1973), pp. 47–60; and a series of essays in Edmund Burke III and Ira M. Lapidus, eds., *Islam, Politics, and Social Movements* (Berkeley: University of California Press, 1988) by Peter von Sivers, "Rural Uprisings as Political Movements in Colonial Algeria, 1851–1914," pp. 39–59; Julia Clancy-Smith, "Saints, Mahdis, and Arms: Religion and Resistance in Nineteenth Century North Africa," pp. 60–80; and Fanny Colonna, "The Transformation of a Saintly Lineage in the Northwest Aurès Mountains (Algeria): Nineteenth and Twentieth Centuries," pp. 81–96.

For some time after 1962, however, the more immediate, interwar roots of the Algerian Revolution received the attention of only a few scholars such as Ali Merad, *Le Réformisme musulman en Algérie de 1925 à 1940: Essai d'histoire religieuse et sociale* (The Hague: Mouton, 1967); Aboul-Kassem Saadallah, *La Montée du Nationalisme en Algérie* (Algiers: ENAL, 1983); and Mahfoud Kaddache, the author of two books on the topic, *La Vie politique à Alger de 1919 à 1939* (Algiers: SNED, 1970); and *Histoire du Nationalisme Algérienne: Question Nationale et Politique Algérienne 1919–1951* (Algiers: SNED, 1980). Virtually the only historical treatment of this period in English was Alf Andrew Heggoy, *Insurgency and Counter-Insurgency in Algeria* (Bloomington: Indiana University Press, 1972).

More recent works, including some by Algerian researchers, have offered insights to this still inadequately understood, but crucially important, era. Benjamin Stora has made three important contributions, *Messali Hadj, pionnier du nationalisme algérien. 1898–1974* (Paris: Editions L'Harmattan, 1984); *Dictionnaire biographique des militants nationalistes algériens: ENA, PPA, MTLD, 1926–1954* (Paris: Editions L'Harmattan, 1985); and *Nationalistes algériens et révolutionnaires français au temps du Front populaire* (Paris: Editions L'Harmattan, 1987). Other relevant studies are Ahmed Koulaksiss and Gilbert Meynier, *L'Emir Khaled, premier za'im? Identité algérienne et colonialisme français* (Paris: Editions L'Harmattan, 1987); and an article by Omar Carlier, "Mémoire, mythe et doxa de l'état: L'Etoile nord-africaine et la réligion du 'watan'," in *Vingtième siècle,* no. 30 (1991), pp. 82–91.

Not surprisingly, in view of the recency of the Algerian Revolution and the emotions it engendered, memoirists and popularizers have, to a large extent, elbowed aside serious historians in dealing with the topic. Since 1976, Guy Pervillé has compiled, in the *Annuaire de l'Afrique du Nord,* an annotated bibliography of material on the Algerian War under the heading "Historiographie de la guerre d'Algérie." Among the better studies of the war are Bernard Droz and Evelyne Lever, *Histoire de la guerre d'Algérie. 1954–1962* (Paris: Editions du Seuil, 1982); and the Marxist interpretation offered by Mohammed Harbi, *Le FLN, mirage et réalité: des origines à la prise de pouvoir 1945–1962* (Paris: Editions Jeune Afrique, 1980). Undoubtedly the most popular English-language book (at least in terms of sales) on any modern North African topic is Alastair Horne, *A Savage War of Peace* (New York: Penguin Books, 1987), a journalistic account of the war which, despite its bulk and its overall high quality, could hardly be said to do its topic justice.

As for Morocco, studies on political activity have centered on the Istiqlal and the party's immediate wartime antecedents. Investigations similar to those cited for Tunisia would almost certainly enhance our view of the growth of nationalist sentiment in the country. On the other hand, Morocco provides the setting for two of the very best examinations of primary resistance to colonial impingement: Ross Dunn, *Resistance in the Desert: Moroccan Responses to French Imperialism, 1881–1912* (Madison: University of Wisconsin Press, 1977), on the tribes of the south at the beginning of the protectorate era; and C. Richard Pennell, *A Country with a Government and a Flag: The Rif War in Morocco, 1921–1926* (Wisbech, England: Middle East and North African Studies Press, Ltd., 1986). Parallel to studies mentioned earlier on Tunisia, the involvement of European liberals in the Moroccan nationalist movement is discussed in Georges Oved, *La Gauche française et le nationalisme marocain* (2 vols.; Paris: Editions L'Harmattan, 1984).

In general, the Spanish protectorate in northern Morocco has received far less scholarly attention than its French counterpart. A general overview is provided by Victor Morales Lezcano, *España y el Norte de Africa: el protectorado en Marruecos (1912–1956)* (2d ed.; Madrid: Universidad Nacional de Educación a Distancia, 1986); while two articles in the *Revue d'histoire maghrébine* by Abdelmajid Ben Jalloun, "La Part prise par le mouvement nationaliste marocain de la zone d'influence espagnole dans le processus de libération du Maroc," nos. 43–44 (1986), pp. 5–42, and "Les Développements du mouvement nationaliste marocain dans la zone nord sur le plan international," in nos. 45–46 (1987), pp. 31–74, consider the activities of Moroccan nationalists in the Spanish-controlled parts of the country.

If the "Copernican Revolution" has not been completely achieved in the study of the colonial history of some parts of the Maghrib, it has hardly begun with respect to either the Western Sahara or Mauritania. Political and cultural variations make the study of these regions' colonial history a rather different task than in the rest of the Maghrib. Nevertheless, it is within that context that they most naturally fit and if historians familiar with North Africa do not devote more attention than they have done thus far to these areas, they will remain obscure and poorly comprehended corners of the Maghrib.

Historians of colonial North Africa have devoted considerably less attention to social and economic than to political themes, although this orientation is clearly shifting. Historians and social scientists have begun to address the broad topic of the colonial state's intervention in, and impact on, highly traditional aspects of the colonized society. Among the most useful English-language works in this field are Arnold Green, *The Tunisian Ulama 1873–1915. Social Structure and Response to Ideological Currents* (Leiden: E. J. Brill, 1978); Nancy Gallagher, *Medicine and Power in Tunisia 1780–1900* (Cambridge: Cambridge University Press, 1983); Allan Christelow, *Muslim Law Courts and the French Colonial State in Algeria* (Princeton, N.J.: Princeton University Press, 1985); Michael Brett, "Legislating for Inequality in Algeria: The Senatus-Consulte of 14 July 1865," in *Bulletin of the School of Oriental and African Studies* LI (1988), pp. 440–461; and Dale Eickelman (writing not as a historian but within a historical framework), *Knowledge and Power in Morocco: The Education of a Twentieth Century Notable* (Princeton, N. J.: Princeton University Press, 1985).

Studies on colonization practices and their long-term impact on development constitute a subdivision of this field of inquiry exemplified for Tunisia by Byron Cannon, "Administrative and Economic Regionalism in Tunisian Oleiculture: The Idarat al-Ghabah Experiment, 1870–1914," in *International Journal of African Historical Studies* XI, no. 4 (1978), pp. 585–628; and "The Beylical Habous Council and Suburban Development in Tunis, 1881–1914," in *Maghreb Review* VII, nos. 1–2 (1982), 32–40; for Morocco by Will Swearingen, *Moroccan Mirages: Agrarian Dreams and Deceptions, 1912–1986* (Princeton, N. J.: Princeton University Press, 1987); and for Algeria by Michael J. Heffernan and Keith Sutton, "The Landscape of Colonialism:

The Impact of French Colonial Rule on the Algerian Rural Settlement Pattern, 1830–1987," in *Colonialism and Development in the Contemporary World,* Chris Dixon and Michael J. Heffernan, eds. (London: Mansell, 1991), pp. 121–152.

## FROM THE COPERNICAN REVOLUTION
## TO THE EXPLORATION OF SPACE

In the decades since the North African countries achieved their independence, the examination of topics previously ignored and the revision of thinking about many others that were objects of earlier study, have created a more honest overall picture of the colonial Maghrib. The "Copernican Revolution" rearranged the elements of North African history in a pattern more closely approximating reality. With that task accomplished—or at least having received widespread recognition as a desirable objective—many historians have now turned their attention to the careful and detailed examination of the elements that make up this reordered Maghribi universe. To continue Sahli's astronomical analogy, they, like the Apollo XI astronauts and the satellites that have probed the outer reaches of our galaxy, are exploring the planets and moons first put into proper perspective by Copernicus.

A number of works of this kind point to fruitful directions for future research on the colonial period. André Adam, *Casablanca: Essai sur la transformation de la société marocaine au contact de l'Occident,* (2 vols.; Paris: CNRS, 1968); Kenneth Brown, *People of Salé: Tradition and Change in a Moroccan City, 1830–1930* (Manchester: Manchester University Press, 1976); Janet Abu-Lughod, *Rabat: Urban Apartheid in Morocco* (Princeton, N.J.: Princeton University Press, 1980); Maria Sgroï-Dufresne, *Alger, 1830–1984: Stratégies et enjeux urbains* (Paris: Recherche Civilisations, 1986); and David Prochaska, *Making Algeria French: Colonialism in Bône, 1870–1920* (Cambridge: Cambridge University Press, 1990) have, for example, focused attention on the impact of French colonial rule in five Maghribi cities, while a more narrowly conceived article by O. Sangiovanni, "La Medina di Tripoli: dal piano regolatore del 1912 ai lavori del 1936–1937," in *Islàm: Storia e civiltà* XXX/IX, no. 1 (1990), pp. 48–58, 92–94, examines Italian policy in the major Libyan urban center. There is, however, room for considerably more work in this field and Tunis, Sfax, Constantine, Tlemcen, or Marrakesh might well serve as subjects for comparable studies.

In a variation on this theme, so might urban centers that experienced very specific kinds of transformations in the colonial era—Bizerte, Oran, and Kenitra, all of which became important modern seaports; or Gafsa, which was the center of southern Tunisia's mining industry. Colonial efforts to develop and then integrate Saharan oasis communities such as Laghouat or Ghardaia would provide a strikingly different context for raising similar questions. Tentative steps in this direction include Kenneth Perkins, "The Transformation of Bizerte, 1881–1914: The Razing of a Traditional Tunisian Community and the Raising of a Modern French Naval Base," in *Revue d'histoire maghrébine* XXI, no. 74 (1994), pp. 53–70; and Jean Lethielleux, *Ouargla, cité saharienne: des Origines au début du XXème siècle* (Paris: Geuthner, 1983) although, as its title indicates, the study ends at precisely the time that the process of transformation wrought by French colonialism was gathering steam. A more pertinent study of this sort is Youssef Nacif, *Cultures oasiennes: Bou Saada, essai d'histoire sociale* (Paris: Publisud, 1986). Also in the Sahara, Biskra, with its attraction as a tourist center, offers yet another possibility.

Probes into cities with political structures that detached them from the remainder of the country—Ceuta, Melilla, and Tangiers come most immediately to mind—might provide interesting contrasts to the more typical communities already suggested. Finally, probes into secondary urban centers, which might prove more manageable as case studies, can sometimes produce equally useful and detailed information. One example of what can be done in such a framework is an article by Salwa Khaddur-Zangur, "Nabeul: de la domination coloniale à la libération nationale, 1881–1954," in *Revue d'histoire maghrébine*, nos. 49–50 (1988), pp. 47–70.

Urban studies of the kinds proposed above cut across a wide variety of social history themes, any one of which would make a suitable topic for further development. To identify only one of many areas, much useful work could be done on education practices in the colonial period. Heretofore, the emphasis in studies on education has been on the emergence of a European-educated elite active in the nationalist movement. Closer looks at important foci of traditional education, such as that provided by Mahmoud Abdel Moula, *L'Université zaytounienne et la société tunisienne* (Paris: Maisonneuve et Larose, 1971) would be invaluable.

In the introduction to his book on agrarian development in Morocco, Will Swearingen notes:

> Conventional wisdom on European colonization and national development processes in former colonies is a surprisingly rickety construction of premature conclusions. Far too few actual case studies have been conducted.[7]

Careful investigations of the impact of European settlers and European agriculture in specific parts of such crucial areas as the Majarda Valley in Tunisia, the Mitidja in Algeria, and the hinterland of Casablanca in Morocco, perhaps modeled on Paul Pascon, *Le Haouz de Marrakesh* (2 vols.; Rabat: CURS, 1977), would begin to address this deficiency. In a somewhat related vein, historians have for some time recognized the need for studies of large indigenous landowners, especially in Algeria but also elsewhere,[8] however few have been forthcoming.

Nor have there been any detailed explorations of the Sociétés Indigènes de Prévoyance—organizations that advanced cash and seeds on easy terms to Muslim peasant farmers who stored portions of their grain in SIP silos—or of other rural institutions, although they had a major impact on rural life. A frequently excellent but little utilized source for the study of rural conditions is the periodic reports of officers of the Bureaux Arabes and the contrôleurs civils, and their correspondence with the indigenous leadership. For obvious reasons, care must be exercised in the use of these documents, but studies by Peter von Sivers, "Indigenous Administrators in Algeria, 1846–1914. Manipulation and Manipulators," in *Maghreb Review* VII, nos. 5–6 (1982), pp. 116–121; Kenneth J. Perkins, *Qaids, Captains, and Colons: French Military Administration in the Colonial Maghrib, 1844–1934* (New York: Africana Press, 1980); and Colette Establet, *Etre caïd dans l'Algérie coloniale* (Paris: CNRS, 1991) indicate how effective they can be in formulating a fairly detailed picture of rural conditions.

Despite the fact that extractive industries often played an important part in colonial development plans while, of course, contributing to the formation of a North African proletariat, they have received relatively little attention. Useful guideposts for studying the emergence of such operations and beginning to assess their impact on national development both during and after the colonial period are contained in two articles by Noureddine Dougui, "La naissance d'une grande entreprise coloniale: la Compagnie des phosphates et de chemin de fer de Gafsa," in *Cahiers de Tunisie* XXX, nos. 119–120 (1982), pp. 123–165; and "La construction et l'exploitation du reseau de chemin de fer de Sfax-Gafsa," in *Cahiers de Tunisie* XXXI, nos. 123–124 (1983), pp. 13–46.

Mining and European agriculture both helped to determine the placement of transportation and communication networks across North Africa. A study of those networks, particularly with reference to the influence of transportation and communication technology on the evolution of colonial political activity, as Allan Christelow has done in "Political Ends and Means of Transport in the Colonial North African Pilgrimage," in *Maghreb Review* XII, nos. 3–4 (1987), pp. 84–89, might prove extremely instructive. Although it focuses on the tropical colonies, especially those of Great Britain, and most especially India, and thus does not directly concern North Africa, a superb study by Daniel Headrick on technology transfer in imperial settings, *The Tentacles of Progress. Technology Transfer in the Age of Imperialism, 1850–1940* (New York: Oxford University Press, 1988) offers considerable stimulation on this question.

Because colonial administrative procedures frequently formed the subject matter of pre-"Copernican" historical inquiry, this topic might well be overlooked in the search for new directions. Yet there are aspects of the topic that have not been fully explored, and on which new methodologies might shed new light. Little work has been done, for example, on such quasi-legislative bodies established in the colonial era as the Tunisian Consultative Conference. Studies of the organizations themselves, and of their composition, might provide important information on relationships within an individual colonial unit, while studies taking all three French North African territories into account might reveal patterns that would make broad policies more comprehensible.

A few random topics which fit neatly into none of the previously mentioned themes or, conversely, run through all of them are also worth noting. Although the issue of French "Berber Policy" has been thoroughly flogged, both before and after independence, there appears to be surprisingly little material that focuses primarily on the Berbers and their responses to the colonial process, whether in terms of administration, economic issues, or social issues. An exception is an essay by Edmund Burke III, "Mohand N'Hamoucha: Middle Atlas Berber," in *Struggle and Survival in the Modern Middle East,* Edmund Burke III, ed. (Berkeley: University of California Press, 1993), pp. 100–113.

This volume is especially noteworthy for its use of biographical sketches of ordinary persons to illuminate important issues and trends in the history of the modern Middle East and North Africa. Aside from the cases of a few very prominent individuals, biography has been largely ignored as a viable approach to understanding North Africa's colonial past, while many of the biographies of North African personalities that have been published are journalistic rather than historic. That a greater use of the "life and times" approach to the period would be an important complement to the development of specific topical studies is demonstrated not only by Burke's study on Mohand, but also by contributions in the same volume by Lisa Anderson, "Ramadan al-Suwayhli: Hero of the Libyan Resistance," pp. 114–128; Julia Clancy-Smith, "The Shaykh and His Daughter: Coping in Colonial Algeria," pp. 145–163; Eqbal Ahmad and Stuart Schaar, "M'hamed Ali:

Tunisian Labor Organizer," pp. 191–204; David Seddon, "Muhammad El Merid: The Man Who Became Qaid," pp. 211–223; and Kenneth Brown, "Muhammad Ameur: A Tunisian Comrade," pp. 251–267.

All of the directions heretofore proposed for future research have centered on the European impact on the Maghrib. In something of a continuation of the "Copernican Revolution," however, there is merit in examining the ways in which North Africa and North Africans had an impact on the colonial powers and their citizens. An essay that raises issues germane to this topic is Jean-Louis Miège, "The Colonial Past in the Present," in *Decolonization and After: The British and French Experience,* ed. by W. H. Morris-Jones and Georges Fischer (London: Cass, 1980), pp. 35–49. One area that offers rich investigative possibilities in all three former North African colonial powers is the political arena, where the emergence of metropolitan parties and the formulation of political orientations were sometimes directly influenced by events in the Maghrib. For example, Danièle Joly, *The French Communist Party and the Algerian War* (New York: St. Martin's Press, 1991) gives an account of the problems precipitated within that organization by the fighting in Algeria.

In a rather different context, the North African territories shaped the French, Italian, and Spanish views not only of Africa and the Muslim world but, in a very real sense, of themselves as they related to those worlds. Although the topic is less tangible than most of those suggested in this section (and perhaps more suitable to practitioners of some other discipline), a study of this question might prove revealing. For an earlier historical period, Ann Thomson has attempted such an analysis in *Barbary and Enlightenment: European Attitudes Towards the Maghrib in the Eighteenth Century* (Leiden: E. J. Brill, 1987), although a volume in the "Maghreb contemporain" collection—coproduced by the Centre de Recherches et d'Etudes sur les Sociétés Méditerranéennes (CRESM) and the *Revue de l'Occident musulman et de la Méditerrannée—Le Maghreb dans l'imagination français: la colonie, le désert, l'exil* (Aix-en-Provence: Edisud, 1985), is more pertinent to the period under consideration in this paper.

Finally, it is essential to close by returning to a point raised earlier. The formerly Italian and Spanish territories of North Africa, as well as Mauritania, have been ill served by postindependence historical research and writing. Many of the broad themes noted above could be applied in these areas, while others more specific to them might also be developed. In either case, there is a crying need for greater attention to be paid to these neglected corners of the Maghrib.

## Notes

1. Many of these English-speaking Maghribi specialists extended their scholarly research into their teaching. The introduction of specific courses on North African history into the curriculum of a number of colleges and universities underscored the paucity of general works on the area in English. To meet classroom needs and also to make information available to the broader public, some general studies were translated from French, but original historical overviews and reference works on each of the countries of the Maghrib have also appeared. Although most are not exclusively concerned with the colonial period, these works nevertheless provide considerable material—albeit of variable quality—on the era of European control in the Maghrib. They include four titles in the African Historical Dictionaries Series published by Scarecrow Press (Metuchen, N.J.): Ronald B. St. John, *Historical Dictionary of Libya* (2d ed.; 1991); Kenneth J. Perkins, *Historical Dictionary of Tunisia* (1989); Phillip C. Naylor and Alf Andrew Heggoy, *Historical Dictionary of Algeria* (2d ed.; 1994); and William Spencer, *Historical Dictionary of Morocco* (1980). The Nations of the Contemporary Middle East Series by Westview Press (Boulder, Colo.) includes Lillian C. Harris, *Libya: Qadhafi's Revolution and the Modern State* (1986); Kenneth J. Perkins, *Tunisia: Crossroads of the Islamic and European Worlds* (1986); and John P. Entelis, *Algeria: The Revolution Institutionalized* (1986). A similar study is John Ruedy, *Modern Algeria* (Bloomington: Indiana University Press, 1992).

2. In the preface to Mohamed Lahbabi, *Le Gouvernement marocain à l'aube du XXè siècle* (Rabat: Editions Techniques Nord-Africaines, 1958), p. 3.

3. David Henige, "On Method: An Apologia and a Plea," in *History in Africa* I (1974), p. 1.

4. Among the more recent volumes are Arnold Temu and Bonaventure Swai, *Historians and Africanist History: A Critique* (London: Zed Press, 1981); Bogumil Jewsiewicki and David Newbury, *African Historiographies: What History for Which Africa?* (Beverly Hills: Sage Publications, 1985); and Caroline Neale, *Writing "Independent" History: African Historiography, 1960–1980* (Westport, Conn.: Greenwood Press, 1985).

5. Two other essays in this collection addressing the same general topic, although in the eastern Arab world, not the Maghrib, are Assem Dessouki, "Social and Political Dimensions of the Historiography of the Arab Gulf," pp. 92–115; and Eric Davis and Nicolas Gavrielides, "Statecraft, Historical Memory, and Popular Culture in Iraq and Kuwait," pp. 116–148.

6. Mongi Warda, "Judhur al-harakat al-yusufiyya," in *Revue d'histoire maghrébine*, nos. 71–72 (1993), pp. 479–563.

7. Will Swearingen, *Moroccan Mirages: Agrarian Dreams and Deceptions, 1912–1986* (Princeton, N.J.: Princeton University Press, 1987), p. 3.

8. See, for example, Michael Brett, "The Colonial Period in the Maghrib and its Aftermath: The Present State of Historical Writing," in *Journal of African History* XVII, no. 2 (1976), p. 297.

# Scholars and Politicians:
# An Examination of the Algerian View
# of Algerian Nationalism

*Omar Carlier*

Centre de Recherches Africaines (Université de Paris)

> *How does one perceive history when one has made it—since men*
> *make their own history? How is history written when so*
> *perceived, since men are not always conscious of the history they*
> *make? What is the distance—or the proximity, perhaps even*
> *the fusion—between what the actors, who are sometimes the chroniclers,*
> *say about themselves and what the professional historians, who*
> *may have been actors themselves, have to say about the past,*
> *especially when it is their own past and deals with politics?*
>
> —FRANÇOIS FURET[1]

The above quotation raises a whole set of problems proper to any "perception"—and any "compilation"—of history, whether academic or popular, since history is forever becoming entangled with its own myths and the irreducible dimension of belief.[2] It should be added that "mythical dimension of history" refers not only to the power of a particular "event" or "moment" to irrevocably fashion, in reality and in the mind of the observer, the Before and the After—defined by that instant when destiny appears to hesitate before the fate of a people or a community—but it also expresses the survival of perceptional structures, sometimes of very ancient ones.[3]

The only ground more fertile for the study of the mythical in history than independence movements and revolutions is religion. This is because faith, like revolutions and nationalist movements, sets aside social disparities through the sacred, another fundamental aspect of human existence.[4] Whether religious or political, the sacred assumes a temporal identity— Gregorian, hegirian, or revolutionary—at once inside and outside of history, that conveys a yearning for eternity.

If the most positivist contemporary historiography, or its oldest Marxist counterpart, so often goes through the set piece of "the making of"—as is the case with Edward Palmer Thompson's major opus on the English working class—it is precisely because historiography has, for a long time, patterned itself on the biological model of life. An entity is born, grows, and dies, as in the fall of the Roman Empire or the decline of classical Islam. To this day, this pattern moves us. It operates as a substitute for the sacred, in the shadow cast upon it by monotheism.[5] History is at once genesis, foundation, and message. Be it American or Russian, national history remains the hostage of its "founding myths,"[6] upheld or preceded in its modifications by the machines of dreams: Griffith and his *Birth of a Nation;* Eisenstein and his *October* and the *Battleship Potemkin.* The range of opposing movies extends from David Lean's *Lawrence of Arabia* to Mustapha Akkad's *The Messenger.*

On the one side, "independence"; on the other, "revolution." What characterizes contemporary Algeria is the melding of the one into the other. No nation in the Arab world so compellingly evokes the twin myths of rupture and rebirth. To the rupture of 1954, which led directly to independence, corresponds the rebirth that it made possible. The revolutionary saga of November thus harks back to the historical resurgence that corresponds to the birth of the national movement. How, then, could the very young Algerian historiography escape its own myths—whether of paralysis or exaltation? How could it exempt itself from the recurring doubts and controversies proper to the historical discourse given as "founding discourse"—a dilemma shared alike by the media and by professionals. Who created modern Algerian nationalism and who was the "first" nationalist: Khaled, Messali Hadj, or Ben Badis?[7] The Etoile Nord-Africaine (ENA) or the Association des Ulémas Musulmans Algériens? As for the ENA, who was in fact its founder, Khaled, Messali, or the international communist movement?[8] These questions are not mere matters of technical or archival scholarship; they reflect a militant concern and express a social imperative for the committed intellectual or the history of the state. One can readily recognize in this an ideological representation of things political, a call for legitimation or delegitimation stemming from the fatigue of a genuine hero, while somewhere in the background lurks the structural figure of the scapegoat. Our revolution and our independence, unlike those of the United States or France, are not two centuries old. Consequently, they cannot yet be fully converted into distant historiographical objects. Although they may already strike us as being far in the past, the phantasmal repetition of the confrontation with the other and with the divided self is unceasingly revived by the continuous reshaping of the divide between adversary, friend, and enemy. Of this Carl Schmidt has made the foundation of politics.[9] Still, this repetition cannot forever ignore the constant renewal of existing knowledge. Our young Algerian history must be built between the conflictual myth at the heart of its memory and the positivist approach inherited from the former masters of this discipline. For this to happen, tension *must* be resolved. The notion of "national movement" has thus prevailed for over twenty years as a common ground between the symbolic and the cognitive.

My subject here will be the political history of this movement—and more specifically of that independence-oriented and radical part of it symbolized by the ENA and the Parti du Peuple Algérien (PPA), both of which were founded in Paris, in 1926 and 1937, respectively. It is upon this background of memory and myth, of ideological and scientific "self-determination," that I shall rely to sketch the elements of a history of Algerian historiography.

## COLONIAL HISTORIOGRAPHY AND THE
## FRENCH HISTORY OF ALGERIA

The appearance in 1962 of *La naissance du nationalisme algérien,* a classic book by André Nouschi, came late in French historiography if one dates the origins of the nationalist movement from the late nineteenth and early twentieth centuries.[10] Not that journalists failed to pay attention to the movement's growth; rather they often sought to circumvent or channel it. A specialized review, the *Bulletin du Comité de l'Afrique française,* and its supplement, *Renseignements coloniaux,* the vehicles for conveying the sentiments of the colonial party, displayed a very precocious awareness of, and lively interest in, anything related to its concerns and their assumed appendages. This included the ideologies of Pan-Islamism, Pan-Arabism, and Bolshevism and was especially focused on the ENA, whose Maghribi vocation and troubling ties with the Komintern elicited both attention and uneasiness.[11] For that matter, until the publication of Nouschi's book, the *Bulletin du Comité de l'Afrique française* remained an essential source for any serious study of the ENA, which became the first organized expression of modern Algerian nationalism just as the "Khaledian," or most radical, wing of the "Young Algerian" movement was ebbing.[12] The reason for this was that the *Bulletin* availed itself of the best information from such sources as the Ministry of the Interior and the Ministry of the Colonies and brought together the best specialists, including Massignon, Desparmet, and Augustin Berque.

When it comes to scholarly publications, however, one would be hard put to find a single work from this period on the political evolution of North Africa in general or the Algerian situation in particular. It is as if this topic could not be left to the initiative of an authentic, scientifically autonomous, and politically independent scholarly community; as if neither the French political class nor the French intelligentsia could or would face the facts at a time when the colonial concept was becoming more important. The "république des professeurs" seemed uninterested in examining or questioning the colonial status quo. The Communist Party, revolutionary communists of the "proletarian revolution" and of Trotskyite allegiance, and the left wing of the Socialist Party all encountered the indifference of the public, notwithstanding its superficial taste for exoticism and colonial folklore. In 1936 and 1937, the "Commission Coloniale" of the Socialist Party did not have the least influence on Socialist ministers or parliamentarians. Daniel Guérin was the only one to hold radical, anticolonialist views.[13] Thus, the near monopoly of *Afrique française* was gone without a successor after the Second World War, and for good reason, since its purpose was rapidly becoming obsolete despite attempts to construct a "Union Française." In any event, the "big names" who, during the 1930s, had applied their skills to the justification of imperial policy abandoned a periodical that had no future.

In fact, only two books published during the 1930s really deserve mention, and those were written by politicians. *L'Algérie vivra-t-elle?* was published in 1931 by Maurice Viollette, a former governor-general of a "liberal" bent whose project of assimilating the indigenous elite served, five years later, both as the framework and as the intellectual and political stake in the struggle among the various protagonists during the Popular Front in 1936.[14] Viollette, who at the time won the support of elected representatives, the ulama, and the Parti Communiste Algérien (PCA), was, along with Michel Rouzé, one of the few to interpret correctly the meager gains obtained by the PPA during the 1936 elections.[15] But in the final analysis, the most consistent work remains the one which two delegates from the Komintern, N. D'Orient and M. Loew, devoted to the "Algerian problem," bringing it to the attention of the Communist militants at the moment of the 1936 Popular Front victory.[16] They were the first to offer a coherent, if debatable, picture of the forces hostile to colonial domination. They depicted the ENA as a "hinge element" in the national movement at a time when the new strategy of the Popular Front had not yet succeeded in erasing the old notion of revolutionary nationalism which had been the basic prescription of the Communist International during the 1920s for countries under foreign domination. The new approach focused on the frustrations of the French-speaking elite and anticipated the activity of *"islah"* (Islamic reformism), as Joseph Desparmet quickly observed in a series of articles in *Bulletin du Comité de l'Afrique française*. The older concept stressed, in the terms of institutional Marxism, the global character of the Algerian crisis born of social ruptures and of structural blockages associated with colonial domination. The one was "reformist," on the left of the Radical-Socialist party; the other was "revolutionary," at the cutting edge of international Communism. As yet another measure of the persistent gap between the scholar and the politician, only one serious study answered the views of D'Orient and Loew. Robert Montagne, known primarily for his writings about Morocco, wrote of "la fermentation des partis politiques en Algérie" in a journal customarily read by members of the political elite. While laying more stress on the religious factor, he developed an analytical framework similar to D'Orient and Loew's; however, he concluded with a call for firmness and repression.[17] In any case, Montagne did not inspire a following. In the mid-1930s, Louis Massignon, perhaps the greatest French Orientalist of the day, adopted increasingly critical views about the colonial system but would not push to their conclusions his "conscientious objections" regarding Algeria.

*Afrique française* was too set in its views to exploit its information and accurately measure the shift represented by the Muslim Congress and the Popular Front. Its political analysis remained mediocre, although it must be acknowledged that a great gap existed between the subtle observations of Desparmet on the ulama movement and the rather coarse analysis of less sophisticated observers such as Ladreit de Lacharrière.[18]

Algeria was, above all, the locus of political class blindness and social-science escapism.[19] Desparmet was never allowed into the University, nor was there room for Charles-André Julien during the 1930s. Julien himself was caught between the contradictions of his time and his responsibilities within the Socialist party, in the cabinet of Léon Blum, and in his functions when head of the Haut Comité Méditerranéen.

Even after the end of World War II brought increasing nationalist militancy, the intellectual climate hardly changed. *Afrique française* grew ever weaker and "colonial science" fell into decay. The best scholars distanced themselves radically from the mainstream but, except for Maxime Rodinson, without moving to the political level. And if prestigious publications such as *Esprit* at first, and then *Les Temps modernes,* started espousing radical political views, they made little room for Maghribi social science. In this context, a 1949 study by Hildebert Isnard, a geographer known for his writings about vineyards, published in no less a review than *Annales,* fails to conceal the impoverished state of North African political studies. One can merely contrast Hildebert's attempt to comprehend the roots of the nationalist movement with more typical works on the topic that appeared in the same year: a rather ambivalent pamphlet by Sylvain Wisner and a classically colonialist book by Paul Emile Sarasin.[20]

Political Algeria so frightened specialists and so inhibited the French intelligentsia that it fell to a newcomer to Algeria—André Mandouze, a renowned authority on Saint Augustine—to stress the depth of the crisis in an *Esprit* article.[21] That raising of the alarm was a prelude to the real historiographic reassessment made by Charles-André Julien in *L'Afrique du Nord en marche* in 1952. This fundamental and unparalleled work[22] accurately depicts the increasing pressure from the three nationalist parties which, under changing appellations but always in the name of a common Maghribi ideal, openly struggled for the independence of their respective countries from the mid-1930s, and which together, in 1950, reached the brink of armed insurrection. Julien's book expressed the support of a large section of academia and of the French intelligentsia for the need to introduce basic reforms into the colonial structure—if not outright independence for North Africa, then at least a redefined interdependence between the region and metropolitan France.[23]

*L'Afrique du Nord en marche* is a masterpiece because of its intimate knowledge of its subject, because of the individuals and issues with which it deals, and because of the author's exceptional ability to convey the richness of history, honed during the writing of an earlier masterpiece, *Histoire de l'Afrique du Nord: Tunisie, Algérie, Maroc* (1931). The former is also remarkable because of its agenda of inquiry. As in his earlier work, Julien makes the Maghrib the epistemological foundation of his study. Thus the Maghrib is seen as the anthropological unity of a thousand-year-old geographical and cultural complex of "total history." An aesthetic unity of time and place gives the narrative the force of classical tragedy. A methodological unity which invites a comparative approach is the key to the political reading of the book.

Of necessity, such a book is dated by the discovery of new sources, by the vagaries of a very broad synthesis, by the pressure of events, and by the ethnocentric aspects of the scholarly approach. Yet it remains irreplaceable and unsurpassed. In the case of Algeria, the principal protagonists, in order of their presentation, are the ulama (who receive the longest coverage and are thus accorded the greatest importance), the ENA, the PPA, the "enlightened people," and the Communist Party, all clearly distinguished from the socialists and the extreme right, which also recruited their own Muslim followers. The book places both the ENA and the PPA at the center of a dynamic of forces which crystallize into an autonomous political movement and which shape historical evolution. The framework sketched out by D'Orient, Montagne, and Isnard was preserved and developed, and Julien drew comparisons, stressing, for each country and with respect to the whole context, the shifting of "turfs" and stakes from one decade to another, from one crisis to another, and from one leader to another.

It must be acknowledged, however, that Julien neglected a few areas in his monumental work. Emir Khaled receives very little attention, although the first edition of Julien's book grants him the status of "the true initiator of a nationalism everyone later claimed to be his own."[24] Julien disposes of the ENA and the PPA in a scant few pages. The latter was born "in the shadow of the Communist party" and was characterized by its "proletarian and revolutionary following" and its "distinct preference for direct action." It was also epitomized by the "simple and direct eloquence of its leader" and by a "basically religious doctrine also marked by an openly nationalist and proletarian outlook."[25] The former is less clearly definable, despite its often-asserted "proletarian" character. What is stressed is the evolutionary side of the program, associated with "spiritual obedience to Chekib Arslan," its growing influence on city and country alike through "the ability to express the aspirations of the native masses," the infiltration of the Amis du Manifeste de la Liberté (AML), the "rivalry between followers of Messali Hadj and the Communists," the awareness of outside influences such as the United Nations, and the strength of the Pan-Arab myth. Mention is twice made of the contention that the PPA was "riddled with policemen."[26] In the most striking omission, Julien says nothing about the tensions within the PPA. He does not see the Berber crisis, nor even the crucial importance of the Organisation Spéciale (OS), the paramilitary wing of the Mouvement pour le Triomphe des Libertés Démocratiques (MTLD) that was dismantled in March and April 1950, even though his book was completed in February 1953.[27] This said, his documentation is considerable and if the nationalist press (such as *El-Umma* or *L'Algérie libre*) is not directly quoted, it is clear that he had access to confidential reports made available to scholars only much later.

Thus, Charles-André Julien established, for a long time to come, both the categories of analysis and the terms of the controversy. Almost as if the successive historiographical reassessments followed a decennial pattern, it was ten years before a historian cum political scientist took the next important step. The work of André Nouschi cannot be reduced, as some have claimed, to the status of a "handbook." Its difference from Julien's is not so much a matter of sources as it is of methods and orientation, although it is true that Nouschi did not have access to the police reports Julien had used. Moved by the pressure of events (writing in 1962) Nouschi could systematically research neither the nationalist nor the colonial press, as Kaddache did later. Therefore, he made far more liberal use than Julien of data gathered in *Afrique française* for the period between the two world wars, along with the research of the most informed observers, principally Albert Paul Lentin and Francis Jeanson, for the following period.[28] (Strangely enough, Mostefa

Lacheraf was not quoted, although his articles in *Esprit* and *Les Temps modernes* were readily available.) In terms of outlook, Nouschi subscribed to the need to "decolonize"—as Julien initially advocated—the views expressed about Algeria in French scholarly historiography. His book thus complements, in dealing with the present, the "rupture concept" that he, Yves Lacoste, and André Prenant had previously applied to the past in their 1960 publication *L'Algérie, passé et présent* (Paris: Editions Sociales), a dramatically revisionist work that clearly differed with virtually all previous assessments. Nouschi's book was a historical and cognitive inventory of evolution, at a time when the very fact of Algerian independence raised and demanded a reconsideration of the question, How did the process reach this point? Throughout the fateful year of 1962, politically and symbolically speaking, a very large number of books on the war in Algeria, its origin and causes, appeared in response to the explosion of this niche in the book market. It was in the area of methodology that Nouschi was an innovator. This stemmed from his pioneering efforts in Maghribi social history, evidenced by his 1961 thesis, "Enquête sur le niveau de vie des populations rurales constantinoises de la conquête jusqu'en 1919." Nouschi made maximum use of his sociological knowledge to offer a synthetic reinterpretation of the political scene by systematically establishing a parallel between the socio-economic situation and the political one in the periods 1919 to 1939 and 1939 to 1954. This method was later broadly applied by Charles-Robert Ageron and then Gilbert Meynier in monumental works of total history. Mahfoud Kaddache also employed it in his *Histoire du nationalisme algérien*. On the other hand, Nouschi abandoned the Maghribi unity approach at the very moment when Jacques Berque based his masterwork of cultural and social anthropology, *Le Maghreb entre deux guerres,* on it.[29]

Widening the scope of the study offered gains in the depth of analysis but, at the same time, losses in the volume of documentation. In fact, Nouschi's study was indicative of a process—already started by Xavier Yacono, Pierre Boyer, and Hildebert Isnard—of returning to the monograph.[30] Isnard set an example with his thesis, at the regional level, and his synthesis, at the national level. There was a further parallel in the work of a political scientist, Pierre Rossignol, whose Université de Paris law dissertation, "Les Partis politiques musulmans en Algérie de leur origine au premier novembre 1954," provided a closer examination of the words and deeds of the main political protagonists. Its clearest contributions concerned the Union Démocratique du Manifeste Algérien (UDMA), the PPA, and the MTLD, while its most complete "case history" was that of Messali Hadj himself, in which Rossignol provided, for the first time, the outline of a biography. He innovated further with his use of interviews and his taking information directly from the source—such MTLD publications as *Commission centrale d'information et de documentation du MTLD en Algérie,* a series of eight booklets issued in December 1951; Abdelghani [M'hamed Yazid], *Le problème algérien de l'émigration en France* (Paris: n.p., 1950); and the parties' newspapers, including *La République algérienne* (UDMA) and, especially, *L'Algérie libre* (PPA).

It then fell to Roger Le Tourneau to reexamine the evolution of North African nationalism as though it were, for him, a way of updating the masterwork of Julien at the same time that the colonization of the Maghrib was drawing to a close.[31] Although remarkably written and documented, the book had neither the depth of views nor the perspective of its model. Although Le Tourneau wrote ten years after Julien, he left the impression of doing so ten years earlier and was closer to Montagne than to Nouschi. His analysis of the ENA and the PPA was not very different, however, from Julien's. Twelve years later, Jean-Claude Vatin offered readers a very complete and perspicacious critical study of the "history of the colonizer" in an excellent book entitled *L'Algérie politique. Histoire et société.*[32]

## ALTERITY AND ALTERCATION:
## HISTORIOGRAPHICAL DEPENDENCY AND THE MAKING
## OF AN AUTONOMOUS AREA OF NATIONAL HISTORY

*Decolonizing History*

When Algeria reached the threshold of independence, it was not altogether without access to knowledge about its own history. Yet it still depended, in the main, on a history written not only by others, but by historians and journalists of the former colonial power, friendly though some of them may have been. Just as in the Hegelian thesis, the slave had been freed, but the master still held the slave's past. By dominating the slave's history, he polluted his memory and perturbed his identity. This, at least, was a widely prevalent feeling within the nationalist intelligentsia, if not within the entire political and intellectual class.

That this was true, and to an extent unparalleled in other Arab countries, was evident in the emphasis given by the "charters"—the fundamental political documents of the party-state drawn up by the Front de Libération Nationale (FLN)—to preparing an authentic national history.[33] It is also apparent in the success enjoyed by a small book by Mohamed Chérif Sahli entitled *Décoloniser l'histoire.* The title, an agenda in itself, sounds like the death knell of things past.[34] In a critique that foreshadowed by some fifteen years the anti-Orientalist tract of Edward Said, Sahli asserted that everything needed to be redone. Sahli did not offer an "Islamist" alternative, as did his counterpart and rival Malek Bennabi. *Vocation de l'Islam,* the latter's best known work, reproached what he called "post-Almohadean" North Africans for having sunken into a state of political and religious decadence that had rendered them "colonizable." For Bennabi, only a cultural revival rooted in the Maghrib's Arabo-Islamic heritage, albeit sufficiently ecumenical to embrace the assets of contemporary science and technology, could reverse this trend and undo the damage it had wrought.[35]

Several facts help clarify this observation. To begin with something of an overstatement, it might simply be said that there was no Algerian history of Algeria because there were no Algerian historians. This paucity was certainly related to the systematic withholding of primary, and especially secondary, education from Muslim children during practically the whole of the colonial period, which minimized the possibility of creating the "breeding ground" necessary for forming a critical cultural mass and of having a sufficient number of high school graduates capable of entering university. The intellectual and cultural deficit also stemmed from the preference of the French-speaking Muslim elites for the "streams" that brought prestige, status, and income: law and medicine.

Exceptions to the aforestated lack of Algerian historians were all special cases. The remarkable works and personality of Mohammed Ben Cheneb themselves underline his exceptional standing in the Algerian intellectual landscape and the colonial university.[36] Much the same may be said of the "Arabist historians" Mubarak al-Mili and Tawfiq al-Madani, who looked upon themselves as unique, not as the founders of a "school." For twenty years, as they contented themselves with the not-inconsiderable task of answering Gsell and Gautier, their names constituted the whole "set."[37]

Second, along with the "group" limitation, there was a "field" restriction. Such a restriction was institutionalized in that the discipline of history was generally beyond the reach of the Algerian student, if not out of his curriculum. It was also a political restriction, because public censorship was reinforced by private self-censorship. Never would Ben Cheneb venture into the area of "contemporary" studies. al-Mili and al-Madani prudently restricted their endeavors, the former to a euphemistic examination of the colonial period, the latter to the fifteenth century. Since they wanted to be read, they needed to be published. Even the Europeans rarely dealt with the recent past, much less with political history—and not only because of a positivist tradition.

Third, the scarcity of Algerian historians had a cognitive nature in its chronological, linguistic, and conceptual aspects. History was a "normative" exercise and left current matters to other disciplines or to journalists, civil servants, and so-called experts. Besides Arabic, three languages are required to master the history of the Maghrib: Latin for Antiquity, Ottoman Turkish for the "Régences barbaresques," and French for the colonial period—not to mention Berber for the oral tradition. As daunting as this may have been for specialists condemned to a narrow division of labor, it was considerably more difficult still for scholars monolingual in Arabic. Moreover, the field of history had undergone, since the 1930s, great changes, many of them linked with the initiatives of the "Annales school." Salvation, then, would come from bilingual, French-speaking Arab historians with a "modern" training.

At first, this training, by leaning heavily on a system of cooperation with France and several countries of the Middle East, notably Egypt, for the entire school program, but especially for secondary and university education, tended to increase the very dependency it sought to remove. So also did the cognitive domination of the French university system, with its degree granting strictures, and the technical and cultural domination of the book market by the former colonizer—a domination that was strengthened by the censorship inherent in the logic of a single party.

Naturally, no one could replace a Julien all at once, nor could independence instantly reverse the course of Algerian historical studies, since the formation of a new contingent of historians would necessarily take time. Mostefa Lacheraf, the key intellectual figure for the generation of the independence movements, was published in Paris by Maspero, as was Sahli. And the first major doctoral dissertation in the field of history since Algerian independence—Ali Merad's thesis on the ulama, which established the basis of noncolonial historical scholarship on that subject—was published in Paris by Mouton.[38]

Typically, the best bilingual Arabic scholars—Ali Merad, Mohamed Arkoun, and Hadi Bencheikh—were lost to the Algerian universities. This heavy blow deeply affected the future of "Arabic letters" at the decisive time of an initial impulse. Thus, ideology won over historical science. The intellectual and political elite of 1962 had no other choice in learning its own contemporary history than to turn to the French history of Algeria—not to say the history of French Algeria. For yet another twenty years, Algerian students and teachers were compelled to use that history as a term of reference—and eventually of opposition—until a new "School of Algiers" changed the accessibility of postgraduate studies by relying on the early Arabization of history teaching.[39]

But in a paradox intolerable to pervasive nationalist sensitivities, it was the very history of nationalism that was written by non-Algerians such as Julien, Nouschi, and Ageron—sympathetic though they may have been. Algerians remained the "other," seemingly forever, inasmuch as Merad and Saadallah did not publish their main works for another six or seven years; Gallissot, Meynier, Stora, and Carlier later still. One might think that a people could not be more dispossessed of their own history. At the same time the fictionalized accounts of Yves Courrière, for example, published in the 1970s and all the more sought after in Algeria because they were censored, even encouraged readers to forget about the war of liberation itself.

When this feeling of alienation reached its climax, it prompted President Houari Boumédienne to launch the Centre National d'Etudes Historiques (CNEH) in 1971 and to define a set procedure for writing history. (An earlier commission, whose work focused mainly on the war of national liberation, never published a report.) For as the country's history was reinterpreted and filtered by the media and the official orthodoxy, which was itself predicated on the meaning of the war as successive victors defined it, what were being kidnapped and held hostage were the myth of the "Founding Fathers," the sacred struggle, and the sacrifices of the *shuhada* (plural of *shahid,* 'martyr').[40] This was a perfect example of the perverse effect analyzed by Raymond Boudon, in which the nationalization of history leads to its denial and makes existing disparities even more acute.[41]

This frame of reference influenced the work of Mostefa Lacheraf, who was the first among his peers to propose another global study centered on the colonial period, foreshadowing the views of Sahli, but offering an alternative analysis that went beyond Sahli's negative attitude.[42] To the stereotype of the perennial brute, the Berber anarchist, the eternal loser dominated by a foreign power, and the "bennabiste" syndrome of "colonizability," Lacheraf opposed a redeeming "dualism." In doing so, he made a clear distinction between the rural patriotism of the peasant and the nationalism of the city dweller—the former preceding, and then joining the latter; the latter taking over the former as it transforms it—thereby giving a key role to the social "actor," the maker of his own history. On the one hand, the peasantry; on the other, the urban and rural masses. Thus we are propelled, all at once, into the "national movement"—the phrase used by the ideologues and anticolonialist organizations of the time. It was indicative of a political framework the PPA had already imposed upon the Algerian elites during the decade between 1936 and 1946 that would contribute to the naming of the Mouvement National Algérien (MNA) after the final crisis within the MTLD (1953–1954). In yet another "first," an Algerian historian says something about Algerian nationalism—in terms of its relation to the very concept of the nation-state, and using the analytical categories of social history clearly associated with Marxism.

Harsh towards everyone—beginning with his own group, which became the Comité Révolutionnaire d'Unité et d'Action (CRUA) and then the FLN—Lacheraf attempted to reconstruct what Julien merely sketched out (although he never quotes Julien)—a "historical sociology" of nationalism—and to connect analytically what Nouschi had separated, the social and the political. Thus, political protagonists were defined socially and culturally in their complexity, their heterogeneity, and their evolution.

According to Lacheraf, Khaled, for instance, "speaks a new language for the period," "gathers together a small group of rival Notables, of civil servants, and of intellectuals" and "attempts to fashion a connection between rural patriotism, considerably diminished, not to say nonexistent, and the emerging and confused urban patriotism." The ENA "harbors several tendencies and several ideologies . . . a superficial Marxism, a sentimental and nostalgic Algerianism, and a rudimentary Islamism." The PPA can reach "the masses, the intellectual and working youth," "create public opinion," and also "rally a fair number of middle class people, and especially progressive lower middle class people" in contrast to the proletarian origins of the ENA. This is the same PPA whose orientation, through lack of culture, sinks into "improvisation, mimicry, tactical religiosity, respectability, and populism."[43] Although hopelessly dated, this book has also never been equaled or replaced. It is a work with neither predecessor nor successor.

*Mobilizing History*

Lacheraf's was a wartime work that gave meaning to war—a critique with a nationalist perspective as well as a farewell to early nationalism. This is so because of the renewed relation between documentation, methods, and analytical categories. But allowance must also be made for a certain measure of utopian euphoria appropriate for a Third World and revolutionary ideology at the time when it reaches a climax with the completion of the decolonization process begun in 1945. Allowance must be made as well for the subsequent worldwide expansion of socialism, whatever the multiplicity of its forms and the intensity of its contradictions. In 1956 and 1957, *Les Temps modernes* published a series of articles by Lacheraf designed to influence the French intelligentsia as the Socialist party waded deeper into the "dirty war" in Algeria. In order to make a convincing historical argument, these articles also offered a coherent and compelling theory of "nationalism." In 1965, Maspero brought them out as *L'Algérie, nation et société,* expanded to include, among other new material, an important introduction bearing directly on current problems with, and having an obviously critical theory of, "populism." With independence a reality, the major battle had come to center on the nature of the new Algerian state and the political form its regime would assume—and this precisely at a time when history was becoming institutionalized and officialized and was being taken over by opposing protagonists who wanted to legitimize, or delegitimize, their respective claims to power. Thus, *L'Algérie, nation et société* had two publishers, two publics, and even two levels of analysis—political and scientific.

History was more than ever politicized, calling both on memory of and knowledge about a controversy that had not only opposed Frenchmen to Algerians, but also Algerians to each other. Before it was relinquished to the still-rare specialists, the politicians monopolized history. Never have Algerians written so much about themselves and their collective adventure as when they first began to take the full measure of its scope in the fateful moments of the self-determination referendum and the ensuing race for power that pitted the "Oudja Group" against the provisional government, the *wilayat* (political subdivisions; states) of the "interior" against the armies fighting at the borders. Some of the protagonists were directly associated with the struggle among the leaders, including such "historiques" as Ait Ahmed and Boudiaf, who were already beginning to move away from the consensus.[44] Others were outside the locus of the FLN, with its PPA-MTLD sociohistoric matrix, although for different reasons. They included Ferhat Abbas, formerly the beacon of the intellectuals, the Fédération des Elus, and the UDMA; and Amar Ouzegane, secretary of the Algerian Communist Party from 1936 to 1948.

Abbas and Ouzegane were eminently experienced politicians and talented speakers and commentators; both were bound to a retrospective outlook that might explain the meaning of history and justify their past political course, despite acknowledged failures and their claim to have advanced ideological and political revisionism. Such a reassessment took place through what Jean-Claude Vatin felicitously called a "paternity search," since it was based on the assumption that the FLN issued from the PPA, which itself derived from the ENA, which was the ultimate source both of good and of evil.[45] Good because the modern idea of independence as an organized political purpose started with the Etoile; evil because Messali Hadj led it into fratricidal divisions and counterrevolution.

The ENA is a good example of a certain vision of history and of the way the "national movement" is viewed. Abbas and Ouzegane echo Lacheraf. In the writings of both, albeit in very different formulations, were parallels to the "false start" Lacheraf attributed to Messali. Abbas contrasted the personality of Messali to that of Khaled in an interpretation that minimized the contribution of the Communist Party, deprived Messali of the prestige associated with the "paternity" of the movement and, by strengthening the later UDMA's inheritance, enhanced that party's position within the FLN.[46] His version, which displayed an elitist bent in spite of the very deliberate humility of the tone, rested on the testimony of a single man, Ahmed Belghoul, a political associate of Khaled and Messali, and proceeded according to a logic of proof that had less to do with the techniques of oral history than with the secular paradigm of witnesses and of *isnad* (chain of authorities for conveying information). Belghoul was also a source of information for a book by Mohamed Lebjaoui, *Vérités sur la révolution algérienne*.[47] Lebjaoui used his testimony, however, only with due caution and within the context of other available sources, as did Mahfoud Kaddache in his dissertation. What matters here is the cultural mode of reference to a witness. A member of the Communist Party and of the CGTU, a founding member of the first Etoile Nord-Africaine, and close to Emir Khaled, Ahmed Belghoul followed, beginning in 1929–1930, the "Khaledian current" among the emigrants. He then moved within the circles of the elected representatives until joining the UDMA after 1945. While maintaining episodic contacts with Messali and certain militants of the PPA, he was a close associate and friend of Ferhat Abbas, an open adversary of Messali and of Communism.

Ouzegane, on the other hand, countered the paternalist concept of the genitor with the notion of a collective initiative inherited from the labor tradition and associative solidarity which, at the time, strengthened the left wing of the FLN and ultimately merged, although arriving by a different route, with Lacheraf's viewpoint. Inspired by the collective memory of the party, Ouzegane's text rejected both the Messalist and UDMA interpretations, as well as the orthodox communist reinterpretation ascribed to Yves Lacoste.[48]

At that time, the Algerian Communist Party lacked an adequate narrative of events of its own. An initial version was embedded in the memory of party supporters but was vitiated by an old quarrel closely connected to Messali himself. He was firmly believed to have been indoctrinated at the communist school in the Paris suburb of Bobigny and was attacked for deserting the internationalist cause and the doctrines of revolutionary nationalism. The written version of these events, however, was a coded one, prompted by higher authorities who decided upon its terms and its timeliness. Yet, despite the polemical accusation, Ouzegane still spoke for Messali on the origins of the independence movement. Only much later did the PAGS formulate a revisionist history in a 1970 pamphlet entitled *Essai d'histoire du mouvement ouvrier 1920–1954*.

On the one hand, political players; on the other, the apparatus of the parties. In both cases, they use the past to settle scores in the present and the present to settle past scores. In between, history searches for itself, despite the evolving works of Lacheraf and Merad. It was a fragile history because of its infancy, timorous and restricted because of its status, and paralyzed or normalized because of what was at stake; for the party-state imposed limits on knowledge and legitimacy through its control of the nationalist story which, regulated by the media, evolved into a conformity.[49]

With the "National Charter," the party-state availed itself of a "handbook" whose subsequent editions offered ad hoc and dated versions, with successive representations of the course of history fashioned by those who selected its basic meaning and prescribed its orientation. With this handbook, they had a prototype whose versions varied considerably—from the social democracy of the 1954 text to the self-management concept of the 1964 text—but remained stable in status, structure and, in the main, vocabulary. Here, then, is a text which was at once introductory and set the terms of the revolution; which established the limits of open debate or of measured controversy; and which, therefore, provided a code of understanding, not only for politicians, whether supporters or opponents, but also for the intellectuals, including members of the academic community.

On the one hand, the Charter formed a corpus within a structure based on a modernist chronology patterned after positivism, along with a social and functional morphology (Marxist or otherwise) and, to borrow a business expression, a list of unique selling propositions presented as the judicial logic of a statement of purpose or system description. On the other hand, the Charter prominently featured the protagonists of the historical play and judged the various elements of the national movement. By so doing, it defined the core of legitimacy which lies at the center of any political power, as well as the scenario which dictated any writing of history.

## THE HISTORIOGRAPHIC RESTRUCTURING OF THE 1970S AND THE OUTLINE OF A "NEW HISTORY"

In Algeria, history is a discipline constantly burdened by the dictates of political power. The historiographic restructuring of the 1970s closely followed this axiom. It fit within a political and ideological context marked by the definitive assertion of the regime born of the coup d'état of June 1965; the setting in place of a core of legitimacy preserving a populist compromise with very ancient roots; the implementation of development strategy influenced by the Soviet model, with priority to heavy industry; and a pro-Arab Third World policy that sought to be the heir of Nasser. Ten years after independence, two major decisions symbolized the Boumédienne era: the nationalization of oil resources—reminiscent of Mossadegh—with its challenge to western imperialism; and the agrarian revolution which went beyond the example of Nasser and self-management to ensure, as Zapata and Franz Fanon advocated, the emancipation of the oppressed while working to prevent the establishment of a landed bourgeoisie. But to the economic and social side of the revolutionary recovery, one must add the aspect of the cultural revolution based on the democratization of education and the Arabization of the schools.[50]

The direct and indirect problems resulting from the general pressure on the teaching of history that then developed were considerable. On the one side, the larger-than-life figure of Ben Badis overwhelmed all others, including ʿAbd al-Qadir, as a reintegrator of the past, a bridge between past and present, and a reconciler for "modernism" and authenticity through a kind of "*nahda* within the *nahda*" ('awakening' or 'renaissance'; often used to refer to the Arab cultural revival of the late nineteenth and early twentieth centuries). Here was the theme of "Arabic as the language of steel and iron," whose initiator was Dr. Taleb Ibrahimi, Minister of Education and son of Sheikh Ibrahimi, the successor of Ben Badis. If the charters limited themselves to the "verdict of the Soummam," the media readily placed the ulama at the start of the independence movement at a time when the Middle Eastern supporters of the Algerian religious right wing watched with concern as the regime moved towards what they considered a variant of "atheistic communism." Thus, there was a prescribed use and, indeed, a double use—internal and external—for this emphasis on the role of Ben Badis as the battle for control of the educational system, the young generation, and the formation of future elites took shape between the secularists, de facto backers of bilingualism, and the Arabists, both Baathists and neo-Salafists.[51] Yet, in another sense, the regime, more secure about its present standing and its followers, was less fearful of a return to a "nationalist" past predating November 1, 1954—a past that could enhance the role of the historic old guard and, with it, the PPA forces within the FLN, resulting in a lessened role for the victors of 1962 and 1965. More to the point, just as the "statist-industrialist left" was taking the offensive, within and outside the country, under the direction of Boumédienne himself, monopolizing a progressive image of the nationalist past was not only useful but necessary, so long as it was done in an attractive, controlled, and balanced fashion.

The writing of contemporary Algerian history cannot escape this polarization or free itself from the social, political, ideological, and mental limitations which constrain its activities. There is a structural dualism that centers around Kaddache and Saadallah, the one a former French-speaking Boy Scout with a PPA background, the other an Arabic-speaking neo-Islahist with a postgraduate degree from the United States. This parallels the dualism between two bilingual graduates of the *madrasa* (traditional school) with postgraduate degrees from Paris—Lacheraf and Bennabi. Both were to become authoritative spokesmen for the discipline of history and masters of the "home-grown" generation of postgraduate students. The Minister of Higher Education and Religious Affairs, Mouloud Kassim, increasingly took on the role of supreme arbiter and "president of the tribunal of history." In fact, this former member of the PPA, educated in the Zitouna and in Cairo, settled the dispute in favor of the neo-Salafists.

In this context—and with considerable naïveté—I began my own research on the Etoile Nord-Africaine. An article on the "first period" of the Etoile brought into better perspective the roles of Khaled and Messali and tried to give substance to what Julien had earlier called "the shadow of the Communist party."[52] Later, a paper stressed, in the "second period," the functional autonomy of radical nationalism and the rise of the "Messalist" ENA.[53] At the same time, Mohammed Harbi published in Paris a book on the origins of the FLN that became a preface of sorts for his fundamental work *Le FLN, mirage et réalité* published in 1980 and unequaled since.[54] As a result, two of the least known and most controversial aspects of the independence movement were at least clarified, if not definitively explained: the founding of the Etoile Nord-Africaine and the crisis within the MTLD—two decisive moments, a beginning and an end.

Although quite independent of them, this initiative was related to other undertakings by virtue of the importance attributed to the social rooting of the processes of the mobilization and formation of elites, the social and ideological reasons for political divisions and power conflicts within the party, and the high points and the mechanisms of crises and conflicts. The party was no longer examined as a monolith opposed to other equally monolithic units, but as a differentiated whole. It was also related through a common reference to the concept of populism and the problem of social classes in a colonized country—a dominant paradigm for left-wing French and Algerian academics since 1968.[55] Yet it was different in other ways—the path followed, the nature of the researcher's rapport with his subject, and its ethnosociological dimensions: the study of political socialization among migrants in one case, and in another, the stress upon political strategies, with an inside view of the interplay between individuals, groups, and clans.

This analysis did not rest merely on the systematic investigation of key times and places but also relied on the use of new written sources and oral contributions. With respect to the Etoile Nord-Africaine, the archives of the Paris Prefecture of Police, whose two cartons of documents relating to the ENA (numbers 55 and 56) are now open for examination, were used for the first time. With respect to the PPA-MTLD, the internal documents of the party were also employed for the first time, introducing a method which later made it possible to compile *Les Archives de la révolution algérienne*.[56] In both cases, the statutes and programs were compared with the speeches and actions of the people involved. And in both cases, key witnesses brought to the researcher the contribution of oral testimony. The historical study of the ENA/PPA sequence was established.

In fact, the resumption of studies about the national movement and the struggle for independence started with Mahfoud Kaddache, whose book *La vie politique à Alger de 1919 à 1939*, published by SNED in 1970, established an analytical framework, a methodology, and an interpretation that blossomed ten years later in a two-volume doctoral thesis published by the same press in 1980 (and in a revised and enlarged second edition in 1993) under the title *Histoire du nationalisme algérien: Question nationale et politique algérienne, 1919–1951*.

With these books, another history—a "shadow history," as it were— became available not only to the Algerian elite, but to the public at large. Relying on the use of the same historical methods, it differed from the French outlook not only in its specifically Algerian and nationalist sensitivity—PPA-oriented in this case—but also in that it told its own story and described its own movement. Dealing with the participants in the movement, Kaddache adopted, in the main, the pattern already established by the classical French historians. As they had done, he underlined the structural opposition between the European and the Algerian communities and, within the latter, the successive emergence of the "decision makers," the "intellectuals," and the "militants." As Nouschi had done, he contrasted economic and demographic evolution with political evolution. But dealing specifically with Algiers, Kaddache underscored the central and exemplary role of the capital, site of the largest urban population in Algeria and where the fundamental battles whose outcome weighed most heavily on the whole of the country took place—particularly those over the Muslim Congress and the Viollette Bill. By shifting the level and bases of his analysis, he moved progressively from the general Maghribi framework of Julien to the regional, but also central, framework of Algiers. Yet, by so doing he changed both the method and the tools, calling upon new sources or using them differently. By searching methodically through the minutes of the Municipal Council and especially by exhaustively reading the Muslim Algerian press of the time, Kaddache was able to determine the behavior of the "decision makers" and to follow, without interruption, the electoral track from the 1919 law to the election of Mohamed Douar, a humble streetcar driver affiliated with the PPA, in 1939.

Using the experience acquired working on Algiers, Kaddache broadened his research to Algerian society as a whole and continued the inquiry up to the outbreak of the war of national liberation in 1954. The initial investigation was preserved but widened through the use of such new sources as the French National Archives, especially the F7 series, and the Overseas Archives in Aix-en-Provence, especially the H series. True enough, other Algerian and French scholars had already exploited these sources, but with the exception of Ageron, they had applied them to fields of inquiry more limited in both space and time.

In 1980, the Algerian reader could thus avail himself of a comprehensive book on twentieth-century political Algeria, from Khaled to Ben Boulaïd, or from Sheikh Ben Badis to Sheikh Ibrahimi. A few years later, the same reader could also examine the first French edition of the rewritten doctoral dissertation of Aboul-Kassem Saadallah, initially defended in the United States in 1965 and impossible to obtain until ENAL published it as *La Montée du nationalisme algérien* in 1983. The book's main interest lay in the importance it attributed to the history of ideas in Algeria, and especially to the intellectual clubs and associations that considerably predated the creation of the Association des Uléma Musulmans Algériens in 1931 and went back to Sheikh Abduh's visit to Algeria. A number of other such organizations were born in response to the celebration of the centennial of the French conquest. The study of this missing link ties in the traditional literati with the men of the Islah, as a counterpoint to the dissertation of Ali Merad. But despite its felicitous use of the Anglo-Saxon press, Saadallah's book is marred by its reliance on secondary sources.

Thus, the books of Kaddache and Saadallah broadly corresponded to the works of the French classical historians, but also to those of Lacheraf and Merad. One author considered the whole sweep of the modern national movement, the other more narrowly stressed the intellectual origins of the Algerian nahda, initially inspired by ideas from the Middle East but soon coming into its own. Indeed, Saadallah puts forward the interesting notion that, owing to its early reaction to foreign intervention and occupation, Algeria could have been at the source of the Nahda.[57] Moreover, the role of Islamic influences from India on the Nahda have become more clear. On this question, see the work of Marc Gaboriau, especially *Islam et société en Asie du sud* (Paris: Ecole des Hautes Etudes en Sciences Sociales, 1986). Both writers make use, although to considerably different extents, of the research of the previous decade. They also endeavor to understand and integrate the views of younger postgraduates, most of them connected to the nationalist and Marxist left.

Indeed, during the 1970s, very fruitful work was done on various periods and participants in the social, political, and cultural movement of the first half of the century at the Faculté des Lettres, and especially at the Faculté de Droit, with the encouragement of René Gallissot, Claude Collot, and Jean-Claude Vatin. The articles of Claude Collot in the *Revue algérienne* stand as a counterpoint to the papers and dissertations written in Algiers on the labor movement, the Muslim Congress and the Popular Front, the Amis du Manifeste et de la Liberté, and others, in the context of ideological effervescence and intense political struggle surrounding the Agrarian Revolution and the student activism that followed the dissolution of the Union Nationale des Etudiants Algériens.[58] All those works bore the mark of contemporary events. Most dissertations in sociology and in economics displayed the same attraction and sometimes the same confusion between science and ideology, partly because of the polarization of the conflict between nationalists and Marxists.

The works of Kaddache and Saadallah concluded a third decade, notable for a bitter ideological and political conflict, the survival of a very old event-oriented scheme, and a persistent fascination with "origins." Depending on the writer, either Messali or Ben Badis came first in the "founding father stakes," by bypassing the debate that had previously divided Kaddache and Ageron. But in both cases, History kept a strongly normative, if not teleological, bias, inspired mainly by the classical axioms of the history of ideas. There was also, undoubtedly, the absence of a dynamic theory, such as the one that gave strength to the works of Lacheraf. Yet above all, in both cases, as in most others, the national category was already a given.

As such, the national movement resembles the fairy tale prince who comes to awaken the sleeping beauty—clear evidence of the paradigmatic and normative function of the National Charter. If the Charter is, indeed, consciously or not, the required model for the Algerian historical vision, it is because it established the framework of a political culture that constrains the very people who attempt to formulate views opposed to it or outside its confines. Despite all that separates Lacheraf and Merad, and then Kaddache and Saadallah, it is this very framework that enables them and their readers to take one another's measure through their opposition. The framework is reminiscent of the French republican model in which scholarly history and a more popularized version converge in the writings of Ernest Lavisse.

Moreover, the four-part (assimilationists, ulama, Messalists, and Communists) and four-value (freedom, identity, authenticity, and sovereignty) model is constantly present. Even when not explicitly referred to, it is implicit in the text, whether through the formulation of a question, the recollection of an event, the presentation of a program or an individual, or even a simple allusion in a footnote. Michelet-like with Lacheraf or neo-Salafist with Saadallah, Algerian history has recovered the patriotic theme to integrate it into a national Algerian assertion against the version offered by classical French historians.

In this intellectual context characterized by a dominant topic, the ENA and Khaled represent an early potential polemic because they disappeared during the most controversial stage—the war and the postwar period. They are absent from the institutional framework which precedes and follows November 1, 1954, and centers on the FLN-ALN. A linguist would say that they are all the more open to controversy in that they are at once contemporary and distant; totally or partially disconnected from the major historic issues that were to come later.

My own work, started in 1972, was not exempt from the impact of these ideological conflicts and methodological controversies, nor did it escape the vagaries of a struggling and immature research. At the beginning of the 1970s, emigration had not been studied in a fashion commensurate with its historical importance. As a context, space, and process shaping modern nationalism; as a societal undertaking bound to the creation of a political party; through its link with a fascination with the origins and central idea of a "greater Maghrib"; through its ability to resurrect topics that had been taboo or greatly constricted by censorship and to revive the most hated and repressed figures of nationalist self-definition, the Communist Party and Messali; and through its involvement in the dispute about paternity and legitimacy, my study elucidated the intriguing, if rather delicate, proposition of power sustained by myth. The article sparked controversy and spawned other studies on the ENA, of which two works, Université de Paris dissertations by Kamel Bouguessa and M'Barka Hamed, made real contributions to the debate and particularly to the argument over the ENA-PC linkage, thanks to their examinations of the archives of the Socialist Party's "commission coloniale" brought back from Moscow.[59] Though different in style, tendency, and orientation, Hamed and Bouguessa followed essentially the same path. The social and political were brought side by side, then separated. On the one hand, they took up the classical studies on emigration; on the other, they innovated with an excellent study of the parties' "nomenklatura." But this is precisely why an examination of the social and intellectual transfer to the political realm is missing, even though major surveys by Gilbert Meynier and Charles-Robert Ageron have laid the foundations for a historiographical reassessment.

In this context, the dissertation of Mohamed Chafik Mesbah signaled both the climax and the termination of a political history corseted by ideology.[60] Although well written and well organized, it was heavily based on secondary sources, notwithstanding useful interviews with older militants and an entirely new discussion of the pro-German attitude of some members of the PPA before the start of World War II. By reinforcing Kaddache's thesis, this dissertation, in its own way, stressed the obsolete character of the old ideological and historical conflict between nationalists and Marxists and the need to open political history to new avenues and new approaches. This coincided with the emergence of a new ideological paradigm, often described as a return to religion and self-identity, which marked the end of the Boumédienne years and exercised an ever-greater influence on society at large and on academia.

It was then that new research topics emerged from the major earlier frames of reference, and sometimes in opposition to them. Thus, during the 1980s, a fourth historiographical reassessment became imperative. Following the generation of pioneers in the social sciences at Algiers were Ahmed Mahiou, Hadi Bencheikh, Abdellatif Benachenhou, Fanny Colonna, Claudine Chaulet, Ali El Kenz, Djillali Liabes, and Mustapha and Zoubida Haddab; at Oran were Nadir Marouf, Tayeb Chentouf, Abdelkader Djeghloul, Ahmed Henni, and Bouziane Semmoud. The Centre de Recherches et d'Informations Documentaires en Sciences Sociales et Humaines (CRIDSSH) and the Unité de Recherche en Anthropologie Sociale et Culturelle (URASC), to mention only institutions in Oran, have contributed greatly to the nurturing and dissemination of new ideas; other important scholars included Noureddine Saadi, Ramdane Babadji, and Mohamed Mahieddine; sociologists such as Lahouari Addi, H. Benbarkat, D. Guerid, Mohammed Hocine Benkheira, and Guy Duvignaud; specialists in oral traditions and popular literature such as H. Meliani, H. Tengour, and M. Yelles-Chaouch; political analysts such as L. Babès and Lahcen Zeghdar; psychologists such as K. Ouadah, and linguists such as L. Ouenzar. This list is far from exhaustive, nor does it attempt to cover all classifications, but it does stress the renewed scope of researchers whose initial findings have chiefly concerned contemporary Algerian history, and more specifically political history. Unfortunately, one cannot help but notice an all but complete lack of interest in economic history, represented today in Oran by a lone specialist, Sid Ahmed Refas. Also noteworthy is a minimal attention to geography.[61]

Here I shall mention only a few of the most significant topics. Warda Tengour has worked on the intellectuals active in the transition to the Islah;[62] Mohamed El Korso has reopened the study of the Association des Uléma

Musulmans Algériens with an original statistical and quantitative analysis of its members' sociocultural roots that gives new insights into the sociology of this elite;[63] and Fouad Soufi, chief curator of the Oran Regional Archives, renewed the investigation of social movements by his novel use of Registry Office records before branching into research on the relationship between history and archives and between memory and written texts.[64] Daho Djerbal, working with Mahfoud Bennoune, evolved an approach to the national movement and the war of liberation based on life histories. Lakhdar Ben Tobbal, a former member of the OS (Organisation Secrète) and direct successor of Zighout Youcef at the head of Wilaya II (the northwestern part of Constantine province), cooperated in this as-yet unpublished project. The model of the biographical dictionary inspired Houari Touati's research. Starting with a regional monograph prompted by the concept of total history, while making full allowance for the evolution of mentalités, Touati also branched out into work on Maghribi hagiography.[65] My own writing in the late 1980s attempted to bring to light the means of acculturation and integration of the political ideas and practices of the 1930s by exploring the interplay of sectional relationships and the effect of the places and forms of sociability and socialization (such as the quarter, the café, or the school).[66]

Thus, behind ideas were found mentalités; behind structures, strategies; behind solid blocks, cracks and fractures; behind practices, inherited habits, learning processes, and innovations. All in all, cultural values had been leavened by modernity in the countless forms of its adaptations and adoptions, and in the tension between resistance through violence and resistance through dialogue. A new program emerged, based principally upon political history, but with changes in the levels, components, categories, and techniques of observation. As a result, the dwelling, the quarter, and even the street, the restricted society, and the anonymous man were legitimized by microhistory. The group, divided by worn-out notions of the tribe and of the cultured class with its classical knowledge, cultural paradigms, and daily habits supported by an ancestral civilization—itself questioned by rationalism, the system, and the State—were legitimized by historical anthropology. Party, national movement, ideology, program, vote, and militants—everything had to be deconstructed in order to push ahead. Everything had to be objectivized to close the gap between history and its telling, between the object and its concept. It is more than ever necessary to read and reread the "classics," but it is no longer acceptable to be content with repeating what their authors have said. In the event of our failure, others will follow us and will do better. No one can yet be sure what the results of this new approach will be, or what illusions it may contain.

## CONCLUSION

When I began my research on the Etoile Nord-Africaine in the early 1970s, none of the questions mentioned in the introduction to this paper had ever been raised. It was not a matter of asking who had created modern nationalism and the ENA, since I naively believed that I had the answers. Messali was the "father," with the sponsorship of the Communist Party. Charles-André Julien and André Nouschi had so written and the old militants had said so in interviews. Besides Messali Hadj himself, these sources of oral history included Akli Banoune, Ahmed Belghoul, Bensmain Boumédienne, Amar Bergad, Mohamed Guénanèche, Amar Kheder, Boumédienne Marouf, Mrs. Odette Marouf (widow of Mohamed Marouf, a founding member of the ENA in 1926), Belkacem Radjef, Mohand Rebouh, and Ahmed Yahiaoui. At the same time, Mahmoud Bouayed, Director of the National Library, Mohamed Guénanèche, and Mahfoud Kaddache recorded and published the recollections of Akli Banoune and Amar Kheder in *Histoire par la bande* (Algiers: Société Nationale d'Editions et de Diffusion, 1974).

The question, then, was to know why and how things had been started by Messali. Of course, the question was not limited to his person, no matter how important he may have been. Althusser, Rodinson, and Bourdieu would not allow it. There was also the issue of emigration and the conflict between various models: party versus brotherhood, behavioral stability versus contextual adaptation, ideological movement versus intellectual probing, and even the system of historical action. In brief, this was a long-term program, parts of which remain relevant today. What was not understood at the time was that another kind of reply lay hidden within the question: the subconscious contents of speech. The "father's image" asserted itself, without, however, throwing into relief the very symbols of creation. Without knowing it, I was in the midst of the realm of genesis, the Adam-like figure of the first man, which is an integral part of the Qur'anic corpus and of Arabic literary tradition.[67] Objectivization came later. And one could not dismiss the hypothesis of a twin survival—of a time-honored scheme of verbal logic, closely affiliated with popular versification; and of an anthropological residue surviving the emergence of a new political memory or, better still, strengthening its functioning and its efficacy. All of this, in a word, pointed to the significance of an ideological track and of a hagiographical mold recognizable in the person of the founding forefather.[68]

By thus searching through memory, one rediscovered history and power, since battles over recollections are also power struggles by virtue of the force attached to the legitimate enunciation of history's meaning. Thus, the recollection of the Etoile entailed, and still entails, in competition with other recollections, ideological stakes of the utmost significance in that it involves the battle between political protagonists—a battle recognizable by the joint effect of polemics, censorship, and forgetfulness, and by its hold on the learned discourse. That recollection interfered with the struggle for influence that conditioned the alignments and realignments, the alliances and mismatches, that marked the restructuring of the ruling elite after independence. Thus, there are as many readings of the ENA as there are readers, as many forms of rejection and of rehabilitation as there are viewpoints. "Liberal" according to Khaled, "Islamist" according to Ben Badis, "communist" according to Hadj Ali, the various memories of the Etoile compete for the crumbs of legitimacy conceded by the history of the FLN and the verdict of November 1954.

Everything took place as if academic history had created the historiographical reassessment of the 1970s on the basis of a conflict of recovered memory (Messali versus the Communist Party, Khaled versus the ulama), deliberately resorting to the classic techniques of modern history, but without the ability to distance itself from the intellectual tools used in the process, much less to bring to light a sort of preexisting historiographical subconsciousness, somewhere between total recall and amnesia, the "writing of history" and giving birth to "political mythology."[69]

Sizing up this problem a decade later, historians recognized the need for a radical revision of the questions being asked and the methods being pursued. Forging ahead in the company of anthropologists, linguists, and social scientists, they initiated new ways of utilizing source materials and new ways of thinking in a process reminiscent of what the *Annales* school had once achieved. The importance of their contributions, and those of their predecessors, in creating Algeria's image of itself suggests that the time is now ripe to plunge headlong into a full-scale history of Algerian historiography.

## Notes

1. *Penser la révolution française* (Paris: Gallimard, 1978).

2. Regarding entanglement with myths, see Claude Levi-Strauss, *Race et histoire* (Paris: Gallimard, 1987) and *De près et de loin* (Paris: Odile Jacob, 1988). On the irreducible dimension of belief, see Michel de Certeau, *La faiblesse de croire* (Paris: Le Seuil, 1987).

3. On the power of an event, see, for example, Pierre Chaunu on the idea of the "turning point" in *Histoire, science sociale* (Paris: Sèdes, 1974). Georges Dumézil talks about the survival of perceptual structures in *Mythe et épopée*, vol. I: *L'idéologie des trois fonctions dans les épopées des peuples indo-européens* (2d ed.; Paris: Gallimard, 1974).

4. On this topic, see Marc Auge, "La réligion entre magie et philosophie," in *Afrique plurielle, Afrique actuelle. Homage à Georges Balandier,* Emmanuel Terray, ed. (Paris: Karthala, 1986), and Alphonse Dupront, *Du sacré. Croisades et pélerinages. Images et langage* (Paris: Gallimard, 1987).

5. Jean Bottero, *Naissance de Dieu. La Bible et l'historien* (Paris: Gallimard, 1986) and *Mésopotamie* (Paris: Gallimard, 1987). Clearly, however, the matter is more complex. The cyclical vision of history, although it still survives, has largely been replaced by an ethnocentrist and evolutionist vision of progress based on the physics of Galileo and the naturalism of Darwin. On the changes in paradigms, see T. S. Kuhn, *The Structure of Scientific Revolutions* (3d ed.; Chicago, University of Chicago Press, 1996).

6. By the same token, some would encourage religious history to remain faithful to its promise, its baptism, and its book. See Elise Marientas, *Les mythes fondateurs de la nation américaine* (Paris: Complexe, 1991).

7. On the Emir Khaled, grandson of ʿAbd al-Qadir, see Charles-Robert Ageron, "Enquête sur les origines du nationalisme algérien. L'Emir Khaled, petit-fils d'Abdelkader, fut-il le premier nationaliste algérien?," *ROMM* (2d semester 1966), pp. 9–49. See also Mahfoud Kaddache, "L'activité politique de l'Emir Khaled entre 1919 et 1925," in *Revue d'histoire et de civilisation du Maghreb* [in Arabic] (January 1968), pp. 19–39; and "L'Emir Khaled (1875–1936). Un maillon de la résistance algérienne," in *Les Africains* (vol. IV; Paris: Jeune Afrique, 1977). A discussion of the subject was renewed in 1980 in *Algérie actualité* with contributions by Charles-Robert Ageron (March 6–12), Abdelkader Boutaleb (April 24–30), Abdelkader Djeghloul (March 27–April 2), and Zouheir Ihaddadene (March 13–19). The last word on the subject is now the book by Gilbert Meynier and Ahmed Koulaksiss, *L'Emir Khaled, premier zaim. Identité algérienne et colonialisme français* (Paris: L'Harmattan, 1987).

8. Jean-Louis Carlier, "La première étoile nord-africaine," in *Revue algérienne des sciences juridiques, politiques, et économiques,* no. 4 (1972),

pp. 907–966. See also Aboul-Kassem Saadallah, *al-Haraka al-wataniyya al-jaza'riyya 1900–1930* [The Algerian Nationalist Movement, 1900–1930] (Beirut: Dar al-Adab, 1969). A revised version subsequently appeared in French, *La montée du nationalisme algérien* (Algiers: ENAL, 1983).

9. Carl Schmidt, *Notion de politique théorique du partisan* (Paris: Calman Lévy, 1972).

10. André Nouschi, *La naissance du nationalisme algérien* (Paris: Editions de Minuit, 1962).

11. See, for example, "La Campagne communiste contre l'Afrique française: Le Congrès anti-coloniale de Bruxelles et les revendications de l'Etoile Nord-Africaine," in *Bulletin du Comité de l'Afrique française* XXXVII, no. 6 (June 1927), pp. 226–235.

12. Charles-Robert Ageron, "Le mouvement jeune algérien de 1900 à 1923," *Etudes maghrébines. Mélanges C.-A. Julien* (Paris: PUF, 1964), pp. 217–243.

13. As for the indifference of public opinion and the "Commission Coloniale" of the Socialist Party (formally, the SFIO, an acronym for Section Française de l'Internationale Ouvrière), see Daniel Guérin, *Au service des colonisés* (Paris: Editions de Minuit, 1954). In the same vein, see Charles-Robert Ageron, "Les colonies devant l'opinion publique française (1919–1939)," originally published in mimeographed form as *Cahiers de l'Institut d'histoire de la presse et de l'opinion*, no. 1 (1972–73), and reprinted in *Revue Française d'histoire d'outre-mer* LXXVII, no. 286 (1st trimester, 1990), pp. 31–73. Also by Ageron is "L'exposition coloniale de 1931—mythe républicain ou mythe impérial?," in *Les lieux de mémoire*, Pierre Nora, ed., (Paris: Gallimard, 1984). See also Raoul Girardet, *L'idée coloniale en France, 1871–1962* (Paris: La Table Ronde, 1973).

14. Maurice Viollette, *L'Algérie vivra-t-elle? Notes d'un ancien gouverneur* (Paris: Félix Alcan, 1931). Also worth noting is the slightly later work of Jean Melia, *Le triste sort des indigènes musulmans en Algérie* (Paris: Mercure de France, 1935).

15. Rouzé wrote in *Oran républicain* about those elections. On the PPA in the Oran region, see Fouad Soufi, "Le PPA en Oranie," *Revue algérienne des sciences juridiques, politiques et économiques* XV, no. 4 (December 1978), pp. 169–195.

16. N. D'Orient and M. Loew, *La question algérienne* (Paris: Bureau d'Editions, 1936).

17. Robert Montagne, "La fermentation des partis politiques en Algérie," *Politique étrangère* (April 1937), pp. 124–147.

18. Jacques Ladreit de Lacharrière, *La crise de l'Afrique du Nord, le péril et les remèdes* (Paris: n.p., 1935).

19. This observation accords with those made about the shunning of Islam by Durkheim and his disciples in Fanny Colonna, "L'Islam

évité: les Durkheimiens et le Musée de l'homme," in *Le Monde arabe et l'entre-deux guerres dans la vision de l'historiographie de la production intellectuelle arabe. Actes du séminaire.* (Oran: URASC, 1990), pp. 46–59.

20. Hildebert Isnard, "Aux origines du nationalisme algérien," *AESC* IV (1949), pp. 463–474; Sylvain Wisner, *L'Algérie dans l'impasse; démission de la France!* (Paris: Editions Spartacus, 1949); and Paul Emile Sarrasin, *La crise algérienne* (Paris: Editions du Cerf, 1949).

21. André Mandouze, "Impossibilités algériennes ou le mythe des trois départements," *Esprit* XV, no. 7 (July 1947), 10–30; and "Le dilemme algérien: suicide ou salut public," *Esprit* XVI, no. 10 (October 1948), pp. 535–566.

22. Charles-André Julien, *L'Afrique du Nord en marche* (Paris: Julliard, 1952; 3d ed., 1972). This distinguished historian liked to recall, as he did in the preface to the third edition, that "one of the most revered leaders of the FLN, Larbi Ben M'hidi, once gave [this] book to a young rebel so that he could know the history of his country." Even today, attempts to write a comparative history of the three countries of the Maghrib are rare. Perhaps the most successful of them is Abdallah Laroui's brilliant and daring synthesis encompassing the totality of Maghribi history, *Histoire du Maghreb: un essai de synthèse* (Paris: Maspero, 1976).

23. See, for example, Louis Massignon, *Opera Minora* (Beirut: Dar el-Maaref, 1963). This attitude was reflected not only in "committed" Christian, Marxist, or progressive reviews such as *Esprit* or *Les Temps modernes,* but also in such prestigious publications as Gallimard's *Nouvelle revue française.*

24. Julien, *L'Afrique du Nord en marche,* p. 101. Julien later modified his initial assessment out of a concern for intellectual integrity, but no doubt mistakenly. See, in the bibliography of the 1972 edition, p. 381.

25. Ibid., pp. 106–107.

26. Ibid., p. 259.

27. On these questions, see Omar Carlier, "La production sociale de l'image de soi. Note sur la crise berbériste de 1949," *Annuaire de l'Afrique du Nord* XXIII (1984), pp. 347–371; and "Aux origines du FLN, l'organisation secrète du PPA (1947–1950). Violence coloniale et mystique insurrectionnelle" (Oran: URASC, 1987), a revised version of which is in the University of Oran's *Majallat at-tarikh,* no. 1.

28. Albert Paul Lentin, "De Bugeaud à Borgeaud, ou l'Algérie sous le signe des ultras," *Cahiers internationaux,* no. 77 (1956), pp. 43–60; and Colette and Francis Jeanson, *L'Algérie hors la loi* (Paris: Editions de Minuit, 1955).

29. Charles-Robert Ageron, *Les Algériens musulmans et la France, 1871–1919* (2 vols.; Paris: PUF, 1968); Gilbert Meynier, *L'Algérie révélée, la guerre de 1914–18 et le premier quart du siècle* (Paris: Droz, 1981);

Mahfoud Kaddache, *Histoire du nationalisme algérien. Question nationale et politique algérienne, 1919–1951* (2 vols.; Algiers: SNED, 1980); and Jacques Berque, *Le Maghreb entre deux guerres* (Paris: Le Seuil, 1979). For a critique of colonial anthropology, see Jean-Claude Vatin and Philippe Lucas, *L'Algérie des anthropologues* (Paris: Maspero, 1974).

30. Xavier Yacono, *La colonisation dans les plaines du Chélif, de Lavigerie au confluent de la Mina* (2 vols.; Algiers: E. Imbert, 1955–1956); Pierre Boyer, *L'évolution de l'Algérie médiane de 1830 à 1956* (Paris: Maisonneuve, 1960). As early as 1950, see Hildebert Isnard, *La réorganisation de la propriété rurale dans la Mitidja* (Algiers: A. Joyeux, 1939).

31. Roger Le Tourneau, *L'Evolution politique de l'Afrique du Nord musulmane, 1920–1961* (Paris: Armand Colin, 1962).

32. Jean-Claude Vatin, *L'Algérie politique: histoire et société* (Paris: Fondation Nationale des Sciences Politiques, 1974).

33. Omar Carlier, "Mémoire, mythe et doxa de l'état: L'Etoile Nord-Africaine et la réligion du 'Watan'," *XXème Siècle,* no. 30 (1991), pp. 82–91.

34. Several other short studies by the same author have exercised a considerable influence over the whole nationalist generation, and especially the PPA militants of the 1940s and 1950s. See Mohamed Chérif Sahli, *Décoloniser l'Histoire: Introduction à l'histoire du Maghreb* (Paris: Maspero, 1965); *Le message de Jugurtha* (Algiers: Imprimerie Générale, 1947); and *Abdelkader, chevalier de la foi* (Algiers: En-Nahda, 1953); but also *L'Algérie accuse: Le calvaire du peuple algérien* (Algiers: En-Nahda, 1949). This, of course, echoes Zola's *J'accuse* and Tha'albi's *La Tunisie martyre* of 1920.

35. Malek Bennabi, *Vocation de l'islam* (Paris: Editions du Seuil, 1954). Similar themes appear in such earlier writings of Bennabi as *Discours sur les conditions de la renaissance algérienne. Le Problème d'une civilisation* (Algiers: En-Nahda, 1949). It should be noted that Bennabi and Sahli shared the same Algerian publisher, En-Nahda. For a study of Bennabi's thought, see Allan Christelow, "An Islamic Humanist in the 20th-Century, Malik Bennabi," in *The Maghreb Review* XVII, nos. 1–2 (1992), pp. 69–83.

36. Ben Cheneb represented the best of the writers and scholars among the hundreds of teachers and madrasa students, who had grown far more numerous than they had been during the first four decades of the century. It was from their ranks that several scholars of the generation coming of age with independence (Lacheraf and Kaddache, for example) would come.

37. Twenty years separated their works from Abderrahmane Djilali, *Ta'rikh al-Jaza'ir al-'am* (2 vols.; Algiers: Dar al-Thaqafa, 1982). Discussions of al-Madani and al-Mili appear in Saadeddine Bencheneb, "Quelques historiens arabes modernes de l'Algérie," *Revue africaine* C

(1956), pp. 475–499. Desparmet had already approached the subject in "Naissance d'une histoire nationale de l'Algérie," in *Bulletin du Comité de l'Afrique Française* XLIII, no. 8 (July 1933), pp. 387–392.

38. Ali Merad, *Le réformisme musulman en Algérie de 1925 à 1940* (Paris: Mouton, 1967).

39. See Gilbert Grandguillaume, *Arabisation et politique linguistique au Maghreb* (Paris: Maisonneuve et Larose, 1963); Gérard Geneste, "L'arabisation des sciences sociales et humaines en Algérie (unpublished doctoral dissertation, 3ème cycle, Université de Lyon, 1983); and Mustapha Haddab, "Arabisation de l'enseignement des sciences et mutation dans le champ sociolinguistique en Algérie," *Annuaire de l'Afrique du Nord* XXIII (1984), pp. 99–104.

40. Carlier, "Mémoire, mythe et doxa."

41. Raymond Boudon, *The Unintended Consequences of Social Action* (New York: St. Martin's Press, 1982), esp. chapter 2.

42. Mostefa Lacheraf, *L'Algérie, nation et société* (Paris: Maspero, 1965).

43. Ibid., pp. 192–193 for Khaled; pp. 195, 196, and 198 for the later parties.

44. On this, see Abdelkader Yefsah, *Le processus de légitimation du pouvoir militaire et la construction de l'état en Algérie* (Paris: Editions Anthropos, 1982); Ramdane Redjala, *L'opposition en Algérie depuis 1962* (Paris: L'Harmattan, 1982); and Mohamed Harbi, *Le FLN, mirage et réalité* (Paris: Editions Jeune Afrique, 1980).

45. Vatin discusses this issue in a revised edition of *L'Algérie politique: Histoire et société* (Paris: Presses de la Fondation Nationale des Sciences Politiques, 1983), pp. 342–348. The matter of continuity or discontinuity in the transition from the ENA to the PPA has often been overlooked. The author's work has repeatedly underlined the discontinuous aspects, and Fouad Soufi presented a paper on "L'Etoile Nord-Africaine" at a conference at the Centre Culturel Algérien in Paris in 1987 that also addresses the subject. As to the relation between "good" and "evil," the strength and virulence of the dispute can be measured by the contradictory and intensely polemical terminologies that affect both militants' memories and the media's interpretations of rival groups' official doctrines.

46. Ferhat Abbas, *La nuit coloniale* (Paris: Julliard, 1962), pp. 136–137.

47. Mohamed Lebjaoui, *Vérités sur la révolution algérienne.* (Paris: Gallimard, 1970).

48. On the coincidence of views between Ouzegane and Lacheraf, see Amar Ouzegane, *Le meilleur combat* (Paris: Julliard, 1962, p. 195). For Ouzegane's differences with Lacoste, see p. 174, n. 2, where he quotes from Yves Lacoste, "L'Afrique du Nord," *Documents EDSCO*, no. 61 (1957).

49. See Carlier, "Mémoire, mythe, et doxa."

50. An analysis of the Algerian political system after independence appears in Jean Leca and Jean Claude Vatin, *L'Algérie politique* (Paris: Presses de la Fondation Nationale des Sciences Politiques, 1975). On the cultural revolution, see pp. 258–262 and also Paul Balta, *La stratégie de Boumédienne* (Paris: Sindbad, 1978). Another overview of postindependence politics is Houari Addi, "Etat et pouvoir dans les sociétés du Tiers-Monde: Le cas de l'Algérie" (unpublished dissertation, Ecole des Hautes Etudes en Sciences Sociales, 1987).

51. See Grandguillaume, *Arabisation et politique linguistique;* Geneste, "L'arabisation des sciences sociales," and Haddab, "Arabisation de l'enseignement." For an opposite view, see Ahmed Rouadjia, *Les frères et la mosquée: Enquête sur le mouvement islamiste en Algérie* (Paris: Karthala, 1990).

52. Carlier, "La première Etoile Nord-Africaine." Julien's characterization is in *L'Afrique du nord en marche*, p. 106. In fact, the expression had already been used by Roger Le Tourneau in a lecture given in 1951.

53. Jean-Louis Carlier, "Individu, groupe et propagandisme. Le procès de politisation de l'émigration algérienne en France entre les deux guerres," (Diplôme des études supérieures, Faculté des Sciences Politiques, Université d'Alger, 1976).

54. The earlier work is Mohammed Harbi, *Aux origines du FLN: La Scission du PPA-MTLD* (Paris: Christian Bourgeois, 1975); his later book is *Le FLN, mirage et réalité, des origines à la prise du pouvoir* (Paris: Editions Jeune Afrique, 1980).

55. This occurred under the joint influence of structuralism, inspired by the linguistics of Michel Foucault and Gilles Deleuze in philosophy and of Louis Althusser in Marxism. For the opposite view, see Perry Anderson, *Arguments Within English Marxism* (London: Verso, 1980); Michael Kelly, *Modern French Marxism* (Baltimore: Johns Hopkins University Press, 1982); and especially Tony Judt, *Le marxisme et la gauche française* (Paris: Hachette, 1987).

56. *Les Archives de la révolution algérienne* (Paris: Editions Jeune Afrique, 1981), collected and analyzed by Mohammed Harbi, is a fundamental documentary source.

57. The fact remains, however, that Egypt was compelled to react to a similar problem of foreign occupation thirty years earlier. The considerable bibliography on this subject includes the diary of al-Jabarti, *Journal d'un notable du Caire durant l'expédition française* (Paris: Albin Michel, 1979). For other references, see Gilbert Delanoue, "Moralistes et politiques musulmans dans l'Egypte du XIXème siècle, 1798–1882" (unpublished doctoral diss., University of Paris IV, 1977).

58. A study of the uneven development of political history research

at the Université d'Alger Faculté des Lettres and the Faculté de Droit would prove extremely useful and would certainly reveal the decisive impulse given by Professors Gallissot, Collot, and Vatin. Among the studies for the Diplôme d'Etudes Supérieures in political science that deal directly with the political history of contemporary Algeria are Abderrahim Taleb-Bendiab, "Le Congrès musulman algérien" (1973); Youcef Beghoul, "Les amis du Manifeste et de la Liberté" (1974); Ben Yelles, "Les courants fascistes de la colonie de peuplement européenne, 1919–1939" (1975); Jean-Louis Carlier, "Le procès de politisation de l'émigration algérienne en France entre les deux guerres" (1976); Ada Foughali, "L'idée de Révolution en Algérie" (1976); Said Chikhi, "L'UGTA 1969–1973" (1977); and Mustapha Messaoudi, "A propos de l'évolution de l'UGTA" (1977). To these must be added the Doctorat d'Etat dissertation of Mohamed Chafik Mesbah, "Idéologie politique et mouvement national en Algérie. Des projets partisans au projet de renaissance nationale, 1936–1956," (1981).

During the same decade there were only two Diplômes d'Etudes Supérieures studies in political history at the Faculté des Lettres, one by Fouad Soufi on the *Oran républicain* (1976); the other by Mohamed Laidi, also on a newspaper, *Liberté,* and the PCA from 1943 to 1947 (1977). A thesis by Redouane Ainad Tabet on the events of May 8, 1945, was defended in the Department of Philosophy and another by Omar Hachi, "Le problème des mouvements nationaux Algériens à travers la presse, 1950–1954" (1980), was written for the Department of French.

59. Kamel Bouguessa, "Emigration et politique. Essai sur la formation et la politisation de la communauté algérienne en France à l'entre deux guerres" (unpublished diss., 3ème cycle, Université de Paris VI, 1979); and M'Barka Hamed "Immigration maghrébine et activités politiques en France, de la première guerre mondiale à la veille du Front Populaire" (unpublished diss., 3ème cycle, Université de Paris VII, 1979). My own attempts to consult the documents of the commission coloniale in the course of my research were repeatedly frustrated by uncooperative officials.

60. Mohamed Chafik Mesbah, "Idéologie politique et mouvement national en Algérie. Des projets partisans au projet de renaissance nationale 1936–1956" (unpublished Doctorat d'Etat, Science Politique, Université d'Alger, 1981).

61. EDITOR'S NOTE: The political upheavals experienced by Algeria during the 1990s have prompted many intellectuals, particularly those with secularist leanings, to leave the country, effectively depriving Algerian universities of some of their most talented and promising faculty.

62. See, for example, Warda Tengour, *La Fin des medersas ou la rai-*

*son d'une aventure coloniale, Tlemcen et Constantine 1850–1880* (Oran: URASC, 1988). Tengour has also undertaken some innovative research on the relationship between social questions and land ownership.

63. Mohamed El Korso, "Essai de caractérisation de la démarche politique de l'Association des ulema musulmans algériens de 1925 à 1940," in Ministère de l'Education, Enseignement, et Recherche Scientifique et Centre National Universitaire de Documentation Scientifique et Technique, *Les Mouvements politiques et sociaux dans la Tunisie des années* 1930 (Tunis: MEERS-CNUDST, 1987), pp. 743–797.

64. On the first of these interests, see Fouad Soufi, "Les Mouvements sociaux en Oranie (1930–1935)," in Ministère de l'Education, Enseignement, et Recherche Scientifique et Centre National Universitaire de Documentation Scientifique et Technique, *Les Mouvements politiques et sociaux dans la Tunisie des années 1930* (Tunis: MEERS-CNUDST, 1987), pp. 569–596; on the second, see "Les Archives et l'histoire régionale," *Majallat al-Tarikh*, no. 19 (1985), pp. 29–40.

65. Houari Touati, *Dictionnaire biographique sur le mouvement ouvrier maghrébin* (Oran: Centre de Recherches et d'Informations Documentaires en Sciences Sociales et Humaines [CRIDSSH], 1983). Touati's dissertation on "Economie, société et acculturation. L'Oranie colonialisée, 1881–1937" (2 vols.; Université de Nice, 1984), leans towards the *Annales* tradition with its research on historic and religious anthropology. See his "Approche sociologique et historique d'un document biographique algérien," *AESC*, no. 5 (September–October 1989), 1205–1228.

66. Omar Carlier, "Espace politique et socialité juvénile. La parole étoiliste en ses quartiers. Contribution à une étude de l'incorporation de nous," in *Lettres, intellectuels, militants en Algérie, 1880–1950* (Algiers: Office des Publications Universitaires, 1987). On the question of socialization and the loci of sociability see Omar Carlier (with the considerable influence of the work of Maurice Agulhon), "Le café maure—Sociabilité masculine et effervescence citoyenne—Algérie 17ème-20ème siècles," *AESC*, no. 4 (1990), pp. 975–1003.

67. See Abdelfatah Kilito, *L'auteur et ses doubles: Essai sur la culture arabe classique* (Paris: Le Seuil, 1985) and Léo Strauss, *La cité et l'homme* (Paris: Agora, 1987).

68. On Maghribi hagiography, see Jacques Berque, *L'intérieur du Maghreb* (Paris: Gallimard, 1978); and his *Ulémas, fondateurs, insurgés du Maghreb* (Paris: Sindbad, 1982).

69. See Raoul Girardet, *Mythologies politiques* (Paris: Grasset, 1987); Claude Lefort, *Les formes de l'histoire. Essai d'anthropologie politique* (Paris: Gallimard, 1978); and Michel de Certeau, *L'écriture de l'histoire* (Paris: Gallimard, 1975).

# PART III

# Theoretical Issues
# and Case Studies

The question of methodology has for some time haunted the study of Middle Eastern and North African history. Although often reluctant to admit it, historians in these fields have tended to feel as though they were the mere country cousins of historians charting various methodological breakthroughs in the areas of European and American history. To add insult to perceived injury, scholars engaged in the study of things Islamic have had to endure a variety of aspersions: they were "philologists masquerading as historians," or they were "area-studies experts" lacking the requisite formal training in the discipline of history. Furthermore, many have had to live with the label of "Orientalist" or "neoimperialist," consciously or unconsciously applied.

The current generation of historians engaged in the study of the Maghrib has witnessed a radical change not only in the political outlook of those working in the field, but also in the methodologies used. It is now much more common to find scholars of the Maghrib pursuing social history, conducting anthropological field work, digging at various archeological sites, or busy with their computers adapting some theoretical model toward an understanding of the complex economic history of the region. The change is due to two forces. The first is the social science revolution of the 1960s, in large part the work of American scholars. Developments in this arena prompted area-studies experts to adapt, modify, challenge, or discard social-science theories developed in the study of western societies to their own fields. More directly related to the study of history, the second influence is that of the *Annales* school of history, which called for the revamping of the historical agenda and the study of society from the bottom up. Over time, straight political history, which was the stock-in-trade of many Maghribi historians, has yielded to new areas of history: urban, class, cultural, popular religious, and the like.

The effects of the "new history" on the study of the Maghrib have been profound, coming as they do on the heels of irreversible political and intellectual changes in the region itself. The most obvious change has been an emphasis on discovering and putting to systematic use new archival sources: not only the archives of Europe, but also the numerous state, religious, and private archives that have accumulated over the centuries in Morocco, Algeria, Tunisia, and Libya. It was once common to hear historians of the Maghrib declare that European history was unique because of the richness of its archives. Now historians of North Africa must readily admit that there is a wealth of evidence that they have yet to exploit or appreciate.

A second effect of the new history has been the reassessment of all aspects of Maghribi social and economic history. Some fifty years ago, historians of North Africa typically viewed Islam as the common denominator of the region: a force which shaped and often leveled society in such a way that history and life throughout the Islamic world had certain given features. These included a powerful state, an army divorced from society, and a mass of people held hostage to a popular religion—riddled with superstition and at the mercy of religious leaders. But the nineteenth-century emphasis on structure and synthesis has given way to a lively and engaging intellectual chaos. Present-day historians of the Maghrib have a keen appreciation for the significance of diversity and regional differences within countries, cultures, and outlooks. The judgments of our historian forefathers upon the Maghribi past now seem much less formidable and have become the subject of endless attacks, revisions, and modifications.

This final section takes note, then, of some of the effects of the new history on the historiography of the Maghrib. Ronald Messier surveys the state of the medieval history of the Maghrib and shows how new methodologies, especially archeology, have served to reframe a host of questions from the nature of the Hilali invasions to the impact of the trans-Saharan gold trade—and the role of the town of Sijilmasa in that commerce. Sami Bergaoui shows the promise of new archival sources for the study of nineteenth- and twentieth-century Tunisian social history and suggests several revisions about the nature of land tenure. Abderrahmane El Moudden explains why historians of Morocco have neglected the eighteenth century and proposes a new fashion of looking at the chronology of precolonial Moroccan history. Finally, Julia Clancy-Smith considers migrants and social marginals as conduits between Europe and the Maghrib in a variety of capacities. All of these contributions seek to show how existing materials can be put to new and innovative use in redefining some of the social categories of the Maghrib and Mediterranean.

# Rereading Medieval Sources
## through Multidisciplinary Glasses

*Ronald A. Messier*
Middle Tennessee State University

### REREADING IBN KHALDUN

Ibn Khaldun was a fourteenth-century historian/sociologist and the first thinker to offer a serious theory regarding the formation of cities. Since his time, historians of the medieval Maghrib have been concerned with the formation of cities and central authority, and with identity based on one's tribal or sectarian affiliation or one's means of earning a living. Being a "modern" historian ahead of his time, Ibn Khaldun, in his *Muqaddimah*,[1] set forth theories that addressed these issues. For example, he talks about the formation and "life span" of dynasties and describes the transition of dynasties from desert life to sedentary culture. When the ruling dynasty is in a state of decline, new dynasties take its place in two ways: provincial governors within the dynasty gain control over remote regions, or a rival from among the neighboring nations and tribes challenges the dynasty.[2] Elsewhere, Ibn Khaldun presents a theory concerning the relationship between the formation of cities and central authority. He asserts that cities are the secondary products of central authority and that the size of cities, their citadels, and their monuments are proportional to the importance, longevity, and jurisdiction of the ruling dynasty.[3] He also describes the various ways of earning a living for a sedentary population, establishing the link between crafts, long-distance trade, and urbanization.[4]

Historians have been testing these theories ever since Ibn Khaldun promulgated them in the fourteenth century. Some have accepted Ibn Khaldun's assessment of the invasion of the nomadic Arabs of the Bani Hilal as a turning point in the history of the Maghrib, with respect to the various processes listed above. Ibn Khaldun writes that the Hilalians ravaged the countryside and "like an army of grasshoppers . . . destroyed everything in their path."[5]

In the twentieth century, a long line of scholars have read this literally, from Georges Marçais, who wrote: "The totality of North African life will be profoundly and permanently affected by the catastrophe [the Hilalian invasion]," [6] to Charles-André Julien, who found the Hilalian invasion to be "undoubtedly the most important event of the entire medieval period in the Maghrib. It was that invasion, far more than the Muslim conquest, that transformed the Maghrib for centuries. Before the Hilalians, the country— Islam apart—had remained profoundly Berber in language and custom. . . . The Bedouin brought with them their language . . . the source of most of the rural Arabic dialects spoken in North Africa today." [7]

This traditional view of the disastrous consequences of the Hilalian invasion was challenged in 1967 by Jean Poncet, who ascribed the collapse to internal factors.[8] Over a decade later, Michael Brett described the "invasion" as legend. He viewed its impact more as a "stage in the Arabization of the region. . . . It may be that they were themselves the product of Arabization to a greater degree than has heretofore been recognized, and that their influence upon the culture of North Africa was more indirect than the concept of their sudden arrival in 1051 would suppose." [9]

Brett criticized Julien, not so much for his literal reading of Ibn Khaldun regarding the Bani Hilal, but rather because he "sets out the syndrome of the Muslim Middle Ages doomed to failure." Starting with the impress of the "oriental" religion of Islam, according to Brett, Julien's Berber "'dough,' fitfully leavened, but incapable of original or permanent political achievement," was deactivated by the destructive Arab nomad.[10]

Jamil Abun-Nasr, in the first (1971) edition of his History of the Maghrib, established a model of the medieval period avowedly based on Ibn Khaldun and his interpreters. He invoked five principles:

> the rise and fall of dynasties from the brotherhood of the desert to the demoralization of the city; religious doctrines as instruments of cohesion; the equation of the city with the state; the suggestion that the only kinds of political legitimacy known before the spread of European influence were the tribal and the Islamic; and the notion of Islam as an urban religion which encourages political centralization.[11]

Brett was dissatisfied with Julien's perception of the medieval period as one of political stagnation, as well as with Abun-Nasr's perception of Islam as a positive influence on behalf of the central government—and both for the same reason. Like Ibn Khaldun, both were too concerned with the central power.

Sixteen years later, in 1987, Abun-Nasr published a substantially revised work entitled History of the Maghrib in the Islamic Period which included an expanded, rewritten, and recast account of the Middle Ages. This volume displayed a new emphasis on social and intellectual history, on the role and personalities of the major cities, and on the complex process of Islamization. There was more coverage of the Fatimids, the Berber dynasties, and Spain, as well as a greater interest in economics than there had been in either the first or the second (1975) edition. A section on the economic role of Qayrawan (p. 58) shows how the production of cereals, olives, dates, and animal products increased internal trade, leading the city to develop from an internal to an external commercial center that linked the Maghrib with the Mashriq and, "like Tahart, Sijilmasa, and Fez . . . was an emporium of the trans-Saharan trade." This information is accompanied by the addition to the bibliography of al-Habib al-Janhani's book on social and economic life in the medieval Maghrib, a study that had garnered high praise as a pioneering work in Arabic utilizing themes and methods developed by the highly respected *Annales* school.[12]

Abun-Nasr revised his date for the founding of Marrakesh, from 1062 in the first and second editions (p. 96 in both) to 1070 in the 1987 work (p. 83), as a result of the addition of Deverdun's work on Marrakesh.[13] He also included both Poncet's and Brett's work on the Hilalian invasion in the bibliography of *History of the Maghrib in the Islamic Period,* somewhat toning down his original interpretation of the negative effects of the Bani Hilal. He omitted the following statement which had appeared in the first and second editions: "The result of the Bedouin domination in the greater part of the Maghrib was a state of anarchy; and as happened in Spain after the disintegration of the Umayyad state, small city states appeared to fill the political gap" (p. 86 in both). However, from the same passage he still retained in the 1987 book the sentence: "One permanent effect which the Hilalian invasion had on Ifriqiyya was that of spreading knowledge of the Arabic language in the countryside instead of it remaining limited to the towns" (p. 70).

A general survey of the Maghrib that more closely approaches the revisionist interpretation is Abdallah Laroui's *History of the Maghrib, an Interpretive Essay,* which appeared in an English edition in 1977, a decade before Abun-Nasr's third edition. Laroui presents a Maghribi viewpoint of the history of his own country and its region. Without denying the effects of the Bani Hilal, he seeks to understand those effects in terms of the preexisting conditions in the Maghrib that made them possible. He sees the conflict that developed between the Bani Hilal and the urban populations of Ifriqiyya as having resulted from "a more and more desperate competition for the profits of a waning trade. It resulted from a special situation, very different from that existing in such cities as Tahart, Sijilmasa, Tlemcen, and Aghmat, where the profits of an active commerce were sufficient to satisfy both the masters of the roads and the masters of the cities" (pp. 155–56).

In acknowledging that the endogenous factors favoring his chosen interpretation had not been isolated and analyzed in a satisfactory way, Laroui admitted that the literature provides both sides with arguments. The controversy goes on, and not only regarding the effects of the Bani Hilal invasion. The interrelationships among all the theories of Ibn Khaldun that were listed at the beginning of this essay are in need of constant review.

What might lead to more conclusive analyses of some of these issues is still another critical rereading of the medieval texts that historians have scoured for generations. But such a rereading will more than likely lead us to the same conclusions we have reached in the past, unless it is done with a new set of glasses, a new perspective. New knowledge might yet come with the discovery of new texts, as when, in the late 1950s, recovered portions of Ibn 'Idhari's *al-Bayan al-Mughrib fi akhbar muluk al-Andalus wa-l-Maghrib*[14] provided a new basis for examining chronicles of Almoravid history. There is, for example, some confusion in the sources concerning the date of, as well as the person responsible for, the founding of Marrakesh. Both Ibn Abi Zar' and Ibn Khaldun place this in 454/1062 and attribute it to Yusuf Ibn Tashfin. In fact, both sources agree that this took place after Abu Bakr appointed Yusuf as his lieutenant in the Maghrib while he himself returned to the Sahara to quell a rebellion. Ibn 'Idhari and the anonymous author of *al-Hulal al-mawshiyya fi dhikr al-akhbar al-marrakushiyya* agree on the date 463/1070 for the founding of the city and on the role of Abu Bakr in choosing the site and laying the foundation before leaving for the Sahara in the following year. Writing in 1067–68, al-Bakri makes no reference whatsoever to Marrakesh. Since he is so thorough and detailed on all other matters, this omission strongly suggests that the city was founded after he wrote and thus favors the date given by Ibn 'Idhari and in *al-Hulal*. The fact that Ibn 'Idhari describes in considerable detail the role of Abu Bakr in the founding of the city, as well as the fact that the portion of the *Bayan* giving this account was discovered relatively recently, both strengthen the argument for the later date.

Several scholars who closely examined the issue in the sixties also favored the later date.[15] More was at stake than merely the precise date of the founding of Marrakesh, for on that date hinges the date for Abu Bakr's final return to the Sahara and the division of the Almoravid empire between the Sahara and the Maghrib with Yusuf Ibn Tashfin in charge of the latter.

How many "new" (that is, yet to be discovered) medieval texts could there be? Vincent J. Cornell says that thousands of manuscripts in both governmental and private collections have come to light describing the lives and political roles of urban and rural religious figures.[16] Abdel Wedoud Ould Cheikh and Bernard Saison describe manuscripts in Tunisia and Morocco which are perhaps attributable to Imam al-Hadrami.[17] A text that would undoubtedly shed new light on Almoravid history is Ibn al-Sayrafi's *Al-anwar al-jaliyya fi akhbar al-dawla-l-murabitiyya.*[18]

## REREADING THE FATAWA

*Fatawa* (plural of *fatwa,* a formal legal opinion based on Islamic law) are increasingly being studied to provide insight into political and social history.[19] A court case from fourteenth-century Fez, for example, that is preserved in the *Kitab al-Mi'yar* of Ahmad al-Wansharisi addresses the status of an endowment established in A.D. 1329 by a certain Fatima bint Muhammad al-Hasani for the perpetual use of her son and his descendants. In the deed, the founder defined a descent strategy whose interpretation became the focus of a dispute among her lineal descendants.

The dispute can be followed over nearly three-quarters of a century, from 1329 to 1390, as various family members contested the rights to endowment revenues. Upon the death of Muhammad I, the endowment's first beneficiary, his son, Muhammad II, had exercised exclusive use of the revenues. Muhammad II's sisters, 'A'isha and Sawanna, did not establish a claim to the endowment during their lifetimes. On the death of Muhammad II, his son Abu al-Qasim claimed exclusive control over the endowment, but the latter's cousins Fatima II and Ahmad, children of 'A'isha and Sawanna, claimed their share of the endowment revenues. Each party sought fatawa supporting its own position. Some time before 772/1370, the Mufti Ahmad al-Qabbab put forth a possible legal precedent for the principle of representation (favoring Fatima II and Ahmad) that he found in the *Kitab* of Ibn al-Mawwaz, a ninth-century doctrinal textbook. The soundness of the analogy was corroborated in the fatwa of 772/1370, issued jointly by six muftis in the service of the chief *qadi* (Muslim judge) of Fez. But the fatwa itself was not binding and Abu al-Qasim retained control over the endowment. Five years later, in 777/1375, Ahmad and Fatima II brought their case to the chief qadi himself, al-Fishtali. The qadi also ruled in favor of Ahmad and Fatima, basing his decision not on the previous fatawa issued in connection with this case, but rather on a fatwa of Ibn Rushd, the famous qadi of Cordova, over two centuries earlier. Five years later, Abu al-Qasim appealed his case to the new qadi, al-Awrabi, who reversed al-Fishtali's decision, again giving him exclusive control over the endowment. A full decade later, with still another qadi in office, the children of Ahmad and the husband of Fatima II made another claim—and won.

This case, according to David S. Powers, points

to a more flexible and more complex understanding of the family than is generally acknowledged in the scholarly literature. In practice, the patrilineal model did not always coincide with the demographic history of the family subsequent to the creation of a family endowment. In order to maximize their personal economic benefit, individuals were willing to make concessions to the model by invoking a cognatic link to a remote ancestor. Thus, the notion of the family seems to have been a shifting and fluid concept capable of expanding or contracting in response to changing social and economic factors. In our case, neither Sawanna's son Ahmad, nor any of her five grandchildren, qualified as agnatic descendants of the first beneficiary, Muhammad I. Yet all claimed entitlement to a share of the endowment revenues on the grounds of descent, and their claim was upheld in at least two fatwa-s and two court cases.[20]

Furthermore, the documents provide insight into the decision-making process of Maliki jurists and the evolution of legal doctrines. These documents indicate that "the decision of a Muslim judge was not absolutely binding and that an informal, nonhierarchical system of judicial review existed in fourteenth-century North Africa."[21]

Individual fatawa were often collected in treatises such as the *Kitab al-Mi'yar* of Ahmad al-Wansharisi (d. A.D. 1508). This work contains approximately 6,000 legal opinions that were issued from the eleventh through the fifteenth century by muftis living in Ifriqiyya, Morocco, and Spain.[22] Vincent Lagardère has thoroughly summarized the Andalusian material in the *Mi'yar* for the Almoravid period.[23] Apart from the value of this summary for the legal and social history of the Almoravids, it presents a view of the chief qadi of each major city, the qadi al-qudah, as an official administrator for the Almoravid state, appointed by and exercising authority in the name of the Almoravid amir (prince). In contrast to the Almoravid military governors, who were, for the most part, related to the Almoravid nobility, *qudah* (plural of *qadi*) were professionals highly trained in Maliki law. Most of those who served in Andalusia were Andalusian by birth; many were nominated by a local governor. But, as is clear from a fatwa of Ibn Rushd, the appointment had to be ratified by the amir to legitimate the qadi's position.[24]

As for the dismissal of a qadi, another fatwa of Ibn Rushd explains the procedure. The residents of Algeciras complained about their qadi to the amir Ali Ibn Yusuf, who submitted the complaint to the qadi of Ceuta for judgment. The latter ruled against the Algeciras qadi and recommended his dismissal. When the qadi demanded to know the identity of his accusers, Ibn Rushd issued a fatwa saying that a qadi's "dismissal did not fall under the jurisdiction . . . of witnesses." [25]

The chief qadi of the city was the most powerful and influential official in the entire administrative hierarchy under the Saharan military governor. His stated role was to "direct matters of religion and to protect the Muslim citizens." That rather broad mission gave him jurisdiction over much of the city's life. As head of the judiciary, he was the chief reviewer of the law, and he advised the Almoravid rulers on how to govern in accordance with the edicts of Islamic Law as interpreted by the Maliki school. He was the superintendent of education, setting the standards for the teachers who, in each of the neighborhood mosques, taught the youth to recite the Qur'an and to respect the law. He supervised the treasury and was called upon to ensure that tax assessors and collectors "weighed with a just scale." [26]

Some of the fatawa of these jurists served the specific interests of the Almoravid ruling elite. For example, a question came to Ibn Rushd from the capital of Marrakesh—should the Almoravids be obliged to remove the *litham,* or veil, from their faces when they prayed? Those Almoravid warriors who settled in Marrakesh, as well as in other urban centers in Morocco and Spain, continued the practice of veiling their faces as they had done in the desert. Ibn Rushd ruled that the Almoravids should retain the veil since it set them apart as defenders of the faith and made the people conscious of their presence, all of which discouraged the infidel and contributed to the strength of Islam. [27] Another question from the capital involved the permissibility of insisting on payment in Almoravid dinars. Ibn Rushd ruled in favor of this practice. [28]

## REREADING THE CITY

Ancillary sciences such as archaeology and numismatics or the social and the natural sciences, insofar as they might help us understand the use of resources, especially in those areas where resources are at critical levels, also provide new lenses for rereading texts. Regarding "the Islamic city," Janet Abu Lughod traces the *isnad* (chain of authorities) of what has been done, beginning with William Marçais's 1928 article and continuing through Georges Marçais, Robert Brunschvig, Gustave von Grunebaum, Roger Le Tourneau, and Jacques Berque. [29] She discusses each of the works, seeing as a common problem their tendency to base their generalizations on French North African sources and studies, particularly those focusing on Fez—that is, a series of studies that looked back on each other. She also identifies a second isnad consisting of the works of Jean Sauvaget and, more recently, Ira Lapidus.[30] Sauvaget's studies concentrate on Damascus and Aleppo; Lapidus adds supporting material on the Mamluk capital of Cairo. In each case, a very tentative set of place-specific comments and descriptions appears. Dale Eickelman sees the Lapidus study as a major breakthrough in the study of cities.[31] Whereas other scholars "tended to get bogged down in descriptivism, enumerating the features that appeared to characterize particular Islamic cities or 'the' Islamic city as an ideal type" and "represented the characteristics of towns as enumerated by Muslim theologians,"[32] Lapidus asked a different set of sociological questions. Rather than searching for social forms that were unique to Islamic cities, Lapidus sought to delineate the social forms found in cities which were Muslim by virtue of the predominance of subcommunities embodying Muslim beliefs and a Muslim way of life. Eickelman himself asked what is undoubtedly the most basic question for this discussion in his article "Is There an Islamic City?"[33]

Abu Lughod proposed a method of approaching the fundamental question of why one might expect Islamic cities to be similar and in what ways. First, she suggested looking for elements in city planning that reflect or facilitate distinctions between classes that are juridically distinct in Islam—for example, the residential segregation of the *dhimmi* (practitioners of other monotheistic faiths who were entitled to the protection of the Muslim authorities). Second, one could look for elements that facilitate gender segregation, which might reflect the distinction between private and public space. Neglect was the third way in which Islam shaped the traditional "Islamic" city, with its failure to concern itself with matters of day-to-day maintenance, thereby encouraging the vitality of other substate units such as the neighborhood. In other words, since such public functionaries as market supervisors were concerned with public space, private space enjoyed a large measure of autonomy within the city.

Fredj Stambouli and Abdelkader Zghal in 1976 outlined four discernible patterns of spatial order in precolonial North African cities: the presence of the central power, often represented by a fortified quarter, or *qasba;* a complex of economic activity, the suq; religious institutions, such as mosques and maraboutic shrines (*marabouts* are venerated persons or saints); and residential quarters.[34]

Studies on the cities continued throughout the 1980s.[35] Amar Dhina began his work with the observation that the city "played an important role in the political, religious, intellectual, artistic, and economic domains" of the classical Muslim world. He defined the principal elements of such a city as the mosque, citadel, baths, and markets. The study included a history of some of the major Islamic cities East and West that called attention to these elements.[36]

A very different approach to the "city" is offered by Charles Redman's work at Qsar es-Seghir, which provides a model for comparing the evidence from history and archaeology to trace the chronological development of a Moroccan city through its successive stages.[37]

## REREADING SILENCES

In a very careful examination of the Arabic sources dealing with West Africa during the Almoravid period, from al-Bakri to al-Maqrisi, David Conrad and Humphrey Fisher found none that unambiguously pointed to the conquest of Ghana by the Almoravids.[38] Much of the case in favor of such a conquest is based on the text by al-Zuhri, which says that Ghana became Muslim during the time of the Lamtuna. Ibn Abi Zar', writing in the early fourteenth century, says that the Almoravid Abu Bakr made himself master of the whole region of the desert, raiding the Sudan and conquering much of it, but does not specifically include Ghana in this conquest. Even Ibn Khaldun, who wrote during the period of the three-hundredth anniversary of the alleged conquest, does not specifically state that the Almoravids conquered Ghana, albeit he talks about Ghana extensively in the geographical discussion.

It was actually the lack of textual evidence on which Conrad and Fisher based their case, but as they considered the more than 1,500 extant specimens of Almoravid gold coinage, an amount that Harry Hazard believed reflects "an extraordinary prosperity,"[39] numismatic evidence again suggests an interpretation. Conrad and Fisher suggested that gold in such quantity could not have come from a conquered Ghana. "Dislocation at the center reflected in a reduction of Ghanaian influence on the periphery (where gold was mined) might actually have reduced the flow of gold. . . . It seems more likely that such a flow of trade was based on a relationship of mutual respect and cooperation between Ghana and the gold producers on the one hand and the Almoravids on the other, a relationship cemented now by a common faith, Islam".[40]

The year after Conrad and Fisher published their thesis, Michael Brett affirmed its conclusion.[41] Since that time, the thesis has been repeated so often that its hypotheses have acquired the aura of demonstrated fact, and authors who overlook "The Conquest that Never Was" have been called to task.[42] Quite recently, however, Sheryl L. Burkhalter has challenged Conrad and Fisher, not only turning the basis of their own argument—the ab-

sence of evidence—against them, but making it the basis of her own refutation.[43] She criticizes their interpretation of al-Zuhri's statement on several
specific points.

First, she claims that silencing al-Zuhri's mention of Azuqqi[44] allows Con-
rad and Fisher to skirt the question of how al-Zuhri comes to designate the
Almoravids as living between Sijilmasa and Waraqlan to the east—or more
problematically, between Ghana and Zafun (Qarafun) to its east—when the
Almoravid capital of Azuqqi lies well to the west of both Sijilmasa and Ghana.
They can then intimate that the Almoravids were subordinate to Ghana.[45]

Second, she criticizes the authors' identification of the leader of the *khu-
ruj* (assault) as the amir Abu Yahya al-Massufi who, according to Ibn al-
Khatib, left the Sahara and was appointed governor of Granada by Ali Ibn
Yusuf in 500/1107–08. To do this, Conrad and Fisher have to assume that
al-Zuhri transposed the name from Yahya Ibn Abu Bakr to Abu Yahya.
They must also read "Massufi" as a *nisba* (an adjective denoting descent or
origin) rather than as "Massufa," an *idafa* (appositive phrase) meaning that the
leader was of the Massufi tribe rather than commander over the Massufa.
Finally, they must assume that al-Zuhri mistakenly transposed the date from
469/1076–77 to 496/1103–04, thus making it fit within the time frame of
the man they identify as the leader. Burkhalter, on the other hand, identifies the leader as Yahya, a son of the second Almoravid amir Abu Bakr. Ibn
'Idhari tells us that Abu Bakr had a son named Yahya and that he also had
a second son named Ibrahim. In fact, Ibn 'Idhari is the only source that tells
about Ibrahim's mission to Aghmat in 469 to reclaim the power he felt
Yusuf Ibn Tashfin had usurped from Abu Bakr. Only numismatic evidence
confirms Ibrahim's governorship (his appointment as amir) over Sijilmasa
from 462–467; the texts are silent on his appointment.[46] Could Abu Bakr
have appointed his other son, Yahya, to lead a campaign into Ghana in the
same year that Ibrahim led an expedition to Aghmat—an appointment that
was also silenced in the texts?[47]

Third, Burkhalter challenges Conrad and Fisher's statement that "when
Abu Bakr himself finally got back to the desert, his story ended there not
with a bang but a whimper."[48] She looks very carefully at verb tenses in a
text by Yaqut written in the third quarter of the thirteenth century, or after
the transfer of power from the Almoravids to the Almohads. She notes that
"Yaqut uses the past tense in referring to Almoravid rule in the Maghrib;
yet in referring to the tribal alignment among the Lamtuna, Gudala, and
Massufa, he uses the present tense: the veiled amirs "ruled" the Gharb,
whereas authority "resides" among the Lamtuna." She suggests that "although Almoravid authority gave way to the north, the tribal coalition seems
to continue, in some fashion, at least, to the south." She also points to the

fact that "the numerous tribes cited by Amilhat continued to recount his saga and lay claim to having taken part in his victories."[49] Additionally, there is archeological evidence, such as the tombstone in Gao in the Middle Niger dated in the early twelfth century A.D. Jean Sauvaget has concluded that the inscriptions are closely related to those of Muslim Spain and, more specifically, to the funerary inscriptions of Almeria.[50]

Most interesting of all is Burkhalter's explanation for the "silences" of the medieval Arab authors who focus on the Almoravids in the Maghrib and Andalusia rather than in the Saharan and sub-Saharan regions. For the Maghribi chroniclers, the historically significant unit was the "state," and "the Almoravid state was the Maghrib and Spain as defined over and against, in the words of Ibn Khaldun, 'the various tribes of veil-wearers . . . who stayed in the desert [and] remained in their primitive state of dissension and divergence'" (brackets Burkhalter's). Her strategy of "listening for silences" comes from Donald Moore and Richard Roberts, who apply it in African studies in the belief that "we need to think about the past containing many voices, often discordant ones."[51]

## REREADING THROUGH ANCILLARY SCIENCES

The importance of trade and the significant role of the central authority in the life of the Muslim urban centers has been widely acknowledged. Stambouli and Zghal felt that understanding patterns of trade in the Middle Ages was crucial to understanding cities. "The principal source of wealth in the towns of the precolonial Maghrib was constituted by trade, notably long distance trade, which depended on the stability of the central power and its capacity to control the main trade routes." They add that "the power of the Maghribi states was, therefore, directly linked to the role they assumed in international trade, particularly Mediterranean and trans-Saharan trade," citing Braudel's assertion that "the gold trade caused new towns to arise in the Maghrib and old centers to expand."[52] Laroui's "interpretive essay" placed a similar, if not an even greater, stress on the importance of understanding trade patterns.[53]

Several revisionist studies also suggested valid approaches for looking at long-distance trade. One, by Timothy F. Garrard, set out to determine when the trans-Saharan gold trade actually began.[54] Opinions range over so wide a period—from third century B.C. to tenth century A.D.—as to be of little use.[55] In conjunction with historical texts, Garrard used coins and weights as evidence, concluding that an irregular gold coinage was issued at Carthage from the end of the third century B.C. and that by the end of the fourth century A.D., significant changes in the North African tax system enabled more gold to be collected. The solidus, a coin first issued in 312, provided the standard used in weighing gold dust in the trans-Saharan trade, which was evidently flourishing before the Arab Conquest, since the Byzantine mint at Carthage produced a copious output of gold between 534 and 695.

The Arabs retained the standard based on the Roman ounce and the solidus for weighing gold dust. Indeed, this standard survived until the nineteenth century in the Western Sudan. Garrard's point in using the weights as evidence is that, south of the Sahara, gold dust rather than coins was being weighed. Since gold dust could be apportioned in any quantity, it could always be weighed with the same set of weights. Thus, there was no compelling reason to change the standard after its initial introduction in the region in the fourth century. Standards of weight north of the Sahara, on the other hand, changed a number of times as new systems of coinage appeared.

Garrard was quite correct in saying that historians and archaeologists have demonstrated scant awareness that there was an eighth-century Arab gold coinage struck in North Africa. He acknowledged that some uncertainty remained as to whether the coinage of eighth-century Arab Qayrawan, or of earlier Byzantium, had been struck from gold crossing the desert from West Africa, but he suggested that scientific tests of numismatic evidence could shed more light on this question.[56]

It is clear that historians of the medieval Maghrib can learn much from their colleagues who study West African history and face the same problem of the paucity of textual sources. Ann McDougall, for example, is studying the relationship between local trade and long-distance trade among communities in the southern Sahara. She suggests doing the same thing in a microstudy of Awdaghust. "Finding a window on to this way of life [in the southern Sahara], made obscure by its itinerant nature and the passage of time, is not easy. . . . In this paper [on Awdaghust] an effort is made to meet these challenges by approaching the subject through the history of an oasis where many strands of Saharan life appear to have crossed."[57]

In the late ninth century, Awdaghust was already a prosperous place. The king of the surrounding Sanhaja lived there and by the following century it was the main southern terminus for trade with Sijilmasa. Devisse describes at least seven levels of occupation, dating from the seventh or eighth century to the seventeenth, at the site.[58] There are indications that toward the end of the twelfth century, important streets had been abandoned to encroaching sands and the following occupation (VI), from the end of the twelfth to the end of the fourteenth century, confirms the onset of a process of desertification. The town's physical dimensions shrank considerably and the signs of a general impoverishment are unmistakable. A significant gap exists between the sixth and seventh occupations, suggesting that the town had been abandoned by the fifteenth century and resettled some two centuries later.

According to McDougall, until recently "analyses have shed more light on North African politics and religion, on Sudanic state building and trade, than on local life."[59] For at least the past thirty years, since Raymond Mauny published his *Tableau Géographique,* the emphasis has been on long-distance trade. Trans-Saharan commerce gave birth to southern Saharan towns; the departure of the merchants struck a death blow.[60]

*Tegdaoust III,* however, begins to direct attention towards local factors: "to the impact of a rapidly growing urban community on a rather fragile environment; to the effect of artisanal activity on supplies of wood and water; to the consequences of domestic animals (especially sheep) for local vegetation; and to the interaction of these developments with changes of a broader nature—regional production, trade, and climate."[61] Robert-Chalieux compares each of the occupations under several headings: carbon-14 datings, characteristic elements, most common objects unearthed, pottery industry, metalworking, daily life, imported goods, relations north and south, and relations east and west.[62]

This same kind of systematic analysis is needed for sites north of the Sahara. But most medieval sites north of the desert are currently inhabited, which precludes such systematic excavations. Charles Redman has executed such a microstudy at Qsar es-Seghir on the northern Moroccan coast, between Tangier and Ceuta. Using material culture evidence, he has successfully documented the occupation of Qsar es-Seghir, beginning in Almoravid times and continuing through the Almohad, Marinid, and Portuguese periods, or from the early twelfth to the mid-sixteenth century. He describes the city's evolution from a dynastic port to an autonomous entrepot, a declining entrepot, a military fortress, and finally a military colony.[63]

A valuable work on the oasis of Ouargla is Jean Lethielleux's *Ouargla. Cité saharienne.*[64] It draws little from the work of Tadeusz Lewicki or Joseph Schacht, both of whom have written extensively on the history of Ouargla, but instead draws heavily on Lethielleux's intimate knowledge of the area— where he has lived most of his life—and of the lives, language, and oral literature of its inhabitants. Descriptions of archeological sites and domestic architecture, as well as plans of oases and towns, accompany the text, reflecting the author's special expertise in the region. This work is certainly of interest for the study of Saharan trade and caravan commerce. In many ways, the history of Ouargla reflects the rise, decline, and rebirth of other great Saharan cities such as Ghadames, Timbuktu, and Sijilmasa.

## REREADING THROUGH ARCHEOLOGY: SIJILMASA

The history of Sijilmasa should figure prominently in any history of the medieval Maghrib, as well as in any serious discussion of "the Islamic city." But, until recently, the treatment of this important city has been based on relatively brief references in medieval texts.[65] One of the most extensive discussions in a scholarly survey was Denise Jacques-Meunie's *Le Maroc saharien des origines à 1670*.[66] The Tafilalt is one of several pre-Saharan regions covered in this useful book. More recently, Larbi Mezzine published an excellent microstudy of this same region.[67] In the first part of this work, Mezzine describes the sources of evidence: geographic texts, chronicles, genealogy studies, and biographic and hagiographic literature. For the period specifically covered in the book, Mezzine uses *ti'qqidin* (plural of *ta'qqitt*), compendia of customary law among southeastern Moroccan Berber tribes that regulate relations among individuals of a *qasr* (a self-contained fortified community), a tribe, or a confederation. The ta'qqitt of the Qasr Larsa, which he examines in the volume, was discovered in 1972. Mezzine presents three documents of another type, called *tayssa*. This term refers to the protection offered by nomads to sedentary populations, as well as to the document offered by the protector to the protected. Mezzine also makes use of oral tradition, popular culture, and aerial photographs.

Boone, Myers, and Redman describe two very distinct urban patterns during North Africa's medieval period: one in which the major source of state surplus is based on the concentration of agricultural production, and the other in which it rests on control of long-distance trade.[68] Sijilmasa might well provide an interesting model in which those two patterns converge. Mezzine explains how, in the region of Sijilmasa, a system of local exchange between nomads and agriculturalists was grafted onto long-distance trade. Under the date palms, residents of the oasis cultivated winter grains, an assortment of vegetables, and spring wheat. A system of rotation was established whereby, after a few years of this kind of production, land was given over to pasture for a time. Among the products of pastoral life were leather and wool which, in turn, gave rise to local industries. Residents traded their surplus in dates, leather goods, and textiles for a variety of industrial products from the northern Maghrib. The benefits of that commerce provided commodities and products for the trans-Saharan trade.

The Ludwig Keimer Foundation organized two archeological and ethnological missions to the Tafilalt in the early seventies, both under the direction of Boris de Rachewiltz.[69] The excavations were done approximately three kilometers north-northwest of Rissani. According to a summary of the report, the first mission uncovered a network of underground canals with associated water mains in glazed terra-cotta, as well as a bridge and a dam near a large reservoir located by Inspector Benshemsi of Meknès. The second season uncovered the remains of walls, a fountain, plant fossils, and human bones. The excavations also produced fragments of fine glass, jewelry, and small tiles in faience. Regrettably, stratigraphic information from these two seasons is unavailable to us.

In 1974, Benshemsi conducted an excavation in "the mosque area." The mud walls exposed in this excavation contained shards that suggest that they probably do not predate the eighteenth century. Although there are numerous ceramics shards from these excavations in the Archeological Museum in Rabat, no useful stratigraphic information could be derived from them.

The joint Moroccan-American missions of 1988, 1992, 1993, 1994, and 1996, under the direction of the author,[70] have made considerable progress in addressing some of the issues raised above. Correlation of data from remote sensing, observation in the field, topographical maps, and oral interviews allowed the geographers to reconstruct the shape of medieval Sijilmasa. Oral tradition identifies the original four gates of Sijilmasa as the points at which one would leave the desert and enter the *g'maman* (oasis) of the city rather than the gates of the city itself. These points help to determine the boundaries of the Sijilmasa g'maman and constitute at least the last mental picture people had of Sijilmasa just before it collapsed. Portions of the walls connecting these gates were observed in aerial photographs and confirmed by field observation. The walls of the city itself, those described by al-Bakri,[71] encircled a long, narrow city no more than one-and-a-half kilometers wide. Oral tradition also identifies a market area at the western edge of the Sijilmasa g'maman called "Ben Akla Tazrout." Visible at this location today are low wall sections and stone foundations, including a few square pillar foundations for what local tradition identifies as a small mosque. Could Suq Ben Akla have been a receiving area for the large caravans coming from the south? An interesting question, but we still don't know.

Satellite imagery further confirmed that the current Oued Ziz is, in fact, a man-made channel. Diversion of the original Oued Ziz, what is today called Oued Amerbou, from its original bed to the east of the oasis to its current channel facilitated agriculture in the western part of the oasis. Jean Margat[72] suggests that the diversion of the Ziz by constructing a dam just south of Erfoud possibly dates from the eleventh century. According to oral tradition, the primary source of water was the Timedrine Spring feeding the Oued Ziz just to the north of Erfoud. al-Bakri tells us that "the cultivated land is irrigated with water from the river collected in basins like those used for watering gardens." Oral tradition identifies three dams, still presently visible on the Oued Ziz, though not in their original form, that were employed in the medieval irrigation system. These dams in their present form, like those along the Oued Gheris to the west of the Ziz, were reconstructed during the Alawite period. The geographers also examined the *khattara* system of underground irrigation (called *qanat* in much of the Arab world) that feeds the oasis. They agree with local sources that khattarat were introduced to the area in the fifteenth century, that is, after the fall of Sijilmasa city. They describe the system as one that decentralized irrigation technology. It may have resulted from the breakup of the city, or perhaps even contributed to its downfall.

This view of medieval Sijilmasa addresses the issue of the very organization of the city. Some scholars maintain that the city was divided into separate "suburbs" somewhat like the *qusur* (plural of qasr, usually *ksour* in Moroccan Arabic) of today; al-Bakri describes Sijilmasa as being "surrounded by numerous suburbs." [73] Separate qusur were definitely the settlement pattern after the civil war of 1393. On the other side of the argument, historical descriptions indicating that Sijilmasa was essentially a single long and narrow city containing most or all the population of the Tafilalt include al-Idrissi,[74] who describes Sijilmasa as consisting of a series of palaces, houses, and cultivated fields stretched out along the Oued Ziz which during the summer resembled the Nile, whose waters were used for agriculture. The tenth-century historian and traveler al-Masʿudi[75] describes Sijilmasa as having a great main artery a half-day's walk long. Oral tradition in the Tafilalt repeats that description. It could well be the case that Sijilmasa conformed to each of these models at different points in time, under different dynastic regimes.

Excavations west of the "mosque" revealed at least two levels of occupation below the eighteenth-century level previously exposed by the Benshemsi excavation of 1974, a level defined by stone pavers above a mud/concrete floor with subterranean drains. The exact nature of the architecture remains undefined, but the abundance of stone building materials suggests structures of major importance. One sounding reveals at least three different floor levels and two series of drains, pits, and cesspools.

Excavations along the Oued Ziz have provided valuable information about the western wall of the city. A tower was excavated revealing two distinct phases of construction. By digging trenches both inside and outside the tower below the base of the wall, we learned that the lower level of the wall rests on an earlier level of occupation, probably of the eleventh or twelfth century. Tracing the western wall approximately three hundred meters north of that tower, we exposed another tower having the same two levels of construction. Several small trenches dug to the north and to the west of the north tower revealed that the outer wall does not continue due north but steps in to the northeast toward the citadel. It remains to be determined whether or not evidence of a continuous exterior wall can be found all along the Oued Ziz. That would certainly help resolve the question of Sijilmasa's being a united or divided city.

Excavations were done in two areas that appear at this point to be residential areas. A sounding approximately 100 meters to the southeast of the north tower exposed two floor levels near the surface, below which was a deposit of midden for one meter and then still another floor level. Although time did not allow us to reach bedrock in this sounding, the lowest levels reached contained eleventh- through fourteenth-century pottery. The architecture remains to be identified. At the southern edge of the central area, a sounding revealed three distinct levels of occupation, the lowest consisting of a solid mud/concrete floor, tentatively dated to the eleventh century by ceramics embedded in the aggregate base of the floor. This sounding had a preponderance of common tableware, cooking ware, and storage vessels suggesting a residential zone.

Aerial photographs revealed areas where we suspect subsurface walls. The excavation team tested an area one to two hundred meters southwest of the mosque with a series of small cuts and discovered that walls were located just below the surface forming a rectangular enclosure, the nature of which is yet to be identified.

Perhaps the most important achievement of the excavation team is the confirmation of the identity of the site's largest major structure, according to the local population, a mosque. A sounding along the south wall revealed the foundation of the mihrab, or prayer niche. The location of the mihrab along the south wall is consistent with most early mosques in Morocco.[76] The structure is located in the central part of the site, which is also the highest part of the site. The Alawite dynasty refortified this area in the late seventeenth century. The walls and structures visible on the surface, including the mosque, date from this later Alawite period. But the orientation of the qibla wall (indicating the direction toward Mecca) of the mosque must have been based on the qibla of an earlier mosque which has yet to be found.

We know that Sijilmasa has been the site of a thriving ceramics industry from the earliest times to the present. During the 1992 season, Lahcen Taouchikt catalogued 1,200 items of diagnostic pottery that he divided into three broad chronological periods: eleventh through fourteenth centuries, which we call Sijilmasian pottery; fifteenth through seventeenth, which we call Filalian pottery; and eighteenth through nineteenth, which we call Bhayr pottery because it was made in the village of Bhayr al-Ansar, immediately southwest of Sijilmasa. All of this pottery displays considerable continuity in form, raw materials, and manufacturing techniques. That some of it was produced for foreign export is apparent in the discovery of Sijilmasian types in excavations at the Qala'at Bani Hammad in Algeria and in Tegdaoust south of the Sahara.

Another important local industry in medieval Sijilmasa was the minting of gold and silver coins. During the 1988 season, Lahcen Taouchikt found three silver coins struck in the name of Mas'ud b. Wanudin, the last independent ruler of Sijilmasa before the Almoravid conquest, that underline the city's intermittent role as an independent capital. Most of the coins that were struck in the mint at Sijilmasa were struck in the name of dynastic rulers outside the city, stressing the city's role as a provincial capital.[77] In the spring of 1992, Donald Whitcomb discovered a hoard of thirty-two dinars in Aqaba, Jordan, twenty-nine of which had been struck in the Sijilmasa mint between A.D. 976 and 1013. Whitcomb speculates that the coins were the purse of a traveler making the pilgrimage to Mecca. In any case, the coins, struck in the name of the Umayyad caliphs of Cordova, document the Umayyad's brief control of the city in the late tenth and early eleventh centuries.

Many questions remain about the city's unity, organization, land usage, and water resources, and about the piggy-backing of long-distance trade on local trade under successive regimes. We propose several more seasons of archeological research at Sijilmasa. Using airborne thematic mapping and color infrared photographics, the remote sensing analyst and cartographer will generate a detailed map of the surface and subsurface architectural plan of this extensive urban area. We are especially anxious to see if this mapping will suggest evidence of a united or divided city. The excavating team will use these data in order to place their soundings into a broader urban context.

The correlation of data gathered from satellite imagery, aerial photographs, ground-truthing, historical documents, and oral tradition will facilitate the study of local agriculture. The carrying capacity of the oasis can be calculated from the maximum area of arable land and the average yield of primary crops. The collection of archeobotanical specimens through a flotation process will provide information about what crops were grown in medieval Sijilmasa. It is also possible to identify the kinds of plant-processing activities carried out at the site and determine whether these activities were spatially restricted within the urban center. Such research will provide evidence not only of agricultural practices, but also of specialization and exchange.[78]

Determining the provenance of the various types of ceramics found at Sijilmasa will enhance our understanding of the city's long-distance trade. Neutron-activation analysis will be used to distinguish between locally made and imported wares. Pottery excavated from other Moroccan sites, as well as from Andalusia and south of the Sahara, will provide a basis for comparison. Neutron-activation studies of several coins minted in Sijilmasa and other mints around the Mediterranean have already determined the extent to which Mediterranean mints drew on gold from West Africa.[79] Newly discovered coins in excavations at Sijilmasa and elsewhere (such as the hoard recently discovered in Aqaba) will add to our appreciation of the role of the Sijilmasa mint.

Ultimately, this archeological investigation will result in a comprehensive view of the entire Sijilmasa landscape, including its economic, political, religious, and residential institutions, its agriculture, and its water resources, all of which were part of the city's ecosystem. The study will address the process of urbanization; the city's role, first as an independent capital and then as a provincial capital; its role as a center of religious ideology, a garrison town, an agricultural oasis, a commercial entrepot, and a link to West Africa.

## CONCLUSION

This essay has not attempted to address all of the themes it has raised in equal detail. The question of central authority, for example, has not been developed, despite the fact that major works on individual dynasties have continued to appear. Among those especially worthy of note are Farhat Dachraoui, *Le Califat fatimide au Maghreb* (Tunis: Société Tunisienne de Diffusion, 1981); Rachid Bourouiba, *Les H'ammadites* (Algiers: Entreprise Nationale du Livre, 1984), which draws extensively on several seasons of excavation at the Qala'at Bani Hammad; Mohamed Talbi, *L'Emirat aghlabide* (Paris: Vrin, 1986); and Mohammed Kably, *Société, pouvoir et religion au Maroc à la fin du Moyen-Age* (Paris: Maisonneuve and Larose, 1986), which covers the Merinids and Wattasids in Morocco.

Rather, the key objective of the essay has been to demonstrate, through discussions of examples drawn from fields that are especially crucial to an understanding of events in medieval North Africa (such as political and social history, religious studies, economics, and archeology), the importance of rereading existing source materials, as well as new ones that continue to come to light, with "multidisciplinary glasses." In my own work on the Almoravid dynasty, which is now very close to completion, I have attempted to present a model for the rereading of existing texts.

In it, I have chosen to tell the story with an omniscient, third-person narrative voice. As in any story, there is conflicting evidence and, potentially, several differing interpretations of a given event or sequence of events, a personality, a motive, a cause, or a result. Compared to practitioners of modern history, the early Arab chroniclers are overly dramatic; they exaggerate the facts of historical events and the qualities of historical personalities. For them, there is a greater truth than factual truth, and that includes the heroism and moral righteousness of their leaders, men who had enough charisma to create a strong sense of Moroccan/Muslim self-awareness. One should be cautious about accepting what each of them says as "historical truth." Indeed, the factual truth regarding the Almoravids is, in some cases, simply unobtainable for us because too few sources have survived. But another form of truth that is just as important is how the personalities and events of Almoravid history were perceived by the writers who originally told the story.

In the account I have written, the narrator's goal of presenting *one* coherent version has forced me to choose one interpretation above another—the one that, in view of the entire inventory of information at my disposal, seems to be most logical or best fits the narrative. As a historian, I have tried to *understand* all of the evidence that I have accumulated from texts as well as from numismatics and archeology and to extrapolate as much of the story as possible from that evidence. At the end of each chapter, I have adopted a different narrative voice—that of an inquiring commentator on the sources who offers alternate or supplementary explanations. I have relied on numismatic evidence and on archeology to fill in some of the gaps. Also, I have "listened for silences."

Much of the work cited in this essay was done by nonhistorians—legal and religious scholars, sociologists, anthropologists and archaeologists, numismatists and ceramists, geographers, geomorphologists, and remote sensing analysts. The questions raised by these experts, as well as some of the answers they have suggested, provide historians with a new set of glasses that should sharpen our understanding of the broad theories of Ibn Khaldun and his interpreters as we utilize them to reread the medieval texts.

## Notes

1. Ibn Khaldun, *The Muqaddimah. An Introduction to History*, trans. by Franz Rosenthal (3 vols.; New York: Pantheon Books, 1958).

2. Ibid., II, p. 129.

3. Ibid., II, pp. 235 ff.

4. Ibid., II, pp. 338 ff.

5. Translated from Ibn Khaldun, *Histoire des Berbères* (2 vols.; Paris: Librairie Orientalist Paul Geuthner, 1927), II, p. 34.

6. Georges Marçais, *La Berbérie musulmane et l'Orient au moyen âge* (Paris: Aubier, 1946), p. 11.

7. Charles-André Julien, *History of North Africa* (New York: Praeger, 1970), p. 73.

8. Jean Poncet, "Le myth de la catastrophe hilalienne," *AESC* XXII, no. 5 (1967), pp. 1099–1120.

9. Michael Brett, "Ibn Khaldun and the Arabisation of North Africa," *Maghreb Review* IV (1979), pp. 9–16. His revisionist view of the Hilalian invasion first appeared in "Fitnat al-Qayrawan," (unpublished Ph.D. diss., University of London, 1970).

10. Michael Brett, "Problems in the Interpretation of the History of the Maghrib in the Light of Some Recent Publications," *Journal of African History* XIII, no. 3 (1972), pp. 489–506.

11. As cited ibid., p. 493.

12. al-Habib al-Janhani, *Al-Maghrib al-Islami: al-hayat al-iqtisadiyya wa-l-ijtima'iyya* (Tunis: Maison Tunisienne de l'Edition, 1978).

13. Gaston Deverdun, *Marrakesh des origines à 1912* (2 vols., Rabat: Editions Techniques Nord-Africaines, 1959). The publication date of this work is sufficiently early that it should have been included in the first edition, but it is certainly a welcome addition to the second. Abun-Nasr's narrative is the only one with which I am familiar that constructs the chronology of Yusuf bin Tashfin's campaign into the Maghrib, his conquest of Fez, and the construction of Marrakesh in the same order as I have in my own work on the Almoravids which is in preparation.

14. Ambrosio Huici-Miranda "Un nuevo manuscrito de 'Al-Bayan al-mughrib'," *Al-Andalus* XXIV (1959), pp. 155–182.

15. Deverdun, *Marrakech*, I, pp. 59–64; Paulo Farias, "The Almoravids, Some Questions Concerning the Character of the Movement during its Periods of Closest Contact with the Sudan," *Bulletin de l'Institut Fondamental d'Afrique Noire* XXIX B, pp. 794–878; and Paul Semonin, "The Almoravid Movement in the Western Soudan," *Transactions of the Historical Society of Ghana* VII (1964), pp. 42–59.

16. Vincent J. Cornell, "Ribat tit-n-Fitr and the Origins of Moroccan Maraboutism," *Islamic Studies* XXVII (1988), p. 25.

17. Abdel Wedoud Ould Cheikh and Bernard Saison, "Vie(s) et mort(s) de al-Imam al-Hadrami," *Arabica* XXXIV (1987), p. 57, nn. 37 and 38.

18. Francisco Pons y Boigues, *Essayo bio-bibliográfico sobre los historiadores arábigo-españoles* (Madrid: S. F. de Sales, 1898) reproduces the following note made by Dozy in his own handwriting on his copy of *Loci de Abadidis:* "L'histoire d'Aben-Ac-Cairafi était parmi les livres que I. E. Humbert a trouvés à Tunis en 1823 et dont les possesseurs ne voulaient pas se défaire, sans néanmoins se refuser à en livrer des copies—Missive du Ministre de l'Instr. A. R. Falch à Hamaker, 21 février 1823."

19. David S. Powers, "Fatwas as Sources for Legal and Social History: A Dispute over Endowment Revenues from Fourteenth-Century Fez," *Al-Qantara* XI, no. 2 (1990), pp. 295–341. In another article, "A Court Case from Fourteenth-Century North Africa," *Journal of the American Oriental Society* CX, no. 2 (1990), pp. 229–254, Powers analyzes a single fatwa that preserves 28 other legal documents issued in connection with a fourteenth-century property dispute. Hadi R. Idris used fatawa to study the institution of marriage. See his "Le mariage en occident musulman d'après un choix de fatwas médiévales extraites du *Mi'yar* d'al-Wansharisi," *Studia Islamica* XXXII (1970), pp. 157–167, and his "Le mariage en occident musulman: analyse de fatwas médiévales extraites du *Mi'yar* d'al-Wansharisi," *ROMM* XII (1972), pp. 45–62; XVII (1974), pp. 71–105; and XXV (1978), pp. 119–138. For the use of fatawa in economic history, see Hadi R. Idris, "Commerce maritime et kirad en Berbérie orientale d'après un recueil de fatwas médiévales," *Journal of the Economic and Social History of the Orient* IV (1961), pp. 225–239.

20. Powers, "Fatwas as Sources," p. 338.

21. Ibid., p. 341.

22. Abu al-'Abbas Ahmad Ibn Yahya al-Wansharisi (834/1430–914/1508), *al-Mi'yar al-mu'rib wa-l-jami' al-mughrib 'an fatawa 'ulama' Ifriqiyya wa-l-Andalus wa-l-Maghrib* (12 vols.; lithograph: Fez, 1314–15/1896–97; repr. 13 vols. Rabat: Ministry of Awqat, 1981–1983).

23. Vincent Lagardère, "La Haute judicature à l'époque almoravide en al-Andalus," *Al-Qantara* VII (1986), pp. 135–228.

24. Ibid., p. 139.

25. Ibid., pp. 140, 172.

26. Evariste Lévi-Provençal, *Seville musulmane au début du XIIè siècle—le Traité d'Ibn 'Abdun sur la vie urbaine et les corps de métiers* (Paris: Librairie Orientale et Américaine, 1947). The Arabic text appears in *Journal Asiatique* CCXXIV (April–June 1934), pp. 177–255.

27. Ibid., p. 153.

28. Ibid., 159.

29. Janet L. Abu Lughod, "The Islamic City—Historic Myth, Islamic Essence, and Contemporary Relevance," *International Journal of Middle East Studies* XIX, no. 2 (1987) pp. 155–176. Articles she cites include William Marçais, "L'Islamisme et la vie urbaine," *L'Académie des inscriptions et belles-lettres, Comptes rendus* (January–March 1928), pp. 86–100; Georges Marçais, "L'urbanisme musulman," in his *Mélanges d'histoire et d'archéologie de l'Occident musulman,* (2 vols.; Algiers: Imprimerie officielle, 1957), vol. I; Georges Marçais, "La conception des villes dans l'Islam," *Revue d'Alger* II (1945), pp. 517–33; Robert Brunschvig, "Urbanisme médiéval et droit musulman," *Revue des études islamiques* XV (1947), pp. 127–55; Gustave von Grunebaum, "The Structure of the Muslim Town," in his *Islam: Essays in the Nature and Growth of a Cultural Tradition* (London: Routledge and Kegan Paul, 1961); Roger Le Tourneau, *Fès avant le protectorat. Etude économique et sociale d'une ville de l'Occident musulman* (Casablanca: SMLE, 1949); Roger Le Tourneau, *Les villes musulmanes de l'Afrique du Nord* (Algiers: Maison du Livre, 1957); Carleton Coon, *Caravan* (New York: Holt, 1951), particularly the chapter on "Town and City"; and Jacques Berque, "Medinas, villesneuves et bidonvilles," *Les Cahiers de Tunisie* XXI–XXII (1958), pp. 5–42.

30. Jean Sauvaget, *Alep: Essai sur le développement d'une grande ville syrienne, des origines au milieu du XIXè siècle* (Paris: P. Geuthner, 1941); and also "Esquisse d'une histoire de la ville de Damas," *Revue des études islamiques* VIII (1934), pp. 421–80; Ira Lapidus, *Muslim Cities in the Later Middle Ages* (Cambridge: Harvard University Press, 1967).

31. Dale F. Eickleman, *The Middle East: An Anthropological Approach* (Englewood Cliffs, N. J.: Prentice Hall, 1989).

32. Ibid., pp. 101–102.

33. In *International Journal of Middle East Studies* V (1974), pp. 274–294.

34. Fredj Stambouli and Abdelkader Zghal, "Urban Life in Precolonial North Africa," *The British Journal of Sociology* XXVII, no. 1 (March 1976), pp. 1–20.

35. See Tarif Khalidi, "Some Classical Islamic Views of the City," in *Studia Arabica et Islamica: Festschrift Ihsan Abbas* (Beirut: American University of Beirut Press, 1981), pp. 265–276; Kenneth Brown, Michèle Jolé, Peter Sluglett, and Sami Zubeida, eds., *Middle Eastern Cities in Comparative Perspective* (London: Ithaca Press, 1986); Abdulaziz Y. Saqqal, ed., *The Middle East City* (New York: Paragon House, 1987).

36. Amar Dhina, *Cités musulmanes d'Orient et d'Occident* (Algiers: Entreprise Nationale du Livre, 1986).

37. Charles L. Redman, *Qsar es-Seghir: An Archaeological View of Medieval Life* (Orlando: Academic Press Inc., 1986).

38. David Conrad and Humphrey Fisher, "The Conquest that

Never Was: Ghana and the Almoravids, 1076," *History in Africa* IX (1982), pp. 21–59.

39. Harry Hazard, *The Numismatic History of Late Medieval North Africa* (New York: The American Numismatic Society, 1952), p. 61.

40. Conrad and Fisher, "The Conquest that Never Was," p. 45.

41. Michael Brett, "Islam and Trade in the Bilad al-Sudan, Tenth–Eleventh Century A.D.," *Journal of African History* XXIV (1983), pp. 431–440.

42. See, for example, Gareth Austin's review of J. F. A. Ajayi and Michael Crowder, *History of West Africa* in *Bulletin of the School of Oriental and African Studies* LI (1988), pp. 618–619.

43. Sheryl L. Burkhalter, "Listening for Silences in Almoravid History: Another Reading of 'The Conquest that Never Was,'" *History in Africa* XIX (1992), pp. 103–131.

44. H. T. Norris, *Saharan Myth and Saga* (Oxford: Clarendon Press, 1972), pp. 80–87, provides a comprehensive discussion of this "capital" and its history as recounted in Arabic texts and local traditions. Bernard Saison's excavations at the citadel of Azuqqi suggest an occupation contemporaneous with the Almoravid movement. See Bernard Saison, "Azugi, archéologie et histoire," *Recherche, pédagogie et culture* IX, no. 55 (1981), pp. 66–74. According to al-Bakri, Yannu Ibn 'Umar al-Hajj, brother of Yahya Ibn 'Umar, the first Almoravid amir, built such a fortress at Azuqqi. See Nehemia Levtzion and J. F. P. Hopkins, *Corpus of Early Arabic Sources for West African History* (Cambridge: Cambridge University Press, 1981), p. 73. This is a superb collection of documents bringing together in a single source much of the material needed for a critical rereading of texts pertaining to West African, including Northwest African, history.

45. Burkhalter, "Listening for Silences," p. 106.

46. Hazard, *Numismatic History,* pp. 99–100, lists four dinars struck in Sijilmasa in the name of al-amir Ibrahim Ibn Abi Bakr in the year 462, two in 465, and one each in 466 and 467. Kassis, "Observations," pp. 320–321, provides an insightful discussion of these coins.

47. Burkhalter, "Listening for Silences," pp. 111–117.

48. Conrad and Fisher, p. 34.

49. Burkhalter, "Listening for Silences," pp. 119–121. The reference to Amilhat is "Petite chronique des Id ou Aich, héritiers guerriers des Almoravides sahariens," *Revue des études islamiques* XI (1937), p. 44.

50. John Hunwick, "Gao and the Almoravids: A Hypothesis," in B. Swartz and Raymond Dumett, eds., *West African Culture Dynamics: Archaeological and Historical Perspectives* (The Hague: Mouton, 1980), pp. 413–430, uses these tombstones as a departure point for establishing a link between West Africa and Spain, from Gao to Tadmakka to Ouargla to Tlemcen to Oran to Alméria, during the Almoravid period.

51. Burkhalter, "Listening for Silences," p. 118. See also Donald Moore and Richard Roberts, "Listening for Silences," *History in Africa* XVII (1990), pp. 319–325.

52. Stambouli and Zghal, "Urban Life," pp. 7–8. See also, Fernand Braudel, *La Méditerranée et le monde méditerranéen à l'époque de Philippe II* (Paris: Librairie Armand Colin, 1949). A microstudy of the trade patterns of a particular city in the modern Maghrib that provides an interesting perspective for looking at a medieval suq is Clifford Geertz, "Suq: The Bazaar Economy in Sefrou," in *Meaning and Order in Moroccan Society: Three Essays in Cultural Analysis* (New York: Cambridge University Press, 1979), pp. 123–313. Geertz takes into account the medieval background of the Sefrou suq.

53. Laroui, *The History of the Maghrib,* especially the chapter on "Islam and Commerce."

54. Timothy F. Garrard, "Myth and Metrology: The Early Trans-Saharan Gold Trade," *Journal of African History* XXIII (1982), pp. 443–461.

55. See, for example, Gilbert and Colette Charles-Picard, *Daily Life in Carthage* (London: G. Allen and Unwin, 1961), p. 217; and D. and S. Robert and J. Devisse, *Tegdaoust I: Recherches sur Aoudaghost* (Paris: Arts et Métiers Graphiques, 1970), p. 139.

56. I have done such tests using techniques developed by Adon A. Gordus of the Department of Chemistry at the University of Michigan. See Ronald A. Messier, "The Almoravids: West African Gold and the Gold Currency of the Mediterranean Basin," *Journal of the Economic and Social History of the Orient* XVII, 1 (1974), pp. 31–47. Other numismatic studies that are valuable contributions to interpreting medieval Maghribi history include Hanna E. Kassis, "Some Unpublished Almoravid Dinars in Madrid and Badajos," *Al-Qantara* III (1982), pp. 457–465; and, by the same author, "Observations on the First Three Decades of the Almoravid Dynasty (A.H. 450–480 = A.D. 1058–1088): A Numismatic Study," *Der Islam* LXII, no. 2 (1985), pp. 311–25. The latter study is an excellent example of rereading medieval texts in light of numismatic evidence. See also Muhammad Abu-l-Faraj al-Ush, *Monnaies aghlabides étudiées en relation avec l'histoire des aghlabides* (Damascus: Institut Français de Damas, 1982), the general catalogue of which is virtually complete, and the best that exists for Aghlabid coins, but the interpretive sections of which leave many questions unanswered.

57. E. Ann McDougall, "The View from Awdaghust: War, Trade and Social Change in the Southwestern Sahara, from the Eighth to the Fifteenth Century," *Journal of African History* XXVI (1985), pp. 1–31. The major work on Awdaghust is a series of publications based on the archeological findings at Tegdaoust between 1960 and 1976. In addition

to Robert, Robert, and Devisse, *Tegdaoust I: Recherches sur Aoudaghost*, see also Claudette Vanacker, *Tegdaoust II: Recherches sur Aoudaghost. Fouille d'un quartier artisanal*, Mémoires de l'Institut Mauritanien de la Recherche Scientifique, No. 2 (Paris: Arts et Métiers Graphiques, 1979); and J. Devisse, D. Robert-Chalieux et al., *Tegdaoust III: Recherches sur Aoudaghost* (Paris: Institut Mauritanien de la Recherche Scientifique, 1983). Other volumes in the series are forthcoming. McDougall lists several other studies in note 3 of her article.

58. *Tegdaoust III*, pp. 554–556.

59. McDougall, "View from Awdaghust," p. 12.

60. Raymond Mauny, *Tableau Géographique de l'Ouest Africain au Moyen Age* (Dakar: Institut Fondamental de l'Afrique Noire, 1960), p. 479.

61. McDougall, "View from Awdaghust," p. 12.

62. Denise Robert-Chalieux, "Tegdaoust V. Recherches sur Aoudaghost. Une concession médiévale, implantation et évolution d'une unité d'habitation" (unpublished diss., University of Paris, 1981).

63. Redman, *Qsar es-Seghir.*

64. Jean Lethielleux, *Ouargla. Cité saharienne des origines au début du XXè siècle* (Paris: Librairie Orientaliste Paul Geuthner, 1983).

65. The main medieval source for the chronological outline of Sijilmasa's history is al-Bakri, *Kitab al-masalik wa-'l-mamalik*. Baron Mac-Guckin de Slane, ed. and trans., *Description de l'Afrique septentrionale* (revised and corrected edition; Paris: Adrien Maisonneuve, 1965) pp. 148–151 and 167 in the text; pp. 282–289 and 315 in the translation, for events through the conquest of the Almoravids. On the Almohad conquest, see Ibn Abi Zar', *Kitab al-anis al-mutrib bi-rawd al-qirtas fi akhbar muluk al-maghrib wa-tarikh madinat Fas*, Carl Johan Tornberg, ed. (Uppsala: Litteris Academicis, 1843–1846). The events of 796/1393 are described in Luis del Marmol Carvajal, *L'Afrique de Marmol de la traduction de Nicolas Perrot, sieur d'Ablancourt* (Paris: L. Billaine, 1667), III, p. 18. A detailed study of the history of Sijilmasa was done as a doctoral thesis at the University of Aix-en-Provence. See Mohamed El Mellouki, "Contribution à l'étude de l'histoire des villes médiévales du Maroc: Sijilmasa des origines à 668 (H)/1269 (JC) (unpublished Ph.D. diss., University of Aix-en-Provence, 1985). The most recent article on Sijilmasa is John Wright, "Sijilmasa, A Saharan Entrepot," *Moroccan Studies,* I (1991), pp. 7–19.

66. Denise Jacques-Meunie, *Le Maroc saharien des origines à 1670* (Paris: Librairie Klincksieck, 1982).

67. Larbi Mezzine, *Le Tafilalt: Contribution à l'histoire du Maroc aux XVIIè et XVIIIè siècles* (Rabat: Publications de la Faculté des Lettres et des Sciences Humaines, 1987).

68. James L. Boone, J. Emlen Myers, and Charles L. Redman, "Archaeological and Historical Approaches to Complex Societies: The

Islamic States of Medieval Morocco," in *American Anthropology* XCII (1990), pp. 630–46.

69. Boris de Rachewiltz, *Missione Etno-Archeologica nel Sahara Maghrebino* (Rome: Instituto Italiano per L'Africa, 1972), p. 567.

70. The teams have worked under an agreement between the Institut des Sciences d'Archéologie et du Patrimoine de Maroc and Middle Tennessee State University. The associate project director is Neil MacKenzie, and the Moroccan associate is Lahcen Taouchikt. Stephen Brown and John Runkle are project cartographers. Archeologist James Knudstad joined the team in 1992, as did geographers Dale Lightfoot and James Miller.

71. Levtzion and Hopkins, *Corpus*, p. 64.

72. Jean Margat, *Mémoire explicatif de la carte hydrogéologique au 1/50,000 de la plaine du Tafilalt* (Rabat: Editions du Service Géologique du Maroc, 1962), p. 191.

73. Levtzion and Hopkins, *Corpus*, p. 64.

74. Edrissi, *Description de l'Afrique et de l'Espagne*, Reinhart Dozy and Michael Jan de Goeje, eds. and trans. (Leiden: E. J. Brill, 1968), p. 70.

75. Abu'l-Hasan ʿAli Ibn al-Husayn al-Masʿudi, *Muruj al-dhahab wa-maʿadin al-jawhar.* Charles Adrien Casimir Barbier de Meynard and Pavet de Courteille, eds. and trans., *Les Prairies d'or* (Paris: Société Asiatique, 1965).

76. Michael E. Bonine, "The Sacred Direction and City Structure: A Preliminary Analysis of the Islamic Cities of Morocco," in *Muqarnas* VII (1990), pp. 50–72.

77. Messier, "The Almoravids: West African Gold," and Ronald A. Messier, "Quantitative Analysis of Almoravid Dinars," *Journal of the Economic and Social History of the Orient* XXIII (1980), pp. 104–120.

78. Susan Pollock, "Progress Report on the Plant Remains from Badis, Al-Basra, Nakur and Qsar es-Seghir," *Bulletin d'archéologie marocaine* XV (1984), p. 357.

79. See supra, note 29.

# The Eighteenth Century:
# A Poor Relation in the Historiography
# of Morocco

*Abderrahmane El Moudden*
Al-Akhawayn University

A topographical metaphor aptly describes the state of Moroccan historiography: in contrast with prominent peaks are deep gullies, which at some points become veritable submarine trenches. The periods which have attracted historiographical attention are the peaks; the many casualties of historiography, which have remained unnoticed or insufficiently studied, are the depressions. It would be very useful to identify the different eras systematically and pose questions as to why they have attracted, or been neglected by, historians. In the present state of historical research in Morocco, however, addressing these weaknesses can only be a fond hope. The results that Moroccan historiography has begun to achieve, appreciable as they are in certain sectors, nonetheless generally remain the product of remarkable efforts by isolated researchers. More can be accomplished only within a framework of coherent programs involving research groups with precise agendas. The following remarks concern the relatively circumscribed period of Moroccan history bracketed by the sixteenth and nineteenth centuries but focus particularly on the eighteenth. Because the eighteenth century was the last period during which Morocco, as well as other regions of the southern Mediterranean, still functioned as an equal of the European powers, any attempt to understand the changes that later occurred ought, logically, to begin there. Although a handful of historians have recognized the crucial importance of the period, this essay argues that the eighteenth century is a poor relation of the rest, one of the troughs in the historiography of Morocco; discusses the probable origins of this phenomenon; and concludes with some practical suggestions for correcting this deficiency.

First of all, it is necessary to define terms. What is meant by the Moroccan eighteenth century? As is well known, the question of periodization has proven most difficult, especially for a history whose historiography is only just emerging. It is, however, essential to take note of gaps in the historical continuum. Needless to say, periodization goes beyond simple arithmetic: The years 1700 and 1799 do not accurately correspond to any particular changes in Moroccan history. Indeed, imposing exact limits is quite impossible. Depending on the perspective, a historical century may stretch beyond a hundred years or terminate with fewer. The perspective adopted for this work centers around macrohistory, the state, and the great movements that affected the whole of Moroccan society and its relations with the world around the Mediterranean littoral.

Within this perspective, the end point presents itself more readily than the point of departure. No reason exists for changing the customarily preferred choice of 1830. The occupation of Algeria reverberated throughout the region like a thunderclap announcing the beginning of a terrible storm. The problem lies in where to begin. Such standard texts as the *Histoire du Maroc*[1] have often opted for the year 1727, the date of the death of Sultan Isma'il, who had consolidated the acquisitions of his two predecessors, the founders of the Alawite Dynasty. But that choice tightly condenses an entire epoch into the life of one sultan and overlooks the fact that the events which devastated Moroccan society in the middle third of the century (1727–1757) had their origins in the last decade of Sultan Isma'il's reign. We know that at some point, around 1720, the sultanic system entered a phase of decay, and that date provides a more suitable point of departure. With the eighteenth century more or less delineated, the treatment that the historiography of Morocco has thus far accorded it can be assessed.

The assertion that the eighteenth century is a weak link in the historiography of Morocco rests on empirical observation. While doing research on nineteenth-century rural communities around Fez, I sought information about the earlier history of these groups in an effort to reconstruct their wanderings and learn how they had established themselves in the region. The meager sources dealing with the eighteenth century surprised me, especially when compared with the relative wealth of studies devoted to the sixteenth and seventeenth centuries on the one hand, and the nineteenth century on the other. To revert to the topographical metaphor, the eighteenth century forms a syncline of sorts.

These evaluations cannot, of course, stop with personal observations. Two useful tools are readily available to test their validity at a broader level and thus confirm or refute their accuracy. These are the journal *Hespéris-Tamuda* and the lists of research completed or currently underway at the Department of History of the Faculté des Lettres at the Université Mohammed V in Rabat.

Of course, these arbitrarily selected instruments of measurement offer only partial insights. *Hespéris-Tamuda* is certainly not the only outlet for historical writing on Morocco. Ideally, one should also survey such prestigious journals as *Studia Islamica, Annales,* the *International Journal of Middle East Studies,* and the *Revue de l'Occident Musulman et de la Méditerranée,* as well as considering the content of less well-known periodicals, such as *Dar al-Niyaba* or *al-Manahil,* which might actually suggest trends even more clearly. Nor is historical research confined solely to history departments. Departments of sociology, economics, political science, and Arabic and Islamic studies, among others, also concern themselves with history. Nevertheless, *Hespéris-Tamuda* remains the most likely place to find studies on Moroccan history. Similarly, in attempting to identify the tendencies of historiography, historians constitute the most logical starting point. One important disclaimer at the outset: This survey does not purport to be either exhaustive or statistically precise; the data are presented with an eye towards suggesting tendencies.

### HESPÉRIS-TAMUDA

*Hespéris-Tamuda* has maintained a regular schedule of publication since 1921, although the journal began as two separate entities. *Hespéris* was published in Rabat, capital of the French protectorate, from 1912 to 1956–1957; *Tamuda* appeared in Tetouan, the capital of Spanish Morocco, much later. An index of articles appearing in *Hespéris-Tamuda* between 1921 and 1971 provides a base for examining the distribution of historical production by epoch over that fifty year period, revealing the inclinations of colonial historiography. In order to develop an understanding of the present historiography of Morocco, Table 2 confines the count to the past three decades (with the omission of a few years for which information was unavailable)—broadly speaking, to postcolonial historiography.

The growth of the rubric "Other," primarily because of the inclusion of many ethnographic studies, underscores the imprecise nature of these figures. Nevertheless, as imperfect as Table 2 may be, it clearly reveals two great "troughs": pre-Islamic history and twentieth-century history. For the eighteenth century, the figures belie the hypothesis and require some explanation.

The interest in the eighteenth century indicated by these figures is, to some extent, misleading. Only a handful of authors are represented, and much of the work appears in the form of short "notes et communications" published as asides to works in progress. Such, for example, are the articles of Jacques Caillé and Pierre Grillon. A small number of faithful contributors to *Hespéris* or *Tamuda* who had for years been studying material in Eu-

TABLE 2

Distribution of Articles in *Hespéris-Tamuda,* 1960–1987

| YEARS | PRE-ISLAM | MEDI-EVAL | 16–17 CENT. | 18 CENT. | 19 CENT. | 20 CENT. | OTHER |
|---|---|---|---|---|---|---|---|
| 1960 | 2 | 4 | 3 | 5 | 2 | 1 | 5 |
| 1961 | | 5 | | 5 | | | 6 |
| 1962 | | | | | | | |
| 1963 | | 1 | 3 | 3 | 2 | | 1 |
| 1964 | | 2 | | 1 | 2 | | 1 |
| 1965 | | 2 | 1 | 1 | 1 | | 2 |
| 1966 | | | | | | | |
| 1967 | | 4 | | | | | 2 |
| 1968 | | 5 | 1 | 1 | 1 | | 6 |
| 1969 | | 1 | 1 | 2 | 1 | | 4 |
| 1970 | 1 | 1 | 2 | | 1 | | 2 |
| 1971 | | 2 | 1 | 2 | | 2 | |
| 1972 | | 1 | 1 | 1 | 1 | | 2 |
| 1973 | | 1 | 2 | 1 | | | 1 |
| 1974 | | | 2 | 1 | | 1 | 2 |
| 1975 | | | | 2 | 1 | | 3 |
| 1976–7 | | | 2 | 3 | 4 | 1 | |
| 1978 | | 2 | 3 | 1 | 1 | | 3 |
| 1979 | | | | | | | |
| 1980–1 | | 2 | | | 2 | | 2 |
| 1982–3 | | 4 | 1 | 2 | 2 | 1 | |
| 1984 | | | | | | | |
| 1985 | | 1 | 3 | 1 | 1 | 1 | 1 |
| 1986 | | 2 | 1 | 1 | 1 | | 1 |
| 1987 | | 2 | | 1 | 3 | 1 | |
| TOTAL | 3 | 42 | 27 | 34 | 26 | 8 | 44 |

ropean archives concerning Morocco in the second half of the eighteenth century also regularly submitted pieces. Mariano Arribas Palau, over whose signature several articles and notes appear, falls into this category. It is hardly astonishing that the themes and the periods addressed show little variety. The reigns of Muhammad b. ʿAbdallah (1757–1790) and his son Yazid (1790–1792) are privileged, as is the time of the stay in Morocco of the French consul Louis Chénier (1767–1782). Naturally, historians work first with the most accessible material and, in that sense, a compelling logic drives them to concentrate their research in these years. By contrast, many important events, especially during the first half of the century, particularly between 1727 and 1757, remain largely unexplored.

The nationality of the articles' authors illustrates the hypothesis even more cogently. In the 1960s, mostly foreigners published in Hespéris-Tamuda; by the mid-1970s, the number of Moroccan authors (Hamid Triki and Abdallah Hammoudi, for example) had become noteworthy. At the same time, however, a noticeable shift in the distribution of articles between the eighteenth and the nineteenth centuries occurred, as the interest aroused by the nineteenth century began to overtake that previously shown in the eighteenth.

In summation, over the past thirty years Hespéris-Tamuda has indeed devoted substantial space to the eighteenth century, at least if measured in terms of the number of articles. With the growing participation of Moroccan historians, the tendency developed to desert the eighteenth century in favor of the nineteenth, on the one hand, and the sixteenth and seventeenth on the other. The recent choices in history research topics at the Université Mohammed V illustrate this trend even more clearly.

## ACADEMIC RESEARCH IN THE HISTORY DEPARTMENT, UNIVERSITÉ MOHAMMED V

In 1980, 1986, and 1987, the journal of the Rabat Faculté des Lettres (Majallat kulliyyat al-adab) published lists of the subject matter of theses defended or in progress between 1963 and 1986. Since few scholars defended theses before 1980, and since most of those registered prior to that date are listed among those defended after 1980, Table 3 focuses on the years since 1980.

Clearly, what the contents of Hespéris-Tamuda hinted at becomes, in these lists, an indisputable fact: the eighteenth century is understudied, its topics squeezed between—perhaps even bottled up by—the sixteenth and seventeenth centuries and the nineteenth. The observations of the few historians who study the eighteenth century confirm these figures. Virtually all of them have called attention in their publications to the paucity of sources in their period.

Among these rare eighteenth-century specialists, Mariano Arribas Palau and Ramón Lourido Díaz are the two most knowledgeable about the Spanish archives and Moroccan sources. Thus far, Díaz has published the greatest number of articles and other works on Morocco in the second half of the eighteenth century. The Moroccan historian Mohamed El Mansour has published a monograph, based on Moroccan and British sources, on the reign of Mawlay Sulayman (1792–1822).[2] As for the first half of the century, Magali Morsy, who has undoubtedly studied it most extensively, has described the era as strikingly neglected.[3] Allan R. Meyers and Norman Cigar have also made significant contributions to that period.[4]

Almost all of these historians have pointed to the lack of historiographical interest in the eighteenth century and have advanced explanations of a technical, historical, or ideological order to account for it. Chief among the technical reasons is the general deficiency of primary materials. For Nor-

TABLE 3

Theses defended and topics registered at Mohammed V University

| YEARS | PRE-ISLAM | MEDIEVAL | 16–17 CENT. | 18 CENT. | 19 CENT. | 20 CENT. | OTHER |
|---|---|---|---|---|---|---|---|
| *Theses defended (Doctorat de troisième cycle)* | | | | | | | |
| 1980–85 | | | 4 | | 9 | | |
| 1985–86 | 1 | 2 | | 1 | 1 | 2 | |
| TOTAL | 1 | 2 | 4 | 1 | 10 | 2 | |
| *Topics registered (Doctorat d'état)* | | | | | | | |
| 1980–85 | | 1 | 1 | | 2 | | |
| 1985–86 | | 1 | 3 | 1 | 4 | 2 | 2 |
| TOTAL | | 2 | 4 | 1 | 6 | 2 | 2 |
| *Topics registered (Doctorat de troisième cycle)* | | | | | | | |
| 1980–85 | 1 | 13 | 13 | 2 | 20 | 6 | |
| 1985–86 | | 7 | 1 | 3 | 11 | 5 | |
| TOTAL | 1 | 20 | 14 | 5 | 31 | 11 | |

man Cigar, "the reason for this oversight is evident and can best be explained by the inadequacy of sources necessary for undertaking any such study."[5] As a step toward filling this gap, Cigar opted to edit a text of exceptional value.[6]

Many other historians of the eighteenth century have felt the pressing need to edit an otherwise inaccessible source or to publish a collection of archival records deemed central to the understanding of the period. Arribas Palau published *Cartas árabes de Marruecos en tiempo de Mawlay al-Yazid, 1790–1792* in 1961;[7] Jacques Caillé, *Les accords internationaux du sultan Sidi Mohammed Ben Abdallah (1757–1790)* in 1960;[8] and Pierre Grillon, *La correspondance du consul Louis Chénier 1767–1782* in 1970.[9] From 1977 to 1986, Muhammad Hajji and Ahmad Tawfiq edited al-Qadiri's *Nashr al-Mathani* in its entirety;[10] and in 1983 Magali Morsy edited *La Relation de Thomas Pellow*.[11]

Although each new edition of a text makes a basic contribution to knowledge about the eighteenth century, the era's documentary wealth continues to lag far behind that of the sixteenth, seventeenth, or nineteenth centuries. *Les Sources inédites de l'histoire du Maroc,* published by de Castries beginning in 1905,[12] provides insights of inestimable value to historians of the sixteenth and seventeenth centuries. One can only deplore the termination (or abandonment?) of this project. As for the nineteenth century, since Jean-Louis Miège devoted his monumental thesis, based on the materials in European archives, to *Le Maroc et l'Europe,*[13] Moroccan sources and archives, the most substantial part of which concern the nineteenth century,[14] have grown increasingly accessible. Is it any wonder, then, that scholars have concentrated their attention on this century?

By itself, however, this technical explanation is insufficient. Other elements, including the attitudes of Moroccan historians themselves, come into play. Since the records for eighteenth-century Morocco are richer and better preserved outside the country than inside it, these Moroccan historians are the scholars most affected by the problems of documentation. For that very reason, more foreign historians than Moroccan have been active in examining this period. But a historic element must also be factored into the equation: The intrinsic attraction of what little is known of the eighteenth century simply cannot rival the appeal of the sixteenth and seventeenth centuries or the challenge of the nineteenth. A brief glance at descriptive phrases applied to the eighteenth century may help to explain why. For Brignon, it is "a century of difficulties and of wavering;"[15] Laroui sees it as a time of "expectation," although his English translator more bluntly refers to "the eve of foreign intervention."[16] The eighteenth century no longer provides a stage for Berque's "founders," nor is it yet the time of the European opening and penetration, or of the fevered reactions that it aroused. All-in-all, an unstable equilibrium with little magnetism.

Ideological motivations have certainly influenced this process of selective attraction. National historians place the same emphasis on the post-Islamic history of Morocco that colonial historians placed on the pre-Islamic period. The times of grandeur and brilliance are privileged to the detriment of those of weakness and obscurity. As the period directly preceding colonization, the nineteenth century holds a special place. Much colonial historiography was predicated on "facts" associated with this period, although its practitioners rarely took the trouble to consult local sources. The decolonization of history has taken the form, first and foremost, of a reappropriation of a people's own voice through local sources.

Today, after four decades of independence, national historiography can no longer survive essentially as an adjunct of ideology. It must be converted into an instrument of knowledge and this is, in fact, happening. In the process of this conversion, the eighteenth century, among other neglected periods, will attract the attention of more and more researchers. Positive action on the practical suggestions which follow would greatly facilitate their work.

The resumption of the editing and publication of the *Sources inédites de l'histoire du Maroc* is imperative. Even for the periods included in the volumes already published, de Castries and his collaborators overlooked numerous important items.[17] However, greater emphasis should be given to the periods not yet addressed and to the archival materials consulted infrequently, if at all. Preliminary exploratory work, albeit fragmentary, holds out the hope of some very rich discoveries in both quantity and quality.[18] Such undertakings would certainly shed new light on these periods.

A single example will suffice. Given the state of his documentation, Lourido Díaz could only conclude that Moroccan-Ottoman relations simply did not exist during the dynastic and social crisis from 1727 to 1757.[19] He was quite astonished, however, that the deys of Algiers did not take advantage of their repeated opportunities during those years to seize power in Morocco. Material that I have collected in the course of a research trip to Istanbul modifies that view in a major way. Not only were relations maintained between Sultan ʿAbdallah b. Ismaʿil and the Sublime Porte, but those contacts may have played a part in protecting Morocco against any meddling by the deys.

This essay has attempted to demonstrate conclusively the scantiness of historic studies treating the Moroccan eighteenth century. Its analysis of historical production—albeit limited to the journal *Hespéris-Tamuda* and the academic research of historians at Rabat—has verified the feeble nature of the historiography of this era in contrast with the immediately preceding and following ones. Such a situation is not peculiar to Moroccan historiography. Similar observations can be made about certain periods of the eighteenth century in the Ottoman Empire.[20] Could there have been a localized golden age during the sixteenth and seventeenth century throughout the whole of the southern Mediterranean? Whether or not that was so, the nineteenth century proved a period of violent challenges for all of these regions before they fell, generally in short order, under the yoke of foreign occupation. The religious, intellectual, and political shock engendered by the threat—and then the reality—of occupation have commanded the priority of national historians anxious to reappropriate their nation's voice and its history. Nevertheless, with the help of new materials and a rethinking by the historical community of the conventional wisdom, the eighteenth century, situated between grandeur and decline (or what is perceived in those terms), should attract greater attention and study, as well as arouse greater interest.

## Notes

1. Jean Brignon et al., *Histoire du Maroc* (Paris: Hatier, 1967).

2. Mohamed El Mansour, *Morocco in the Reign of Mawlay Sulayman* (Wisbech, Eng.: Middle East and North African Studies Press, Ltd., 1990).

3. For an essay particularly germane to this article, see Magali Morsy, "Réflexions sur le discours historique à travers l'examen d'un document sur le Maroc au milieu du XVIIIè siècle," *ROMM* XX (1975), pp. 67–102.

4. See, for example, Allan R. Meyers, "Sidi Muhammad ibn Abdallah ou le faux départ du Maroc moderne," in Charles-André Julien et al., *Les Africains* (Paris: Editions Jeune Afrique, 1977), pp. 231–259; Norman Cigar, "Société et vie politique à Fès sous les premiers 'Alawites (ca. 1660/1830)," in *Hespéris-Tamuda* XVIII (1978–1979), pp. 93–172; and idem., "Recently Discovered Moroccan Chronicles in the Bodleian Library, Oxford," in *ROMM* XXIV (1977), pp. 111–123.

5. Cigar, "Société et vie politique," p. 94.

6. Muhammad ibn al-Tayyib al-Qadiri, *Nashr al-Mathani,* Norman Cigar, trans. (London: Oxford University Press, 1981).

7. Mariano Arribas Palau, *Cartas árabes de Marruecos en tiempo de Mawlay al-Yazid, 1790–1792* (Rabat: Université de Rabat, Publications de la Faculté des Lettres, 1961).

8. Jacques Caillé, *Les accords internationaux du sultan Sidi Mohammed Ben Abdallah (1757–1790)* (Paris: Librairie Général de Droit et de Jurisprudence, 1960).

9. Pierre Grillon, *La correspondance du consul Louis Chénier 1767–1782* (2 vols.; Paris: SEVPEN, 1970).

10. Muhammad ibn al-Tayyib al-Qadiri, *Nashr al-Mathani,* Muhammad Hajji and Ahmad Tawfiq, eds. (4 vols.; Rabat: Maktabat al-Talib, 1977–1986.)

11. Magali Morsy, *La Relation de Thomas Pellow. Une lecture du Maroc au 18è siècle* (Paris: Editions Recherche sur les Civilisations, 1983).

12. Henry de Castries et al., eds., *Les Sources inédites de l'histoire du Maroc* (26 vols.; Paris: E. Leroux, 1905–1961).

13. Jean-Louis Miège, *Le Maroc et l'Europe* (Paris: PUF, 1961–1963).

14. See Germain Ayache, "La question des archives historiques marocaines" in *Hespéris-Tamuda* II (1961), pp. 311–326; idem., "L'utilisation et l'apport des archives historiques marocaines," ibid. VII (1966), pp. 69–85; idem., "Archives et documentation historique arabe au Maroc," in *Les Arabes par leurs archives*, Jacques Berque and Dominique Chevallier, eds. (Paris: CNRS, 1976), pp. 37–45; and Daniel Schroeter, "The Royal Palace Archives of Rabat and the Makhzan in the 19th Century," in *Maghreb Review* VII, nos. 1–2 (1982), pp. 41–45.

15. Brignon, *Histoire du Maroc,* p. 256.

16. Abdallah Laroui, *L'Histoire du Maghreb* (Paris: Maspero, 1976), Chap. XII.

17. J. F. P. Hopkins, *Letters from Barbary, 1576–1774: Arabic Documents from the Public Record Office* (London: Oxford University Press, 1982), p. 7.

18. Magali Morsy and A. R. Meyers, "L'Apport des archives britanniques à la connaissance de l'histoire du Maroc aux XVIIè–XVIIIè siècles," in *Hespéris-Tamuda* XIV (1973), pp. 17–193, for the British archives and Andrew Hess, *The Forgotten Frontier*, (Chicago: University of Chicago Press, 1978) on the Turkish and other archives.

19. Ramón Lourido Díaz, "Relaciones del alawi Sidi Muhammad ibn Abdallah con el imperio turco en la primera mitad de su sultanato (1757–1775)," in *Cuadernos de la Biblioteca española de Tetuán* XXIII–XXIV (1981), p. 314.

20. Stanford J. Shaw, *History of the Ottoman Empire and Modern Turkey*, (2 vols.; Cambridge: Cambridge University Press, 1976), I, p. 324 for the reign of Abdul Hamid I (1774–1789).

# An Aspect of Tunisian Historiography
# in the Modern and Contemporary Periods:
# Research in the Notarial Archives

*Sami Bergaoui*
Université de Tunis

A few years ago, a historian taking stock of the recent historiography on Tunisia's modern period made a cogent point.

> Because, on the one hand, the sources of Tunisian history merely reflect the reality of political power in its various forms and because, on the other, they express even better the contingencies of business and diplomacy, they generally allow only rather brief incursions into the exploration of their endogenous substance.[1]

A dark picture, perhaps, but not entirely black. It would worsen if research efforts were limited to commercial and diplomatic archives and to the state archives of Tunisia. Indeed, were this to occur, "the material and psychological structures of Tunisian society would not be evident" and "vast stretches of Tunisian history would be doomed to obscurity."[2] One might go even farther and say that the reality of political power itself, as it related to Tunisian society and to foreign countries, would never be entirely clear since our perspective would always be one-sided.

The same may be said of the colonial period. Neither the archives of the Tunisian administration, nor diplomatic archives, nor police reports, much less the newspapers, can tell us, in a totally satisfactory way, about the material foundations of Tunisian society or its daily life. Regrettably, however, the inventory of sources likely to shed light on this hidden side of Tunisian history is still unfinished.

Among the most important of these promising sources are the notarial archives. Unfortunately, these records are not complete. Although they remain essentially intact for the years since 1875 (thanks to a government decree issued by Khayr al-Din), only a portion of them has survived from the earlier period. They do not constitute a distinct archival grouping but consist of several sets of notarial deeds housed in disparate archival repositories. Moreover, the documents from before 1875 deal almost exclusively with land ownership. Only since 1875 are there records, maintained by the Ministry of Justice, that cover almost all notarial transactions. A brief overview of these various archives will reveal the truly enormous prospects that they open to historical researchers.[3]

The archives of the state domain include:

1 PROPERTY OF THE FORMER HABUS (PIOUS ENDOWMENTS) COUNCIL (1874–1957)
   a. Property deeds of estates managed by the Council date primarily from the nineteenth and twentieth centuries, but some are from the eighteenth, seventeenth, and occasionally even the sixteenth centuries (dozens of uninventoried cartons).
   b. Accounting records of the Council's holdings, by year and by property, from 1874 to 1957 (several hundred uninventoried records).

2 PROPERTY OF THE BAIT AL-MAL (TREASURY)
   Inventories of the estates of persons deceased without heirs; devolution of assets to the Bait al-Mal (a few dozen uninventoried cartons).

Other archives include:

1 ARCHIVES OF THE LAND REGISTRY (ESTABLISHED IN 1885)
   Several thousand files, consisting mostly of property deeds, primarily from the nineteenth and twentieth centuries, but also from earlier times.

2 ARCHIVES OF THE GOVERNORATES
   Notary deeds of habus properties used by the Committees for the Redistribution of Habus (starting in 1957) with a view towards establishing the rights of claimants and dividing the estates. Unfortunately for the historian, many of these deeds have been returned to their owners.

3 GENERAL ARCHIVES OF THE TUNISIAN GOVERNMENT
   These contain several cartons of notary deeds related to the property of the beylik, of various beys and members of the beylical family, and of high dignitaries and leading citizens. They are being inventoried.

4 COURT ARCHIVES
   Local court archives hold the most important and varied trove of notarial archives—several thousand records—all later than 1875.

To these various archival sources must be added deeds privately held by families of notaries and particularly by landowners' families. Several studies have shown the importance of these deeds for historians,[4] but their accessibility remains extremely limited and selective.

Although the focus of research undertaken on the basis of these notarial archives invariably pertains to economic and social history, it has produced quite diverse results. Although outlining the scope of these various studies is a bit difficult—especially since the notarial archives are sometimes their chief source, while at other times they serve to complement other archival materials—the following descriptions of three main areas of current research highlight the most important contributions. A fairly complete list of studies based on notarial archives appears at the end of this article.

## OWNERSHIP

The interest taken in ownership goes back at least to the 1950s and the pioneering studies of Jean Poncet, which dealt mainly with European property in Tunisia.[5] Research on property deeds began after Mohammed Hédi Chérif demonstrated, in 1968, that such documents could shed light on the profound changes in society and in the political regime during the Muradid era.[6]

The examination of notarial archives has somewhat shifted the focus of studies on ownership. Instead of a global approach (as in Poncet) or a static view (as in Valensi[7]), these records allow for more detailed and dynamic analyses in that they focus on the transfer of property which was, after all, the main form of wealth in colonial and precolonial Tunisian society. Thus far, studies in this field have dealt with the history of ownership in Tunis[8] and the surrounding area[9] or Sfax and certain inland towns and villages of the Sahel.[10] Some studies have taken a more specific interest in family patrimonies[11] or in religious institutions.[12] Yet another—and newer—approach is to trace the evolution of the beylik's land holdings through the modern period, from the beginning of the seventeenth century to the twentieth century.[13]

These studies clearly show the extent of economic and social disparities in cities and in rural areas, the importance and limits of the control of property by urban people and members of the privileged classes, the vitality of some of these groups and the intensity of the rivalries between them, the breaks and continuities in the social structure, and the effects of shifts in the economic context on society. They also show the diversity of the factors, including family relationships, that governed social interaction, especially in the cities. But at least as important as kinship were such factors as geographical affinities, ethnic origins, professional affiliations, and social standing. Many of these works deal with the habus properties of religious institutions or with private habus, revealing the economic and social importance of this practice. By examining the problems stemming from this particular form of property transfer—often running counter to Islamic law—this research paves the way for the study of the social and ideological relationships resulting from such transfers.

## METHODS OF EXPLOITATION

Closely related to the review of ownership and, like it, seeking to better explain problems of social stratification and the interaction of social groups, are several studies that have stressed the importance of understanding the methods of exploitation of both labor and capital. Apart from a few *fiqh* (Islamic jurisprudence) agreements or compilations of *nawazil* (legal actions), no other source allows for the systematic study of these problems. Regrettably, the notarial archives that provide information on this subject start only in 1875. On the positive side, it is an enormously rich lode whose study in this context is only beginning. As it is, research in this field has already demonstrated the profound divisions within rural communities, not only between owners and nonowners, but also between workers and employers of labor, whether in suburban areas, villages, or tribes. The great majority of peasants, who appear to have owned neither land nor flocks, had little choice but to hire themselves out as laborers in order to survive. Hence, the multiplication in notarial records of labor contracts with the *khammas* arrangement (share-cropping, with one-fifth of the crop going to the peasant laborer), generally prominent in the northern part of the country, and the *musaqah* contract (by which the laborer irrigated a piece of land in return for a share of its produce) and grazing contracts more in evidence in the oases. Although these studies are only beginning, they call into question Valensi's conclusions on rural Tunisia at the end of the nineteenth century by illustrating that independent farmers were far from the majority of the rural population.

Special attention should be given to the evolution of these relationships following the "colonial trauma." Their degradation was so slow that "traditional" labor contracts, albeit modified and adjusted, were used by both colonists and modern Tunisian farmers until 1956. Until at least that time, wage earners remained a marginal group (at least among Tunisian farmers) and derived no profit from the demise of tribal society.

Urban society remains somewhat beyond the scope of these studies.

What needs to be examined is how participants perceived these divisions and this evolution. Notarial documents permit a study of ideologies and thought processes regarding labor relations and conflicts, as well as many other kinds of litigation that could burden daily life. Such bitter disputes, and their tragic consequences, bring to light complex motivations in a wide variety of situations. This is an avenue yet to be explored.

## FAMILY AND KINSHIP

Although research to date on family and kinship has been limited, what has been done is of the most original and most innovative order. Still restricted to the urban context, it has considered, among other questions, the so-called "Arab" marriage (between parallel cousins), polygamy, and endogamy, which have proven to be rather marginal practices.[14] But scholars have also gone beyond these questions to focus on the study of matrimonial strategies that created alliances favoring elevation within the society, strengthened established positions, or preserved and increased the family patrimony. Scholars are also taking an interest in the family group—its daily life, its structure, and the status of women, with a particular interest in the changes of that status, which accelerated through contact with colonial society. Finally, scholars have succeeded in identifying networks of family alliances and family constellations held together not only by matrimonial bonds but also by wealth, profession, and culture. The confluence of these new emphases might be regarded as the birth of a history of intimacy.

The birth of Tunisian social historiography has coincided with the spread, among American and European scholars, of the segmentary model, which is thought to best explain the social structure of the Maghrib. Tunisian historiography has not failed to consider this question, but the reply of scholars who have analyzed notarial documents tends to contradict the model, primarily by contesting two of its basic tenets. The first tenet is that of equality. Contrary to what the segmentary model seeks to prove, equality is a marginal phenomenon; indeed, a nonexistent one. This is true with respect to the workplace, to wealth, and to political power (whether it be at the level of community-related or of state-related institutions). The second contested tenet is that of statism and stability. Contrary to the model, what is significant is the drive and vitality of this society; its complexity, its social mobility, and the rivalries between its component groups. This drive is not limited to a few people but is inherent in the structures of a society receptive to private ownership, trade, and the profitable use of labor and capital.

In short, this is not so integrated a society that it has a single model of behavior. The segmentary model can only partially explain relations between individuals and social groups and is but one pattern governing society, influencing social behavior, and contributing to shaping the forces that determine social relations. In any event, these forces seem larger, more varied, and more contradictory than the segmentary model would suggest. Without entirely invalidating it, notarial studies have made it possible to define the model more succinctly, to give it some nuances, and to ascribe to it a more modest role in a more complex overall social structure.

These studies go beyond the framework of a sterile segmentary theory unable to account for historical reality. They assume close connections among politics, culture, and economics and seek, behind the political event, its social equivalent. For example, it is becoming clear that the "de-Turkification" of political power in Tunisia throughout the eighteenth century, and especially in the nineteenth, was followed by the shrinkage of the landed wealth of alien groups and a corresponding increase in that of indigenous groups, not only in the cities, but also in the provinces and the tribes.[15] Similarly, during the nineteenth century, seizure of power by the mamluks (slaves of the royal family trained to serve in administrative and military positions) was accompanied by the slow loss by the state of its landed property. Starting in 1881, with the collapse of the Tunisian state, the dependent social groups lost most of their land. Although Tunisians in general lost much to the Europeans, some of them quickly adjusted to the new circumstances and actually increased their fortunes. This was especially true for urban groups of provincial background, for people in the provinces, and for some members of the beylical aristocracy.[16] Thus, this historiography breaks with the unanimity that has characterized some studies on colonial society and the nationalist movement. All too often, such studies have set up an excessively cut-and-dried distinction between European colonial society—which alone, except for a tiny minority of Tunisians, profited from the colonial regime and always supported it—and the overburdened mass of the Tunisian people, who were always exploited, always in crisis, and always opposed to that regime.

Curiously, while the Arabo-Islamic world engages in a frantic search for a basic identity, the work presented here seeks identification with what researchers regard as of universal importance—change and movement. Perhaps the central problem with segmentary theory is that it is an approach that freezes the society, thereby marginalizing it with reference to European or western history. That is precisely why it is necessary to look to the past for signs and evidence of hope for the future. Therein resides, whatever the limits of this form of historiography may be, its profound originality in comparison with the ideas that now dominate both local and western historiography on modern and contemporary Tunisia.

In conclusion, the problem of command over the mass of documents in this research, which in most cases far exceeds individual (or even human) capability, must be acknowledged. The obvious solution—and one towards which there is movement—is computerization. An initial endeavor in this direction has been the "Patrimoines, Familles et Alliances à Tunis (XVIIIème–XXème siècle)" project under the aegis of the Comparative Research Program at the Centre National de la Recherche Scientifique (CNRS), which has brought together historians and sociologists. A second, similar, project was begun in 1989 at the CNRS.

## Notes

1. Taoufik Bachrouch, "L'historiographie tunisienne de 1968 à 1985. L'époque moderne," *Revue de l'Institut des Belles Lettres Arabes* L, no. 159 (1987), pp. 75–90.

2. Ibid., p. 77.

3. Since 1974, Mohammed Hédi Chérif has drawn the attention of scholars to the importance of these archives. See his article "L'Histoire économique et sociale de la Tunisie au XVIIIème siècle à travers les sources locales: enseignements et perspectives" in *Les Arabes par leurs archives (XVIe–XXe siècles)* (Paris: CNRS, 1976).

4. See, for example, Mohamed al-Aziz Ben Achour, "Catégories de la société tunisoise dans la deuxième moitié du XIXème siècle: les élites musulmanes" (Thèse du doctorat, Université de Paris IV, 1986).

5. Jean Poncet, *La Colonisation et l'agriculture européennes en Tunisie depuis 1881* (Paris and The Hague: Mouton, 1961).

6. Mohammed Hédi Chérif, "Introduction de la piastre espagnole (ryal) dans la Régence de Tunis au début du XVIIIème siècle" in *Cahiers de Tunisie*, nos. 61–64 (1968), pp. 45–53. See also Chérif's later work "Propriété des oliviers au Sahel des débuts du XVIIème à ceux du XIXème siècle" in *Actes du 1er Congrès d'histoire et de civilisation du Maghreb* (Tunis: CERES, 1979), pp. 209–247.

7. Lucette Valensi, *Tunisian Peasants in the Eighteenth and Nineteenth Centuries* (Cambridge: Cambridge University Press, 1985).

8. At the heart of this work is the project "Patrimoines, Familles et Alliances à Tunis (XVIIIème–XXème siècle)," bringing together historians and sociologists under the aegis of the Comparative Research Program of the CNRS. Also of importance is the doctoral dissertation of Abdelhamid Henia, "Propriété et propriétaires dans la région de Tunis du début du XVIIIème siècle au XXème," at the Université de Tunis under the direction of Mohammed Hédi Chérif.

9. Sami Bergaoui, "Propriété foncière et rapports de production dans la région de Tunis (1875–1914)" (Thèse de D.R.A., Université de Tunis, Faculté des Sciences Humaines et Sociales, 1982). [In Arabic].

10. Chérif, "Propriété des oliviers."

11. These include the CNRS joint history-sociology project; Ben Achour, "Catégories de la société tunisoise;" and Abdelhamid Henia, "Origine et évolution d'un patrimoine familial tunisien (XVIIème–XIXème)" in *IBLA*, no. 154 (1984), pp. 201–247 and no. 155 (1985), pp. 3–17.

12. al-Azhar Kesraoui, "Les confréries religieuse à Sfax aux XVIIIème et XIXème siècles" (Thèse de D.R.A., Université de Tunis, Faculté des Sciences Humaines et Sociales, 1985). [In Arabic].

13. Jamal Ben Taher, "La Propriété foncière beylicale" [provisional

title] (Doctoral Thesis, Université de Tunis, Faculté des Sciences Humaines et Sociales, in progress).

14. See the CNRS joint history-sociology project and Lili Blili Ben Temime, "Structure et vie de famille à Tunis à l'époque pré-coloniale et coloniale (de 1875 à la veille des années 1930)" (Thèse de D.R.A., Université de Tunis, Faculté des Sciences Humaines et Sociales, 1986).

15. Data collected in the CNRS joint history-sociology project have underscored this process.

16. As demonstrated in Bergaoui, "Propriété foncière."

## Bibliography of Studies Making Use of Notarial Archives

### Thèses d'Etat

Ben Achour, Mohamed al-Aziz. "Catégories de la société tunisoise dans la deuxième moitié du XIXème siècle: les élites musulmanes" (Université de Paris IV, 1986. Published under the same title, Tunis: INAA, 1989).

Ben Taher, Jamal. "La Propriété foncière beylicale." (Provisional title). In progress, Université de Tunis.

Henia, Abdelhamid. "Propriété et propriétaires dans la région de Tunis du début du XVIIIème siècle au XXème." In progress, Université de Tunis.

### Thèses de D.R.A. (Unpublished unless otherwise noted)

Bergaoui, Sami. "Propriété foncière et rapports de production dans la région de Tunis (1875–1914)." Université de Tunis, 1982. [In Arabic].

Blili Ben Temime, Lili. "Structure et vie de famille à Tunis à l'époque pré-coloniale et coloniale (de 1875 à la veille des années 1930)." Université de Tunis, 1986.

Henia, Abdelhamid. "Les rapports du Grid avec le Beylik de Tunis (1676–1840)." Tunis: Publications de l'Ecole Normale Supérieure de Tunis, 1980.

Karray, K. "Situation foncière dans la région de Sfax du début du XIXème siècle à 1929." Université de Tunis, 1986. [In Arabic].

Kesraoui, al-Azhar. "Les confréries religieuses à Sfax aux XVIIIème et XIXème siècles." Université de Tunis.

### Other Publications

Bergaoui, Sami. "Le phénomène de l'usure dans la Tunisie de 1881," in Réactions à l'occupation française de la Tunisie en 1881. Tunis: Editions CNUDST, 1983.

———. "Rente foncière et prix agricoles en Tunisie (1920–1945)," in IBLA, no. 158 (1986), pp. 297–319.

————. "L'Etat, le lazzam et les producteurs d'huile au milieu du XIXème siècle," in *Revue d'histoire maghrébine*, no. 43–44 (1986), pp. 223–238. [In Arabic].

Chérif, Mohammed Hédi. "Introduction de la piastre espagnole (ryal) dans la Régence de Tunis au début du XVIIème siècle," in *Cahiers de Tunisie*, nos. 61–64 (1968), pp. 45–53.

————. "Propriété des oliviers au Sahel des débuts du XVIIème à ceux du XIXème siècle," in *Actes du 1er Congrès d'histoire et de civilisation du Maghreb* (Tunis: CERES, 1979), pp. 209–247.

Henia, Abdelhamid. "Origine et évolution d'un patrimoine familial tunisien (XVIIème–XIXème)," in *Revue de l'Institut des belles lettres arabes*, no. 154 (1984), pp. 201–247; and no. 155 (1985), pp. 3–17.

R.C.P. 549. "Patrimoines, familles et alliances à Tunis (XVIIIème–XXème siècle)." Comparative Research Program of the CNRS. Study in progress.

# The Maghrib and the Mediterranean World in the Nineteenth Century: Illicit Exchanges, Migrants, and Social Marginals

Julia Clancy-Smith
University of Arizona

*When the rooster crows in Malta, he awakens the sleepers in Tunis.*

—MALTESE PROVERB

*The Frenchman marched against [Algiers] and took her.*

*It was not one hundred ships that he had, nor two hundred;*

*He proudly has his flotilla defile before her,*

*Surging forth from the high seas, with powerful armies . . .*

—SHEIKH ʿABD AL-QADIR[1]

## INTRODUCTION

In his classic study of the sixteenth century, the late French historian Fernand Braudel maintained that the civilizations of the Mediterranean Basin "shared a common destiny," characterized by cultural unity and historical coherence,[2] but studies viewing the Mediterranean from a "Braudelian" perspective for later centuries are few and far between.[3] Indeed, for the medieval era, we have a more finely grained portrait of Mediterranean commerce and social relations than we do for later periods, largely due to the research of Abraham L. Udovitch, S. D. Goitein, and Robert Lopez.[4] Much of what Braudel says for the age of Philip II, Sulayman, and Khayr al-Din was true in the last century as well. Yet monographs on states or peoples bordering the Middle Sea during the era of imperialism almost exclusively employ the nation-state as a unit of analysis, which obscures larger, more important relationships and interconnections.[5]

The Maghrib's involvement with the Mediterranean world is as ancient as it is intense. In his introduction to *The Tunisia of Ahmad Bey*, L. Carl

Brown noted that Ahmad was the son of a female Christian slave captured in 1798 by Tunisian corsairs raiding the island of Sardinia.[6] More than two decades ago, Lucette Valensi pointed out that North African demographic patterns in the seventeenth and eighteenth centuries were subject to epidemic cycles whose origins lay not only in other parts of the Mediterranean, but also farther afield in Asia.[7] In *On the Eve of Colonialism,* Valensi further noted that no comprehensive study existed on the question of North African trade with the Mediterranean world during the eighteenth century.[8] In the following century came more epidemic diseases, as well as newcomers and intruders, to the Maghrib.

With the possible exception of Egypt-oriented studies, recent historical works of northern Africa during the colonial moment have disregarded the presence of European colons and traders, while paradoxically decrying settler colonialism and economic imperialism. More than the interior, the Maghrib's coastal cities hosted the newly arrived Europeans, many of whom resided there permanently, sometimes for generations. Thus far, historians of nineteenth-century North Africa have been somewhat slow to examine the Maghrib's relation to the Middle Sea; however, the number of periodicals and journals now appearing which adopt a trans-Mediterranean perspective suggests a move to rethink the nation-state grid imposed upon the entire region.[9]

Here it will be argued that the nineteenth-century Maghrib must be considered from a vantage point other than simply that of the nation-state; it has to be relinked with sea-wide systems and processes. In this period, the Mediterranean was—as it always has been—utterly promiscuous, a privileged terrain for complex interactions involving many of the cultures around its rim. Yet the Mediterranean, too, should be conceived of differently. It forms a gigantic internal waterway surrounded by Afro-Eurasia but divided into smaller seas in terms of ease of navigation. And the Mediterranean has always constituted more of a highway than a border. If, today, Maghribi worker migration to the north has made Mediterranean Africa into Europe's southern frontier, in the nineteenth and early twentieth centuries, the migratory impulse ran in the opposite direction.

From 1830 on, the Sea became increasingly an expressway distributing migrants willy-nilly from Europe to North Africa. The Maghrib, therefore, represented a frontier for certain classes of Europeans, a pole of attraction for those seeking socioeconomic opportunity, in much the same way that the Americas did. While the patterns isolated by historians of migration, such as Bernard Bailyn in *The Peopling of British North America,* could have relevance for North Africa in its multiple relationships with the Mediterranean, scholarly obsessions with population movements to the New World have deflected attention away from other sites of peopling.[10] Moreover, the arrival of Europeans on the Mediterranean's southern littoral in the course of the colonial enterprise represented the largest transfer of populations between the two continents since the Reconquista of centuries earlier.

As the century progressed, western commodities flooded North African markets as economic props to European political hegemony in the region. While some manufactured products came into the Maghrib "legally"—that is, in accordance with diplomatic and commercial treaties often imposed by force upon unwilling rulers—many others were introduced as contraband through complex, clandestine trading networks that spliced one side of the Mediterranean with the other. What needs to be assessed are the world-historical implications of these countless illicit operations linking the African coast from Tangier to Alexandria with Livorno (Leghorn), Marseille, Palermo, and Valetta.[11]

By probing into the related issues of migration and migrants, illegal exchanges or contraband, and social marginals, this essay reviews past scholarship on, and plots out future research directions for, the nineteenth-century history of the Maghrib, concentrating mainly on Tunisia and Algeria.[12] In addition, it argues that the ethnic and social groups under consideration may not have been marginal at all; rather their activities, in the aggregate, displace our current understanding of centers and peripheries. Finally, North Africa, which is often omitted from conventional treatments of world history, can take its rightful place as a crossroads region linking Europe, the Mediterranean Basin, and Africa. If events—whether barely perceptible changes or the more conspicuous large-scale transformations—on the Sea's northern lip had an impact on its southern edge, the reverse was also true.

## MIGRANTS, SOCIAL MARGINALS, AND CONTRABAND

The nineteenth century witnessed the mass movement of southern Europeans, often outside of official or authorized colonization schemes, to the Maghrib. These migrations, sub rosa and spontaneous, first to Algeria and Tunisia and later to Morocco, have hardly been studied; yet they constitute a crucial chapter in global migration history. The countless local exoduses—subsistence migration—from Naples, Pantellaria, the Italian Piedmont, Sardinia, Corsica, and elsewhere raise significant issues in the Maghrib's history for its political relationship with Europe and the Mediterranean world; for the evolution of local economies; for the growth of the state; for the politics of identity in the nineteenth century; and for world market integration. Many of the subsistence migrants were also political marginals in that they were somewhat outside of the prevailing system of nation-states while loosely under the pro forma protection of one or another of the major European powers. They were thus part both of European and of North African societies, yet apart from them; the Maltese residing in Tunisia and Algeria are perhaps the best example of this.

As stated above, recent literature on the Maghrib during the colonial period ignores, for the most part, the multiple interactions of these European "squatters"—colonies within colonies—and even those residing there with official approval of North African societies. When the European communities that took root in the Maghrib are examined, attention is usually conferred either upon settlers or high-ranking officials.[13] However important the land-hungry colons were for the evolution of French imperialism and the ideology of conquest, the fact remains that by the nineteenth century's close most resident Europeans were city dwellers. Hugging the Mediterranean coast from Tangier to Djerba, they occupied the middle ranks of the colonial social order, although in terms of social marginality, the lower ranks of the colonizers often bled into indigenous society. And social marginals, whether European or North African, have hardly been studied for this era.

The corpus of colonial literature devoted to certain classes of Europeans residing in the Maghrib is, not surprisingly, quite large, yet remains to be exploited. One noteworthy example is Gaston Loth's *Le Peuplement italien en Tunisie et en Algérie,* published in 1905, which remains the only detailed study of Italian emigration.[14] For Tunisia, Jean Ganiage has done the most research in his demographic studies, some of which were completed over three decades ago—for example, his *La Population européenne de Tunis au milieu du XIXè siècle.*[15] And for Morocco, Jean-Louis Miège's four-volume *Le Maroc et L'Europe (1830–1894)* remains a classic, although it was published thirty years ago.[16] Much new documentation has come to light since these works first appeared, and substantial theoretical advances into questions of identity, ethnicity, class, race, and gender have been made. Thus, the classics need to be supplanted or supplemented by new studies.

A recent work which contributes greatly to our understanding of transplanted European society in Algeria is David Prochaska's *Making Algeria French: Colonialism in Bône, 1870–1920.*[17] Prochaska traces the construction of a distinctly pied-noir society in Bône, formed of variegated human material from all over the Middle Sea region. The work raises critical issues regarding the relationship between class and 'race' in the formation of the social pecking order in Bône. In this and his other studies, Prochaska makes a substantial contribution to our understanding of the crystallization of a unique pied-noir mentalité and popular culture, with crucial political ramifications for Maghribi history. However, the absence of any discussion of women—and without them a settler colonial society cannot, by definition, exist—is regrettable and will be addressed below.

Refugees and migrants share a number of characteristics, although both represent imprecisely defined social groups. As the French conquest of Algeria progressed, waves of Algerian refugees poured into Tunisia and Morocco. In their host countries, they were, for the most part, socially marginalized—the elites and religious notables aside.[18] Very little recent research has been devoted to Algerian refugee communities in either Tunisia or Morocco, although two prominent nationalists, Tawfiq al-Madani and 'Abd al-'Aziz al-Tha'alibi, were from Algerian families residing in Tunisia. While the importance of the exiles is noted, for example, in Roger Le Tourneau's *Fès avant le protectorat* or Charles-Robert Ageron's study of the Algerian exodus from Tlemcen, "L'émigration des musulmans algériens," it has not been explored in depth, once again mainly due to the nation-state paradigm which largely fails to accommodate migrants, exiles and refugees.[19] For Tunisia, Georges Marty's long 1948 essay, "Les Algériens à Tunis," represents an important, if dated, study of Algerians in that capital. And abundant archival documentation exists for further investigations of Algerians driven into exile.[20]

Many of the more enterprising Algerian refugees of ordinary rank engaged in various and sundry contraband operations, particularly the illicit gunpowder and armaments traffic between Tunis, Tunisian border towns, and eastern Algeria or between the Oranais and Morocco, to make an "honest" living. Nor were they alone, for Europeans of humble station residing along the North African coast also engaged in smuggling and contraband activities to offset their frequently precarious economic situation. In fact, illegal exchanges often united the two groups, native North Africans and Europeans. And these exchanges linking the Maghrib to Europe and to the eastern Mediterranean made contraband the nineteenth century's peculiar brand of piracy.

Contraband exchanges during the colonial century appear, in some cases, to have directly superseded piracy and privateering, although the relationships between these variant forms of commerce have yet to be investigated.[21] It does seem that legitimate trade, for example between England and the Caribbean in the late sixteenth and early seventeenth centuries, often grew directly from privateering. For the eighteenth century, works on the so-called "Barbary pirates" abound, although most fail to place the North African corsairs in a wider context of privateering all over the Mediterranean, Atlantic, and Caribbean.[22] And if corsair activity was a venerable system of forced exchange in which Christian and Muslim states, diplomatic allies and foes all participated, contraband, too, was a Mediterranean-wide phenomenon. It involved a huge array of shady types—among others, gunrunners, tavern owners, spies, and Maltese smugglers—as well as more or less upright folks of humble station eking out a living under less-than-favorable circumstances. While the pirate and, to a lesser extent, the bandit have captured our imaginations, their no less flamboyant successors, the contrabbandisti—either in North African countries or in others around the Basin's rim—have remained on the margins of historical inquiry.[23]

Pirates, bandits, and smugglers share a number of characteristics in terms of how transactions are effected; moreover, the latter two often shade off into one another. Bandits and banditry were initially pushed to the foreground of social-science consciousness by Eric Hobsbawm in his *Bandits* (1969).[24] While colonial archival documentation exists for studying banditry, only a few studies have appeared to date. Jean Déjeux's "Un Bandit d'honneur dans l'Aurès" was one of the first to investigate the "noble robber" as folk hero and avenger of wrongs in the Aurès Mountains during the First World War.[25] More recently, David Hart's *Banditry in Islam* applied Hobsbawm's model of the bandit to case studies from precolonial Morocco and Algeria to see if the ostensibly universal paradigm fit the North African data.[26] In addition, Hart sought to determine to what extent social banditry in the Maghrib was a product of colonial domination. Not surprisingly, he found that the global model proposed by Hobsbawm needed considerable adjustment for the Maghribi cases. "The question of the role played by colonialism in the phenomenon of social banditry is to underscore the often fine line of distinction in reality between the social bandit and the resistance leader."[27] If the lines were frequently blurred between the local political activist and the noble robber, those demarcating Mediterranean smugglers and contrebandiers from bandits or from "honest" small-time retailers were also blurred.

In his 1980 study of Bu Hmara (Abu Himara), Ross E. Dunn drew attention to the political significance of the contraband arms trade in Morocco.[28] Dunn's inquiry focused mainly on the role that access to European firearms played in the rise to power of local warlords in the Moroccan northeast as the noose of formal colonialism tightened over the country. Mohammed Kenbib's 1984 study, "Contrabande d'armes et 'anarchie' dans le Maroc précolonial," reopened the question of the arms traffic in the Sharifian empire from the Battle of Isly (1844) until the imposition of the formal French protectorate.[29] As Kenbib found for Morocco, and this author has found for Tunisia and Algeria, the shifting fortunes of the central state and local economies in the Maghrib were both cause and consequence of the contraband trade.

The fact that some economic and commercial activities previously ignored or unregulated by the state came to be branded as "extralegal" partially explains the apparently spectacular growth in the contraband traffic.[30] Thus, in one sense, contraband existed in the eye of the beholder—the wielders of power, whether indigenous or European. And the creation (or preservation) of intricate "illegal" commercial networks and black markets crisscrossing the Middle Sea represented a calculated riposte by once economically semiautonomous communities to the heightened intrusions of central governments. It was also a response of social groups marginalized by the consolidation of nation-states on the Mediterranean's northern and southern edges. In this regard, both Tunisia after 1837 and French Algeria were engaged in roughly the same experiment in state expansion. And it was no accident that as the colonial state was woven together, albeit of heterogeneous elements, the two adjacent Muslim states, Tunisia and then Morocco, began progressively to unravel.

The literature on the building of the state in French Algeria, both of colonial and of more recent date, is extensive; the best known examples are the numerous works by Charles-André Julien, Charles-Robert Ageron, and André Nouschi. Fanny Colonna, Kenneth J. Perkins, and Peter von Sivers, to name only a few, have made substantial contributions on specific dimensions of the process whereby colonial mechanisms of control—the institutions of power—were worked out.[31] The undoing of the Sharifian Empire has also received considerable scholarly attention; one of the first in-depth reconstructions of that process was *Prelude to Protectorate in Morocco* by Edmund Burke III, which related changes in world market forces with popular protest in Morocco.[32]

After the body of scholarship devoted to the nationalist movement, the corpus of historical work on the evolution of the nineteenth-century Tunisian state and economy is the most extensive. Leading the way was L. C. Brown's 1974 study of the political culture of Ahmad Bey and his era. Supplementing Brown's work are two more recent studies which also complement each other; Khelifa Chater's *Dépendance et mutations précoloniales* and Taoufik Bachrouch's *Le Saint et le prince en Tunisie*.[33] Abdelhamid Henia's *Le Grid: ses rapports avec le beylik de Tunis (1676–1840)* reversed the state-centered perspective to investigate the impact of changes in fiscal administration on the geographical periphery constituted by the Jarid.[34] Mention must also be made of the considerable contributions of Lucette Valensi and Mohamed Hédi Chérif to our understanding of the state and of rural society in both the eighteenth and nineteenth centuries.[35]

However, by definition, many of these works tend to focus upon either the official world of colonial administrators, indigenous religious notables, and urban elites, or that of local big men who either resisted the colonial regime or accommodated themselves to it (or sometimes both). Local North

African cultural brokers and intermediaries have received less attention; yet for the politics of identity and for the construction of a colonial vulgate on the nature of Islamic Maghribi society, these countless mediators and middlemen were critical. Allan Christelow's *Muslim Law Courts* revealed how the *qudah* (plural of *qadi*, a Muslim judge) emerged after 1854 not only as legal but also as political and cultural brokers since the courts represented one key point of intersection between rulers and ruled.[36]

Another group of critical intermediaries were the *qadat* (plural of *qa'id*, the head of a tribal confederation) and sheikhs recently studied by Colette Establet in *Etre caid dans l'Algérie coloniale*.[37] Chosen by France to act as links between colonizer and colonized, the qadat and sheikhs of the Nemencha confederacy in the cercle of Tebessa (in northeastern Algeria) generated an important body of documentation—Arabic correspondence with the officers of the Bureau Arabe and other officials in the Constantinois. Utilizing these archival materials, the author reconstructs the daily life of both the qadat and their subordinates, as well as the frequently contradictory relationships between indigenous administrators and the colonial hierarchy. While France sought, via the qadat, to construct a modern lower-level bureaucracy loyal to her perceived interests, the qadat strove to best local rivals and enlarge their own spheres of power. Moreover, the local qa'id was frequently implicated in the contraband trade—hand-in-hand with European allies—as this 1856 report from Bougie reveals:

> Contraband has been occurring on a large scale and for a long time in the cercle of Bougie, or rather in the cercle of Jijalli. Each time that the unloading of contraband takes place, one or two fires appear on the coast. The most active individual in this illegal commerce is Juan Onoffre, a [European] tobacco merchant in Bougie; he is associated with the qa'id of Mansouriah.[38]

What better way to supplement a meager salary than by either engaging actively in illicit nocturnal exchanges or at least turning a blind eye, for a certain sum, to the contrebanders, whether native or European, operating within one's administrative purview. Evidence for similar sorts of complicity among local beylical officials, European traders, and Mediterranean smugglers exists in abundance for Tunisia.[39] A quarter of a century ago, Jean Ganiage in his *Les Origines du protectorat français en Tunisie, 1861–1881* alluded to the importance of contraband and the role in the traffic of Europeans residing in the beylik.[40] What is significant in many of the Tunisian and Algerian cases is the frequent collusion between Europeans and indigenous agents in these illicit exchanges and the fact that local French nationals or

European protégés were working at cross-purposes with France's imperial interests.

Thus, contraband increased in volume and extent as the European states vying for hegemony in North Africa established direct or indirect control over the Mediterranean's southern shore.[41] Contraband also grew with the unification of the Italian peninsula, the creation of more modern, centralized states in Tunisia and Egypt, and the demographic boom in Malta as the island became Great Britain's chief coaling and supply base in the central Mediterranean.[42] While some literature on Malta and the Maltese exists, a thorough study of the scattered Maltese community in its multiple relationships with North Africans is still a desideratum. Two recent works are Jacques Godechot's *Histoire de Malte* and Charles Owens' *The Maltese Islands;* Ramire Vadala's *Les Maltais hors de Malte. Etude sur l'émigration maltaise,* published in 1911, remains most central to the questions under consideration here.[43]

As was the case with Maltese emigrants to Algeria, Tunisia, and Egypt, island peoples of the Mediterranean were crucial in the water transport side of contraband since they controlled small-scale cabotage operations, drawing upon a long tradition of seafaring. In the seventeenth and early eighteenth centuries, the island of Malta was perfectly situated for privateering—indeed, her balance of payments depended upon plundered shipping. By the following century, the island's location, her burgeoning population, and her free-port status made her into an exporter of men and women to the Maghrib—and elsewhere in the Mediterranean—as well as a smuggler's paradise.[44]

The contrebandiers par excellence were the Maltese residing mainly in Tunisia and Algeria. In 1850, in Bône alone, out of approximately 7,000 resident Europeans, at least 2,500 were Maltese, if official statistics can be given any credence.[45] In Tunisia, the Maltese formed the largest European presence, numbering some 7,000 in 1856; they lived in small communities scattered along the coastline from Djerba to Tabarka and also in the capital. Their nimble *speronare* and *chebecs* (Arabic: *shabbak,* a shallow-draft boat) could be dragged ashore in the dark of night or in secluded coves in the full light of day at places like Djerba, Zarzis, Gabès, and along Cape Bon during the spring and summer Mediterranean sailing season. Indeed, Djerba became a haven for smugglers channeling Tunisian products such as wheat, olive oil, and dates out to Malta and funneling prized British gunpowder and other commodities into the beylik and eventually to Algeria. The natives of Djerba, too, sailed their small craft to colonial Bône to barter their pottery there, taking the opportunity to traffic in contraband military stores as well.

If a single vector or internal impetus for the contraband trade were to be sought, it would be the French military pacification of Algeria and the construction of the colonial state. Undoubtedly, Algerians viewed this as a disaster of apocalyptic proportions, but the twin forces of conquest and state building, combined with Mediterranean-wide processes, also opened up new opportunities for cunning local entrepreneurs in the Maghrib. And neither indigenous North Africans nor their European associates of ordinary social status were slow to seize the initiative, to become populist redistributors. North African elites or notables—the best example being the Amir 'Abd al-Qadir—were also associated with this social underworld, principally to obtain ample supplies of western armaments, much of it hand-me-down firearms.[46]

Significantly, religion and culture did not necessarily constitute a barrier to participation in the contraband trade, since the vaguely Catholic Maltese worked closely with North African Muslims or Jews. Regarding the texture of daily relations between indigenous Jews and Muslims, two historians in particular have made the most valuable contributions to this important subject—Lucette Valensi and Daniel J. Schroeter. Schroeter's *Merchants of Essaouira* and his "Trade as Mediator in Muslim-Jewish Relations" reveal how ethnoreligious boundaries actually facilitated exchanges between the two communities.[47] Moreover, we know from *Merchants of Essaouira* how relations between European Jews, European diplomats, and the local Jewish community evolved in the course of the critical period between 1844 and 1886. And as Valensi and Udovitch observed for the Jews of Djerba, "the marketplace is also the locus of the most frequent and varied contact between Jews and Muslims, and consequently the arena in which important aspects of identity, self-image, and mutual perceptions are defined and enacted."[48] In the past century, commercial transactions, whether clandestine and illegal, licit, or transpiring in the murky area between, drew the Maghrib, its indigenous peoples, and its resident foreigners into an untidy knot of trading relations, often brokered by small-time Mediterranean commercial pirates, which transcended national boundaries and worked at times against imperial agendas.

As the colonial administration frantically passed decrees after 1840 to limit Algeria's contacts with the outside, French citizens cum contrabandiers—of which Juan Onoffre is only one example—appear to have been stealthily undermining France's efforts to establish commercial hegemony over its African départements. And while aggressive European consuls and merchants struggled to construct exclusive spheres of economic and commercial influence in the Maghrib for their home governments, some of their own countrymen—or diplomatic protégés—were quietly undermining them.

Contraband, therefore, serves as a complicated vehicle for flushing out a whole constellation of transactions that at times ran counter to the aims of centralizing North African states or colonial powers. But this is only part of the story. Illegal exchanges and illicit marketing offer a glimpse into a partially hidden social universe which, in turn, raises issues of world market integration and social marginality. The first has received some scholarly attention; the second very little.

The social universe of contraband exchanges was forged by, and depended upon, spies, bandits, smugglers, counterfeiters, corrupt local port officials, black marketeers, caravan leaders, tavern keepers, and colporteurs—the riffraff of the Mediterranean's European and African shores. Coming largely from the lower ranks of society, the dealers in forbidden goods were economic actors who functioned as conduits for "illegal" transfers of military supplies and other commodities—British textiles, tobacco, hardware, and coffee—between western Europe and North Africa. Thus, migrants, refugees, and contrebandiers constituted a varied ethnocultural lot whose importance to history has been largely overlooked by scholars. Moreover, these types of exchanges were often combined with, or shaded off into, other unsavory activities, such as drug dealing and prostitution, that most ancient of illicit encounters, which the state attempted to regulate.

Studies of socially marginal groups in the past are not abundant for either the Maghrib or the Mashriq. *Struggle and Survival in the Modern Middle East,* a collection of lives as texts, edited and introduced by Edmund Burke III, brings the people without history to the foreground of historical inquiry. As Burke observes, ". . . we know very little of the lives of ordinary Middle Eastern men and women. Instead we see the Middle East over the shoulders of diplomats, military officers, entrepreneurs and bureaucrats."[49] Seven of the twenty-five biographies deal with North Africans in the precolonial, colonial, and contemporary periods; four of the seven concern the period under consideration here. David Seddon's piece on "The Man Who Became Qaid" is particularly apt. Not only does the Moroccan qa'id, "a wily opportunist," resemble his Algerian counterparts studied by Establet, but he was also quick to seize the opportunities for personal advancement presented by European imperialism in Morocco to become a self-made man.[50] Had not the invaders come from across the Middle Sea, Muhammad El Merid would probably have remained a nobody, his story untold.

Another recent and very important contribution to the genre of social history is made by the Tunisian historians Dalenda and Abdelhamid Largueche in their *Marginales en terre d'Islam,* which investigates women, gender, and class.[51] The history of women, whether in the Maghrib, the Arab world, or in Islamic civilization, is only beginning. In her chapter devoted to the Dar Joued (house for disobedient females), Dalenda Largueche argues that women's history also raises issues of social marginality.[52] For centuries, marginality was the fate of women consigned to a profound silence behind the walls of the Muslim city.[53] No institution betrays this better than the Dar Joued which, paradoxically, reveals while attempting to conceal individual women's revolt against the patriarchal order of things. A place of forced retreat found in Tunisian cities for females who either refused to accept an undesirable husband selected by their families or had fallen out of love with their spouse, it was a sort of prison for "crimes of the heart." Here, unloving females were confined, sometimes for months at a time, to house arrest under the watchful eye of an older female guardian, until their behavior complied with conjugal duty and with the wishes of the patrilineage.

Thus, the Dar Joued unveils two contradictory sociocultural processes and two opposing concepts of space in North African Muslim society. On the one hand, this institution demonstrates the powerlessness of individual women, their marginality in the face of the armature of patriarchy; yet it also shows the centrality of females, as "pivots of the family, guarantors of honor and morality and of the entire social order," to the construction of patriarchal systems.[54] Ordinary women of European origins were also essential to the building of a distinct pied-noir cultural identity in Algeria although, once again, there is little recent scholarship on this question. And we need to comprehend exactly how the two systems of patriarchy, one indigenous, the other European, reinforced—or undermined—each other.

The dialectic between social marginality and centrality is also addressed in Abdelhamid Largueche's chapter in the same work, entitled "Anthropology of Prostitution in the Arab City: Tunis in the Nineteenth Century."[55] If discussion of most sexual matters is restricted in Islam, the topic of illicit sexual encounters represents the ultimate taboo. Despite the relative rarity of written sources, Largueche offers not only a portrait of the capital's prostitutes, who were integrated into a larger underworld of socially marginalized groups, but also of the totality of the urban fabric itself. In tracing the historical trajectory of organized prostitution and of certain city festivals associated with "public women," Largueche posits that the origins of these popular carnivals, seemingly connected to fertility rites, may lie in the ancient Mediterranean world's culture.

Prostitution in the Maghrib's ethnically heterogenous precolonial and colonial cities and popular quarters was supposed to observe the boundaries erected between different groups. "The Muslim prostitute was solely the domain of the Muslims. Any [sexual] contact with Christians or Jews was strictly forbidden and severely punished."[56] In 1744, a riot broke out in Tunis after Muslim prostitutes shared their charms with French nationals. Some of the capital's prostitutes came from among the lower orders of Algerian refugees or those impoverished Algerian groups which had traditionally migrated to Tunis in search of work. Thus, the most marginal of social marginals—females and prostitutes—were fundamental to the politics of identity in a city which had long welcomed migrants from all over the Mediterranean.

The impact of increased southern Mediterranean migration to Tunisia or Algeria after mid-century also needs to be investigated in terms of links to crime and other unsavory activities, as well as to the construction of socio-cultural borders and frontiers and to representations of the other. In the 1860s, many of the Sicilians arriving in Tunisia were draft-dodgers, bandits, and criminals fleeing the Italian police; a few were lovers escaping unhappy marriages arranged by their families.[57] By 1897, the Italians had become more numerous than the Maltese; the more than 60,000 Italians who resided in Tunisia represented a four-to-one ratio with Frenchmen.[58] And since the peddlers of sexual favors were often located in those quarters where taverns and cafés were found, more research into the urban topography of the nineteenth-century Maghribi city or town would probably reveal a certain degree of interplay between the dealers in contraband goods and those engaged in other forbidden exchanges.[59]

The contraband traffic linking Mediterranean islands or southern Europe with the Maghrib was often organized along domestic lines—that is, run out of households or modest home-based businesses such as taverns. Consequently, it was all the more difficult to detect and stamp out. In these informal—even dual—underground economic sectors, women of modest substance played no small part. For some women (and men) living in expatriate circumstances in Tunis or other coastal cities, involvement in contraband offered new opportunities to act as freelance, small-scale traders, retailers, and distributors. They thus forged commercial, and therefore social, spaces for themselves in black market or "out-the-back-door" enterprises. Anna Borg, a British-Maltese protégée, was an entrepreneur who participated in the clandestine trade in illegal tobacco. Moreover, she perhaps did so with greater impunity than her male counterparts, since both British officials and Tunisian authorities were reluctant to arrest women. In 1881, no ordinary year in Tunisia, the French holder of the tobacco monopoly in Tunis reported that

> The fermier de tabac learned that there were twenty-six sacks of tobacco hidden in the basement of a dwelling inhabited by Anna Borg, a British-Maltese protégée. The fermier obtained permission to inspect her premises, but upon arriving there and asking to search the room, Anna refused them entry and said that she could only allow the British Janissary, a Tunisian named Hamda, to enter. The Janissary arrived and went into the room; he later emerged and claimed to have found nothing. But the delegation from the French monopoly saw

leaves of tobacco scattered around the dwelling and insisted on going together into Anna Borg's room to search. The British Janissary refused, saying he did not have an order to do this. The British consulate and the English Janissaries know perfectly well that Anna Borg is habitually involved in contraband and that four or five searches have already been made at her house.[60]

Thus, it would appear that Mediterranean folk of humble station also served as commercial mediators, via participation in the contraband traffic, between Europe and North Africa. In addition, one could argue that this class of Europeans may also have functioned as the principal cultural brokers between indigenous and western society—more so than high-level European diplomats stationed in capital cities who disdained and avoided the menu peuple of whatever ethnoreligious background. Nevertheless, we know very little either of the lives of these transplanted Europeans or of their multiple daily interactions with their North African neighbors. Of paramount significance, however, to the internal social dynamic of French imperialism in the Maghrib is the role of female settlers. Here the gap in the available literature is perhaps the most glaring.

Over the past decade, studies of the British Raj and other European overseas possessions have increasingly emphasized the decisive, complex part played by gender and sex in the elaboration of the culture of colonialism. Laura Ann Stoler and Margaret Strobel, among others, have laid bare the gendered boundaries of rule as well as the contradictory ways in which European women in the colonies both challenged and buttressed the subordination of the colonized.[61] Yet virtually nothing has been done for the Maghrib. For much of the nineteenth century, two measurements for calibrating "native" inferiority were employed by male colonial writers examining things North African—political institutions and levels of technology. As the century drew to a close, Muslim female status became increasingly influential as a benchmark for judging the culturally different, subordinate "other." Malek Alloula's striking work The Colonial Harem provides visual evidence of this trend.[62] An examination of the production of picture-postcard images of Algerian women, increasingly popular by the century's turn as a source of "pseudo-knowledge of the colony," reveals not only how European society represented the other, but also the growing obsession with the veiled, for the most part sexually inaccessible, Muslim female. Finally, the entry of European women settlers, such as Marie Bugéja, into the debate over education for North African females, represented a political and cultural sea change, particularly for Algeria.[63]

Once again, relatively little is known of the lives of either indigenous Maghribi women or their European counterparts—of whatever class— during the early colonial period.[64] Ursula Hart's slim volume *Two Ladies of Colonial Algeria* sketched the lives of perhaps the two best-known European women in French North Africa, Aurélie Picard and Isabelle Eberhardt; chapters in Gabriel Camps's *L'Afrique du Nord au féminin* and Jean Déjeux's *Femmes d'Algérie* are also devoted to Picard and Eberhardt, as well as to North African heroines, writers, and legendary figures from the past—distant and near.[65] As regards Eberhardt, the so-called "Passionate Nomad," judging by the number of titles currently in print, the field suffers from an embarras de richesse of studies on her.[66] Disorderly western women like Eberhardt, who entertained illicit sexual and other liaisons with the natives, were seen as threats to the increasingly lithified colonial boundaries separating resident Europeans from indigenous North Africans. Her case, while important, was somewhat exceptional (as was Picard's) and its very singularity has deflected attention away from less dramatic but perhaps more significant points of interaction between gender and colonial politics.

Peering into the underworld of migrants, social marginals, and contrebandiers bestows a face—still half concealed perhaps—upon people who have remained largely faceless until now, but who were ensnared by, and participated in, world market forces. The fact that just about everyone was engaged in contraband in the nineteenth-century Mediterranean—not only social marginals or ordinary folk—reveals the behind-the-scenes maneuvers of those European officials ostensibly opposed to such operations. Thus, these clandestine exchanges could be viewed as a form of undeclared commercial warfare, as nocturnal, behind the scenes and "out-the-back-door" commerce or banking, as the Mediterranean world's own extralegal maritime barter economy.[67]

In Tunisia and Algeria (until the 1889 Naturalization Law was passed), the sociolegal status of diaspora communities of Maltese and others was ambiguous, and this ambiguity conferred considerable economic advantage, if parlayed in the right manner. Much the same could be said for Algerian refugees residing in either Tunisia or Morocco. The legal trade in imported gunpowder, tobacco, and other items was, in theory, a state monopoly which excluded ordinary people of whatever ethnoreligious background from trading in these goods without state licenses. Yet, both the Tunisian government and European diplomats claiming jurisdiction over communities like the Maltese lacked the means or the will (or both) to superintend those groups strategically placed to tap into illicit networks.

Therefore, some Mediterraneans in the Maghrib carved out what appear—at first glance—to be rather modest economic niches; they accomplished this precisely because they straddled the socioeconomic boundaries between indigenous North African society and the official European world. Nevertheless, these niches, in the aggregate, had immense political ramifications, particularly when the transfer of weapons and gunpowder from western Europe to Africa was involved.

The newly arrived Europeans hailing from around the Mediterranean Basin could not have succeeded in their unlawful enterprises had they not been associated with local North Africans—with oasis smugglers from the Suf in southeastern Algeria, with Tunisian pastoralists like the Awlad Bu Ghanam, with the inveterate smugglers found along the borders, or with Maltese clans, such as the Bartolo, longtime inhabitants of Gabès whose family members were well assimilated into the local society and economy. Due to Tunisia's location vis-à-vis the Middle Sea, her coastal topography, and her relatively greater affinity for Mediterranean ties, the beylik represented a singular pole of attraction for illicit trade, at least during the fifty-year period stretching from 1830 to 1881. Reimagining North African history in the longue durée suggests that, just as Tunisia was, in Goitein's words, "the hub of the 19th century Mediterranean," so she constituted the "hub" of nineteenth-century contraband networks.[68]

After roughly 1850, Algeria was economically integrated into the imperial trade zone of the métropole, her products admitted largely duty-free to French soil. This only encouraged enterprising Tunisian and Algerian contrebandiers to introduce some of the beylik's commodities fraudulently into France via Algeria by passing them off as Algerian goods. Much the same pattern occurred after 1880 when Tunisian products, similar to those from southern Italy and Sicily, were admitted duty free to French territory, while Italian goods either were excluded or paid higher customs duties in France.[69] And if the Maltese, and to a lesser extent Italians and Sicilians, made maritime smuggling into a national specialty, they were certainly not alone, for Greek vessels plied the waters off Djerba in the 1860s with gunpowder, as did Tripolitanian traders and even boats from Smyrna (Izmir).

In the imperial imagination, above all that of France, contraband represented a danger akin to rebellion; the surveillance of illicit exchanges between Algerians, Tunisians, and the Mediterranean Basin developed into an obsession which colonized the collective imperial consciousness of French officials in Algeria and diplomats in Tunisia. As much effort was expended in chasing after the contrebandiers, spying on them, and attempting to impound their ill-gotten goods as in dampening insurrection; indeed, in the imperial mind set, revolt and contraband were intimately intertwined, the one feeding the other.[70] In 1867, French officials even went so far as to advocate taking "possession of the isle of Djerba which would be of very great importance to us. It would enable us to occupy a point from which Arab and Maltese contrabandists operate to supply English gunpowder and arms to our Algerian tribes in the south."[71] Thus, the multifarious activities of untold numbers of ordinary people as agents in the Mediterranean-wide contraband trade shaped the thinking and strategies of imperial elites.

## CONCLUSION

If contraband constituted a nightmare for French officials in Algeria and modernizers in Tunisia during the past century, it also poses certain challenges for historians today. The American consul in Tunis observed in 1864, admittedly a singular year, that: "I am assured by trustworthy merchants who possess ample means for obtaining practical knowledge that the exports and imports of the regency are probably five or six times greater than represented [in official records]."[72] Also during the reign of Muhammad al-Sadiq Bey (1859–1882), it was calculated that imports into Sfax should be doubled or even tripled to account for smuggling, while exports from southern Tunisia's most important port had to be increased substantially to account for clandestine commercial operations.[73] Balance sheets derived from official statistics and treaties theoretically regulating trans-Mediterranean commercial relations, such as the 1838 Anglo-Ottoman trade treaty, were akin to the leaky boats navigating between Valleta and Tunis, Bône, or Tripoli with prohibited goods.[74]

The hundreds of accounts of contraband exchanges found in archives around the Mediterranean, however partial or fragmentary, provide evidence for historical processes and relationships which have been consigned to the half-light, or semidarkness, of scholarly work on the nineteenth-century Maghrib. Taken as individual testimonies, these texts suggest the ways that people, many of ordinary stations, shaped their own destinies. At times, their actions contradicted the grander schemes of modernizing North African rulers, imperial strategists, or world-market capitalists; at others they inadvertently buttressed or complemented them. The social biographies of marginals, migrants, and contrebandiers, related for the most part by those seeking to circumscribe their actions, can "give voice to the masses of people who left few written records"—if used properly.[75] Furthermore, while political resistance in all its variant guises has governed inquiries into "Domination and the Arts of Resistance," economic resistance—or mere subsistence coping—has much less frequently been the subject of inquiry.[76]

If eighteenth-century piracy was much more than mere robbery committed at sea, nineteenth-century contraband and its multiple agents represented something beyond unregulated commerce or proscribed transactions concluded in the dead of night or through alternative markets. The very scale of these operations and their persistence throughout that century raise issues of world market incorporation. For the most part, scholars such as Hobsbawm and David Landes have focused solely upon the conquering bourgeoisie—the "Bankers and Pashas," high-ranking diplomats, and international merchants operating on the Mediterranean's other shore as the bearers and mediators of capitalism.[77] Might not those of humble rank be considered—in their own peculiar way—as tacit agents of imperial capitalism abroad? And could not integration have been also the work of socially marginal communities? In his study *Egyptian Textiles and British Capital, 1930–1956* (1989), Robert Tignor pointed out the "power of the periphery." The multifarious activities of smugglers, gunrunners, and contrebandiers of all nationalities suggest not only the unsuspected power of the peripheries but also the existence of multiple centers, some of them rather marginal to dynamic, expansionist Europe.[78]

In the final analysis, what I am arguing for is somewhat analogous to medievalist Jacques Le Goff's long-standing plea: "pour un autre moyen-âge"—for another view of the nineteenth-century Maghrib and Mediterranean World. Or to use John E. Wills' recent reappraisal of maritime Asian trade in the period 1500–1800, I am suggesting that we need a "paradigm shift" for Mediterranean North Africa during the long nineteenth century, stretching from the Napoleonic Wars to the Great War.[79] The stories of migrants, extralegal transactions, and social marginals help to restitch together both sides of the Mediterranean and suggest a somewhat different—or at least more complex—historical cartography of the grander and smaller processes at work in the nineteenth century.

Notes

1. As quoted in Alf A. Heggoy, *The French Conquest of Algiers, 1830: An Algerian Oral Tradition* (Athens: Ohio University Press, 1986), p. 32.

2. The question should be raised regarding the differing natures of geographic, temporal, and cultural unity in the Mediterranean; on this as it relates to the Indian Ocean, see K. N. Chaudhuri, "The Unity and Disunity of Indian Ocean History from the Rise of Islam to 1750: The Outline of a Theory and Historical Discourse," *Journal of World History* IV, no. 1 (Spring 1993), pp. 1–21.

3. An exception to this is Andrew C. Hess's "The Forgotten Frontier: The Ottoman North African Provinces during the Eighteenth Century," in *Studies in Eighteenth Century History,* Thomas Naff and Roger Owen, eds. (Carbondale and Edwardsville, Ill., Southern Illinois University Press, 1977), pp. 74–87. The title of Hess's article, however, indicates the state of the art.

4. See Abraham L. Udovitch, "International Commerce and Society in Mid-Eleventh Century Egypt and North Africa," in *The Economic Dimensions of Middle Eastern History: Essays in Honor of Charles Issawi,* Haleh Esfandiari and A. L. Udovitch, eds. (Princeton: Darwin Press, 1990), pp. 239–53; S. D. Goitein, *Mediterranean Society* (5 vols.; Berkeley: University of California Press, 1967–88); and Robert S. Lopez and Irving W. Raymond, *Medieval Trade in the Mediterranean World* (New York: Columbia University Press, 1955).

5. A recent exception to this is John McNeill's *Mountains of the Mediterranean* (Oxford: Oxford University Press, 1993).

6. L. Carl Brown, *The Tunisia of Ahmad Bey, 1837–1855* (Princeton: Princeton University Press, 1974), p. 3.

7. Lucette Valensi, "Calamités démographiques en Tunisie et en Méditerranée orientale aux XVIIIè et XIXè siècles," *AÈSC* XXIV, no. 6 (1969), pp. 1540–1562.

8. Lucette Valensi, *On the Eve of Colonialism: North Africa before the French Conquest, 1790–1830,* Kenneth J. Perkins, trans. (New York: Africana, 1977), pp. 137–138.

9. To cite but a few, *Peuples méditerranéens* has been published since 1977, the *Revue de l'Occident musulman et de la Méditerranée* since 1966, although after 1988 it assumed the slightly different title of *Revue du monde musulman et de la Méditerranée.* The *Mediterranean History Review* appeared in 1986 and in 1990 Kenneth Brown launched *Mediterraneans;* that same year the *Mediterranean Quarterly: A Journal of Global Issues* appeared.

10. Bernard Bailyn, *The Peopling of British North America: An Introduction* (New York: Vintage Books, 1988).

11. The local archives in Alexandria, Egypt, are apparently full of documentation on contraband (or contrabbando as it was sometimes

referred to in the Arabic documents) for the nineteenth century; boat-loads of contraband French spirits were frequently impounded in Alexandria, for example, and the manifests for vessels thus impounded exist in abundance.

12. The term "contraband" is used as a shorthand device to cover a whole constellation of extralegal or illegal kinds of exchanges, bargains, transactions, and markets. I know of no other published work devoted to this topic, although several scholars, including Eric Wolf and Philip Curtin, allude to the importance of contraband in other historical contexts. Some studies exist for the Atlantic world. For example, Joyce Lorimer, "The English Contraband Tobacco Trade in Trinidad and Guiana, 1590–1617," in *The Westward Enterprise: English Activities in Ireland, the Atlantic, and America, 1480–1650*, K. R. Andrews, Nicholas P. Canny and P. E. H. Hair, eds. (Liverpool: Liverpool University Press, 1978), pp. 124–50.

13. Relatively more recent research has been done for settler colonialism in the agrarian sector in Morocco than for Algeria or Tunisia; an outstanding example is Will D. Swearingen, *Moroccan Mirages: Agrarian Dreams and Deceptions, 1912–1986* (Princeton: Princeton University Press, 1987). Mention should also be made of Marie Cardinal, *Les pieds-noirs* (Tours: Belfond, 1988) which, while not a work of history by any means, contains invaluable photographs of European society in Algeria.

14. Gaston Loth, *Le Peuplement italien en Tunisie et en Algérie* (Paris: Colin, 1905).

15. Jean Ganiage, *La Population européenne de Tunis au milieu du XIXè siècle: Etude démographique* (Paris: PUF, 1960); and "Les Européens en Tunisie au milieu du XIXè siècle (1840–1870)," *Cahiers de Tunisie* XI (1955), pp. 388–421. Sources on European migration to the Maghrib exist from the nineteenth and early twentieth centuries; Ganiage, *Population*, pp. 94–96, notes some of them.

16. Jean-Louis Miège, *Le Maroc et L'Europe (1830–1894)* (4 vols.; Paris: PUF, 1963).

17. David Prochaska, *Making Algeria French: Colonialism in Bône, 1870–1920* (Cambridge: Cambridge University Press, 1990); his bibliography, pp. 310–324, contains a good listing of sources on European migrants, mainly for Algeria.

18. For a study of religious notables from the Algerian Rahmaniyya *tariqa* (brotherhood) who took refuge in the Tunisian Jarid, see Julia Clancy-Smith, *Rebel and Saint: Religious Notables, Populist Protest, Colonial Encounters (Algeria and Tunisia), 1800–1904* (Berkeley: University of California Press, 1994).

19. Roger Le Tourneau, *Fès avant le protectorat: Etude d'une ville de l'Occident musulman* (Casablanca: Société Marocaine de Librairie et

d'Edition, 1949), pp. 198–200; and Charles-Robert Ageron, "L'émigration des musulmans algériens et l'éxode de Tlemcen (1830–1911)," *Annales, économies, sociétés, civilisations* XXII, no. 5 (1967), pp. 1047–1066.

20. Georges Marty, "Les Algériens à Tunis," *Revue de l'Institut des belles lettres arabes* XI, nos. 43–44 (1948), pp. 301–334. For North African emigration to the Ottoman Empire, see Pierre Bardin's *Algériens et Tunisiens dans l'empire ottoman de 1848 à 1914* (Paris: CNRS, 1979). Extensive archival documentation on Algerian refugees is found in the Quai d'Orsay, Nantes, and Aix-en-Provence collections.

21. Peter Earle, *Corsairs of Malta and Barbary* (London: Sidgwick and Jackson, 1970), p. 6, defines a corsair or privateer as a "private individual granted a license by his sovereign to fit out a ship to attack his sovereign's enemies." Normally, the corsair's license was legitimate only in times of war. And legally, piracy was distinguished from privateering in that the corsair had been granted a license to engage in armed attacks against certain ships or specific groups. In addition, "corsale" was a recognized profession in that social system. Moreover, he points out that "privateering was just another system of exchange" (p. 16). It could also be conceived of as another form of social mobility for the downtrodden of the Mediterranean world who, in the seventeenth and eighteenth centuries, could not hope to migrate en masse. Thus, there was a link between the end of privateering and the opening of mass migration for Mediterranean peoples to other parts of the globe.

22. Two exceptions to the generally poor quality of English language works, recent or otherwise, on the Barbary pirates are William Spencer, *Algeria in the Age of the Corsairs* (Norman, Okla.: University of Oklahoma Press, 1976); and Sir Godfrey Fisher, *Barbary Legend: War, Trade and Piracy in North Africa, 1415–1830* (Westport, Conn.: Greenwood Press, 1974). Approaching the Barbary legend from another angle, that of intellectual history and collective attitudes, is Ann Thomson, *Attitudes towards the Maghreb in the 18th Century* (Leiden: E. J. Brill, 1987). A select bibliography of works on privateering is found in Valensi, *On the Eve of Colonialism*, pp. 136–37.

23. The number of works on pirates is steadily mounting for the Atlantic world; two recent examples are Robert C. Ritchie, *Captain Kidd and the War Against the Pirates* (Cambridge, Mass.: Harvard University Press, 1986); and Marcus Rediker, *Between the Devil and the Deep Blue Sea: Merchant Seamen, Pirates, and the Anglo-American Maritime World, 1700–1750* (Cambridge: Cambridge University Press, 1987).

24. Eric Hobsbawm, *Bandits* (London: Weidenfeld and Nicolson, 1969).

25. Jean Déjeux, "Un Bandit d'honneur dans l'Aurès de 1917 à 1921: Messaoud ben Zeimad," *ROMM* XXVI, no. 2 (1978), pp. 35–54.

26. David Hart, *Banditry in Islam: Case Studies from Morocco, Algeria and the Pakistan North West Frontier* (Wisbech, Cambridgeshire: Middle East and North African Studies Press, 1987).

27. Ibid., p. 2. David Prochaska's "Fire on the Mountain: Resisting Colonialism in Algeria," in *Banditry, Rebellion and Social Protest in Africa*, Donald Crummey, ed. (London: James Currey, 1986), pp. 229–252, demonstrates how social protest in the forests of the Bône region was mistakenly branded as "banditry" by colonial observers.

28. Ross E. Dunn, "Bu Hmara's European Connexion: The Commercial Relations of a Moroccan Warlord," *Journal of African History* XXI, no. 2 (1980), pp. 235–253.

29. Mohammed Kenbib, "Contrabande d'armes et 'anarchie' dans le Maroc précolonial (1844–1912)," *Revue Dar al-Niaba: Etudes d'histoire marocaine* I, no. 4 (1984), pp. 8–16.

30. Contraband was not a phenomenon confined to the nineteenth or twentieth century; military stores and supplies had long been regulated by early modern states. The importation into Christian states of saltpeter (potassium nitrate or *millah al-barud*) produced by Morocco was generally forbidden in the sixteenth century due to its uses in warfare. In the sixteenth century, after refined sugar, saltpeter—coming from the Marrakesh region and the Sous—was the second most important item on a list of Moroccan exports to England in 1574–75 and 1575–76. And saltpeter was exchanged or bartered for other war materials from European Christian sources. According to Paul Berthier, *Les Anciennes sucreries du Maroc et leurs réseaux hydrauliques* (Rabat: Imprimeries Françaises et Marocaines, 1966), pp. 255–256, the export of saltpeter was tied to the "contrebande de guerre" trade. Exports of gold coins from Morocco were also part of the contraband traffic in this period.

31. Fanny Colonna, *Instituteurs algériens, 1883–1939* (Algiers: Office des Publications Universitaires, 1975); Kenneth J. Perkins, *Qaids, Captains and Colons: French Military Administration in the Colonial Maghrib, 1844–1934* (New York: Africana, 1981); and numerous articles by Peter von Sivers, among them, "Insurrection and Accommodation: Indigenous Leadership in Eastern Algeria, 1840–1900," *International Journal of Middle East Studies* VI, no. 3 (1975), pp. 259–275.

32. Edmund Burke III, *Prelude to Protectorate in Morocco: Precolonial Protest and Resistance, 1860–1912* (Chicago: University of Chicago Press, 1976).

33. L. Carl Brown, *Tunisia of Ahmad Bey;* Khelifa Chater, *Dépendance et mutations précoloniales: la Régence de Tunis de 1815 à 1857* (Tunis: Publications de l'Université de Tunis, 1984); and Bachrouch, *Le Saint et le prince en Tunisie: Contribution à l'étude des groupes sociaux dominants (1782–1881)* (Tunis: Publications de l'Université de Tunis I, 1989).

34. Abdelhamid Henia, *Le Grid: ses rapports avec le beylik de Tunis (1676–1840)* (Tunis: Publications de l'Université de Tunis I, 1989).

35. Lucette Valensi, *Fellahs tunisiens: l'économie rurale et la vie des campagnes aux 18è et 19è siècles* (Paris: Mouton, 1977) remains the classic study of the countryside; Mohamed Hédi Chérif, *Pouvoir et société dans la Tunisie de Husain bin ʿAli (1705–1740)* (2 vols.; Tunis: Publications de l'Université de Tunis. 1984–1986). Both Valensi and Chérif have published numerous articles on wide-ranging topics.

36. Allan Christelow, *Muslim Law Courts and the French Colonial State in Algeria* (Princeton: Princeton University Press, 1985).

37. Colette Establet, *Etre caid dans l'Algérie coloniale* (Paris: CNRS, 1991).

38. Archives du Gouvernement Général de l'Algérie, Archives d'Outre-Mer, Aix-en-Provence, 1 H 13 (1856). This report was written by a French ship captain reporting from Bougie, Algeria, in March 1856 to the Admiralty; his information was based upon intelligence gathered over the previous year by paid spies.

39. See chapter 5 of Clancy-Smith, *Rebel and Saint,* for a full treatment of contraband in Tunisia after 1830.

40. Jean Ganiage, *Les Origines du protectorat français en Tunisie, 1861– 1881* (2d ed., Tunis: Maison Tunisienne de l'Edition, 1968), pp. 40–53. He also pointed out that three-quarters of the Europeans residing in the beylik at mid-century were originally from a few Mediterranean islands.

41. In the seventeenth century, for the Dutch, British, and other European powers excluded from areas in the Americas claimed by Spain and Portugal, contraband, smuggling, and piracy represented a mechanism for establishing indirect colonial control over parts of the Caribbean and Central America. Immanuel Wallerstein, *The Modern World System II. Mercantilism and the Consolidation of the European World Economy, 1600–1750* (New York: Academic Press, 1980), pp. 158–161.

42. Malta fell first to the French when Napoleon, then headed for Egypt, seized the island from the Knights of Saint John in 1798. In 1800, the British fleet took Malta, and it remained in British hands until well into the twentieth century. Malta's great natural harbor, Valetta, was Great Britain's chief naval base in the Mediterranean and contained a vast arsenal; its deeply indented harbors, the island's most coveted assets, were well suited for unregulated commerce by small ships heading for the Tunisian coast. After the opening of the Suez Canal in 1869 and the reversion of British commercial and strategic interests back to the Mediterranean, Malta became a vital link in the long sea chain to India. In addition, Malta was a free port between 1803 and 1813, provoking a boom in the island's economy and attracting merchandise from all over the Mediterranean Basin. Some information on Malta

and the Maltese in North Africa can be found in Prochaska, *Making Algeria French,* pp. 149–150.

43. Jacques Godechot, *Histoire de Malte* (Paris: PUF, 1970); Ramire Vadala, *Les Maltais hors de Malte. Etude sur l'émigration maltaise* (Paris: Rousseau, 1911); and Charles Owens, *The Maltese Islands* (London: David and Charles, 1969). Mention should also be made of periodical literature devoted to the Maltese, including Lucette Valensi, "Relations commerciales entre Tunis et Malte aux XVIIIè siècle," *Cahiers de Tunisie* XLIII, no. 3 (1963), pp. 71–83.

44. Earle, *Corsairs,* pp. 97–100, points out that by the late eighteenth century, the population of Malta had risen to a point that the island's peasants could only produce wheat and barley sufficient for four months' consumption; the rest had to be imported either from Sicily, where grain exports to Malta were regarded as a privilege to be granted or withheld, or from the Maghrib. In the nineteenth century, the balance between grains and population must have been even more unfavorable. Moreover, in the eighteenth century, as French commercial interests in Malta grew, the island became France's main window to the central Mediterranean as Livorno was for English commerce or Zante for the Venetians. Indeed, as French commercial interests in Malta grew in the course of the eighteenth century, privateering came to be an activity of diminishing importance for the island's economy.

45. Prochaska, *Making Algeria French,* p. 86.

46. A comprehensive study of the amir's complex movements is still needed; Raphael Danziger, *Abd al-Qadir and the Algerians: Resistance to the French and Internal Consolidation* (New York: Holmes and Meier, 1977) only takes the narrative up to the mid-point of the Algerian leader's career. Moreover, given the enormous theoretical advances in scholarship on popular protest and political movements in the past fifteen years, a more up-to-date study is in order.

47. Daniel J. Schroeter, *Merchants of Essaouira: Urban Society and Imperialism in Southwestern Morocco, 1844–1886* (Cambridge: Cambridge University Press, 1988); and idem., "Trade as a Mediator in Muslim-Jewish Relations: Southwestern Morocco in the Nineteenth Century," in *Jews Among Arabs: Contacts and Boundaries,* Mark R. Cohen and Abraham L. Udovitch, eds. (Princeton: Darwin Press, 1989), pp. 113–140. On Tunisian Jews, see Lucette Valensi, "Religious Orthodoxy or Local Tradition: Marriage Celebration in Southern Tunisia," ibid., pp. 65–84; and Abraham L. Udovitch and Lucette Valensi, *The Last Arab Jews: The Communities of Jerba, Tunisia* (New York: Harwood, 1984).

48. Udovitch and Valensi, *The Last Arab Jews,* p. 101.

49. Edmund Burke III, *Struggle and Survival in the Modern Middle East* (Berkeley: University of California Press, 1993), p. 1.

50. David Seddon, "Muhammad El Merid: The Man Who Became Qaid," ibid., pp. 211–223.

51. Dalenda and Abdelhamid Largueche, *Marginales en terre d'Islam* (Tunis: CERES, 1992). Until very recently, prostitution was not deemed of adequate significance to be the object of historical inquiry, although studies of the problem were undertaken by colonial authorities in the Maghrib; for example, Edouard Duchesne, *De la prostitution dans la ville d'Alger depuis la conquête* (Paris: J.-B. Baillière, 1853). Allan Christelow, *Muslim Law Courts*, pp. 82–106, discusses the social problems rife in the colonial urban milieu and suggests new avenues for research on questions of gender and social marginality. In addition, Christelow briefly alludes to the growing use in Algerian cities of hashish and other drugs, some introduced legally, others as contraband.

52. For a recent appraisal of the state of the art of women's history for the Middle East, see Nikki R. Keddie and Beth Baron, eds., *Women in Middle Eastern History: Shifting Boundaries in Sex and Gender* (New Haven: Yale University Press, 1991). In tracing the evolution of this "house for disobedient females," Largueche delved into a wide array of written sources—manuals of jurisprudence, court records, municipal police archives, etc.—and oral ones. As regards the latter, she encountered a partial wall of silence. In the popular collective mind, this institution, which endured until the present century, was conflated with group disgrace and shame; moreover, the Dar Joued had been mistakenly associated with other institutions of female correction, such as the Dar 'Adal or women's prison.

53. Largueche, *Marginales*, p. 7.

54. Ibid., p. 85.

55. Ibid., pp. 13–80; see also his "L'institution municipale, la restructuration urbaine et la dépendance à Tunis dans la seconde moitié du 19ème siècle," *Revue d'histoire maghrébine* XLVII–XLVIII (1987), pp. 15–29.

56. Ibid., p. 24.

57. Ganiage, *Les Origines*, p. 41.

58. Loth, *Le Peuplement*.

59. Another unexplored topic which relates to trans-Mediterranean exchanges and the politics of identity within the heterogeneous popular culture of the Maghrib's cities is the theater. French theater was introduced to Syria and then Egypt, from whence it was brought to Tunisia by Syrian Christian migrants in the course of the nineteenth century. There is very little recent work on this important social-history subject, aside from Hamadi Ben Halima, *Un Demi siècle de théâtre arabe en Tunisie (1907–1957)* (Tunis: Publications de l'Université de Tunis, 1974).

60. Dar el-Bey, Tunis. Série H, Carton 96, Dossier 141 (Corres-

pondance au sujet de la contrabande de tabac). Letter from J. Rousseau, 1881.

61. Laura Ann Stoler, "Rethinking Colonial Categories: European Communities and the Boundaries of Rule," *Comparative Studies in Society and History* XXXI, no. 1 (January 1989), pp. 134–161; Margaret Strobel, *European Women and the Second British Empire* (Bloomington: Indiana University Press, 1991); and Nupur Chaudhuri and Margaret Strobel, eds., *Western Women and Imperialism: Complicity and Resistance* (Bloomington: Indiana University Press, 1992).

62. Malek Alloula, *The Colonial Harem*, Myrna and Wlad Godzich, trans. (Minneapolis: University of Minnesota Press, 1987).

63. Marie Bugéja, the wife of a colonial administrator in Bougie, wrote at least ten books and forty-seven articles, many of them devoted to the question of Algerian Muslim female status and assimilation. While her story belongs more to the interwar period—she began publishing in 1918—nevertheless, the relationships between European settlers and indigenous North African women (or men) are raised by Bugéja's career. On her, see the important work in progress by Jeanne Bowlan, "Prescribing Civility: French Colonialism and Gender in Algeria, 1919–1939," (Paper presented at the Ninth Berkshire Conference on the History of Women, Vassar College, Poughkeepsie, N.Y., June 11–13, 1993).

64. There are at least two general studies of women in Algeria which concentrate mainly on the late colonial period: Peter R. Knauss, *The Persistence of Patriarchy: Class, Gender, and Ideology in Twentieth Century Algeria* (Westport, Conn.: Praeger, 1984); and David C. Gordon, *Women of Algeria: An Essay on Change* (Cambridge, Mass.: Harvard University Press, 1968). However, the former does not make use of the substantial theoretical literature on class and gender, while the latter work is dated.

65. Ursula K. Hart, *Two Ladies of Colonial Algeria: The Lives and Times of Aurélie Picard and Isabelle Eberhardt* (Athens: Ohio University Center for International Studies, 1987); Gabriel Camps, *L'Afrique du Nord au féminin: Héroines du Mahgreb [sic] et du Sahara* (Paris: Perrin, 1922); and Jean Déjeux, *Femmes d'Algérie: Légendes, traditions, histoire, littérature* (Paris: La Boîte à Documents, 1987).

66. For a partial listing of works devoted to Eberhardt and a critique of those sources, see Julia Clancy-Smith, "The 'Passionate Nomad' Reconsidered: A European Woman in L'Algérie Française (Isabelle Eberhardt, 1877–1904)," in *Western Women and Imperialism: Complicity and Resistance*, Nupur Chaudhuri and Margaret Strobel, eds. (Bloomington: Indiana University Press, 1992), pp. 61–78. For a study of an extraordinary Algerian female, who also befriended Eberhardt, see Julia Clancy-Smith, "The House of Zainab: Female Authority and Saintly

Succession in Colonial Algeria," in *Women in Middle Eastern History: Shifting Boundaries in Sex and Gender,* Nikki Keddie and Beth Baron, eds. (New Haven: Yale University Press, 1991), pp. 254–274.

67. One could even argue that health and disease conditions were influenced by migrants, refugees, and illicit exchanges. Nancy E. Gallagher, *Medicine and Power in Tunisia, 1780–1900* (Cambridge: Cambridge University Press, 1984) demonstrated the processes leading to the collapse of Arab medical institutions, mainly in Tunis, and the link between medicine and colonial domination.

68. S. D. Goitein, *Studies in Islamic History and Institutions* (Leiden: E. J. Brill, 1966), pp. 308–328.

69. Loth, *Le Peuplement,* p. 63, points out that the differential in customs duties levied upon Tunisian, as opposed to Italian, products admitted to France provoked a rise in Italian emigration to Tunisia.

70. A few examples are: Archives du Ministère des Affaires Etrangères (AMAE), Tunisie, Correspondance Politique, Vol. 7 (1843); Archives de la Résidence Générale de France à Tunis (Nantes), Carton 423 (1866–1874); and Archives du Gouvernement Tunisien, Carton 207, Dossier 102, no. 101 (1870). Illicit exports from Tunis to Malta are reported by Richard Wood, Tunis, September 10, 1863, in Public Record Office, Tunisia, FO 102/68, among other sources. The impact of the increased export duties in 1868 was reported by Botmiliau to Paris, August 25, 1868, in AMAE, Tunisie, Correspondance Commerciale, vol. 59. While the Maltese dominated the Mediterranean leg of the contraband trade, they were not alone; smugglers from Leghorn (Livorno) also participated actively in smuggling between Italy, Tunisia, and Algeria; French Foreign Minister to Governor-general of Algeria, May 1834, Archives du Gouvernement Générale de l'Algérie, F 80 1420.

71. Archives du Ministère des Affaires Etrangères, Mémoires et Documents, Tunisie, vol. 13, March 1867.

72. Perry to Secretary of State Seward, April 21, 1864. Department of State, Despatch Book, Vol. 7 (January 1858–1864), National Archives, Washington, D.C.

73. Ibid.; and Ganiage, *Les Origines,* pp. 50–53.

74. Sevket Pamuk, "The Middle East in the Nineteenth Century World Trade," in *The Economic Dimensions of Middle Eastern History: Essays in Honor of Charles Issawi,* Haleh Esfandiari and Abraham L. Udovitch, eds. (Princeton: Darwin Press, 1990), pp. 199–213, points out (p. 200) "the poor quality of underlying data on trade and population," for the Middle East and North Africa.

75. Suzanne Desan, "Crowds, Community, and Ritual in the Work of E. P. Thompson and Natalie Davis," in *The New Cultural History,* Lynn Hunt, ed. (Berkeley: University of California Press, 1989), p. 55.

76. James C. Scott, *Domination and the Arts of Resistance: Hidden Transcripts* (New Haven: Yale University Press, 1990).

77. David S. Landes, *Bankers and Pashas: International Finance and Economic Imperialism in Egypt* (Cambridge, Mass.: Harvard University Press, 1958).

78. Robert L. Tignor, *Egyptian Texiles and British Capital, 1930–1956* (Cairo: The American University in Cairo Press, 1989).

79. John E. Wills, "Maritime Asia, 1500–1800: The Interactive Emergence of European Domination," *American Historical Review* XCVIII, no. 1 (February 1993), pp. 83–105.

# Conclusion:
# Toward an Authentic and Balanced
# Historical Perspective

As these essays underscore, a considerable diversity—indeed, divergence
—of opinion exists among historians of North Africa on a variety of
critical issues, some of them as fundamental as the definition of history itself. Matters of method, conceptualization, and choice of subject are very
much open to debate, creating a profuse variety of ongoing research. There
are many histories of the Maghrib, no one of them definitive, each one of
them contributing to deepening our understanding of a region the construction of whose history is very much a work in progress, shaped not only
by the past, but also by the present.

In these respects, historians of the Maghrib are no different from their
colleagues who study the past of the Middle East, East Asia, Europe, North
America, or any other area. Thus, their evaluations of major developments
in their field (some of which have parallels elsewhere, others of which are
unique to the Maghrib) and their assessments of how best to cope with the
challenges surrounding an intellectually rigorous reconstruction of the past
are food for thought for all practitioners of the historian's craft, whatever
their specialization.

Despite their diversity, however, historians of North Africa share, to a
remarkably high degree, a sense of participating in a common endeavor.
There is among them, as well, a striking convergence of views on what
needs to be done to guarantee that their enterprise continue to function in
the future with the same high standards and levels of productivity that have
been the rule in the decades since independence. All of the following recommendations designed to achieve those goals could, with minor adaptations, be applied equally well in efforts to facilitate and strengthen the study
of history in other parts of the world.

a) The provision of technical assistance to libraries and archives in the
Maghrib to expedite the preservation, storage, retrieval, and classification of documentation of all genres. Much of this precious material is scattered, in poor condition, and all-too-often neglected. Some
of it is in real danger of being lost without prompt and appropriate
attention.

b) The development of more, and better, facilities and cadres, especially within the Maghrib but outside it as well, capable of supporting historical studies, preservation efforts, and scientific analysis, thus making it possible to build upon the laudable progress made in the years since independence.

c) The promotion of the study of areas and periods of history hitherto ignored or recently neglected, and the training of specialists in these areas. Chief among these are the pre-Islamic Maghrib, the early Islamic period, and the Ottoman era. Similarly, much work remains to be done on the Spanish and Italian presence in North Africa.

d) The fostering of women's history, the history of the family, and the history of traditionally marginal components of Maghribi society, none of which has yet received adequate attention and each of which deserves a high priority in all geographical areas and chronological periods.

e) The encouragement of continued dialogue and cooperation with anthropology, archeology, and other disciplines allied to the study of history.

f) The production of more local and regional studies for all periods in order to test prevailing interpretations and fill the many critical gaps in the current understanding of North African history, particularly regarding the rural sector and everyday life outside the centers of wealth and power which have customarily been the main foci of historical attention.

g) The organization of conferences that provide an opportunity for North African historians, from both the Maghrib and elsewhere, to meet colleagues in their own and allied fields, exchange information, debate issues, and discuss ongoing projects. The level of cooperation, dialogue, and understanding that such meetings make possible is an invaluable asset to individual scholars and readily translates into significant advances in conceptualizing the North African past.

The successful implementation of measures such as these will position historians of North Africa to understand more fully, and so interpret more effectively, its past. In doing so they will certainly advance the interests of the scholarly community but, perhaps even more importantly, they will also serve the people of the Maghrib, whose heritage is, after all, embedded in that past.

# Contributors to this Collection

SAMI BERGAOUI holds a Diplôme de Recherches Approfondies from the Ecole Normale Supérieure of Tunis and is currently a junior lecturer in the Faculté des Lettres (La Manouba) of the Université de Tunis I. He is the author of *Landed Property and Production Relationships in the Region of Tunis* (published in Arabic by the Ecole Normale Supérieure in Tunis in 1989) and of articles that have appeared in such journals as *Revue de l'institut des belles lettres arabes, Revue d'histoire maghrébine, Cahiers de Tunisie, Cahiers de la Méditerranée,* and *Arabica.* He has also contributed a chapter on "Land Circulation in Tunis (18th–20th Century)" to Sophie Ferchiou, *Hasab wa nasab— Parenté, alliance et patrimoine en Tunisie* (Paris: CNRS, 1992).

L. CARL BROWN is Garrett Professor Emeritus in Foreign Affairs at Princeton University, where he long served as director of the interdisciplinary Program in Near Eastern Studies. He is the author of *The Tunisia of Ahmad Bey, 1837–1855* (Princeton: Princeton University Press, 1974); coauthor of *Tunisia: The Politics of Modernization* (New York: Praeger, 1964); editor of *State and Society in Independent North Africa* (Washington: Middle East Institute, 1966); and translator (with commentary) of *The Surest Path: The Political Treatise of a 19th Century Muslim Statesman* (Cambridge: Harvard University Press, 1967).

OMAR CARLIER earned a Doctorat d'Etat in Political Science from the Université de Paris in 1994. Between 1969 and 1993 he served on the faculty of the Université d'Oran. During the last eight years of his tenure at Oran, he held the position of chef de laboratoire at the Unité (subsequently Centre) de Recherche en Anthropologie Sociale et Culturelle (URASC; then CRASC) and oversaw the center's publications. He is the coauthor, with Fanny Colonna, of *Lettrés, intellectuels, militants en Algérie, 1880–1950* (Algiers: Office des Publications Universitaires, 1988) and the author of *Entre nation et jihad. Histoire sociale des radicalismes algériens* (Paris: Presses des Sciences Politiques, 1995). Articles by Professor Carlier have appeared in such journals as *Le Mouvement sociale, Vingtième siècle,* and *Annales, économies, sociétés, civilisations.* His current projects include a study of the discipline of history in colonial Algeria.

MOUNIRA CHAPOUTOT-REMADI is a professor of history at the Université de Tunis. Her articles on a variety of medieval Islamic topics have appeared in *Journal of the Economic and Social History of the Orient, Annales, économies, sociétés, civilisations,* and *Cahiers de Tunisie,* of which she was editor-in-chief from 1981 until 1988. In addition, she also contributed two essays to *Les Africains, sous la direction de Charles-André Julien* (Paris: Editions Jeunes Afriques, 1977–), one in Volume IV on the Mamluk chronicler al-Nuwayri, the other in Volume X on the Mamluk sultan Shadjar al-Durr.

JULIA CLANCY-SMITH received her Ph.D. in modern North African and Middle Eastern History from the University of California, Los Angeles, in 1988. She is currently an associate professor of history in the Department of Near Eastern Studies at the University of Arizona. Her first book, *Rebel and Saint: Notables, Populist Protest, Colonial Encounters (Algeria and Tunisia, 1800–1904)* (Berkeley: University of California Press, 1994), received the 1995 Alf Heggoy Book Prize from the French Colonial Historical Society; the 1995 Phi Alpha Theta Book Award from the International Honor Society in History; and Honorable Mention in the 1995 Albert Hourani Book Award from the Middle East Studies Association. She is currently editing a volume with Frances Gouda entitled *Gender, Race, and Family Life in the Dutch and French Empires, 1800–1962*. Dr. Clancy-Smith is also working on a monograph entitled "Displacements: Women, Migration, and Identities in the 19th Century Mediterranean World."

MICHEL LE GALL holds the Ph.D. degree in Near Eastern Studies from Princeton University and teaches at St. Olaf College in Northfield, Minnesota. His primary interest lies in the field of late nineteenth-century Ottoman history and, in particular, late Ottoman Libya, about which he has written a number of articles in such periodicals as the *International Journal of Middle East Studies, Asian and African Studies* (Haifa), and *Princeton Papers in Near Eastern Studies*. He is currently finishing a monograph entitled "An Imperial Fin de Siècle: Ottoman Rule in Tripolitania and Cyrenaica, 1881–1911" and is preparing a documentary history of slavery and the slave trade in North Africa, Egypt, and the Sudan in the nineteenth and twentieth centuries.

AMMAR MAHJOUBI, a specialist in ancient Roman history, received his Doctorat d'Etat from the Université de Paris-Sorbonne in 1974. He is a professor in the Faculté des Sciences Humaines et Sociales of the Université de Tunis and is director of the Institut Supérieur d'Histoire du Mouvement National. He is the author of *Les cités romaines de Tunisie* (Tunis: Société Tunisienne de Diffusion, 1967); and *Recherches d'histoire et d'archéologie à Henchir el-Faouar. I: La cité des Belalitani Maiores* (Tunis: Faculté des Lettres, 1978); as well as chapters on "Le Haut Empire" in *Histoire générale de la Tunisie, Vol. I, L'Antiquité;* and "La Période Romaine" in the UNESCO *Histoire générale de l'Afrique* (Paris: UNESCO, 1980). In the past, he has served as the director of the Centre des Recherches Archéologiques at the Institut National d'Archéologie et d'Arts de Tunis (1962–1967); of the Ecole Normale Supérieure de Tunis (1976–1985); and of the Institut Supérieure de l'Education (1985–1987).

MOHAMED EL MANSOUR holds a Ph.D. degree in history from the University of London School of Oriental and African Studies and is currently professor of history at the Université Mohammed V in Rabat, Morocco. He is the author of *Morocco in the Reign of Mawlay Sulayman* (Cambridgeshire: MENAS Press, 1990) and the coeditor of two volumes, *The Atlantic Connection: 200 Years of Moroccan-American Relations* (Rabat: Edino, 1990) and *al-Tarikh wa adab al-nawazil* (Rabat: Faculté des Lettres, 1995). Dr. El Mansour is a former vice-president of the Moroccan Association for Historical Research and was a Middle East Studies Association visiting scholar in the humanities in 1991.

RONALD A. MESSIER is a professor of Middle East history and historical archeology at Middle Tennessee State University in Murfreesboro. He received his M.A. and Ph.D. degrees from the University of Michigan. His teaching and research focus on medieval Islam, North Africa, medieval architecture, and archeology. Since 1987, he has directed an ongoing excavation of the medieval city of Sijilmasa, a community in southeastern Morocco famous for its gold trade and its contacts with Timbuctu and other West African centers. He has published some dozen articles, coedited a book entitled *Jihad and its Times* (Ann Arbor: University of Michigan Center of Middle Eastern and North African Studies, 1991) and has recently completed a manuscript on the Almoravid dynasty of Morocco and Muslim Spain. He has won several teaching awards, including the Council for the Advancement and Support of Education award as Tennessee Professor of the Year for 1993.

ABDERRAHMANE EL MOUDDEN earned his Ph.D. in Near Eastern Studies/History at Princeton University in 1991 and is a member of the faculty of al-Akhawayn University in Ifrane, Morocco. His scholarly interests encompass modern Moroccan social and political history; Islamic international and intercultural relations; and translation projects. He has published a number of articles and notes in Arabic, French, and English in such journals as *Majallat kulliyat al-adab bil-Rabat*, *Hespéris-Tamuda*, *The Maghreb Review*, *Bulletin économique et social du Maroc*, and *Studia Islamica*. Dr. El Moudden is author of *al-Badawi al-maghribiyya qabl al-isti'mar* (Rabat: Faculté des Arts, 1995) and editor of *al-Magharib fil ʿahd al-ʿUthmani* (Rabat: Faculté des Arts, 1995). He is currently working on a book entitled "Sharifs and Padishahs: Moroccan-Ottoman Relations from the 16th through the 18th Centuries: Contributions to the Study of a Diplomatic Culture."

KENNETH PERKINS is a professor of Middle Eastern and North African history at the University of South Carolina. He holds the Ph.D. degree in Near Eastern Studies from Princeton University. A specialist in the nineteenth- and twentieth-century history of the Maghrib and of the Sudan, he is the author of *Qaids, Captains, and Colons: French Military Administration in the Colonial Maghrib, 1844–1934* (New York: Africana Press, 1981); *Tunisia: Crossroads of the Islamic and European Worlds* (Boulder: Westview Press, 1986); *Historical Dictionary of Tunisia* (Metuchen: Scarecrow Press, 1989); and *Port Sudan: The Evolution of a Colonial City* (Boulder: Westview Press, 1993); and the translator and annotator of Lucette Valensi, *Le Maghreb avant la prise d'Alger* as *On the Eve of Colonialism: North Africa Before the French Conquest* (New York: Africana Press, 1977). Professor Perkins has also published articles in *Revue d'histoire maghrébine, African Studies Review,* and *Middle East Studies* (London).

WILFRID J. ROLLMAN received his Ph.D. from the University of Michigan (1983) in Middle Eastern and North African History. He has taught this field at Harvard University, Wellesley College, the University of Virginia, and Boston University. He is currently an affiliate in Research at the Center for Middle Eastern Studies (Harvard) and works as a bibliographical specialist in Arabic at the Harvard Library's Middle East Division. He is general editor of *Western Books on Islam and the Middle East,* a microform series being published by Harvard University and Primary Sources Media, Inc. and is completing a manuscript on "Reform, State and Society in Pre-Colonial Morocco."

HOUARI TOUATI received the doctorat en histoire from the Université de Nice in 1984. He is currently maître de conférence at the Ecole des Hautes Etudes en Sciences Sociales in Paris and was previously maître assistant at the Université d'Oran and a researcher at its Unité (subsequently Centre) de Recherche en Anthropologie Sociale et Culturelle (URASC; then CRASC). Professor Touati is the author of *Entre Dieu et les hommes. Lettrés, saints et sorciers au Maghreb (XVIIè siècle)* (Paris: Ecole des Hautes Etudes en Sciences Sociales, 1994) and of articles in such journals as *Revue maghrébine d'études politiques et religieuses* and *Annales, économies, sociétés, civilisations.* In 1994 he was awarded the Ibn Khaldun Prize by the Social Science Research Council.

# List of Abbreviations

AESC        *Annales, économies, sociétés, civilisations*
AFDA        Association française des arabisants
AIEMA       Association Internationale pour l'Etude de la Mosaïque
            Antique
AIMS        American Institute of Maghrib Studies
CDTM        Centre de Documentation Tunisie Maghreb (Tunis)
CEMAT       Centre d'Etudes maghrébines à Tunis
CERES       Centre d'Etudes et de Recherches Economiques et Sociales
            (Tunis)
CERMAA      Centre d'Etudes et de Recherches du Monde Arabe et
            Africaine (Paris)
CEROMDI     Centre d'Etudes et de Recherches Ottomanes, Morisques,
            de Documentation et d'Information (Zaghouan)
CNRS        Centre National de la Recherche Scientifique (Paris)
CNUDST      Centre National Universitaire de Documentation
            Scientifique et Technique (Tunis)
CRESM       Centre de Recherches et d'Etudes sur les Sociétés Méditer-
            ranéennes (Aix-en-Provence)
CRIDSSH     Centre de Recherches et d'Informations Documentaires en
            Sciences Sociales et Humaines (Oram)
CSIC        Consejo superior de investigaciones científicas (Madrid)
CURS        Centre universitaire de la recherche scientifique (Rabat)
ENAL        Entreprise Nationale Algérien des Livres
EPHE        Ecole pratique des hautes études (Paris)
IBLA        *Revue de l'Institut des belles lettres arabes*
IHAC        Instituto Hispano-arabe de cultura (Madrid)
IHEM        Institut des Hautes Etudes Marocaines (Rabat)
IJMES       *International Journal of Middle East Studies*
INAA        Institut National d'Archéologie et d'Art (Tunis)
IREMAM      Institut de Recherches et d'études sur le Monde Arabe et
            Musulman (Aix-en-Provence)
MESRS       Ministère de l'Enseignement Supérieur et de la Recherche
            Scientifique (Tunis)
PUF         Presses Universitaires de France
ROMM        *Revue de l'Occident musulman et de la Méditerrannée* (since 1966,

<table>
<tbody>
<tr><td></td><td>although after 1988 it assumed the slightly different title of Revue du monde musulman et de la Méditerranée)</td></tr>
<tr><td>SEVPEN</td><td>Service d'Edition et de Vent des Publications et de l'Education</td></tr>
<tr><td>SMLE</td><td>Société Marocaine de Librairie et d'Edition (Casablanca)</td></tr>
<tr><td>SNED</td><td>Société Nationale d'Edition et de Diffusion (Algiers)</td></tr>
<tr><td>SOAS</td><td>School of Oriental and African Studies (London)</td></tr>
<tr><td>SUNYP</td><td>State University of New York Press (Albany)</td></tr>
<tr><td>TALM</td><td>Tangier American Legation Museum</td></tr>
<tr><td>UEAI</td><td>Union européenne des Arabisants et Islamisants</td></tr>
<tr><td>URASC</td><td>Unité de Recherche en Anthropologie Sociale et Culturelle (Oran)</td></tr>
</tbody>
</table>

Printed and bound by CPI Group (UK) Ltd, Croydon, CR0 4YY

13/04/2025

14656494-0003